The Elephant Path

The Elephant Path
Attention Development and Training in Children and Adolescents

MICHELLE G. BISSANTI M.ED.,
DANIEL P. BROWN, PH.D.,
& JAE PASARI, PH.D.

FOR MUSTANG BON FOUNDATION

*We dedicate this book to all children,
that their sense of wonder, innate wisdom and compassion
will shine brightly for the benefit of all beings.*

About the Authors

Daniel P. Brown, Ph.D. is an Associate Clinical Professor in Psychology, Dept. of Psychiatry, at Harvard Medical School at Beth Israel Deaconess Medical Center. He teaches a variety of clinical assessment and treatment courses and also a course on performance excellence for physicians, CEOs, and judges. In graduate school at the University of Chicago he studied Sanskrit, and at the University of Wisconsin he studied Tibetan, Buddhist Sanskrit, and Pali. In the 1980s he wrote *Transformations of Consciousness* with Ken Wilber and Jack Engler. He is also the author of *Pointing Out the Great Way: The Stages of Meditation in the Mahamudra Tradition*. More recently, under the guidance of H.H. Menri Trizin, he and Geshe Sonam translated Bru rGyal ba g.Yung drung's *The Pith Instructions for the Stages of the Practice Sessions of Bon rDzogs Chen [Great Completion] Meditation*, and a collection of eleven advanced yogic texts, Shar rdza bKra' shis rGyal mtshan's *sKu gsum rang shar [Self-Arising Three-fold Embodiment of Enlightenment]*.

Michelle G. Bissanti, M.Ed. is an elementary educator, a yoga and meditation teacher, and founder of HeartSeed Wisdom Practices. She has worked in both public and independent schools since 1992 and created, developed and implemented an innovative yoga and meditation program for children ages 4 through 12. Currently, she is consulting and developing programs with school communities, as well as corporate, family, and individual clients committed to supporting the heart-mind of children. Michelle holds a Masters in Elementary Education from Lesley University in Cambridge, Massachusetts and lives in the Boston area with her son. You can learn more about her background and work at www.heartseedwisdompractices.com.

Jae Pasari, Ph.D. holds a degree in Molecular Environmental Biology from the University of California, Berkeley, as well as masters and doctoral degrees in Environmental Studies from the University of California, Santa Cruz. He served as a high school and college educator for many years, and currently works as a sustainability advisor to impact investors, philanthropists, and academics.

Table of Contents

Acknowledgments xvii

The Vision Behind this Work by Michelle G. Bissanti, M.Ed. 1

INTRODUCTION: Scope of the Book 11

**PART I – The Development and Training of Attention East
and West** 15

Chapter 1: The Development of Attentional Systems in Childhood
and Adolescence by Daniel P. Brown Ph.D. 17
The Alerting Attentional System 18
The Orienting Attentional System 20
   The Exogenous Orienting System 21
   Orienting and the Maternal Environment 26
The Development of the
Endogenous Attentional System 31
The Development of the
Executive Attentional System 32
The Development of Selective Attention 34
The Development of Sustained Attention: Attention as a
   Steady State 35
Sustained Focused Attention in Free Play 37
Free Play With Background Distractors 38
The Effects on Television Viewing on Sustained Attention 40
The Spotlight 43
Vigilance: Sustained Focus During Task Learning in the
   Presence of Distractors 44
Inhibition of Conflicting Responses and Behaviors 49
Effects of Cueing and Anticipation in Visual Orienting 52
The Development of Strategies of Executive Attention 55

The Development of Meta-cognitive Awareness of
  Attentional Strategies 58
Integration of Attentional Dimensions in the Executive
  Attentional System 58
Brain Development and the Primary Attentional Systems 64
Predictors of Sustained Attention or Significant Distraction 68

Chapter 2: The Varieties of Dysfunctional Attention in the Modern
  Western World by Daniel P. Brown Ph.D 71
Mindlessness 71
Distracted Concentration 74
Developmental Trends in Attention Span 75
The Illusion of Duration of Sustained Attention 76
The Problem of Apportioning Attention 79
Inattentional Blindness as the Cost of Sustained and Selective
  Focus 80
Factors That Aggravate Distraction From Sustained
  Concentration 81
The Home Environment 81
Multimedia Exposure 82
Individual Differences in Distractibility 84
Mind-Wandering 87
Multitasking 92
    The Myth of Multitasking 92
    Super Multitaskers 97
    Why is Multitasking Typically Associated With Poor
      Performance? 97
    The Neuroscience of Multitasking 98
    Multitasking in Children 99
Reactivity 99
Lack of Coherence of Mind; Psychic Entropy and the Disordered,
  Noisy Ordinary Mind 104
Lack of Meta-cognitive Awareness 108
Lack of Working Memory 111

The Effects of Multimedia 118
   The Rapid Rise of Multimedia Exposure 118
   The Effects of Word Processing and Multimedia Learning 120
   The Harm and Benefits of Videogaming 120
   The Effects of Web Browsing on Learning 124
   Smart Phones and Other Mobile Devices 130
   Not Working Memory; The Negative Effects of the Internet on
      Working Memory 133
   Summary of the Potential Effects of Multimedia Exposure 134

Chapter 3: Training Attention and Related Skills in Children
      Two Broad Categories of Training Attention
      by Daniel P. Brown Ph.D. 137
Training Mindfulness in Children; Effects of Attentional
   Systems 141
Effects of Mindfulness Training on Dimensions Other Than
   Attention 144
Effects of Mindfulness on Academic Performance 146
Reviews on the Effects of Mindfulness 146
What Does Mindfulness Actually Train? 147
Concentration Training; Selective and Sustained Attention 150
Training to Reduce Mind-Wandering 154
Training Multitasking 157
Training to Reduce Reactivity 160
Training Meta-cognitive Monitoring 160
Training in Mentalization 162
Training Working Memory 165
Training Executive Functions 171
What Do We Want to Target for Training and Why? 173

Chapter 4: Training Concentration in Adults
      by Daniel Brown Ph.D. 177
The Basic Skills of Concentration 177
The Stages of Concentration Training 182

Table of Contents

PART II – Concentration Meditation Training According to Developmental Age 197

Chapter 5: Adapting Training to the Developmental Age of the Child by Daniel P. Brown Ph.D. 199
  The Main Considerations of Early Preoperational Development 200
  The Main Considerations of Late Preoperational Development 201
  The Main Considerations of Concrete Operational Development 201

Chapter 6: Introduction to the Program for Children ages 4 Through 12 by Michelle G. Bissanti, M.Ed. 205
  The Three-fold Practices—Body, Mind, Heart 205
  Body Practice—A Sound Body 207
  Mind Practice—A Conscious Mind 214
  The Elephant Path 216
  The Three Jewels—Buddha, Dharma, Sangha 219
  Heart Practice—Conduct of a Compassionate Heart 222

Chapter 7: The Practice for Early Preoperational Children (Ages 4-6) by Michelle G. Bissanti, M.Ed. 225
  Elephant Path Preparation 225
  Personal Space 226
  Arriving to the Mat: Rock Pose 226
  Rock Garden 227
  The Singing Bowl Meditation 228
  Breath work 228
  Mindful Sharing 231
  Focus Friends 232
  Heart Meditation; Resting Attention in the Heart—Seeing Through the Eyes of the Heart 232
  Savasana 235

Table of Contents

Chapter 8: Concentration Development for Late Preoperational Children (Ages 7-9) by Michelle Bissanti, M.Ed. 237
Goals and Objectives 238
Defining Personal Space and Setting Up the Posture 239
Setting the Intention 240
Singing Bowl 241
Sitting Posture 241
Breath work 241
Sphere Breath 242
Mindful Sharing 243
Moving Meditation 244
Walking Meditation 245
Shake It Standing Meditation 245
Concentration 1: Following the Breath; Identifying with the Meditator in The Elephant Path 246
What is the Mind? Identifying with the Elephant on The Elephant Path; Clouds in the Sky 248
Cloud Meditation 249
Monkey Mind; Identifying with the Monkey on The Elephant Path 249
The Mind Jar; Noticing the Workings of the Mind 251
Concentration 2: Noticing the Activity of the Mind; Identifying with the Elephant and the Monkey on The Elephant Path 252
Deepening Practice 254
Baby Bird Visualization Meditation 255
Resting Attention in the Heart and Silence Meditations: Noticing Feelings and Emotions as they Arise 256
Feeling and Emotion as Movement 257

Chapter 9: Concentration Development for Concrete Operational Children (Ages 9-12) by Michelle Bissanti, M.Ed. 261
Goals and Objectives 263
Preparational Practices 264
Breath work 266

Table of Contents

Setting Intention and Developing Motivation 267
Preparation for the Concentration Session 268
Concentration 1: Following the Breath, Noticing the Mind and Redirecting 269
Concentration 2: Noticing the Movement of the Mind and Identifying Distractions 272
Concentration 3: Strategies and Activities for Dealing with Distraction and Sustaining Concentration; Intensifying 274
    The Flame and Intensifying Activities 274
    Singing Bowl Activity 274
    Foggy Mountain Road Activity 275
    Tree Pose Activity 275
    The Deer Spotting Activity 276
Intensifying Meditation 276
Metaphors to Illustrate the Activity of Mind 277
    The Practitioner's Rope 277
    Dog on a Leash Metaphor 277
    Fishing Line Metaphor 277
    The Rabbit of Subtle Dullness 278
    Ocean and Waves 278
    Bubbles Around Thoughts 279
    Freight Train 279
Deepening Practice: Sharpening Meta-cognition On and Off the Mat 279
Favorite Clouds 279
Favorite Cloud-Jar Activity 280
Gauging Progress: Talking About the Practice 280
The Benefits of Concentration 281
Impermanence 282
    Buddha Board Activity 282
    Painting with Water Activity 282
The *Mandala* Project 283
Mandala Meditation Activity 284
Awareness Activities 285

Listening with Awareness 285
    Pairs or Small Group Listening Activity 285
    Large Group Listening Activity 286
  Mirroring with Awareness 287
  Drawing with Awareness 287
  Assignments and School-Work with Awareness 288
  Tea Time with Awareness 288
  Understanding Anxiety and Stress 289
Heart Practice: The Conduct of a Compassionate Heart 290
  Before You Speak, Before You Act 290
  Intention 291
  Namaste—Closing the Practice 291
  Spontaneously Arising Practice 292
  Heart Meditations 292
  Mantras 293
  Heart Rocks 294
  Prayer Flags 294
  Daily Wishes; Nuggets of Goodness 295
  Reflection 296

Chapter 10: A Concentration Training Program for Adolescents
              in a Public School by Jae Pasari 299
  Adolescence; Developmental Considerations 299
  Setting the Context 300
  Design Considerations 301
  Curriculum Overview 302
  Table 1: Jedi Mind Control Overview 306
  A Video Guide to Jedi Mind Training 308
  Week 1: Matt Killingsworth: Want to be happier? Stay in the
      moment 308
  Week 2: Donald Hoffman: Do we see reality as it is? 308
  Week 3: Tan Le: A headset that reads your brainwaves 309
  Week 4: Daniel Goleman: Focus, flow, and frazzle 309
  Week 5: Dan Harris: What do we have all wrong about meditation?
      and Hack your brain with meditation 309

Table of Contents

Week 6: Andy Puddicombe: All it takes is 10 mindful minutes 310
Week 7: Instant Egghead: Meditation changes the brain and ASAP Science: The scientific power of meditation 310
Week 8: Rick Hanson: How to change your brain 310
Week 9: Cliff Nass: Are you multitasking your life away? 310
Week 10: Dandapani: Unwavering focus 311
Week 11: Isaac Lidsky: What reality are you creating for yourself? 311
Week 12: Srikumar Rao: Plug into your hard-wired happiness 311
Week 13: Richard Davidson: The four constituents of well-being 311
Week 14: Alia Crum: Change your mindset, change the game 312
Week 15: Abigail Marsh: Why some people are more altruistic ... 312
Concentration and Meta-cognitive Training 312
Sample Guided Meditations 315
Preparations 315
Exemplar Practice 315
Directing Concentration to the Three-Point Object 316
Supplemental Counting 316
Intensification (magnification) 316
Seven-Point Object 317
Training Meta-cognitive Detection of Distracting Thought; The Spinning Sword Exercise 317
Closing 318
Reporting Back 318
Outcomes and Implications 318
Final Comment: Implementing these Practices in Educational Settings 319

Bibliography 323

The Elephant Path: Attention Development and Training in Children and Adolescents

Acknowledgments

The authors would especially like to thank His Holiness, the thirty third Menri Trizin, the spiritual leader and lineage holder of the Bon, for his vision and making these teachings available to the West, to Rahob Tulku, Thupten Kalsang Rinpoche, an emanation of Padmasambhava, for his vision and making these teachings available to the West, and to the late Denma Locho Rinpoche, Abbott of Namgyal Monastery in Dharamsala, who taught Dan Brown Asanga's Nine Stages of Staying. We would also like to thank Triodos Bank N.V. and Adeline van Waning, M.D., Ph.D., who gave a grant to the authors to assist in the development and writing of this book. We would also like to extend our deepest gratitude to the Pointing Out the Great Way Foundation for their support in writing and producing this book. We would also like to express our deepest appreciation to Evelyn Tribole, MS., RDN and Anita Cook, Ph.D., who carefully did the copy-editing on this manuscript. Our sincere thanks to Susan Pottish who did the final stage of copy editing on this manuscript. Deepest gratitude to Dustin DiPerna and Bright Alliance for publishing this book, and to Brad Reynolds for all his care with the type-setting and final printing of this book. Finally, we would like to acknowledge with much gratitude the children that we have had the privilege of teaching.

The Vision Behind this Work

by Michelle G. Bissanti, M.Ed.

Over 10 years ago I (MB) wrote a motivation statement to convey why I wanted to bring the practices of yoga and meditation to children. This vision is what flowed quickly and clearly from my heart. After endless hours of practice, research, collaboration, and instruction with children, the motivation remains the same.

Imagine a world where children discover, listen to, and live through their inner teacher; where the development of the external world is balanced with the development of the internal mind; where kindness, compassion, and awareness of the interconnectedness of all beings is ever-present; and where a child's innate awareness remains fluid through childhood and into adulthood.

This is the fruition of these practices. They are vitally important in our efforts to nurture and support the development of strong, aware, and meta-cognitively intelligent individuals who move with compassion and kindness through this world.

Over more than twenty years as an educator and a mother, I have come to realize the deep importance and responsibility we have in supporting and nurturing the body/mind connection and social-emotional health of our children. The world is ever-changing and the busyness that has become a mainstay of Western society challenges our internal rhythm and very being. It can be seen in a multitude of ways how children struggle with the many demands placed on them both in the educational system and the world at large.

Over the course of my first ten years teaching in the public schools I saw a dramatic increase in the attention deficit disorder (ADD and ADHD). In some instances, classroom supports were put in place such as student aides. In many cases, however, such a diagnosis resulted in prescription drugs. At the time, these had some positive effects but also many frustrating and concerning effects on the children and families trying to negotiate them. At the same time, state standards were strongly guiding our teaching, and a multitude of standardized tests were coursing their way back into the repertoire. As an educator who was very involved in the development of curriculum, I became increasingly concerned. Days had become busier with more requirements and less time for creative ways to bring education to children. Behavior issues and the ability to manage and support our children became a challenge. While we were deeply committed to teaching to the whole child, there seemed to be a real disconnect. Over the past twenty years the technology revolution has become the latest challenge for our children. While there are wonderful opportunities for connection and learning, it comes with a sense of bombardment, a continuous flow of too much information that comes so quickly it often does not allow for reflection or thoughtful clear response. It can frazzle children, throw them off, and pull them away from their center.

"A 2010 Kaiser Foundation study showed that elementary aged children use an average of 7.5 hours per day of entertainment technology. Sedentary bodies bombarded with chaotic sensory stimulation are resulting in delays in attaining child developmental milestones. The impact of rapidly advancing technology on the developing child has seen an increase in physical, psychological and behavioral disorders." (Rowan, 2017) Obesity, anxiety, and attention disorders are among the diagnoses facing children today. There is an urgent need to restore a sense of balance and to truly support the development of a healthy, whole child.

The ancient practices of yoga and meditation offer balance and a healthy mind/body connection. They come naturally to children and are applicable to an educational program that values the well-being of its children. I spent ten years developing a program for elementary students, which honors the mind, body, and heart through the practices of yoga, meditation, and social-emotional skills development. Coupling the needs and mission of a school community with the richness and depth of these practices is essential and enables an organic program to emerge. These practices support the development of a strong body, mental pliancy, concentration, attention, and awareness. They point the way to

The Vision Behind This Work

one's innate goodness and inner knowing through the teacher within each of us. Children are able to progress at their own pace, encouraging self-awareness, fostering self-esteem and creating a strong community of practitioners supporting one another.

The practices of yoga and meditation have been around for thousands of years. They follow lineage traditions, in which they are passed down from generation-to-generation by great masters. Understanding how these practices originate for children, and how they are taught to children, has been important in ensuring that the practices are authentic and as close to the original teachings as possible. It has been important to me to honor and uphold the integrity of these practices while also making them accessible and relevant to the Western child.

Over the course of my years creating, developing, and implementing a yoga and meditation program which honored the mission, goals, and needs of an independent school community of children ages 4 through 12, I had the opportunity to travel to both Tibet and Nepal. These travels gave me the opportunity to reflect on the program that I had created and to understand more deeply how these practices develop for children in the cultures in which they originated. I traveled to Rahob Monastery in Eastern Tibet with Rahob Tulku Rinpoche and The Pointing Out the Great Way Foundation. This Foundation is inspired by the work of Daniel P. Brown, Ph.D. Its mission is to promote an exchange of gifts between the East and West. The Foundation acts as facilitator for the gifts of the precious teachings of the Bon and Buddhist Indo-Tibetan meditation lineages through its support of meditation practices and translation of sacred texts for Western practitioners. In return the Foundation partners with friends and mentors to preserve and revitalize these precious teachings in their indigenous settings. While in Rahob Village, I interviewed the boy monks and their main teacher to gain a greater understanding of how children in these indigenous communities learn these practices and develop attention skills and working memory. While yoga is not a large part of their studies and practice in this tradition, their upbringing, the values held within their communities, and the development of their meditation practice is vital to the education of the child. The children are cared for by extended family members and neighborhood elders.

They practice with their family and are considered a part of the "sangha," a practice community. The local agricultural and nomadic community face many challenges, but their communities are strong and intact. The people are very devotional. They are hard-working, warm-hearted, and live their spiritual practice in daily life.

One of the most revealing questions I asked the monks' teacher was "How do you deal with distraction and misbehavior?" My translator turned to me various times asking me to reword the question. This went back and forth multiple times until finally the translator explained that he hadn't understood the question because it was not an issue. The only connection he could make to the question was that sometimes the boys got tired, and a simple tug of their ears pulled them back to the moment. I looked at the boys realizing that they'd been sitting here for almost two hours as we shared conversation with their teacher. There were no interruptions, no misbehaving, and no need for the teacher to give them reminders to listen, be attentive or respectful. They were not statues, as they shifted, shared smiles, and frequently expressed little giggles. They were typical kids in that way but seemed to have complete control over their actions, bodies, and choices.

Maybe most of what I learned from these interviews and my time within this community was the feeling I had while being in their presence. Their devotion, presence of mind, and warm-hearted nature were palpable and visible in their actions and the way they interacted with one another and with us. In regard to their meditation practice I learned that daily memorization of prayers trained attention, concentration, and working memory. I also learned that once children reach the age of 9 or 10 they have the opportunity to further their education by attending a school that offers formal concentration practices, such as the "elephant path of concentration." Children that do not proceed along this path can return to the village school to continue their education. Either way, the practices of concentration meditation are built into the learning curriculum for children. In this way, they are raised with these practices, which are embedded and ingrained in their very being. They live their practice.

The Vision Behind This Work

As a result of this trip I was invited by the Foundation to go on a subsequent trip two years later to Jomsom, Nepal to evaluate a school there and was able to deepen my understanding of how these practices are traditionally taught to children. The Foundation sponsors Tibetan children living in Nepal, supporting the re-learning of their indigenous Tibetan language and practices. They wanted an independent evaluation of the quality of education that these children would be receiving.

I had the good fortune to interview Geshe Sonam Gurung who founded the Himalayan Children's Home in Mustang, a boarding school for Tibetan children. His mission was to establish and strengthen his indigenous Tibetan culture and educate the local children living in very rural areas in their indigenous Tibetan language and meditation practices. These children were currently working the farms and fields with their families. Not only were they not attending school, but they were losing their language, culture, and traditions. At the time, twenty-five children lived together at the Himalayan Children's Home and attended the nearby public school. In the hours before and after school, Geshe Sonam taught the children Tibetan language, meditation practices, and culture. He begins with morning prayers and meditation consisting of the teaching of prayers with specific focus on memorization. The memorization teaches focus and concentration and nurtures within the children the deep and beautiful understanding of the prayers. They begin with a one-line mantra, the Three Heart Mantra. They pay careful attention to the words and the rhythm. They continue attention training by teaching more prayers. He also uses sound meditation to focus on the sound, rhythm, and feeling that arises. This helps them to identify when they feel peace of mind arising. In learning how to focus they cultivate positive thinking that brings their mind into a positive state. His hope is that the Tibetan culture and language will remain alive and flourish for these children and families for generations to come. Geshe Sonam feels it is important to foster the sharing of traditional stories. Storytelling is an important part of developing and carrying forward the traditions of these indigenous people. He feels strongly that the children should have time with their families. The bond and connection that the children have with their mothers and families is important, and he creates times during the year when children return home, or families come to the Himalayan Children's Home.

Again, in developing my program, it seemed important to incorporate the body practice of yoga alongside a concentration practice for the Western child. Unlike the children in villages in Tibet and Nepal, Western children are growing up with a multitude of very different challenges. Cultivating an awareness of the body, a sense of respect and care for the body, is important. There are so many challenges facing Western children today such as the amount of time they are often expected to sit, the fast-paced daily flow, and the often-over-scheduled life of young people. The pressures and expectations placed on children growing up in the West also play a critical part in the development of body image issues and obesity. Teachers are continually exploring ways to address and support children around bullying and other social emotional issues. The use of social media, technology, and the culture of materialism are all challenges that we, as parents and educators, must embrace as we help children navigate them in healthy ways. It became clear that beginning with a yoga practice was essential to the Western child. Yoga means "to yolk the body and the mind." Cultivating a yoga practice builds the ground from which a meditation practice naturally arises. The body is the vessel within which one can rest in the mind. From meditation practice the mind settles, and the heart naturally opens. Geshe Sonam expresses beautifully that the fruition of his sound meditations with children is the ability to "feel peace arising".

As a young adult discovering these practices, I was deeply moved by the invitation to recognize my breath, to develop a relationship with it, and to allow it to be a path to the present moment. I remember wondering how different my life might have been if I'd been introduced to this as a child. I felt an urgency to make the introduction for them. If we could teach children the sacred relationship they have with their body, their breath, and their mind, children would be free to navigate and move through this world with their innate wisdom, awake and aware.

My vision for these practices in a school setting was that they offer a

The Vision Behind This Work

moment in the school day where children can have space to step out of the routine and happenings in their classroom to connect with the most sacred parts of themselves, that they would have a moment to witness and come to know their most sacred teacher, their teacher within. My hope was that children would then begin to carry these practices with them confidently throughout the rest of their school day. In time, over their years of practice, they would truly begin to incorporate the goodness of these practices into their way of being, and we could begin the commitment to a more awake, kindhearted, compassionate world.

Students and teacher at Rahob Monastery in Eastern Tibet with Daniel P. Brown, Michelle G. Bissanti and Forrest Bissanti.

The Vision Behind This Work

Students and teacher, Geshe Sonam Gurung, at
The Himalayan Children's Home in Mustang, Nepal

The Elephant Path: Attention Development and Training in Children and Adolescents

Introduction:
A Guide for Readers

This book is written for parents, teachers, psychologists, researchers, community leaders, child advocates, and anyone committed to supporting the heart/mind of our children. It is divided into two main parts, and is written in two different styles. The first half of the text presents extensive scientific research into various kinds of attentional capacities and the effects/consequences of their presence or absence in children, and the second half presents detailed practical means for developing those capacities from early childhood through adolescence. We expect that educators may want to delve right into the practical methods about training attention in children, and that some may be less interested in the detailed scientific research that gives solid grounding to these practical exercises. We also expect that researchers may be more interested in the scientific evidence, and less interested in the practical exercises. Yet, by writing the book this way, we hope that educators will read the scientific review sufficiently to appreciate the scientific grounding of these practices, and we hope that researchers will read the practice-based chapters enough to appreciate exactly how the science has been implemented in the classroom.

Part I of this book is written from a scientific perspective. The first chapter begins with a detailed and comprehensive review of the scientific research on the development of attention, from neonates, throughout childhood, adolescence, and then into adulthood. This review includes the development of both the alerting system and the orienting attention systems, which first develops as an outside-oriented exogenous orienting system, then develops as an inside-oriented endogenous attention system, and finally develops as an executive attention system that continues to develop and stabilize throughout adolescence and early adulthood. We include in this review a section on the development of metacognitive awareness in childhood, because this research has shown that metacognitive awareness plays such an important role in effective learning and problem-solving. We also include a section on the neuroscience, namely on the brain development of the various attention systems. Our intention has been to give strong scientific grounding to the development and training of attention in children and adolescents.

The second chapter reviews many types of dysfunctions of attention systems: mindlessly losing track of the task at hand, distracted concentration, individual differences in distractibility, the illusion of sustained attention, the problem of apportioning or dividing attention, mind-wandering, multi-tasking, reactivity to immediate experience, lack of coherence of mind, poor metacognitive awareness, and poor working memory. To make this review relevant to the younger generation, we have included a detailed review of the effects of multimedia on attention, such as a review of the positive and negative effects of word processing, videogaming, web browsing, and mobile devices on attention systems.

The third chapter contains a comprehensive review of studies on training various attention skills, such as training to reduce mind-wandering, multitasking, and reactivity, and training in: mindfulness, concentration, metacognitive monitoring, working memory, and executive functions. We make a strong argument for the importance of concentration and metacognition training in effective learning and performance.

The fourth chapter reviews a comprehensive system of concentration training adapted from Asanga's Indo-Tibetan Buddhist concentration training, the *Nine Stages of the Mind Staying* (Tibetan: *sems gnas dgu*), otherwise referred to as "*the elephant path.*" We have taken the main concentration practices from this Buddhist system, adapted them to the Western mind, and also adapted them to the developmental level of the child or adolescent.

Part II delves into the practical application of these practices and includes a number of case studies. It is written in a more user-friend-

Introduction

ly style designed for educators less involved in the sciences. It offers a large variety of specific, carefully-worded instructions for children for concentration practices, body practices, and supportive activities; and is organized based on developmental age.

The fifth chapter bridges Part I and II by addressing the main considerations for adapting training to the developmental age of the child; the early preoperational child, ages 4-6, the late preoperational child, ages 7-9, and the concrete operational child, ages 10-12.

Chapters six through nine address practices for children ages 4-12 as created, developed, and implemented by Michelle Bissanti. Her work has been taught within an independent school setting, to small groups, and one on one. Each section gives detailed accounts of the wording of the instructions and case examples of the students' responses. We hope that the exercises are described in sufficient detail that the reader actually gets a clear sense of how these are actually implemented in the classroom.

The sixth chapter offers an introduction to the program for children ages 4-12. It introduces the three-fold practices of body, mind, and heart that are cornerstones to the program. This chapter also includes key concepts in Indo-Tibetan Buddhism that are a foundation for the development of these practices with children.

The seventh, eighth and ninth chapters present the development of practices for the early preoperational, the late preoperational, and the concrete operational child. While these chapters include body and heart practices, the focus is on the development of concentration practices.

The tenth chapter gives a comprehensive look at a program of concentration training for high school students in a public school setting as developed and implemented by Jae Pasari.

This book is meant to give both a solid scientific foundation for, an overview of, and detailed examples of these practices. Although we have tried to describe practices for children in sufficient detail, as a window into their implementation in different educational settings, it is not our intention that some who reads this book tries to immediately implement them from this book alone, without any experience or training. We must emphasize that it is important to develop a first-hand experience in concentration practice and the body and heart practices that accompany these programs before introducing and implementing them with children or in a school community. When introducing these practices in any setting it is important to understand the mission, values, population, and goal of the school, organization, or individual and adapt the practices in a supportive way to meet the needs of the community.

Part I

The Development and Training of Attention East and West

Chapter 1

The Development of Attentional Systems in Childhood and Adolescence

by Daniel P. Brown, Ph.D.

Most researchers concur that a variety of attentional systems develop throughout the childhood years. A common distinction is drawn between involuntary stimulus-driven attention to salient stimuli and voluntary control over selecting, sustaining, and engaging attention (Corbetta & Shulman, 202; Knudson, 2007; Ruff & Rothbart, 1996). Neuroscientists concur that the involuntary stimulus-driven attentional system is associated with the maturation of the posterior parietal system and the voluntary selective, sustained attentional system is associated with the prefrontal cortex (Corbetta & Shulman, 2002; Ptak, 2012).

The most widely accepted model for the development of attention in children is the work of Michael Posner and his associates—research that developed over several decades (Posner & Petersen, 1990; Petersen & Posner, 2012; Rothbart, Posner, & Boylan, 1990). According to this model, there are three distinct attentional systems that develop independently and at different rates throughout childhood: the alerting system, the orienting system, and the executive attentional system. The alerting system entails the "ability to prepare and sustain alertness to process high priority signals" (Petersen & Posner, 2012, p. 35). The orienting system pertains to acoustic and visual orienting, pattern recognition, and target selection. The executive attentional system pertains to executive control, selective attention, sustained attention, and self-regulation over attentional systems. Self-regulation entails "the ability to comply with a request, to initiate and cease activities according to situational demands, to modulate the intensity, frequency, and duration of verbal and motor acts in social and educational settings, [and] to postpone acting upon a desired object or goal and to generate socially approved behavior" (Kopp, 1982, p. 199). The executive attentional system pertains to top-down regulation of the other attentional systems (Sarter, Givens, & Bruno, 2001, p. 157).

Each of these three systems are independent systems, as justified by the fact that each is associated with its own neurocircuitry pattern. The alerting system is associated with the reticular activating system in the brain stem (Posner et al., 2014) and the thalamus (Fan et al., 2005). The orienting system is associated with the fronto-parietal system consisting of the parietal cortex and frontal eye fields, and also with the primary sensory and motor regions (Fransson et al., 2011). The executive attention system is associated with the cingulo-opercular system (Lauria & Homskaya, 1970; Posner et al., 2012). The alerting system develops in the first months of life, so that modulation of arousal level is well developed by the second or third month (Kopp, 1982). The orienting system is well developed by 7 months. Goal-directed attention is well developed by 12-18 months (Kopp, 1982, p. 205), and by 24 months the capacity for control over attention develops (Kochanska, Coy, and Murray, 2001). By 4 years of age the executive circuitry is sufficiently developed, such that the executive attentional system begins to dominate (Posner et al., 2014).

THE ALERTING ATTENTIONAL SYSTEM

According to Posner and Petersen (1990) the alerting system entails "the ability to prepare and sustain alertness to process high priority signals" (p. 35). In the first days and weeks of life the neonate spends a good deal of time sleeping. In the first two weeks of life, for example, neonates spend only 11-19% of the day alert (Ruff & Rothbart, 1996, p. 34). As each day passes the neonate spends longer and longer time awake and alert, and during these extended episodes of alertness the neonate spends time gazing (Wolff (1965). "The time infants spend looking at interesting objects during alert periods increases from birth to 3 months" (Ruff & Rothbart, 1996, p. 36).

Chapter 1: The Development of Attentional Systems in Childhood and Adolescence

As the weeks pass the neonate begins to show signs of increasing stability of an alert focused state. For example, Becker and Thoman (1983) directly observed neonates in the home environment at 2-, 3-, 4-, and 5-weeks of age. The various states observed were waking and alert; waking and non-alert; fussing or crying; drowsy; and asleep. They found that over this span of weeks "Infants showed considerable range in state stability over weeks. State stability when alone was significantly correlated with state stability when with the mother" (p. 405). However, according to Moss et al. (1988) there were marked individual differences in infants' state shifts. They observed and gave behavioral ratings to 3-month-old infants of state shifts. They discovered essentially two groups. One group of infants could be aroused rapidly from sleep to alertness. These infants rarely got upset during the examination. They held a steady state for longer duration during the examination, and seemed to react appropriately to internal and external stimulation. A second group failed to show these healthy state changes, sustained steady state, and did "not react adaptively to such [internal and external] signals" (p. 1218).

An upright posture is also associated with increased alertness in the infant. For example, Korner & Grobstein (1966) found that when crying infants are picked up and put on the mother's shoulder, "they not only stop crying but they frequently alert and scan the environment… Each infant alerted and scanned in the majority of trials when put to the shoulder" (p. 867). The shift to greater alertness, however, did not occur when the infant was sitting up or lying on his or her back. Not only does being held upright lead to greater alertness, it also leads to greater visual scanning of the environment. Fredrickson and Brown (1975) observed 3-day-old neonates in three different postures—lying down, sitting up, and being held upright on the mother's shoulder. They found that "each position has little effect on amount of time the eyes were open, [but] the on-shoulder position significantly increased the quality of visual behavior" (p. 579), as measured by his ability to fixate and follow a stimulus.

The alerting system is well developed by the second and third month (Kopp. 1982). Episodes of alert focus as a steady state improve from 3-7 months. The immediacy of alerting to visual cues develops more slowly. For example, Morrison (1982) studied the development of alertness in older children, namely 5-, and 8- year-olds and in adults. They found that 5-year-olds "alerted more slowly than older groups and sustained optimal alertness less well" (p. 187). In contrast 8-year-olds and adults alerted more quickly and sustained optimal alertness better than the 5-year-olds" (p. 197). They found that the alerting system "appears to reach adult levels during the early school years" (p.197). Similarly, Rueda et al. (2005) found no significant changes from ages 6 to 10 in the development of the alerting system. This is the earliest attentional system to develop and the first to reach maturity.

The Orienting Attentional System

The orienting attentional system develops in several stages. The first orienting system to develop is the exogenous orienting system. As the name implies, the exogenous orienting system refers to largely reflexive or involuntary orientation of attention and the gaze to certain features of visual stimuli, wherein the orienting response is activated by the external visual features of objects or locations themselves. In other words, the neonate is hard-wired to respond to certain visual cues on the surrounding environment, and the specificity of these cues activates exogenous orienting changes over time. Over time the orientation of attention to selected visual stimuli becomes independent of the gaze. This is called covert exogenous orienting.

Eventually, the infant develops some internal capacity for modulating the orienting response. This is called the endogenous orienting system. Posner et al. (2012) define the orienting system in terms of "the ability to prioritize sensory input by selecting a modality or location" (p. 75). Ruff and Rothbart (1996) emphasize the critical importance of exogenous orienting as the foundation of exploratory behavior in infancy (p. 42). Posner et al. (2012) emphasize the "importance of orienting as a control system in early development" (p. 823).

The Exogenous Orienting System

Exogenous orienting refers to "the involuntary orienting of atten-

Chapter 1: The Development of Attentional Systems in Childhood and Adolescence

tion to locations signaled by a salient stimulus-difference, such as a brief flash of light that functions as a cue" (Brodeur, 1990, p. 219). Within the first days of life the visual system is already programmed to orient involuntarily to certain kinds of visual patterns over other stimuli. For example, neonates younger that five-days-old "consistently looked more at black-and-white patterns than at plain colored surfaces…[and showed an] ability to perceive form" (Fantz, 1963, p. 256). He adds, the length of gaze at a target and "selective visual responses were related to pattern rather than hue or reflectance" (p. 257). Similarly, Ruff and Rothbart (1996) say, "a newborn will look longer at some pictures or designs than at others" (p. 5), and over time "attend to different aspects of pictures, objects, and events as they develop" (p. 6). They add, "The orienting network is strongly related to the movement of attention to specific locations in the environment" (p. 41).

Preferences for visual patterns clearly change over the first weeks. For example, Ruff and Turkewitz (1975) showed 6- to 24-week-old infants pairs of stimuli—either a bull's eye or a striped pattern varying in size. Infants 6-10 weeks-old "mostly respond to larger size" whereas infants 10-24 weeks old "looked more at the bull's eye regardless of size," (p. 705), and older children responded mainly to "differences in the pattern" (p. 708). By the second month of life infants selectively scan external contours of stationary objects, show an ability to selective certain visual patterns over others, and show some rudimentary capacity to restrict scanning to certain locations. During this transitional period from 2-3 months of age infants develop the ability to visually track moving objects. Exogenous orienting toward selected patterns, location, and movement is well developed by the third month, but "young infants may have trouble looking away from a highly salient object once their attention has been engaged (Ruff & Rothbart, 1996, p. 35).

During that same period, from 2-3 months, infants develop the ability to anticipate the reappearance of a previously presented visual pattern. Canfield and Haith (1991) found, for example, that 2- and 3-month olds "form an expectation about reappearance of a previously presented target….[and]…quickly develop a crude representation of the spatial, temporal, and possible numerical parameters of stimulus sequences to anticipate future events" (p. 198). By 4 months the number of objects in the immediate visual field captures attention. Cohen (1972) found that when 4-month-old infants looked at a checkerboard with varying size and number of squares, the "duration of looking was determined more by number than by size" (p. 869). By 5.5 months infants can detect discrepancies based on changes in previously shown visual patterns (Bhatt, Bertin, & Gilbert, 1999).

The third month of life marks a "major developmental transition in the development of the exogenous orienting system (Ruff & Rothbart, 1996, p. 35). From 2 to 6 months of age, the infant develops a clear preference for exogenous orienting to novel, as compared to repetitive visual stimuli (Fantz (1964). Ruff and Rothbart (1996) state:

> Over the rest of the year, attention is governed in important ways by the novelty of objects and events encountered by the infant. Repeated experience reduces novelty, but also leads the infant to notice new and different details and features… visual features give way to graspability and texture by 3 to 4 months (p. 6)

Visual preference for novelty becomes a moderately stable dimension of exogenous orienting by 6 to 8 months of age (Rose & Feldman, 1987). This strong preference for novel visual stimuli also suggests that selectivity of attention is beginning to develop. For example, Walker and Neisser (1981) presented 4-month-old infants with two films superimposed on the same screen, one with a soundtrack and one without, but the soundtrack from the first film was playing. Then, each film was shown separately. They found, "the infants looked mostly at the previously silent film, suggesting that it was novel for them" (p. 377). They concluded, "infants, like adults, can selectively attend to one complex, visual event while ignoring another superimposed upon it" (p. 389).

Researchers have given considerable thought on how to assess attention in infants who have not yet developed the capacity to speak and therefore cannot describe how they pay attention. For example, Colombo (1993) discovered four highly correlated ways to assess attention in infants. He also found that infants who scored high on these four measures had higher infant intelligence scores. The four measures consist of: 1. duration of time that an infant fixates on a visual object; 2. preference for novelty; 3. memory retention of learned responses; and 4. reaction time (p. 102). Like the previously mentioned researchers, Colombo also noted clear preferences for some visual stimuli over others. He says, "Some visual properties were inherently more attractive or salient to the infant than others" (p. 30), and that even young infants demonstrated "selective looking" (p. 32). Colombo found that duration of fixation on a visual stimulus was "the best metric" (p. 47) to assess "the length of time the infant spends looking at the stimulus" (p. 45). Ironically, he also found that fixation duration generally decreased, not increased with age, but that children could be classified into long- and short-lookers. The short-looking infants, as compared to the long-looking infants, tended to show a stronger preference for novelty and to engage in greater exploratory behavior (p. 57).

Most researchers on infant attention concur that fixation of attention, head turning, fixation of the gaze, reduced motor response, and heart rate deceleration are highly interrelated ways that preverbal infants express their capacity to pay attention (Ruff & Rothbart, 1996, p. 101). Porges (1974), for example states:

> Since the neonatal period is characterized by a lack of meaningful verbal communication, physiological and motor responses have long been proposed as indicators of underlying psychological processes…heart rate…sucking, body movement, and eye movement have been common [p. 231]… Heart rate deceleration has been interpreted as a component of the orienting reflex [p. 233]…a decrease in heart rate variability is related to sustained attention in children and adults in response to demanding tasks [p. 234]… spontaneous heart rate variability may be able to serve as an assessment index of the newborn's attentional responsivity. (p. 251)

In other words, when an infant pays attention the head turns and the eyes fixate, motor output diminishes, and heart-rate slows.

An important dimension of preverbal attentiveness in preverbal infants is head turning and gazing. Enns (1990) clearly states, "attention can be studied in infants through an evaluation of their looking behavior" (p. 15). As Rufff and Rothbart (1996) say, "The shift to greater cortical control around 2 to 3 months makes it possible for processes of attention to assume greater control of eye movements" (p. 39). Hood and Atkinson (1993) for example studied the amount of time it took for 1.5-, 3-, and 6-month old infants to look toward a peripheral target. Somewhere between 1 and 3 months the capacity to control making shifts in eye movements toward the target had matured (p. 421). By 6 months of age the infant was able to maintain the gaze on a central target for longer duration, as well as to readily shift the gaze to another target (Hood, 1993). According to Ruff and Rothbart (1996) there are "steady changes in patterns of looking...from 3 to 9 months [and] selective visual attention is strongly influenced by novelty" (p. 41). Between 6 and 18 months of age, the infant becomes able to adjust the gaze contingent on a change in an adult's focus (Butterworth & Cochran, 1980). A major developmental change is that the infant begins to respond more to cues from the mother (Ruff & Rothbart, 1996, p. 268).

Visual fixation and the gaze, as part of the exogenous orienting system, rapidly matures from 6 to 7 months of age. By 6 months the posterior parietal cortex associated with exogenous orienting is fully developed and by 8 months "many of the functions [of the exogenous orienting system] have reached adult levels" (Ruff & Rothbart, 1996, p. 41).

Lewis, et al (1966) first noted that as early as 2 months of age, the "length of time the infant fixates on the array is directly related to the degree of [heart rate] deceleration" (p. 63). Around the same time Graham and Clifton (1966) discovered that heart rate deceleration was "part of the orienting reflex" (p. 305). Since this earlier research, it has become well established that "Deceleration of heart rate seems to reflect attention to external events...[and the best] index of sustained attention...is a decrease in heart-rate variability" (Ruff & Rothbart, 1996, p. 21). Von Bargen (1983) reviewed the studies on infant heart rate variability. He found that repeated measures of heart rate changes in infants showed remarkable test-retest reliability (r=0.96) over a 24-hour period and also showed high consistency from 2.5 to 5 months. The period of 2-3 months of age constituted "a major developmental change in the control of autonomic functioning" (p. 118), wherein heart-rate deceleration became a stable measure of infant attention. He concluded, "The evidence that the decelerative heart-rate response is an orienting response is quite strong" (p. 130). However, the magnitude of heart rate deceleration accompanying episodes of infant exogenous orienting increases with age. In younger infants HR deceleration is generally 3-6 beats per minutes (BPM) lower, 8-10 bpm lower in older infants and 24 bpm lower in adults during episodes of fixation attention. Heart-rate deceleration is significantly correlated with the size but not the duration of the infant smile. The more rapid the heart-rate deceleration the larger the smile accompanying exogenous orienting (Brock, Rothbart, & Derryberry, 1986, p. 403).

Casey and Richards (1988) studied infants 14-, 20-, and 26-weeks of age. These infants were shown complex patterns on a television screen. When infants fixated on these patterns, heart-rate generally slowed down. The magnitude of heart-rate decoration increased with age. Infants were at times presented with two competing visual stimuli, sometimes when they were focusing on the first stimulus, and sometimes when they were not focusing. They found that during episodes of heart-rate deceleration the infant was "less likely to be distracted by a secondary stimulus" (p. 1519), and that older infants sustained heart-rate deceleration in a stable way during periods of sustained attention (p. 1519). In another study of heart-rate variability in infants watching *Sesame Street*, Richards and Casey (1991) found that infants showed heart-rate deceleration when selectively orienting their attention, and decreased heart-rate variability when sustaining attention over time to the same stimulus (p. 43).

Another dimension of preverbal attentiveness pertains to motor output. According to Ruff and Rothbart (1996), "concentration of attention is linked to a reduction in many forms of motor activity" (p. 99). In other words, when an infant under 5 months of age is being attentive, it is typically accompanied by a drop in motor output. However, after 5 months of age motor output becomes coordinated with attentiveness, in the form of visually guided reaching. According to Bushnell (1985), visually guided reaching is first exhibited sometime between 3 and 5 months of age (p. 139) and by 9 months of age all reaching is visually guided. Starting at around 5 months of age, if an infant is presented with two different objects, the infant will show a preference in the form of reaching for one object instead of the other (Ruff & Rothbart, 1996, p. 18).

Episodes of exogenous orienting in infants are also accompanied by the facial display of interest. Langsdorf (1983) studied the facial display of interest in 2-, 4-, 6-, and 8-month-old infants looking at either a live female, a female mannequin, or an inanimate object. The duration of fixation time was longer in 8-month olds than the other age groups for the live female, then, the mannequin, and less so for the inanimate object (p. 37). Heart-rate deceleration was also larger in the 8-month-old infants as compared to younger groups. According to Langdorf, "Interest accounted for a substantial percentage of the variance" of the orienting response (p. 384).

ORIENTING AND THE MATERNAL ENVIRONMENT

Parrinello and Ruff (1988) studied the effect of maternal intervention on 1-month-old infants' attention to external objects. Infants were randomly assigned to either a condition of low, medium, high, or no maternal intervention in what the infant attended to. They found that the duration of time infants spent attending to external objects increased in medium intervention compared to other conditions, especially when the infant was not attending to anything at the time of the maternal intervention. However, if the infant was already paying attention the maternal intervention added little to the level of attention already shown by the infant. Overall, "the results show that level of intervention interacts with the child's spontaneous tendency to focus attention on objects" (p. 1125).

In the first 2 months, infants will look at their caretakers' faces some of the time, but at other times will "fail to establish eye contact." Infants after 2 months are more likely to make eye contact (Ruff & Rothbart,

Chapter 1: The Development of Attentional Systems in Childhood and Adolescence

1996, p. 37). The duration of social looking increases over the first few months. Starting around 3-4 months the infant and caregiver engage in spontaneous reciprocal facial display of affects. As early as 3 months of age the infant can discriminate smiling/pleasant and frowning/unpleasant facial affective displays made by either the mother or a stranger, but there is a clear preference for facial affective displays made by the mother as compared to the stranger (Barrera & Maurer, 1981). Mutual affective displays between infant and mother are rhythmic and interactive, and are based on mutual regulation and turn-taking (Enns, 1990, p. 124). If the mother expresses her facial affective display as a way to capture the infant's attention it has little effect, but if the mother and child are already engaged in an interactive pattern of mutual facial affective display, if the mother exaggerates her facial affective display it has the effect of holding the infant's attention longer (Fogel, 1977).

By 6-months of age social referencing begins to develop. Social referencing entails the child spontaneously looking in the direction of the mother during free exploration in order to re-establish the mother as a secure base during exploration of the immediate environment. Social referencing becomes a way of checking in with the mother during free exploration. Social referencing is well developed by the end of the first year of life (Walden & Ogan, 1988).

As the infant-mother bond develops as a mutually regulated system, the mother begins to play an important role in directing and sustaining the infant's attention. By the end of the first year of life infant and mother begin jointly to attend to the same object of attention (Ruff & Rothbart, 1996, p. 8). Belsky, Goode, and Most (1980) state, "maternal stimulation is operationally defined as maternal efforts to focus the infant's attention on objects and events within the environment" (p. 1169). They observed various strategies mothers used to direct attention in 9-, 12-, 15-, and 18-month-old infants. They found that mothers frequently used verbal and physical (e.g. pointing) attention-directing strategies to direct and sustain the infant's attention. They conclude, "Maternal stimulation teaches the child how to focus his or her own attention and thereby enhances his or her exploratory competence" (p. 1176).

Landry, Chapieski, and Schmidt (1986) studied the effects of maternal attention-directing strategies when the child was playing with toys in the presence of the mother. All infants were 12-months of age, and the sample consisted of both pre-term and full-term infants. In both groups, mothers used verbal and nonverbal strategies to help focus their infants' attention during play behavior. However, there was a difference in strategies used by pre-term and full-term mothers, in that mothers of pre-term infants followed, more than directed, infant's attention, and mothers of full-term infants tended to use more verbal techniques (p. 257-259). Other patterns of individual difference also occur. For example, Ruff and Rothbart (1996) found differences in the way that some infants direct their attention during free play in the absence of their mothers, and when in the presence of their mothers. They say, "…the attention of some infants is not strongly engaged by objects and toys when they play by themselves. Their attention will increase, however, when stimulated, aroused, instructed, and/or restricted by their mothers during joint play with objects" (p. 229).

Between 6 and 9 months joint coordination of attention by the infant-mother dyad is well developed. Bakeman and Adamson (1984) conducted a longitudinal study in 6- to 18-month-old infants of "sequences of 'engagement states' observed in the home environment during joint play" (p. 1279). They found that infant-mother engagement with each other declined with age, "while coordinated joint engagement increased" (p. 1278). However, maturation of joint states of engagement occurred rather late, by 15-18 months (p. 1286). However, such joint coordination of attention is an important predictor of the subsequent development of intelligence. For example, Bornstein (1985) studied infants and mothers longitudinally at 4 months, 1 year, and 4 years of age. They found that mothers who more frequently encouraged infants to attend to the properties, objects, and events in home environment significantly predicted both subsequent language and intellectual development.

However, the positive effect of jointly coordinated attention is contingent on a positive encouraging response from the mother toward her child. Hornik, Risenhoover, and Gunnar (1987) studied maternal response to 1-year-old infants while engaged in play behavior. The experiment varied three toy conditions—pleasant, ambiguous, and aversive—and three conditions of maternal response—positive, negative, and unresponsive. They found, "In response to negative but not positive or neutral maternal displays during toy behavior...infants... "played less with the stimulus toys" (p. 942). Breznitz and Friedman (1988) studied free play between toddlers and mothers in a home-like environment. The study used both depressed and non-depressed mothers. They found, "Children of depressed women focused attention on more objects for shorter durations...Depressed women initiated and terminated more instances of attention to objects than well mothers" (p. 267) and depressed mothers exhibited "more controlling behavior" (p. 275).

The period from 9 to 12-months marks a "major transition point in development" (Ruff & Rothbart, 1996, p. 42). One aspect of this transition pertains to the development of the motor system and its impact on object examining and manipulation. The other aspect is the outgrowth of motor development, namely a leap in the child's capacity for exploratory behavior. Looking becomes more and more coordinated with pointing, grasping and manually examining objects in the immediate environment. Pointing at an object or following where someone else pointed developed by 14 months (Ruff & Rothbart, 1996, p. 91). During this period the frequency of simple manipulation of, and mouthing of, objects in the immediate environment increases (Belsky & Most, 1981, p. 630). Crawling and locomotion increases (pp. 46-47). Tipper, Lortie, and Baylis (1992) describe the selective reaching that emerges as an example of "action-centered attention" (p. 891), so that through selective reaching the child can begin to manually attend to an object. Ruff et al. (1992) studied mouthing of and manually examining objects in 5- and 11-month-olds. They found, "Exploratory mouthing decreased with age and examining increased... Mouthing peaks at 7 months and then declines to 11 months. In contrast, the trend is for examining to increase from 5 to 11 months." (pp. 851, 859).

According to Ruff (1986) examining and manipulation of objects exemplifies sustained attention at this age. Oakes and Tellinghuisen (1994) studied 7- to 10-month old infants examining toy trucks. They found that infants of this age were less distractible during episodes of manually examining than during episodes of non-examining (p. 754), and that overall distractibility decreased from 7 to 10 months of age (p. 755). They concluded that manually "examining reflects a higher level of attentional engagement than does non-examining" (p.755). Ruff and Dubiner (1987) found that manual manipulation of objects became a stable state of engagement between 9-12 months (p. 1100).

The second major aspect of the 9-12-month-old transition is a marked increase in exploratory behavior. Kaye and Fogel (1980) studied video recordings of infant-mother face-to-face play with infants 6, 13, and 26 weeks-old. They found that the average proportion of time infants oriented to mother's face, and state of attention toward mother declined with age to 70% at 6 weeks, and to 33% by 26 weeks (p. 457). They also replicated previous finding that the mother's exaggerated facial display was not especially effective in attracting, but was effective in holding infant's attention. By 26 weeks the frequency of inter-subjective face-to-face interactions had become significantly reduced, as infants spent more time actively exploring the environment (p. 463). Belsky, Garduque, and Hrncir (1984) studied free play in the home environment longitudinally at 12, 15, and 18-months. Secure vs. insecure attachment had been assessed using the Strange Situation. They found that securely attached as compared to insecurely attached children had greater exploratory behavior over time (p. 406).

Ruff and Rothbart (1996) summarize the developments of the exogenous orienting system in the first year of life as follows:

> By 4 months infants seem to have much more control over the shifts of attention, making their attention more flexible... Thus, in the first year of life, infants orient to novel and otherwise salient events; they sustain attention to those events for the purpose of exploring and learning. They gradually gain more control over their attention and can shift more easily from one focus to another. A system of attention, which we refer to as the orienting/investigative system becomes functional early and governs attention in the first year. (p. 6)

Chapter 1: The Development of Attentional Systems in Childhood and Adolescence

What begins to emerge is greater control over orienting. Smith (2008) studied exogenous orienting to stimuli in space. He found exogenous orienting evolved in first 6 months. He says, "Between 3 and 6 months of age, infants develop more complex control of their orienting abilities...the ability to vary the size of the spotlight...to focus narrowly at 4 months and at 7 months globally respond to whole object" (pp. 1285-1286). This greater control makes a natural transition from exogenous to endogenous orienting.

THE DEVELOPMENT OF THE ENDOGENOUS ATTENTIONAL SYSTEM

Exogenous orienting entails being drawn to an object by external stimulus features. According to Brodeur (1990) exogenous orienting peaks at 8 months and declines by 12 months (p. 219). Gradually by the beginning of the second year exogenous orienting is replaced by endogenous orienting, wherein orienting is guided more by internal strategic selection. The "spotlight of attention" becomes more internally directed (Brodeur, 1990, p. 223). Brodeur defines endogenous orienting saying, "Endogenous orienting, on the other hand, refers to the strategic choice of an observer attending to a particular region of visual space" (p. 213). With endogenous orienting the child can discern more complex relationships between features in the visual field, can begin to filter out distractors, begins to develop strategies of attention, and can attend to more complex visual displays, such as television. (Riff & Rothbart, 1996, p. 48) The endogenous orienting system develops steadily from 12 to 40 months. (p. 241) Endogenous orienting entails greater internal control over attention:

> Infants during the first year of life are thought to be able to exercise little volitional control over their allocation of attention...Towards the end of the first year of life, the capacity to exercise attentional control—i.e., the capacity of an individual to choose what is paid attention to and what is ignored—is

thought to emerge as the neural circuitry substantiating these cognitive functions matures. (Wass et al., 2012 p. 362)

Gerhardstein and Rovee-Collier (2002) studied visual search in 1- to 3-year-olds. They found that the exogenous orienting system was well developed by the end of the first year of life. Endogenous orienting, which involved the ability to select the target over an increasing number of distractors, increased from 1- to 3-years of age (p. 210).

An important feature of endogenous orienting is the ability to attend to more complex relationships. For example, Smith (2008) studied visuo-spatial attention, i.e., orienting to stimuli in space. He found that exogenous orienting evolved in first 6 months. By the 7th month infants start to respond to the whole object globally, rather than to selected areas (p. 1286). Switching from part to whole shows itself in toy preference. By 1-year-of age infants begin to focus on multiple, over single toys (Ruff & Caozzi, 2003). The shift from local to global attention gradually develops over time. For example, 3 year-olds prefer selected features of drawings while 5-year-olds prefer global perception (Vinter, Pusitawati, & Witt, 2010). 5-year-olds favor local while 9-year-olds favor global perceptual features (Poirel et al, 2008, p. 245). Perceiving objects globally entails the skill of building up whole objects from simpler feature perception (Thompson & Massaro, 1989), and this reflects a developing skill in perceptual organization (Scherf et al., 2009).

THE DEVELOPMENT OF THE EXECUTIVE ATTENTIONAL SYSTEM

Ruff and Rothbart (1996) define the executive system as follows:

> Focus in the first year, when the orienting/investigative system is operating, is observed most often during exploratory activity. Focus is engaged rapidly when the infant encounters something novel, but it also habituates rapidly. The higher level process is critical for the more voluntary control of attention, however, it begins to emerge at the end of the first year,

These take a giant step forward at 18 months and continue to develop throughout the preschool years, leading to longer and more complex actions guided by plans and goal-oriented attention. Thus, focused attention is no longer as vulnerable to habituation and can be sustained for long periods, if necessary for the completion of planned sequences of activity." (p. 131)

Executive attention entails a "shift in the balance from dependence on external control for regulation of attention to more independent control.... [and the] development of self-control" (p. 133). Ruff and Rothbart add, "By 24 months, children regulate their behavior according to a goal, but are not nearly as likely as older children to correct their actions along the way. After 30 months, children are more likely to monitor and correct specific details of their actions as they progress toward goal-oriented relationships" (p. 150). They add, "As the infant develops into a toddler, a new system of attention emerges. Now, selectivity is less influenced by novelty, and more by what others attend to. Sustained attention in naturalistic settings increases dramatically as children play with toys or watch television....Attention comes to be related more to planned, self-generated activity with objects than to exploration...such as building a house with blocks" (Ruff and Rothbart, 1996, p. 6).

Executive attention entails moving beyond novelty to focus on even uninteresting stimuli, if they serve some important goal (Ruff & Rothbart, 1996, p. 29). Executive attention also entails greater capacity to selectively attend to a target stimulus while resisting distracting and conflicting stimuli (Berlyne, 1970), and voluntarily to sustain attention to the target for longer duration. According to Rueda, Rothbart, and Posner (2005), who used the Child Attention Network Test (ANT) to investigate the development of executive attention in children, there is "substantial development of executive attention between 3- and 7-years of age" (p. 14931).

Bullock and Lutkenhaus (1988) studied the development of task-oriented volitional behavior in toddlers. They found that toddlers begin to monitor their own activity regarding an anticipated outcome around 17-months of age, and that "attention to producing a specific outcome matures around 26-months (p. 670).

THE DEVELOPMENT OF SELECTIVE ATTENTION

According to Enns (1990) much of the research examining selective attention has tended to use "filtering tasks...where a target stimulus is selected from distractors" (p. 199). According to Ruff and Rothbart (1996) "The development of selective attention is critical to maintaining organized activity in the face of extraneous events or potential distractors relationships" (p. 118). Central to the development of executive attention is "the ability to attend to distant goals and block interfering responses to keep attention and action directed toward reaching those goal-oriented relationships" (p. 127).

The earliest forms of inhibitory mechanisms begin to develop as early as 6 months, in the form of reduced responsiveness to peripheral distractors (p. 122). However, genuine selective executive attention, the ability to resist distractors, and organize attention around goals, develops more strongly by the fourth year of life. "At least by 4 years, children can resist distractions in order to attend to a tasks in relationships" (Ruff & Rothbart, 1996, p. 152). Jones, Rothbart, and Posner (2003) studied children's ability to inhibit unwanted responses using a Simon Says-type of task where the commands were given to stuffed animals. The "emergence of error detection" and the "ability to inhibit responses to inappropriate animals" on the task emerged around four years of age. The researchers concluded that the results indicate "changes in self-regulation during fourth year of life" (p. 498). By ages 5-7 the child shows improvements in the ability to filter out involuntary intrusions and task-irrelevant stimuli. By ages 6-7 the child can be observed to systematically inspect a visual display. By ages 8 and 9 the child shows "increasing control over selective attention, including both the facilitation of task-relevant stimuli and the inhibition of task-irrelevant stimuli, throughout young adulthood" (Plude et al., 1994, pp. 254-255). "By the age of 10, the ability to inhibit attention to irrelevant stimuli and perseveratory responses was fairly complete" (Passler, Isaac & Hynd, 1985, p. 349). Reaction time in selective attention/distractor tasks reaches adult performance levels by age 11 (Enns, 1990, p. 205).

Chapter 1: The Development of Attentional Systems in Childhood and Adolescence

THE DEVELOPMENT OF SUSTAINED ATTENTION: ATTENTION AS A STEADY STATE

The overall duration of exogenous orienting "shows modest stability between 3 months and 6 months, and quite strong stability across assessments at 6, 9, and 12 months" (Ruff & Rothbart, 1996, p. 179). However, there is some evidence to suggest that longer duration of looking is not the typical state in the developing child. Ruff and Rothbart (1996) observed clear individual differences between short-looking and long-looking children (p. 180). Contrary to the assumption that long-looking is "better," Colombo (1993) found that the "average duration of looking" tends to decrease across age in infancy, so that developmentally 'mature' performance is measured by shorter, not longer, looking (p. 57). It cannot be readily assumed that even when an infant stares at a visual display the infant's attention is necessarily being engaged, or that longer duration of looking is an adequate index of attention span (Ruff & Rothbart, 1996, p. 181). They add, "infants who look longer do so because they require a longer time to acquire sufficient information for visual recognition" (p.181). It seems as if the typical development of sustained attention in childhood is best characterized as frequent mini-episodes of engagement, disengagement, and re-engagement during a seemingly single period of sustained attention (Ruff & Rothbart, 1996, p. 93). It may be best to describe attention span as prolonged periods of investigation with many episodes of disengagement and re-engagement in a single episode:

> Selection and intensity are integrated through the concept of focused attention relationships [p. 110]....Whether we observe an infant absorbed in exploring an object, a toddler trying hard to put two Lego blocks together, or a 4-year-old concentrating on completing a puzzle, there is a characteristic downward cast of the eyes, a posture that seems to enclose the activity, a serious facial expression, and a quieting of motor activity extraneous to the task at hand relationships... Such periods of investigation can be considered a prolongation of the orienting response (Ruff & Rothbart, 1996, p. 114).

With respect to the exogenous orienting response, Van Hover (1974) described three distinct states. The first is the state of surprise characterized by cardiac deceleration, reduced motor output, and no change in heart-rate variability. The second is a state of sustained attention, characterized by heart-rate deceleration, reduced motor output, and reduced heat-rate variability. The third is internal attention, characterized by heart-rate acceleration, increased motor-output, and reduced heart-rate variability (p. 337).

According to Mahone (2005), "Children demonstrate rapid, steady development of attentional skills between ages 3 and 6, including the ability to shift attention more fluently, and inhibit unnecessary motor behaviors to allow for response" (p. 216). There is a gradual improvement in the ability to utilize various attentional skills from years 2 to 5, and a marked improvement in skill development around age 7 or 8 (Ruff & Rothbart, 1996, p. 53-55). The capacity for sustained selective attention is strong around age 7 or 8, and the ability to sustain attention while resisting distraction becomes stable at around age 7, and reaches near-adult levels by age 10 (Rueda et al., 2004). However, no matter what the age of the child, the capacity for sustained, selective attention varies according to what captures the child's interest. As Ruff and Rothbart state, "The amount of focused attention is strongly governed by situational demands" (p. 184). For example, Moyer and Gilmer (1955) reported an attention span of over 30 minutes in younger children, provided that the children were given age-appropriate toys and optimal play conditions (cited in Turnure, 1973, p. 17).

SUSTAINED FOCUSED ATTENTION IN FREE PLAY

Power, Chapieski, and McGrath (1985) studied the interaction of exploratory behavior and attention span in 12- and 24 month-olds. They defined *developmental level* as "the degree to which infant exploration and play is developmentally advanced or delayed" (p. 975). *Exploratory style* referred to "differences in the ways that infants at the same developmental level explore and play" (p. 975). They defined *attention span* as "the amount of time that infants spend playing or persisting with an object before becoming distracted or losing interest…the total amount of time that the infant spent attending to, exploring, or playing with toys during the entire session" (p. 976). From their observations they concluded that attention span and exploratory behavior were independent dimensions of child behavior, and that shorter attention span was associated with greater exploratory behavior.

Others have found that exploratory free play is related to attention span. For example, Krakow, Kopp, and Vaughn (1982) found that free play at 1-year was related to sustained attention at 2-years of age. Ruff and Rothbart (1996) found that the first signs of sustained attention are typically related to novelty until 1 year of age, but then sustained attention becomes more goal-oriented after that. Ruff and Lawson (1990) studied sustained attention in children 1-, 2-, 3.5-, and 4.5 years of age during free play with toys. The found that all children of various ages showed some ability to sustain attention appropriately but that there was "a significant increase in focused attention over age…more construction and problem-solving in older children" (p. 85) and a capacity to "sustain attention longer as the child got older" (p. 89). Attention span nearly doubled between ages 2.5 and 4.5 years of age. Researcher global ratings of attentiveness at age 1, and maternal ratings of their child's level of attentiveness at ages 1 and 2 predicted attention deficits and perceptual reactivity at age 3.5. The best predictor of attentional problems at age 3.5 was level of distraction and duration of focused attention at younger ages.

Sarid and Breznitz (1997) studied sustained attention in 2- to 6-year-old Israeli children during free play and also in structured tests (e.g. recalling contents of pictures shown). They found that "the ability to sustain attention increased until the age of 4 years, after which a plateau in development appeared" (p.303). There were no age differences on the structured tests. They conclude, "free play may be a sensitive measure of preschool aged children's ability to sustain attention" (p. 303).

FREE PLAY WITH BACKGROUND DISTRACTORS

Ruff and Capozzoli (2003) studied free play under distracting conditions in 2- and 4-year-olds. The children played with toys under several conditions of auditory and visual, or both kinds of distractors. Overall, they found, "children become less distractible with age" (p. 877). They described three kinds of attentional states—casual, settled, and focused. Casual attention occurred when the child looked at a toy but did not engage with it. Settled attention occurred when an instance of casual attention was immediately followed by engagement with the toy. Focused attention occurred when the child sustained attention to the toy and showed minimal extraneous motor output (p. 879). They also found that "the number of times the child turned from toys to distractors was greater at 1-year than 2-years...but time spent in focused attention not different between 1 and 2 year-olds" (p. 880). Ages 2-3 marked a "transition between attention related to stimulus-features and novelty to planned, goal-directed play more under executive control" (p. 887). They further found, "focused attention increased substantially from 26 and 42 months" (p. 882), which tends to suggest that play over time becomes "self-initiated planned activity" as "the child created or discovered interesting and relatively complex activities with the toys" (p. 886). There was also a "strong trend toward less distractibility with age" (p. 887).

Oakes, Tellinghuisen, and Tjebkes (2000) conducted a study with 7-month-old children playing with either a single-component or a multi-component toy, under conditions of visual distractors (colored shapes) and auditory distractors (tones). More casual attention was found for single-component toys and more sustained focused was found for multi-component toys. Both visual and auditory distractors had a larger distracting effect when the infants were in a more focused as compared to a casual state of attention (p. 347), as measured by duration of overall looking at the toy. This age marks the transition from exogenous to endogenous attention so it was found that "infants' attention allocation was jointly influenced by the characteristics of the initial stimulus, the characteristics of the distractors, and attentional state" (p. 358).

Gaertner, Spinrad and Eisenberg (2008) studied focused attention

Chapter 1: The Development of Attentional Systems in Childhood and Adolescence

in independent play with blocks. Observer ratings were used to assess the duration of toddler free play with toys in presence of and interaction with the mother, and in a task assigned by the teacher namely, doing a difficult puzzle. The toddlers were observed at 18-months of age and then a year later. They found "greater levels of focused attention at 30 months in free play and on the puzzle task but not in play in interaction with mother" (p. 15). Early negative emotions predicted decreases in levels of focused attention across time." By 30 months, "Children began to assume and desire more responsibility for autonomous self-regulation across toddlerhood, which coincides with the development of executive systems of effortful control" (p. 14).

Kannass, Oakes, and Shaddy (2006) studied multiple object free play in the presence of distractors with 7-month-old infants and 31-month-old toddlers. Distractors consisted of various shaped and colored objects for the younger children, and for the older children a version of Sesame Street appearing on a television monitor in the background during free play. They found that "at 31 months children who were effective in inhibiting responding to the distractor in the distractibility task also were effective at maintaining their attention for longer durations" (p. 401). The comparison of the two age groups showed "emerging and increasing influence of endogenous or 'top-down,' self-regulated factors on attention toward the end of the first year and into early childhood" (p. 403). Seven months of age corresponds to a period when exogenous factors appear to heavily govern attentional control, 9 months of age corresponds to a period when endogenous control of attention is beginning to emerge in a gradual manner, and 31 months of age corresponds to a period when endogenous control of attention is continuing to increase" (p. 404).

The Effects on Television Viewing on Sustained Attention

Evans-Schmidt et al. (2008) investigated the effects of background television on free play with toys in 2-, 3-, and 4-year-olds who had a 1-hour free play session with toys. Half the time a TV game show played in the background and the other half of the time there was no television as a background distraction. The results showed that "background TV significantly reduced toy play episode length as well as focused attention during play...even when they pay little overt attention to it" (p.1137). Furthermore, they found, "there was less play overall, shorter play episodes, and shorter bouts of focused attention in the presence of background television" (p. 1147)...all ages had reduced play episodes and focused attention lengths" In the presence of the background television (p. 1148). Similarly, Christakis et al. (2004) found that parents' estimates of children's TV viewing significantly predicted parental report of attention disorder symptoms at age 7. Approximately 10% of children had attentional problems at age 7. They found, "Hours of television viewed per day at both ages 1 and 3 was associated with attentional problems at age 7" (p. 708).

The characteristic that sets television and film apart from earlier forms of media is the predominance of visual movement as a stimulus. According to Greenfield (2014), "Movement can help children learn, because, first, it attracts their attention to the screen" (p. 19). This passage assumes, however, that what is on the screen has learning potential. Most television, unless explicitly educational, has little learning potential. Even in shows that are explicitly educational, "educational TV does not equal educational content" (Fisch, 1999). Therefore. Greenfield adds, "The predominance of television and film in children's media diet means that children are not being given models of reflective thought" (p. 63).

In a study of children viewing *Sesame Street* on television Anderson and Levin (1976) found that the duration of sustained attention while watching Sesame Street increased across age, from 1- to 4-years of age. They found, "By age 4, parents report that children spend about a third of their waking hours viewing TV" (p. 806). When children watched *Sesame Street* in a room where toys are visible and readily available, there was an age-related preference for TV over the toys. Anderson and Levin say, "From 1 to 4 years of age, there was a dramatic increase in attention to television [as compared to the toys]....Older children...appeared to more deliberately 'watch' television" (p. 810).

Chapter 1: The Development of Attentional Systems in Childhood and Adolescence

Anderson and associates also found that an age-related preference for TV depended on whether or not the child understood the content of the TV show being watched. Anderson et al. (1981) conducted a study on TV program comprehensibility as related to attention in 3- and 5-year-olds. Children watched a *Sesame Street* program under three conditions: with either its original dialogue, a substituted incomprehensible foreign language dialogue, or with the original dialogue played backwards. Results showed significantly lower visual attention to the foreign or backwards dialogue conditions compared to the original dialogue condition (p. 151). Anderson et al. conclude, "a major determinant of young children's visual attention to a television program is the degree to which they are able to comprehend it" (p. 156).

In another study Anderson, Choi, and Lorch (1987) investigated 3- to 5-year-old children's capacity to maintain focused attention to TV viewing. They found, "the longer a viewer continuously maintains an episode of visual attention, the more likely it becomes that he or she will continue to do so." (p. 798). No age differences were found. In other words, for both 3- and 5-year-olds, "The longer the duration of being absorbed the greater the probability it would be maintained in the face of distractions, especially if the look was maintained for greater than 15 seconds" (p. 803).

Richards and Turner (2001) studied children 6,- 12,- 18,- and 24-months-old watching *Sesame Street* on TV, while simultaneously being distracted by either a second *Sesame Street* on another TV screen, or watching a show on computer generated distracting patterns on a screen. The researchers used hear-rate deceleration as a measure of attention since duration of the exogenous attentional look significantly correlates with hear-rate deceleration. Richards and Turner found, "The time taken to turn toward distraction was a function of length of the look occurring before distractor onset" (p. 963)…Length of look increased with age, but there were no age differences for distractibility" (p. 970).

In another study Anderson et al. (1981) investigated the influence of peers on sustained attention to TV in 3-, to 5 year-olds watching

TV in presence of distracting slides. They found, "Peers viewing the TV together influenced each others' behavior in a synchronized fashion: When one child looked at the TV, looked at the distractor, or demonstrated overt involvement with the TV, the other child tended to do the same thing" (p. 446). They concluded that peers had an "organizing influence" on another child's attentiveness to TV (p. 447), and that "viewing the TV program is controlled in part by the ongoing social interaction" (p. 452).

In a study of amount of TV viewing across age, Anderson et al. (1986) found that the "Percent of visual attention to television increased greatly across the preschool years, leveled off at 70% during school-age years, and declined into adulthood...The increase in visual attention to television during the preschool years is consistent with the theory that TV program comprehensibility is a major determinant of attention in young children" (p. 1024). Children 2- to 3-years of age watched an average of 28 hours/week of television. Children 6- to 11-years of age watched an average of 25 hours/week of television. Overall, the results demonstrate a "dramatic rise in visual attention to television in the years from 1 to 5" (p. 1025).

The increasing influence of television in modern children's lives is problematic. While studies clearly show age-related increases in sustained attention to TV, there may be a cost associated with sustained attention to TV in terms of cognitive and intellectual development. For example, Gadberry (1980) found that restricting first graders' TV viewing during leisure time had positive effects on development. Gadberry says, "TV restriction enhanced Performance IQ, reading time, and reflective Matching Familiar Figures scores" (p. 45).

THE SPOTLIGHT

One dimension of the executive attentional system is the ability to focus attention like a spotlight on a target or expand the focus of attention. Eriksen and Eriksen (1974) studied this attentional filtering mechanism in adults. In this paradigm adults are required to focus on a target letter and to ignore distractor letters that flank the target. The subject "must inhibit his response until he is able to discriminate exactly which letter is in the target position" (p 143). Using a similar research paradigm with children Enns and Girgus (1985) investigated the "spotlight or zoom lens properties of attention" in 8-, 9-, 10- and 17-21-year-olds. They found that "younger children were unable to contract and expand the zoom lens" (p. 319), but that the ability to utilize the spotlight "improves with age in the school years" (p. 319). True voluntary control over the spotlight and the size of the stimulus area began to develop in 8-10 year-olds but was much more developed in 17- to 21-year-olds.

In later childhood there is an important developmental shift in the use of the spotlight—from narrow focus to global awareness. For example, Poporino et al. (2004) observed an important developmental change from selective attention to a more global form of perception. He found that 6- and 8-year-olds showed greater reaction time for global over local targets as compared to older children ages 10 to 12 and adults, who both had similar reaction times. Poporino et al. conclude, "the processes involved in global perception undergo a meaningful change between 8- and 10-years of age" (p. 363). Enns et al. (2000) state that local and global perception involve "different underlying processes" (p. 41). Moses et al., (2002) in an fMRI study of global and local processing in children 12- to14-years of age found greater right tempero-occipital activation in global as compared to local perception. Barrett and Shepp (1988) conducted a visual search task for target when target features could either be integrated into a whole or separated into different stimuli. The study was conducted with 7-, and 10-year-old children and adults. They found younger children favored impressionistic but not integrated "holistic properties," but with increasing age…[older children became] increasingly proficient in extracting either featural or holistic properties" (p. 395). Shepp and Saywitz (1976) assessed the speed in a card-sorting task, wherein the cards depicted either integrated or non-integrated stimulus dimensions. Both 5- and 9-year-olds sorted integral features of the stimulus cards like an adult. However, only the 9-year-olds, but not the 5-year-olds, sorted non-integrated features like an adult because the 5-year-olds sorted separable features on the non-integrated stimulus cards as if they were holistic (p. 73). The authors concluded attention becomes selective of certain features in 9-year-olds but not in 5-year-olds. Shepp and Barrett (1991) studied how 6-, and 8-year-old children and college-age adults integrated stimuli. As subjects initially perceived the stimuli as wholes, yet the features became more accessible with increasing age (p. 434), the authors conclude that "both holistic and featural properties become available with increasing age" (p. 449). Mondloch et al. (2003) presented 6-, 10-, 14-year-old and adult subjects with hierarchical shapes and asked the subjects whether the two shapes were the same or different at global or local level. All groups responded faster to global than local trials especially in the 6-year-old group. 10-year-old children were less able than adults to attend to local as compared to global perception. They conclude, "Sensitivity to local features develops between 10 and 14 years" (p. 37). Overall, the studies consistently show that the selective/featural and global/integrated dimensions of the spotlight develop independently but in parallel.

VIGILANCE: SUSTAINED FOCUS DURING TASK LEARNING IN THE PRESENCE OF DISTRACTORS

Another dimension of the executive attentional system is the capacity to maintain focus and resist distraction. Psychologists typically study sustained attention in the presence of distractors with some sort of vigilance or continuous performance task. Jerison (1970) gives a very clear definition of the requirements of a vigilance, or continuous performance task to study sustained attention:

> An observer is presented with stimuli, some of which are signals to be reported, and others of which are non-signals and usually are not actively reported. The special features of the vigilance experiment are in the parameters. First, the vigil is maintained without interruption for periods of a half-hour or longer. Second, signals are presented infrequently and without forewarning. Third, the signals are strong in a psychophysical sense (nearly always reported correctly with almost no false alarms in a two-alternative forced-choice setting), but

Chapter 1: The Development of Attentional Systems in Childhood and Adolescence

they would be described as weak by most observers because they are not "attention-demanding." Under these conditions the observer has to be almost continuously alert in order to be able to detect and report all signals, and detection failures can be identified with failures of attention, rather than sensory inadequacy....The major vigilance effect is the "decrement function," a reliable drop in the average number of correct reports as the vigil progresses. (p. 124)

Likewise, Stroh (1971) defines vigilance as "the ability to sustain attention" (p. 1). Historically, Stroh says, "vigilance research resulted, initially, from the introduction of assembly-line methods into industry... later research [emphasized]... sustained attention to radar-scanning in WWII." (p. 1) Stroh enumerates a number of variables that affect vigilance performance: the number of signals; stimulus frequency; task complexity; knowledge of results; reducing novel stimulation during vigilance to complex tasks or enhancing novel stimulation during vigilance to simple tasks; amount of background noise; change in the size of the field in which stimuli are to be detected; and reframing the vigilance task as not monotonous but as an interesting challenge. He adds, "a decrement in vigilance performance can be prevented by introducing, during the vigilance session, short periods of rest, conversation, mild physical or mental exercise, or sensory restriction" (p. 38). A major problem with sustaining attention during a vigilance task is the propensity to get distracted. Another problem is a decrement in alertness over time after sustaining attention in a vigilance task. According to Stroh, "Vigilance situations often result in lower levels of arousal after the first half-hour of vigilance" (p. 81).

With respect to vigilance tasks in children Richards, (1989) had 14-, 20-, and 26-week-old infants view complex target patterns with distractors in the background. How vulnerable the infants were to distraction was a function of whether they were or were not attentive to the target at the time of the distraction. Richard says, "infants were not as easily distracted by the interrupting stimulus when the presentation occurred at the point of maximal heart rate deceleration as when the presentation occurred at the end of the heart rate response. Infants with large amounts of...heart rate variable...in baseline recording were less distractible during the deceleration-defined trials than were infants with low amounts" (p. 422). Richards also found that heart-rate deceleration, a measure of focused exogenous orienting, increased from 14 to 26 weeks, but that heart-rate variability, a measure of sustained attention, had little stability in these young infants.

Using a wide range of tasks, Yarrow et al. (1982) found that 13-month-old infants "engaged in persistent, task-directed behaviors about 60% of the time" during a variety of mastery tasks (p. 131). A number of variables predicted sustained attention: maternal stimulation of the infant and maternal responsiveness.

Choudhury and Gorman (2000) investigated sustained attention in 1.5- to 2-year-old toddlers during simple tasks, like stacking cups and sorting toys by shape, after free play period. They found that what seemed like continuous sustained attention was best characterized as frequent mini-episodes of engagement/disengagement/re-engagement during longer episodes of sustained attention. They say, "Toddlers with more frequent off-task glances had longer attention spans.... [p. 127] Frequent brief breaks...may actually help to focus attention and facilitate cognitive processing [p. 141], [and that] "breaks [were] related to enhanced performance" (p. 142). The overall attention span of toddlers was about 2 minutes, with an average of 5 episodes of disengagement/re-engagement during that interval. They also found, "Those toddlers with longer duration sustained attention were more successful at problem solving and had higher intelligence scores" (p. 127).

While these studies utilize many specific types of tasks, the common factor is to vary the number and/or complexity of the target of selective attention (perceptual load) and the ease or difficulty of detecting distracting stimuli. Using a classic vigilance task, Weissberg, Ruff, and Lawson (1990) investigated the development of voluntary control over attention in 3.5-year-olds. They measured reaction time to a sound of a bell in a sustained vigilance task. Their results show that "voluntary self-control seems to develop during the 18- to 30-month period" (p. 63).

Chapter 1: The Development of Attentional Systems in Childhood and Adolescence

However, the main development of voluntary control develops from 7 to 9 years of age. Levy (1980) investigated vigilance using a visual continuous performance task. He found "clear development in capacity for sustained attention (vigilance) in normal children between 4 and 6 years [and] also motor inhibition in same time frame" (p. 83). Gale and Lynn (1972) studied children ages 7 to 13 in a sustained attention auditory vigilance task. They found the "greatest improvement between the ages of 8 and 9" (p. 2600). There was no significant correlation between sustained attention and intelligence. Similarly, McKay et al. (1994) sustained attention showed "no appreciable development" between 7 to 11 but "significant growth" between 11 and adulthood" (p. 121). Greenberg and Waldman (1993) described age-related changes in response to a vigilance task. They found that sustained attention from ages 6 to 16 "developed in a non linear manner, changing rapidly in early childhood and leveling off during later childhood and adolescence" (p. 1019). Printz, Tarnowski, and Nay (1984) used a task analogous to those common in a classroom, a work task done in the presence of distractors by 7- and 9-year-olds diagnosed with attention deficit disorder. There were no significant distractor effects. Donnelly et al. (2007) had children from 6-7 and 9-10 years of age, and adults engage in a visual search for targets among field of distractors. They found visual search was "well established for exogenous stimulus features like color by 6-7 reflecting more bottom up control." However, by ages 9-10 it took less time to reject distractors. They found that top-down control "is functional from age 1 year…with increasing age, children became able to consider multiple dimensions when making relevant comparisons " (p. 121). They concluded that 6-7-year-olds have "either a smaller capacity for the top-down component of their attentional systems or an inability to guide search appropriately….[but there is] development from middle to late childhood in both top-down and bottom-up components of attentional systems" (p. 135). Fjell et al. (2012) studied age-related changes in vigilance using a flanker task. They found the "ability to inhibit responses and impose cognitive control increased rapidly during preteen years. The surface area of the anterior cingulate cortex accounted for a significant proportion of the variance in cognitive performance" (p. 19620).

Turnure (1971) studied the effects of extraneous distraction on task performance in 3- to 5-year-olds. He found that resistance to distraction "would fall between the ages of 5 to 7 years" (p. 17). Children 6- to 7-years of age are "capable of working effectively in potentially distracting conditions" (p. 16). In this study children as young as 3.9-years but not 3.3-years of age were capable of resisting distraction (p. 20). Higgins and Turnure (1984) found that performance of a vigilance task was more disrupted for preschoolers as compared to school-aged children. They studied 4-5-, 7-8-, and 10-11-year-olds using a visual discrimination task where children had a choice between a target square or other simple visual shapes randomly presented. The children were also presented with more difficult tasks by varying the task difficulty of the distractor shapes or background color. Extraneous auditory distracting simulation was created by high and low conditions of extraneous background noise. Results showed that "extraneous stimulation impaired the performance of younger children, but facilitated the performance of older children, for subjects performing easy and difficult tasks" (p. 1806).

Fortenbuagh et al. (2015) presented visual stimuli in a continuous performance task, wherein the visual images varied in terms of clarity of the image. Participants ranged in age from 10- to 70-years of age, and the study included a sample of over 10,000 subjects. The researchers found a "rapid development of sustained attention ability between 10 and 16 years of age then a period of relative ability until approximately 43 years of age, and finally a decline in ability across old age" [p. 5] [and]… Sustained attention peak[ed] in one's 40s" (p.12).

Lopez, Menez and Hernandez-Guzman (2005) investigated developmental trends in sustained attention while potentially being distracted by peer social interactions in the live pre-school classroom. Tasks were structured by the teacher "that demanded sustained attention" (p. 133). Children 4, 5, and 6 years old were used in the study. They found, "Duration of sustained attention to learning tasks increased with age… while distraction by peer social contact decreased with age especially between ages 4 and 5" (p. 134).

In vigilance tasks, the capacity for sustained attention and resistance to distraction was highly correlated. Paus (1989) had children of 8, 10, and 12 years old select a target during an auditory vigilance task while at the same time inhibiting responses to non-target signals. "A positive correlation was found between the number of signals detected (sustained attention) and the number of successfully suppressed reflexive saccades to the peripherally located target…sustained attention and inhibition highly correlated" (p. 51). Carlson and Moses (2001) and Carlson, Moses, and Claxton (2004) found that the ability to inhibit response to distractors was significantly correlated with meta-cognitive monitoring.

INHIBITION OF CONFLICTING RESPONSES AND BEHAVIORS

Reed, Pien, and Rothbart (1984) investigated inhibitory self-control using a Simons Says-type game requiring behavioral inhibition of extraneous responses in children ages 40 to 49 months. They found "behaviors possibly related to internal inhibition also appear to change around age 4" (p. 134) and later childhood is marked by a "transition from internal to more voluntary inhibition" (p. 143). Williams et al. (1999) used a stop-signal procedure requiring the ability to stop a planned or ongoing thought or action. This ability increased from 6-8 to 9-12 years of age, which signified "developmental improvements in inhibitory control" (p. 211). Christakou, Brammer and Rubia (2011) used a temporal discounting task that required the "ability to refrain from preference of immediate rewards, in favor of delayed, larger rewards…ability to delay gratification" (p. 1344). The age-related changes that occurred in later adolescence were related to development of certain brain neurocircuits, such as the anterior cingulate cortex (ACC) associated with selective attention, and the dorsolateral prefrontal cortex, associated with meta-cognition. They conclude, "maturational mechanisms within the fronto-striatal circuitry underlie the observed post-pubertal reductions in impulsive choice" (p. 344).

The Stroop interference task is another common way to study sustained attention in the presence of conflicting or distracting stimuli. Comalli, Wapner, and Werner (1962) studied Stroop color-word interference effects in children, adults, and elderly adults. They found, the "degree of interference greatest in young children (age 7)... [and that] young children have greater difficulty screening out interfering stimuli" (p. 47). Tipper et al. (1989) studied the Stroop effect in 8-year-olds and 19-year olds. Although the capacity to resist color interference began to develop in the younger children this skill was significantly more developed by late adolescence. They say, "adults unlike children were actively inhibiting the to-be-ignored color names from trial to trial" (cited in Enns & Aktar, 1989, p. 1190). Posnansky and Rayner (1977) investigated responses to a picture-word interference Stroop-like task in 6, 8, and 11 year olds, wherein the text and picture did not necessarily match. They found a greater interference in 6-year-olds as compared to the older children, and the least interference effect in the oldest 11-year-olds. Similarly, Hanauer and Brook (2003) used a modified Stroop test in 4 to 11 year olds. They found that "interference effects [got] progressively weaker with age...as executive functions increase" (p. 359). The performance of 9 to 11 year olds was already similar to that of adults. When children and adults with and without ADHD from ages 9 to 41 were given the Stroop test, reaction time was significantly slower in children with ADHD compared to the other groups (Schwartz & Verhaeghen, 2008).

MacLeod (1991) reviewed a half-century of research on the Stroop effect. The conclusion drawn was, "Interference begins early in the school years, rising to its highest level around grades 2 to 3 as reading skill develops. With continued development of reading, interference declines through the adult years until approximately age 60, at which point it begins to increase again" (p. 185).

In another study Nigg et al. (1999) found that Stroop performance at age 7 or 8 significantly predicted behavioral problems and problems of social competence 2 years later using developmental/behavioral teacher rating scales.

Another common strategy to assess the ability to select attention is to use sustained attention to a target stimulus, while the target stimulus is flanked by distracting stimuli similar to or dissimilar to the target of attention. This is called a flaker task. Enns and Akhtar (1989) investigated visual filtering utilizing five measures of visual filtering: attentional

Chapter 1: The Development of Attentional Systems in Childhood and Adolescence

set; encoding interferences; feature number; feature size response; and competition stimulus generalization. The subjects included 4-,5-, 7-, and 20-year-olds who were instructed to sustain attention to the target and resist distraction by flanking distractors. Interference with maintaining the attentional set and interference by the number of features were found in all age groups of children but not in the 20-year-olds. Subjects of all age groups were unable to avoid interference by flanking distractors, "even when the target appeared in a known location" (p. 1195). Maintaining the attentional set was hardest for the youngest age group, but this ability improved around 8-9 years of age (p. 1198). Overall, the capacity to resist distraction by task-irrelevant stimuli as part of the executive attentional system develops in later childhood (p. 1188). Huang-Pollack et al. (2002) used a flanker task wherein perceptual load, i.e., total amount of task-relevant information, was varied. They found that performance was similar to that of adults with high, as compared to the low load condition. Another study by Couperus (2011) clarified these results. Subjects from 7-9, 10-12, 13-15, 16-18 and greater than 19 years of age participated in a study that varied perceptual load. They found, "When perceptual load increases, selection occurs earlier in processing ...increase[ing] load decreased distraction" (p. 1435) presumably because increasing the load required more intense focus on the targets.

Fisher et al. (2013) investigated sustained attention in a visual search task among distractors of varying confusability with 3-, 4-, and 5-year-old preschoolers. The research design was set up to discriminate between exogenous and endogenous factors in sustained attention. They found, "performance on the selective sustained attention component of...[the] task in younger children [3- and 4-year-olds] is influenced by exogenous factors to a greater degree than the performance in 5-year-olds. Specifically, younger—but not older—children exhibited higher tracking accuracy [when]... target objects were more salient than distractors... compared with... [when] target and distractor were equally salient.... These findings support the general notion that development of executive control of selective sustained attention follows a protracted developmental course" (p. 290).

Martin, Razzo, and Brooks-Gunn (2012) investigated sustained attention at age 5 using a sustained attention task that entailed matching an object to a target object without accidentally selecting the wrong unmatched object. Poorer sustained attention and increased failure to inhibit erroneous responses at age 5 significantly predicted attention problems at age 9, as rated by observations by mothers.

Luna et al. (2004) investigated processing speed, voluntary response suppression and spatial working memory in children and adolescents of 8-9, 10-11, 12-13, 14-15, 16-17, 18-19, and 20-25-year-olds. They found, "voluntary/cognitive control of behavior continues to develop throughout adolescence...followed by a plateau in late adolescence and early adulthood....[there was] strong evidence that processing speed, voluntary response suppression, and spatial working memory mature in middle to late adolescence" (p. 1366). "Voluntary response suppression matures around age 14" (p. 1367). "Spatial working memory accuracy matures around 14" (p. 1368). These three measures—processing speed, voluntary response suppression, and spatial working memory—are "three independent though concurrent processes" (p. 1368).

EFFECTS OF CUEING AND ANTICIPATION IN VISUAL ORIENTING

Another way to study the executive attentional system is to study cueing and anticipation of target location in visual spatial orienting tasks. Spatial orienting tasks are a good way to see how the orienting attentional system transitions into the executive attentional system. Pearson and Lane (1990) investigated speed of eye reorientation in a visual reorientation task in 8- and 11-year-old children and adults. Subjects were cued and learned to orient attention to a target location, and then were cued to redirect attention either to the right or left peripheral field. They found "developmental changes in ability to attend to a spatial location" in that "speed of attention reorientation improved with age."

Akhtar (1988) used a visual reorientation task with 5-,7-, and 9-year-old children and 24-year-old adults. Subjects viewed a target location with or without a pre-cue flash. Large age differences occurred when there was no pre-cue, in children of all ages but in adult subjects. Even

Chapter 1: The Development of Attentional Systems in Childhood and Adolescence

if there was a pre-cue, "young children were unable to focus attention voluntarily as well as adults… attention can be focused for them automatically [but not voluntarily by a pre-cue and] then [there are] no distractor effects" (cited in Enns & Akhtar 1989).

Brodeur and Enns (1997) investigated responses to exogenous cues as compared to voluntary control of attention in 7-, 8-, 10-year old children, and in 22- and 73-year-old adults. Subjects were either presented with an abrupt stimulus-cue, namely a flash on a screen that required no voluntary response, or a voluntary information cue, namely arrows as cues to the target location, using a visual spatial orienting task. The main measure was speed of visual orientation with eye movements. Subjects of all ages showed an orienting effect in response to a stimulus cue size. Exogenous orienting was largest for young children and smallest for young adults. Younger children could use information cues but "had difficulty sustaining their attention in the cued location. "Orienting to information was slower than orienting to a presented stimulus in younger children, especially in 6-10-year-olds" (p. 31). The authors state, "Information-based orienting relies more heavily on the parietal and pre-frontal cortex" which develops in later childhood and adolescence (p. 32). Brodeur and Boden (2000) used a visual orientation task wherein various locations were either accurately or inaccurately cued. The study used 6- and 8-year-old children and 21-year-old adults and compared responses to exogenous, automatic orienting to voluntary executive attention using information strategies. Whereas young children largely used exogenous orienting, adults had voluntary control over the strategies they used. Adults had the unique ability to engage in "orienting in such a way that is limited to conditions where it improves their task efficiency" (p. 37). In terms of neurocircuitry exogenous orienting was associated with posterior parietal cortex activation, and executive voluntary use of information was associated with activation of the anterior cingulate cortex and medial prefrontal cortex. Brodeur (1990) says, "attentional strategies develop between 7 and 13 years and continues into adulthood. By 10 to 13 the development of strategies approximates adults" (p. 235). He adds, "Many of these routines become available relatively early in childhood, but their optimal application in complex tasks awaits the development of greater information processing efficiency" (p. 241).

Waszak, Li, and Hommel (2010) used a visual cue-orienting task along with flanker distractors. The cue immediately preceded the target, and was either in the same or different location from the target. The study investigated exogenous orienting and executive attentional ability to inhibit responses to flanker distractors in 6-7-, 8-9-,10-11-,12-13-, 13-15-, 16-21-year-olds and adults. They found that exogenous orienting reaction time decreases and reaches a plateau with adult-like performance by around age 10. The executive ability to resist distractors in the flanking task improved throughout childhood and reached adult-like levels by age 14 to 15 (p. 343). Likewise, Goldberg, Maurer, and Lewis (2001) investigated endogenous orienting and found that this attentional system reached adult-like performance levels by ages 8-10 (p. 217), and also that performance was nevertheless "limited to certain aspects of the visual field" (p. 215).

Ridderinkhof et al. (1997) found a "developmental decrease in interference from irrelevant information from ages 5-7 to 8-9, [and that performance] reaches a plateau around age 10-11 [p. 315]. The results showed an age-related improvement in selective attention" (p. 316). They say, "as children grow older they are less vulnerable to the influences of response competition while at the same time they are more efficient in overcoming inhibition once the target response is selected" (p. 338).

Woods et al. (2013) studied visual search when targets and distractors share common features in children ages 2 to 17years of age. They found the most extensive improvements occur around age 12 and reach a plateau by age 17. These specific age-related patterns "suggests maturation of DLPFC may play a key role in age-related improvement of search organization" (p. 198).

THE DEVELOPMENT OF STRATEGIES OF EXECUTIVE ATTENTION

The development of strategies for paying attention initially stem from the dyadic interaction between the infant and the mother. For example, Wertsch et al. (1980) observed 2.5-, 3.5-, and 4.5-year-old chil-

Chapter 1: The Development of Attentional Systems in Childhood and Adolescence

dren and their mothers engaged in a problem-solving task, for example making a puzzle. The dyadic interaction was video recorded, especially the episodes of the child's gaze toward the mother, and the mother's verbal and non-verbal cues to the child where to put a piece. They found that younger children looked to the mother for strategies and older children selected and inserted puzzle pieces on their own. The age-related changes revealed a transition from other-regulation to self-regulation.

Miller and Harris (1988) used a same or different judgment task to study attentional strategy use in 3- and 4-year-olds. The 3-year-olds had some early but insufficient development of attentional strategies, while the 4-year-olds showed much more efficient use of attentional strategies on the judgment task. Miller and Harris say, "preschoolers can gather information systematically and by age 4 the majority are producing, and benefiting from, a strategy that is very efficient for the same-different task" (p. 631).

Lane and Pearson (1982) reviewed all of the research findings on age-related differences in the ability to use strategies to ignore irrelevant information in four kinds of tasks: 1. Same-difference judgments. Results of these studies showed "gradual development of an ability to establish a 'set' as a means of selecting only relevant stimuli" (p. 322). 2. Classification as quickly as possible during sorting tasks. The results showed "the perception of younger children is organized around a similarity structure, as opposed to the dimensional structure of adults" (p. 327). 3. Selective listening ability, such as the ability to repeat words of one voice while not getting distracted by a second voice. Again, the results showed an age-related trend with clear strategies used in older children. 4. Incidental learning tasks. The results showed a curvilinear relationship between age and incidental learning. Lane and Pearson conclude, "the presence of irrelevant information affects the performance of young children more than it affects the performance of older children…[performance is] more of a function of a different perceptual organization than of attention allocation… [older children can] tune out irrelevant information by age 11" (pp. 333-334).

Pick and associates did a series of experiments documenting improvement in executive selective attention as a function of using informational strategies. Pick, Christy, and Frankel (1972) studied how the use of information strategies affected the development of selective attention. They studied 7- and 11-year-old children. The task entailed selecting wooden animal shapes with relevant and irrelevant information for sorting. They found "a developmental trend toward greater selectivity of attention" (p. 165) because the older children "improve in their ability to focus attention exclusively on relevant information when they have knowledge of the relevant information" (p. 165). The older children had faster reaction times because of "a developmental change" in the use of selective attention strategies. "The older children...better able...to exclude or filter out irrelevant information" (p. 173). The overall results demonstrate "a developmental trend toward greater flexibility in deploying attention...[and the capacity to] exclude irrelevant information better and recall only relevant information due to development of strategies by 11 years of age" (p. 173). According to Pick and Frankel (1973) by age 11 children have developed effective strategies for the task at hand (p. 348) and show an "increasing ability to avoid perceiving irrelevant information" (p. 349). They add, "Older children make more effective use than do younger children of knowledge about what information is relevant for a task. A strategy seems to be acquired" (p. 355).

Patterson and Mischel (1975) studied 4- to 5.5-year-olds while performing a repetitive task while being distracted by a talking "clown box" with rotating drums displaying toys. They found that "children given either 1 or up to 3 plans to resist distraction worked longer on the task" (p. 369). An example of a plan or strategy to resist distraction was to have the child say, "No, I can't. I'm working"; to pretend there was a wall between the distracting clown box and the task; or the have the child think to delay response to the clown box and keep on working in order to enjoy the toys later. They conclude, "providing preschool children with plans for how to resist distraction in a self-control situation can enhance their subsequent self-control" (p. 377).

Miller, Woody-Ramsey, and Aloise (1991) studied 5-, 6-, 7- and 11-year-old children on a dual performance task with and without the use of attentional strategies. The task entailed a box with numerous

Chapter 1: The Development of Attentional Systems in Childhood and Adolescence

doors to open. They found that "younger children sometimes spontaneously reported strategies, but [were] not necessarily effective, and that even when younger subjects spontaneously came up with a strategy to open the doors but their strategies required more effort than older children" (p. 160). Furthermore, "producing a relevant strategy does not mark the end of strategy development. Rather, it marks the beginning of the development of a proficient, low-effort strategy" (p. 163).

In a related study Miller and Zalenski (1982) investigated 3- and 4-year-olds' understanding of distraction. The children were asked "to choose noise or quiet to increase the child's attention to which array was more conducive to attending…Most of the 3- and 4-year-olds understood that the variables of noise and interest affect how much a child learns….[yet] it is unlikely that they consistently apply this knowledge in all real life situations" (p. 874). Similarly, Pillow (1988) investigated children's knowledge about attentional capacity limits. Three- and four-year-old children were observed two puppets telling stories either at the same time or one at a time. He found that even 3-year-olds "appeared to know the conversational rules forbidding simultaneous speech…but willingness to listen to simultaneous recordings indicates that they do not appreciate the difficulty of comprehending simultaneous messages" (p. 38).

O'Sullivan (1993) studied meta-cognition about the role of effort and incentives on recall as 4-year-old children made judgments about the influence of high vs. low effort and incentives on recall. They found already by age 4 "young children have well established meta-memory about these variables including the belief that recall increases with effort and with incentive value" (p. 396). On the other hand, this meta-cognition was not always accurate in the 4-year-olds. Four-year-olds had a "naïve belief that by the power of effort they could recall" (p. 411). Accuracy about the meta-cognitive believes about the efficacy of strategies improves during later childhood between 7- and 9-years of age (see Weil et al., 2013).

The development of attentional strategies is contingent on the development of the prefrontal cortex around age 7-8. For example, Shallice and Burgess (1991) observed that when subjects had traumatic injuries to prefrontal structures they were unable to manifest strategies to carry out even simple tasks.

THE DEVELOPMENT OF META-COGNITIVE AWARENESS OF ATTENTIONAL STRATEGIES

Fernandez-Duque, Baird, and Posner (2000) make a distinction between two kinds of meta-cognitive ability—meta-cognitive knowledge and meta-cognitive strategy use (p. 288). They see the development of the frontal lobes as a major contributor to the maturation of meta-cognition, namely the anterior cingulate cortex, the orbital frontal cortex, and the dorsolateral prefrontal cortex. Conflict resolution and error detection is a function of the development of executive attention between ages 3 and 5, and meta-cognitive awareness of attentional strategies reaches peak development at age 7 or 8 (p. 297). Initial development of the DLPFC occurs from 7.5 to 12 months of age, wherein the infant develops some capacity to observe internal state changes (Diamond & Goldman-Rakic, 1989). However, the major period for the development of the DLPFC doesn't occur until 8-9 yeas of age, and isn't complete until late adolescence (Paus, 2005). According to Weil et al. (2013), "meta-cognition improved between 11 and 17, and shows a long developmental trajectory during adolescence" (p. 264). Meta-cognition in paired-associate learning reaches a ceiling effect around 10 years of age, while meta-cognitive self-evaluation and mentalizing reaches a peak in late adolescence.

INTEGRATION OF ATTENTIONAL DIMENSIONS IN THE EXECUTIVE ATTENTIONAL SYSTEM

One of the main features of the executive attentional system entails the integration of the various dimensions of executive attention as inter-related functions. Psychologists typically assess the degree of integration of executive attentional dimensions by studying correlations between scores using multiple test batteries, wherein different tests tap different dimensions of executive attention.

For example, Levin et al. (1991) found that developmental changes in performances on tests purported to measure frontal lobe development in 7-8-, 9-12, and 13-15-year-olds showed, "Major gains were fond primarily between the 7-8- and 9-12-year-old groups...further advances in performance in the 13-15-year-old age range" (p. 37).

Isquith et al. (2005) say, "Executive functions...can be construed as central or overarching self-regulatory abilities that orchestrate basic or domain-specific cognitive processes (e.g. language, attention, sensory input, motor output} to achieve goal-oriented problem solving...and behavior" (p. 210). They pioneered new methods to assess a variety of executive functions in preschoolers ages 3-4 and 4-5-years of age. The multi-dimensional test battery, the BRIEF-P, had instruments to assess: response inhibition; goal-oriented problem-solving; the ability to shift cognitive set; emotional control; working memory; and planning and organization in preschool children. They found that the ability to shift cognitive set and inhibit response to distractors emerges around 5 years of age.

Rebok et al. (1997) administered four attentional measures to children between the ages of 8 and 13. The four dimensions of attention assessed with 12 different tests were: focused attention; sustained attention; shift in focus; and encoding. They found, "the most rapid changes in attention occurred between ages 8 to 10 years with more gradual changes occurring between ages 10 to 13" (p. 28). On the continuous performance tasks there were less errors in the 8- to 10-year-olds as compared to the scores of the younger children. Overall, "children demonstrated improved performance from age 8 to age 10 on all measures in the attention battery" (p. 36), so that 8 to 10 years of age seems to be a peak in executive attentional development. The ability to make correct responses in distraction tasks was found to "develop rapidly in the early elementary school years, then show stability through the middle school years" (p. 41).

Korkman, Kemp, and Kirk (2001) conducted a cross-sectional study of 800 children from ages 5 to 12 on a battery of executive function tests. Across the battery of tests the children "showed significant age effects in the 10- to 12-year age range. This suggests that neurocognitive development is rapid in the 5-to 8-year range and more moderate in the 9-to 12-year age range" (p. 332). The battery of tests included a measure of auditory attention. Performance on this test showed a rapid increase from to 5 to 7 years of age, and then reaching a plateau around 8 years of age. Scores on a measure of visual attention, for example, selecting a target cat among an array of distracting figures showed rapid development from ages 5 to 9 then reaching a plateau. Performance on complex attentional tasks showed steady improvement throughout adolescence. Performance across the majority of executive function tests reached plateau by age 10 (p. 350), and this improved performance was presumably related to the fact that "neurocognitive development is rapid up to 9 years of age and more moderate after that" (p. 351).

In an Australian study, Anderson et al. (2001) assessed a variety of executive skills in 11-,12-,13-,14-,15-, and 16 to 18-year-olds. Executive functions assessed included tests of: attentional control; cognitive flexibility; working memory; eliciting attentional shifts; self-monitoring; goal setting; and planning or problem-solving (p. 386). The dimension of attentional control as measured by the Digit Span test reached a plateau between the ages of 11-14, and then there was a growth spurt around age 15 (p. 398). The dimension of problem solving and planning showed a growth spurt around 12 years of age (p. 401).

In a Finnish study by Klenberg et al. (2001) on the inter-relationship between various executive functions they found, "the development of basic inhibitory functions precedes the development of more complex functions of selective attention, and executive functions continue to develop into adolescence" (p. 407). Overall, the development of the executive control system is a "multistage process in which different components develop at different times" (p. 409). According to Welsh, Pennington, and Groisser (1991) "planning begins around age 6. The capacity for focused attention reaches maturity around age 10 and then plateaus [p. 420]. Intellectual fluency develops by mid-adolescence" (p. 426).

Kochanska, Murray, and Harlan (2000) used a battery of child neuropsychological tests to measure the development of effortful executive control in children approximately 2- and 3-years-old. Effortful attention was assessed by a Stroop-like task. Control over attention entailed slowing down immediate motor output and attenuating voice to an extraneous external stimulus, and initiating active attention and sustaining attention to the target. The authors found that between ages 2 and 3 "effortful control improved considerably… [p. 220]… and that degree of focused attention at 9 months predicted effortful control in the 3 year-olds" (p. 220).

Luciana and Nelson (1998) studied sensori-motor capacity in 5- to 7-year-olds using a battery of neuropsychological tests. The performance of both age groups of children was essentially the same as adults on basic sensorimotor functions. Results also showed some episodic "spurts in prefrontally-guided behaviors between 5- to 7-years of age. From 5- to 8-years of age there were improvements in attentional set shifting, but attentional strategy use lagged behind these improvements in other dimensions. By 8 years of age, children began to develop complex strategies to solve problems. Working memory developed mainly around 8 years of age and became stable by early adulthood." Luciana and Nelson say, "cognitive functions mediated by the prefrontal cortex emerge in a dimensional fashion from early-to-middle childhood" (p. 289). They add, "the dorsolateral PFC appears to be involved in strategic self-monitoring" (p 286). Hippocampal-based recognition memory skill developed mainly in middle childhood. Many cognitive functions mediated by the prefrontal cortex emerge in a dimensional fashion from early-to-middle childhood (p. 288).

Betts et al. (2006) specifically studied sustained attention utilizing a battery of nine neuropsychological tests, such as those assessing: reaction time; continuous performance; working memory, and so forth in children between the ages of 5 and 12-years of age. The battery of tests allowed the researchers to vary perceptual load. They found, "sustained attention showed development from 5-6 to 11-12 years. For every index (speed, errors, accuracy, and variability), performance was in the expected direction, with increased age associated with improved performance. On some indices, evidence for a plateau in development was present. For example, on indices of speed and accuracy, the 8-9 year-olds' performance was significantly better than that of 5-6-year-olds, but similar to that of 11-12-year-olds….8-9 year olds hav[e] one or two years of rapid development left before they reach 11, the age at which the plateau is evident" (p. 217).

Welsh, Pennington and Groisser (1991) conducted a study on the development of executive functions throughout childhood from 3 to 12 years of age. The specific executive functions assessed were goal-directed behavior, planning, and impulse control. Goal-directed behavior and planning reached a functional level around age 6 and self-regulation of impulsiveness around age 10. Anderson (2002) studied four dimensions of executive functioning: attentional control, cognitive flexibility, goal setting, and information processing. Attentional control (selective attention and the inhibition of responses to distraction) emerges in infancy and develops rapidly in early childhood (around 5 years of age; p. 71). Cognitive flexibility, goal setting, and information-processing reached a critical period between 7 and 9 years of age and was relatively mature by 12 years of age (p. 71).

Brocki and Bohlin (2004) studied the development of executive functions from ages 6 to 13. They found three distinct stages of development: (1) 6- to 8-years-old; (2) 9- to 12-years-old; and (3) early adolescence, starting around age 13 (p. 571). The three dimensions of executive function investigated were: disinhibition, as measured by the Stroop Test; speed of processing and alertnesss, as measured by a continuous performance test; and working memory as measured by the backwards Digit Span Test (p. 58). Disinhibition advances from ages 7.5 to 9.5 and then again from ages 9.5 to 11.5, and then reaches a plateau (p. 588). Speed of processing showed a major gain between ages 6 to 7.5 and then again from 7.5 to 9.5. Working memory first developed around age 8, and then there was another growth spurt around age 12 (p. 588). Brocki and Bolin conclude, "The results strongly support the view of inhibition-disinhibiton and working memory as two salient aspects of executive functioning" (p. 590).

Van der Sluis, de Jong, and van der Leij (2007), studied executive functions in 9- to 12-year-olds. They conducted a factor analysis of the various dimensions of executive functioning. They found evidence for shifting and updating factors, but not an inhibition factor in this age group of children. Updating ability was significantly related to reading, arithmetic, and verbal and non-verbal reasoning (p. 44).

Davidson et al. (2006) studied the development of executive functions from 4- to 13-years-old. Children were tested with a computerized battery of neuropsychological tests. They found, "Even the youngest children could hold information in mind, inhibit a domain response, and combine those as long as the inhibition required was steady-state and the rules remained constant. Cognitive flexibility (switching between rules), even with memory demands minimized, showed a longer developmental progression, with 13-year-olds still not at adult levels" (p. 2037)... Inhibitory control was sufficiently problematic for very young children that they took especially long on all trials requiring inhibition....Inhibitory control improved with age, memory demands started to exact a greater cost than inhibitory ones. Beginning at 10 years of age, increased memory demands (holding of six versus two arbitrary, hardtop-verbalized rules) took a greater toll on accuracy than did consistently inhibiting the tendency to respond on the same side as the stimulus...[p. 2073]... working memory and inhibition were highly correlated...Cognitive flexibility... showed a long developmental progression" (p. 2074).

De Oliveira et al. (2012) investigated developmental changes in executive functions in adults of various ages. Performance on a number of neuropsychological tests was assessed in 19- to 39-years-olds and 40- to 59-year-olds. They found, "The younger adult group performed better than the middle-aged group on tasks that involved mainly processing speed, cognitive flexibility, and lexical search" (p. 29). Similarly, Moraes, Moreas, and Lima (2010) showed that in adults working memory, processing speed, and visuo-spatial skills suffer greatest change with increasing age (cited in de Oliviera et al., 2012, p. 32).

Gathercole et al. (2004) specifically investigated the multi-dimensional structure of working memory in children from ages 4 to 15. They found, "the basic modular [tripartite] structure of working memory is present from 6 years of age and possibly earlier" (p. 177). On all measures there was a progressive increase in performance scores across the three main measures of working memory, i.e., linear increases in performance on measures of the phonological loop, the visuo-spatial sketchpad, and the central executive system from 4 years through adolescence (p. 18). For the most part, the main scaffolding of the phonological loop, and visuo-spatial sketchpad, and the central executive "are in place by 6 years of age at least" (p. 187). All "three main components of... working memory are in place by 6 years of age" (p. 188). Similar results were found in a study by Turner, Henry, and Lucy (2000). Specifically, they studied the extent to which 5-, 7-, and 10-year-old children used long-term memory to assist performance on working memory tasks. Utilizing long-term memory as a strategy to assist working memory did not occur in 5-year-olds, but did develop by age 7. Despite these clear age-related performance trends, Bayliss et al. (2005) in his study of working memory in 6-, 8-, and 10-year-olds found a "considerable amount of age-related variation in working memory" (p. 594). According to Klingberg (2009) the areas of the frontal and parietal systems associated with working memory start to develop at 7 months, and by 12 months of age the child can locate a hidden toy after several seconds.

Pennington and Ozonoff (1996) conducted a review on how deficits in executive functions are related to developmental psychopathology. They found, "executive function deficits are consistently found in... ADHD [including]... impairments in motor inhibition... [and these deficits] especially implicate role of prefrontal cortices" (p. 51).

Brain Development and the Primary Attentional Systems

The development of the three primary attentional systems correlates closely with what is known about the development of the neurocircuitry of attentional systems throughout childhood. Approximately 50% of all of the synaptic density found in adults is already present by the first and second year of life (Huttenlocher, 1979). According to Hudspeth and Pribram (1992) there are five stages in the development of the brain throughout childhood and adolescence. There is an initial period of global brain development from ages 1 through 6. There is a second period of more regional brain development from ages 6 to 11. From

Chapter 1: The Development of Attentional Systems in Childhood and Adolescence

ages 11-12 there is a further period of development of the visuo-spatial neurocircuitry. The somato-sensori cortices develop from 13 to 14. The executive frontal system matures in middle to late adolescence. According to Casey, Giedd, and Thomas (2000), "Increasing cognitive capacity during childhood may coincide with a gradual loss rather than formation of new synapses and presumably a strengthening of remaining synaptic connections" (p. 241). Menon (2013) describes the development of five functional brain networks throughout childhood and adolescence: 1. The development of network topology by age 7; 2. The development of the cortical hubs for the functionality of the sensory and motor areas; 3. The development of hierarchically organized functional brain networks for top-down executive control; 4. The weakening of short-range and the strengthening of long-range neural connections from middle childhood to adulthood; 5. The development of the central executive network (including the dorsolateral prefrontal cortex (DLPFC) and the supramarginal gyrus); the salience network, such as the insula and anterior cingulate cortex (ACC), and default mode network DMN (posterior cingulate cortex (PPC), medial prefrontal cortex, the temporal lobes, and the angular gyrus). Romine & Reynolds (2005) conducted a meta-analysis of studies on frontal lobe development and found that frontal lobe development occurred in three phases. They found, "The greatest period of development appears to occur between 6 and 8 years of age. More moderate increases are evident between the ages of 9 and 12, and performance approximates adult levels between adolescence and the early 20s" (p. 190).

The alerting system associated with the reticular activating system and the thalamus develops in the first months of life, so that modulation of arousal level is well developed by the second or third month (Kopp, 1982). The orienting system associated with the frontal visual systems and the posterior parietal system is well developed by 7 months. The executive control system associated with the anterior cingulate and prefrontal cortex develops around 7 to 8 years of age (Posner et al., 2012, p. 827). By the second and third month of life most of the neurocircuitry associated with the exogenous orienting system has developed, which includes the parietal, temporal, and primary visual cortices, the basal ganglia, and the cerebellar hemisphere (Chugami, 1998, p. 184). According to Ruff and Rothbart (1996) the orienting circuitry associated with the parietal cortex "become fully functional in the first year of life" (Ruff & Rothbart, 1996, p. 7). Posner et al. (2012) concur that the parietal system associated with exogenous orienting is well developed in the neonate. As the prefrontal system starts to develop, along with the previous developement of the superior parietal cortex, the child now has the capacity for sustained attention during vigilance tasks (Pardo, Fox, & Raichle, 1991). The prefrontal areas "become more functional toward the end of the first year" (Ruff & Rothbart, 1996, p. 7). The anterior cingulate cortex starts to develop by 7 months and is fully developed by middle childhood (Rothbart & Posner, 2015). According to Romine and Reynolds (2005) there are three stages in the development of the prefrontal control system. They say, "The greatest period of development appears to occur between 6 and 8 years of age. More moderate increases are evident between the ages of 9 and 12, and performance approximates adult levels between adolescence and the early 20s " (p. 190). This means that the capacity to sustain attention and inhibit conflicting responses develops more clearly between 8-12 years of age. By 8 years of age the predominate attentional system shifts from endogenous orienting to executive attentional control. Posner et al. (2012) say, "during infancy, control is principally exercised by the orienting network but by 3 to 4 years of age this control shifts primarily to the executive network" (p. 828). Similarly, Paus (1989) says that the ability to sustain attention and inhibit conflicting responses develops most clearly from ages 8 to 10 years of age. He says, "An important period in the development of both functions is between 8 and 10 years of age" (p. 51) due to the maturation of the frontal systems.

Casey, Giedd, and Thomas (2000) conducted a fMRI study on 9- and 11-year-old children while performing a working memory task. The children showed activation of the dorsolateral prefrontal cortex (DLPFC) and the anterior cingulate cortex (ACC) during the task. Casey et al. (2005) state, "cortical function becomes fine-tuned with development" (p. 104). The brain regions serving sensory and motor functions develop

Chapter 1: The Development of Attentional Systems in Childhood and Adolescence

first, then temporal and parietal systems develop associated with spatial attention, then higher order systems like the prefrontal and lateral temporal cortices develop, peaking at 2 to 6 years old.

Meta-cognition, the awareness of state of mind and monitoring of strategies used to approach tasks and problem-solving, is associated with the dorsolateral prefrontal cortex (DLPFC). Initial development of the DLPFC occurs from 7.5 to 12 months of age, wherein the infant develops some capacity to observe internal state changes (Diamond & Goldman-Rakic, 1989). However, the major period for the development of the DLPFC doesn't occur until 8 to 9 years of age, and isn't complete until late adolescence (Paus, 2005).

Rueda et al. (2004) used the Attentional Network Test (ANT) to measure the three primary attentional networks in 4-9 year-olds, 10 year-olds, and adults. They found, "Alertness showed evidence of change up to and beyond age 10, while conflict scores appear stable after age seven and orienting scores do not change in the age range studied" (p. 1029). Four-year-olds were unable to filter out distracting stimuli but there was "clear improvement from 6 to 7 years of age" (p. 1035).

According to Luna et al. (2001) brain activation in frontal, parietal, striatal, and thalamic regions increased progressively from childhood to adulthood. The prefrontal cortex becomes more active in adolescence than in childhood (p. 786), and because of the late development of the prefrontal system "efficient top-down modulation...may not be fully developed until adulthood" (p. 786). Reductions in gray matter occur between childhood (7 to 12) and adolescence (14-16), most dramatically in dorsal frontal lobes and parietal lobes (Sowell et al. 1999). The somatosensory and visual cortices develop in the first year of life, but the higher order association cortices, associated with thought and reasoning do not fully develop until adolescence (Gotgay et al., 2004).

There are remarkable changes in brain development throughout adolescence. For example, Blakemore and Choudhury (2006) describe a "second wave of frontal synapse development starting with puberty and throughout adolescence" (p. 307). According to Caballero, Granberg, and Tseng (2016) the prefrontal cortex continues to develop throughout adolescence, and as the prefrontal cortices mature the impulsivity typically associated with adolescence declines. Spear (2000) reviewed the evidence on adolescent brain development from 12-18- years of age. He noted a "gradual period of transition from childhood to adulthood" (p. 417). He also noted, "Prominent neural alterations to brain regions such as the prefrontal cortex (PFC) occur during adolescence" (p. 418). There is also a "Major transformation of cognitive thought leading to abstract reasoning" (p. 423). Overall, The medial prefrontal cortex is "remodeled during adolescence" (p. 439).

PREDICTORS OF SUSTAINED ATTENTION OR SIGNIFICANT DISTRACTION

Carlson, Jacobvitz, and Sroufe (1995) analyzed a subset of data from the Minnesota Longitudinal study. In that study, children were given the Strange Situation Paradigm at age 12 and again and at 20 months. Children found to have insecure attachment in the second year of life were significantly more likely than securely attached children to develop significant attentional problems two decades later. This study is important in that it assessed the relative contribution of both nature (genetic, predispositional) and developmental (mostly early child/caregiver interactional patterns) to the development of significant attentional problems by late adolescence. Notably, genetic/temperament factors only contributed a small amount to the over variance of atttentional problems later in life, and most of the variance was explained in terms of two kinds of child/caregiver interactional patterns. First, children with insecure as compared to secure attachment in the second year predicted significant attentional problems two decades later. Second, direct observations of mothers interacting with their children during the Strange Situation Paradigm demonstrated that mothers who frequently interrupted their children during exploratory play as compared to those who did not were significantly more likely to have a child that developed attentional problems several decades later. In other words, secure children learn to sustain attention better when they are carefully attended to in the context of a secure attachment relationship, wherein the mother

Chapter 1: The Development of Attentional Systems in Childhood and Adolescence

supports the child's sustained attention during exploratory play without the need to disrupt the child from focus in that exploratory play. Since the Minnesota Longitudinal Study is the only study whose design allows for a comparison of temperament and infant/caregiver attachment to later onset significant attentional problems it is noteworthy that the quality of attachment contributes much more than temperament to the development of significant attentional problems in late adolescence and early adulthood. Simply put, a child learns to sustain attention and resist distraction better in the context of a secure attachment relationship where the caregivers are carefully and consistently attuned to the child.

Additionally, Graziono, Calkins, and Keane (2012) studied the relative contribution of material comfort and responsiveness to 2-year-old children by video recording and coding mother/child interactions in a laboratory. Children watched a 5-minute video about a dog exploring the neighborhood. Ability to suppress distracting behavior was assessed by seeing a clear box with a prize toy inside that the child could see but not open for 2 minutes. Maternal comfort and responsiveness significantly predicted the duration of sustained attention at age 4.5, whereas children's high level of avoidance of maternal responsiveness and degree of maternal intrusiveness was associated with lack of sustained attention at age 2, as well as significantly predicting lack of sustained attention at age 4.5.

These studies provide strong support that quality of the infant/caregiver attachment relationship, or lack thereof, predicts duration of sustained attachment or significant attentional problems in later childhood and adulthood. As Ruff and Rothbart (1996) say, "Given the importance of social structuring in the child's early development, the unavailability of parental support may lead some children to develop lower levels of attentiveness and weaker controls on attention and behavior than children who have more parental support" (p. 226).

Chapter 2

The Varieties of Dysfunctional Attention in the Modern Western World

by Daniel P. Brown, Ph.D.

MINDLESSNESS

William James once said that most people throughout life get their work done "in the interstices of their mind-wandering" (James 1890/1951, p. 417). Episodes of mindlessness are defined as losing track of the task at hand or failure to maintain an attentional set. Mindlessness can be distinguished from distraction in that when being mindless the individual loses track of the task or attentional set, but when distracted the individual maintains the set or knows what the task at hand is, yet becomes distracted while trying to carry out that task. Everyday behavior becomes mindless when we lose track of why we are engaging in a given behavior (Langer, Blank, & Chanowitz ,1978).

Mindlessness occurs frequently in everyday life. According to Reason (1984) mindless episodes are most likely to occur in "highly routinized activities" (p. 515). As for examples of everyday mindlessness he adds, "Those who have stepped into their baths still wearing some garment, or struggled to open a friend's front door with their own latch key, or switched on the light as they left the room in the daytime, or attempted to pour a second kettle of water into a pot of freshly made tea...will recognize the species" (p. 527). He defines these "lapses" as "actions deviated from intention" (p. 521) and explains their occurrence as "the performance of a highly automatized task in relatively predictable and familiar surroundings liberates the central processor from moment-to-moment control. As a consequence, focal attention tends to be 'captured' by some pressing but parallel mental activity or by some unrelated external event..." (p. 521). These lapses are typically "associated with either internal preoccupation or with some external distraction" (p. 522). Through an analysis of subjects' daily diaries of everyday lapses Reason was able to identified no less than 30 types of lapses, the most frequent being: doing something without full attention, forgetting a plan, forgetting the intention, having the feeling that you should be doing something but forgetting what is was, and acting differently than what had been intended. Slips of mind were more commonly reported than slips of behavior. Most of these lapses could be accounted four using four broad categories: repeating the same action mindlessly; doing an intended action with respect to the wrong object; unintended thoughts or actions intruding on the task at hand; and omitting intended actions. Reason explains these lapses as temporary suspension of an executive attentional system resulting in some kind of cognitive or action system failure.

One way that scientists have studied mindlessness is through self-report of episodes of mindlessness. For example, Broadbent et al. (1982) created the Cognitive Failures Questionnaire (CFQ) that investigated the frequency of self-reported lapses in perception, memory, and motor functions. They found that episodes of self-reported mindlessness in adults were fairly consistent over long time periods. They concluded that episodes of mindlessness are likely to reflect a general failure in executive monitoring and control over attention. These episodes of mindlessness tend to occur more when an individual is sleepy or when bored (Wallace, Vodanovich & Restino, 2003). In fact, boredom appears to be the main factor predicting "an inability to engage and sustain attention" (Carriere, Cheyne, & Smilek, 2008, p. 836). Another reason for losing track of the task at hand occurs when the individual becomes preoccupied with the past (Langer, 1992).

Brown & Ryan (2003) studied mindlessness using the Mindful Attention Awareness Scale (MAAS). They defined mindfulness as "the presence or absence of attention to and awareness of what is occurring in the present... present-centered awareness" (p.184). Cheyne, Carriere, and Smilek (2006) used the MAAS to study the relationship between episodes of mindlessness and cognitive errors. They created the Attention-Related Cognitive Errors Scale (ARCES). Used in conjunction with the MAAS they found that attentional lapses on the MAAS were significantly correlated with cognitive errors on the ARCES. Additionally, they found that such episodes of mindlessness tended to occur especially during "highly practiced, familiar, repetitive, or tedious tasks" (p. 580), i.e., in situations that become boring. In other words, boredom leads to mindlessness, and mindlessness leads to carelessness (p. 581). They emphasize that this entire pathway begins with the "inability to sustain attention" (p. 582).

Another way that scientists have studied mindlessness is by investigating mindlessness as it occurs during performance on vigilance tasks. For example, while subjects performed a grid game vigilance task, Giambra (1995) found that these subjects frequently reported involuntary shifts away from the vigilance task toward internal task-unrelated images and thoughts. These spontaneous unwanted thoughts and images tended to distract the subjects from the task and seemed to represent "an uncontrolled switching of attention from external stimuli to the contents of consciousness due to "poor inhibitory control" (p. 16). Robertson et al. (1997) add that these episodes of mindlessness tend to occur when there is "insufficient attention to tasks" (p. 747).

These moments of mindlessness are especially apparent during dull yet demanding tasks (Robertson et al., 1997). Scientists developed the Sustained Attention to Response Task (SART) wherein subjects search a display for target numbers that are presented randomly in one of five fonts and are required to press a key for each number except the number three. That vigilance task was purposely constructed to require frequent response to non-targets in a display wherein targets occur very infrequently. Under such conditions of low probability of target occurrence "attention tends to drift away from task relevant material" (p. 683). Manly et al. (1999) interpret mindlessness on the SART saying, "To be absent-minded is to be inattentive to ongoing activity, to lose track of current aims and to become distracted from intended thought or action by salient but (currently) irrelevant stimuli" (p. 661). They add that since the SART is a brief test, then "Inefficiencies in the maintenance of attentional control may be apparent over much briefer periods than is traditionally considered using vigilance measures" (p.661). In other words, it doesn't take long for someone to get bored and drift away from the task at hand especially if the task is repetitive.

Smallwood et al. (2004) investigated disengagement from the task and the occurrence of task-unrelated thought in vigilance tasks "where demands exceed ability to perform the task" (p. 658). Under such conditions attention is said to become "decoupled" from the task at hand and invested in "task unrelated thought" (p. 658). Performance on demanding yet boring tasks like the SART, according to Smallwood et al. "is associated with a higher frequency of verbal reports reflecting task disengagement" (p. 675), especially when the duration of the task is longer. Smallwood et al. add that such lapses in attention to the task are sometimes but not always associated with meta-cognitive awareness. They call this phenomenon the "Oops" response wherein "the individual's failure to detect a target is available to awareness" (p. 687).

Except for the finding that mind wandering decreases with age (Giambra, 1993), there have been very few studies on age-related differences in mindlessness, so we don't know much about the nature and frequency of mindless episodes in children. However, Smallwood, Fishman, and Schooler (2007) have studied the effects of mindlessness on educational performance. They argue that wandering from the task and drifting off into internal thought is especially likely to affect reading and reading comprehension. They add that getting students to think out loud diminishes them drifting off into task irrelevant thought, and that training students to become more meta-cognitively aware of when the drift off also helps.

Distracted Concentration

Mindlessness and distracted concentration are similar but there is an important difference. When someone is mindless the attentional set has been lost and the task-at-hand is forgotten. When someone is distracted the attentional set is not lost, but while attempting to carry out the task-

Chapter 2: The Varieties of Dysfunctional Attention in the Modern Western World

at-hand the individual is distracted by something else.

The ability to concentrate entails two related skills: 1. the capacity to sustain attention for the duration of the task; and 2. the ability to resist distraction while engaging in the task-at-hand. In children, psychologists measure sustained attention in terms of the duration of free play or the duration of time attention is sustained in an assigned task. In both children and adults sustained attention is typically measured with a continuous performance task (CPT).

It is quite clear that duration of sustained attention is in part a function of interest. Someone may appear to be absorbed for hours in an activity that captures his or her interest, but show a very short attention span for task that is of little personal interest. Therefore, estimates of the duration of sustained attention that fail to take into account level of interest in the task-at-hand show great variability. For example, 5-6 year-olds were found to spend on average 10-15 minutes of sustained attention on an activity of interest, but only 5-10 minutes of sustained attention to assigned classroom tasks that were uninteresting (earlyinterventionsupport.com).

DEVELOPMENTAL TRENDS IN ATTENTION SPAN

Many pediatricians have said that the average duration of a child's attention span in minutes is equivalent to their age plus 1-2 minutes. Thus a four-year-olds' average duration of sustained attention in free play or watching television is estimated to be 5-6 minutes, although the duration would be less for engagement in a task that holds little interest. There is some evidence to suggest that the duration of attention span in early years predicts duration in later years. For example, Yarrow et al. (1982) assessed 6-month-old infants' attention spans' while playing with toys. The duration of sustained attention during free play at 6 months predicted persistence of attention at tasks assigned to the children at 13 months. At 13 months of age the children were asked to engage in 11 mastery tasks. They found "13-month-old infants engaged in persistent task-directed behaviors about 60% of the time during 11 mastery tasks" (p. 131). The study also showed that mother-child interactions affected the duration of sustained attention. Yarrow et al. say, "Significant relationships were found between persistence at 1 year and three aspects of maternal care when the infant was 6 months…the amount of maternal kinesthetic stimulation, auditory stimulation, and social mediation of play. These correlations suggest a link between a stimulating, responsive early environment and later persistence at tasks" (p. 138). On the negative side Breznitz and Friedman (1988) studied the negative effects of maternal depression on toddler's concentration. They found "that when depressed women played with their toddler-age children, they initiated and terminated interactions with objects more frequently than the well women. This relatively controlling behavior on the part of depressed women may have led their children to engage with more objects for shorter durations than did children of well mothers" (p. 275). Clearly, maternal responsiveness, and lack of responsiveness, affects the duration of sustained attention in young children. Thus, while there may be a genetic contribution to the duration of sustained attention, it is also clear that maternal attunement and responsiveness entrains the infant's focus and duration of attention to objects in the immediate environment. For example, during periods of free play mother's who consistently focused the child's attention on certain objects or toys significantly predicted the child's duration of attention later in development (Hornik, Risenhoover, & Gunnar, 1987).

THE ILLUSION OF DURATION OF SUSTAINED ATTENTION

Longer duration of sustained attention is not a reliable measure of attentional capacity in children. For example, Ruff and Rothbart (1996) studied 2.5-, 3.5-, and 4.5-year-old children's attention to videotaped puppet skits. The skits were "intended to be moderately interesting but not absorbing" (p. 152). While it was true that "older children looked at the screen more than younger children…all age groups showed decreasing attention over [4] trials. The fact that older children were able to maintain their looking to the screen, despite declining engagement, is likely a consequence of their greater compliance and voluntary control (p. 153). Likewise, average duration of looking tends to decrease

Chapter 2: The Varieties of Dysfunctional Attention in the Modern Western World

across age in infancy, so that developmentally "mature" performance is measured by shorter, not longer, looking (Colombo, 1993). Additionally, "although an infant may be looking at a display, measures of heart rate and distractibility suggest that the infant's attention is not necessarily engaged.... Thus, long looks are not an adequate reflection of attention span" (Ruff & Rothbart, 1996, p. 181). They add, "infants who look longer do so because they require a longer time to acquire sufficient information for visual recognition" (p. 181). Thus, duration of sustained attention as a measure of concentration in children is an illusion.

Haider (1970) reviewed the findings of early continuous performance research and concluded that "fluctuation of attention" was common (p. 419). He documented two main types of attentional fluctuations observed in continuous performance research. Short-term phasic fluctuations occur in a continuous performance task when the subject has a brief duration episode of disengaging and then re-engaging the target stimulus. Longer-term tonic fluctuations occur due to a drop in overall alertness level from trying to sustain attention too long and becoming bored (p. 430).

While it is generally accepted that the duration of sustained attention improves with age, there is some evidence to suggest that the duration of sustained attention is an illusion and that phasic very brief fluctuations in attention are extremely common and frequent. If, for example, an assessment shows that a given individual sustains his or her attention to a task-at-hand for 30 minutes, this does not mean that the task captured the person's attention for the entire 30 minutes. Rather than sustaining a steady state of 30 minutes of uninterrupted attention to the task, some research findings suggest the likelihood that the individual had numerous mini-episodes of becoming distracted for very brief intervals from the task, each time re-engaging in the task such that the overall effect seemed to be sustained attention for 30 minutes.

The illusion of a steady state of sustained attention was discovered by observing children attending to toys during free play sessions in contrast to attending to television. In each case the findings were remarkably similar. Choi and Anderson (1991) observed 5-year-olds engaged in free play. They found that the child's initial engagement with a toy was very tentative, but after 12-15 seconds the child became engaged with the toy. After 15 seconds, once engaged and absorbed, the child became significantly more resistant to distraction. They refer to this increase in resistance to distraction the "attentional inertia effect" (p. 41). However, when they assessed the time course of seemingly deeply engaged play they discovered the child frequently disengaged for brief intervals and quickly immediately re-engaged with the toy. Essentially they discovered the child engaged in a "large number of extremely short play episodes" (p. 51). Similarly, when observing these children watching TV they found that while the child seemed to watch the TV program for an hour, "the child made on average 150 episodes of looks at/looks away/looks again at the TV screen in that hour" (p. 43). Most episodes of engagement/disengagement/re-engagement of the TV program lasted on average 3 seconds. Attentional inertia was the "glue" that linked the numerous mini-episodes of disengagement/re-engagement into a seeming single, long duration of sustained attention (p. 44), but that was more of an illusion. During free play the average episode length was "about a minute in length...so that there is a preponderance of short episodes" (p. 60). Overall, they found striking "parallels between toy play and looks at TV" (p. 60). They say, "Each activity, therefore, might be viewed as a chain of schematic elements... Attentional inertia provides the glue by which involvement with the medium across successive schematic elements or even full schemas can be sustained" (pp. 61-63). Thus, the reality of long episodes of steady, undistracted, sustained attention are highly unlikely (p. 55). (See also Anderson and Lorch (1983) and Anderson, Choi, and Lorch (1987). Anderson et al. 1985 observed a 3-year-old girl viewing TV in her home for 4.4. hours. She looked away 352 times during a period in which she had 38% of actual viewing time to the TV.

In a study of the attention span of toddlers engaged in simple tasks like stacking cups, Choudhury & Groman (2000) found that the attention span of 1.5 to 3-year-old toddlers was about 2 minutes (range 0.5-2.5 minutes), but that there were "frequent off-task glances" even in these brief episodes of sustained attention. However, these frequent episodes of disengagement were not necessarily negative. Frequent disengagement was significantly related to enhanced problem-solving performance. More-

Chapter 2: The Varieties of Dysfunctional Attention in the Modern Western World

over, "Toddlers with more frequent off-task glances had longer attention spans" (p.127). They add, "Frequent brief breaks... may actually help to focus attention and facilitate cognitive processing" (p. 141).

Kaye and Fogel (1980) made video recordings of face-to-face play of mothers and infants at 6, 13, and 26 weeks of age. Mean proportion of time that these infants oriented toward their mother's faces, and also the duration of their state of attention toward mother, declined with age from 70% looking at the mother at 6 weeks to 33% at 26 weeks (p. 457). By 26 weeks the frequency of face-to-face mutual exchanges during play had become substantially reduced and was replaced by predominately object play by the infant. During sustained play Kaye and Fogel noted that infants showed very frequent inattentive periods and that episodes of play had become shorter (p. 463). As in the Choudhury and Gorman study, Kaye and Fogel found that seeming sustained periods of play were characterized by frequent, brief duration disengagement of attention.

These studies in both children and adults strongly suggest that long periods of absorbed attention are mostly an illusion, and that periods of sustained attention are marked frequent yet brief episodes of disengagement and re-engagement.

THE PROBLEM OF APPORTIONING ATTENTION

Berlyne (1970), one of the early pioneers in Western research on attention, developed the idea of "degree of concentration." He defines degree of concentration:

> At one extreme, all the information from one source can be transmitted perfectly and all the information from other sources eliminated. At the other extreme, part, but not all, of the information from every source may reach the output end. (p. 29)

Variations in the degree of concentration have not been studied much in modern Western psychology. A similar construct, in Buddhist meditation is the problem of partial staying. Take, for example, a meditator engaged in concentration meditation using the rising and falling of the breath as a concentration object. The initial task of concentration meditation is to staying concentrated on the breath as the concentration object for increasingly longer periods of time, i.e., to extend the duration of concentration span over time, while resisting chasing after thought and other distractions. Once achieving some mastery over continuous staying over time, the meditator eventually realizes the problem of partial staying, namely that at any given point in time, cross-sectionally, the meditator has been unwittingly dividing or apportioning attention between the breath as the concentration object and the background noise of thought or other distractions in such a way that concentration on the breath as the concentration object has been piecemeal or patchy, and the meditator never really had fully disengaged from distraction. In other words, the meditator had continued to engage distracting thoughts. Now, the new challenge becomes training the mind in complete staying at any given time, cross-sectionally—no longer dividing attention between the concentration object and the background noise.

Fluctuations in degree of concentration are widespread. In the West problems with the degree or depth of concentration are classified as interference effects in divided attention tasks, so we will address this topic again in this chapter under the section on multitasking.

INATTENTIONAL BLINDNESS AS THE COST OF SUSTAINED AND SELECTIVE FOCUS

A second problem with sustained attention is that whenever the spotlight of attention is intensely focused on a particular object, there is a greater likelihood of failing to perceive other important objects or events in the same field of awareness. Failure to perceive objects in full view in the immediate environment is called inattentional blindness. Mack and Rock (1998) used a high-speed visual search task with a tachistoscope wherein Ss were presented with a fixation point at the onset as the visual search. When an unexpected object was present at the same time of the fixation point (a cross) the Ss failed to perceive the unexpected object presumably because of their focus on the fixation point. If the cross was presented at the fixation point, 25% of the Ss failed to detect the unexpected object. If the cross was presented at some peripheral point that required the S to suddenly switch attention to track the location of the cross, 75% of the Ss failed to detect the unexpected object (p. 13). According to Mack and Rock inattentional blindness "is most likely to occur during moments of intense concentration or absorption. During these moments, even though our eyes are open and the objects before us are imaged on our retinas, we seem to perceive very little, if anything" (p. 1).

Simons and Chabris (1999) were able to show how extreme inattentional blindness can be in daily life. In their experiment, they used a videotaped staged event wherein college Ss viewed several players passing a basketball. Subjects were required to monitor and count the number of basketball passes (easy task) or keep track of the number of aerial passes and bounce passes (difficult task). Two unexpected events were used: a woman walking across the set carrying an umbrella, or a woman in a gorilla suit walking across the set during the basketball passes. Across all conditions "46% failed to notice the unexpected event" (p. 1068). The authors conclude, "Approximately half of observers fail to notice an ongoing and highly salient but unexpected event while they are engaged in a primary monitoring task" (p. 1069). The fact that nearly half the Ss failed to notice the gorilla directly in their field of awareness is strong demonstration of inattentional blindness.

There have been few studies on inattentional blindness in children. For example, Memmert (2006) tested 8-year-old children using the basketball-unexpected gorilla paradigm. A total of 60% of the 8 year-old children failed to see the unexpected gorilla while focusing on the basketball counting task.

FACTORS THAT AGGRAVATE DISTRACTION FROM SUSTAINED CONCENTRATION

THE HOME ENVIRONMENT

We have learned that most children grow up with what seems to be age-related increases in the duration of sustained attention, but that extended periods of seemingly sustained attention is a kind of illusion, in that extended periods of sustained attention are typically marked by frequent mini-episodes of distraction and re-engagement. However, some children grow up with additional factors that pose a strong disadvantage to the development of sustained attention. For example, Wachs (1993) assessed the of quality of the home environment in 2-year-old toddlers, and found that "high levels of noise, crowding, or person traffic patterns in infants' homes are associated with less involved and less responsive caregiving parents" (p. 81), and that mothers who had "a higher probability of being less responsive, less involved, and less vocally stimulating were less likely to show or demonstrate objects... and more likely to interfere with infant exploratory activities" (p. 82). In other words, such noisy, over-crowded, high-traffic home environments necessarily interfere with the development of sustained attention in these disadvantaged children. In another study Wachs (1989) added that a high number of siblings in the home dilutes the quality of maternal attunement and responsiveness to a child in a way that also potentially interferes with the development of sustained attention.

MULTIMEDIA EXPOSURE

In modern society, another factor that is highly likely to interfere with the development of sustained attention is multi-media exposure. Anderson and Pempek (2005) conducted a national survey of childrens' television viewing. They asked parents to rate how much television their children watched. They found that in the 1990s television shows were developed specifically targeted to toddlers like Baby Einstein and Teletubbies. Since these shows were mostly comprehensible to toddlers, toddlers in that generation substantially increased the amount of time they spent watching television. At 2.5 months of age toddlers watched on the average of 2 hours/day of television: 50% toddler programming; 40% adult programming; and 9% pre-teen programming (p. 507). The daily time spent by these toddlers watching videotapes or DVDs averaged around 1.5 hours per day, and about half of the videos were not made for children (p. 509). They found that "the duration of attention to

Chapter 2: The Varieties of Dysfunctional Attention in the Modern Western World

television increases with age and peaks about 12 years of age" (p. 508). Anderson and Pempek also discovered that "Children learn less from television than from equivalent real-life experiences. We refer to this as the video deficit... which was defined in terms of "deficits in language, learning, and emotional learning" (p. 511). In support of this view that too much exposure to television and DVDs in childhood interferes with the development of sustained attention, Christakis et al. (2004) found "a small positive association...between viewing at age 1.5 years and having symptoms of attention disorders... [p. 516]... [and] there is very little evidence that children younger than 2 learn anything useful from television. The evidence indicates that learning from television by very young children is poor and that exposure to television is associated with relatively poor outcomes [p. 518]. [Christakis et al. add that with the introduction of home theaters and big screen televisions into homes more recently] It seems likely that the disruptive effects of background TV will only be magnified" (p. 519).

More recently children's exposure to browsing the Internet has aggravated the problem of sustaining attention even more. Browsing the Internet entails jumping frequently from one site to another and training attention to do so. Most internet users spent less than a minute on any one site before jumping to anther site. Regularly "surfing" actually shapes the mind to have a much shorter attention span. In one news report regular surfers of the Internet were found to have an attention span comparable to a goldfish (BBC News, 2002).

On the other hand, not all video behavior is associated with interference of attention span. For example, Green and Bavelier (2003) compared the performance of seasoned action videogame players (VGPs) to Ss not involved with action videogames of 18-23 years of age on a flanker task that measured the extent of distraction by flankers similar to targets in a search task. They found, "VGPs possess enhanced attentional capacity" (p. 534). These findings suggest that for at least some seasoned videogame players the game actually trained working memory and sustained attention, depending on the nature of the game and the level of experience with the game.

INDIVIDUAL DIFFERENCES IN DISTRACTIBILITY

While it may be true that most normal children and adults rarely have long periods of sustained concentration without frequent interruptions, there are a minority of children and adults who have more severe, clinically significant problems with sustained attention, namely children and adults with attention deficit hyperactivity disorder. About 3-7% of children have ADHD, which is identifiable as a clinical condition around age 7 (Barkley, 1997). Some researchers believe that ADHD represents a developmental lag and that most children will eventually grow out of it, but others assert that "There are patterns of cortical activity and abnormality in some ADHD children that are not normal at any age" but while this question has not yet been fully resolved, the important question is "which environment and interventions can best suit the development of the ADHD child, and [which] help them turn their negative traits into positive outcomes (Steffert, 2014, p. 12, 14).

However, precursors to ADHD are typically identifiable by mothers in early childhood years. Campbell et al (1986) conducted a longitudinal study on 2- and 3-year-old hyperactive children. They observed the children and mothers during play periods at intake and 1 year later. They found, "Mothers of problem children provided more redirection initially and made more negative control statements at follow-up (p. 425)... [and were] "more likely to refocus their youngsters' play behavior by suggesting alternative activities" (p. 437). Similarly, Cunningham & Barkley (1979) observed normal and hyperactive 6-12-year-olds in free play and also in structured tasks. They found, "Mothers of hyperactive boys were less likely to respond positively...imposed more structure and control...[and that] ...the controlling intrusive style observed among mothers of hyperactive boys, while initially a response to the child's overactive, impulsive, inattentive style, may further contribute to the child's behavioral difficulties" (p. 217). Similarly, Mash and Johnston (1982) observed mother-child interactions in 4- and 8-year-old normal vs. hyperactive children in unstructured play and in structured tasks. They found, "Mothers of hyperactives were generally more directive and negative during play and less responsive to child-initiated interac-

Chapter 2: The Varieties of Dysfunctional Attention in the Modern Western World

tions... During the structured-task situations mothers of hyperactives were more directive and negative and less interactive and approving" (p. 1371). These studies consistently establish that mothers of children with ADHD behave differently with their children than mothers of normal children. However, it remains unclear whether or not these mothers act differently in reaction to their childrens' ADHD, or whether their controlling unresponsive style is formative of, or aggravating of, their children's ADHD.

A number of studies have demonstrated that children and adults with ADHD have clinically significant deficits in sustained attention. For example, Sykes et al. (1971) studied normal and hyperactive 5- to 12-year-old children's responses to a continuous performance task. Hyperactive as compared to control children were "deficient with respect to their ability to maintain attention to a task... and made more incorrect responses to non-significant stimuli" (p. 136). Using a similar continuous performance task Seidel and Joschko (1990) found "difficulties in the ability to sustain attention can be demonstrated in [6- and 10-year-old] children with ADHD" (p. 217). Printz, Tarnowski and Nay (1984) assessed a variety of attentional measures in 7- to 9-year-old boys diagnosed with ADHD to demographically matched non-ADHD boys during distraction and non-distraction conditions. The ADHD as compared to the non-ADHD boys had significant attentional problems on selective and sustained attention, but distraction was a problem for both groups, not especially for the ADHD group (p. 254). Teachers reported that ADHD as compared to non-ADHD boys took significantly longer time on given tasks. The authors concluded that a failure of sustained attention is a good way to discriminate between ADHD and non-ADHD students. Similarly, Hooks, Milich, and Lorch (1994) investigated response to a continuous performance task in 7- and 12-year-olds and their results were "indicative of a sustained attention deficit" and also a speed classification deficit in ADHD as compared to boys without ADHD. However, Tsal, Shalev, and Mevorach (2005) found that "ADHD may reflect a variety of attention deficits...[which include] deficits of sustained attention [that were] most pronounced" but also deficits in selective executive, and orienting attention in 8-year-olds (p. 142). Barkley,

Grodzinsky, and DuPaul (1992) found that "tests of response inhibition more reliably distinguished ADD/+H from normal children" (p. 163). ADHD children made more errors than normal children on continuous performance tests and on Stroop-like interference tests. Because ADHD children as compared to normal children show greater failure of inhibition motor response and inhibit distractors to sustaining attention in continuous performance and Stroop-like interference tasks, Barkley et al. consider ADHD to be a "disinhibition disorder" (p. 172). Ceci and Tishman (1984) describe a kind of "attentional diffusion" in 8-year-old ADHD boys defined as a "tendency to under focus their attention" (p. 2192) and "a diffuse or unselective manner of processing" (p. 2201).

Barkley (1997) describes "three primary systems" in children with ADHD—"poor sustained attention, impulsiveness, and hyperactivity" (p. 65). He sees "poor behavioral inhibition as central impairment" in ADHD (p. 66). "The hyperactive-impulsive behavior pattern seems to emerge first in development during the preschool years, whereas the symptoms of inattention associated with it appear to have their onset several years later…the essential impairment in ADHD is a deficit involving response inhibition… inhibition is assessed by performance on cognitive and behavioral tasks that require withholding of responding, delayed responding, cessation of on going responding, and resisting distraction or disruption by competing events" (pp. 67-68). He adds,"The inattention in ADHD can now be seen as not so much a primary symptom as a secondary one: it is a consequence of the impairment that poor behavioral inhibition and interference control create in the self-regulation or executive control of behavior" (p. 84).

According to Berger et al. (2015) overall brain development is delayed in ADHD. More specifically, Barkley, Grodzinsky, and Du Paul (1992) have shown that delayed development of the frontal lobes is implicated in ADHD, and that tests of response inhibition are the best way to discriminate ADHD, for example, the Stroop interference test or tests of continuous performance that include distractors. Even more specifically, Bush et al. (1999) have shown that the anterior cingulate cortex (ACC) is under-active in ADHD, and Sykes et al. (1971) have shown that drugs like Ritalin selectively activated ACC and put it back on line.

Chapter 2: The Varieties of Dysfunctional Attention in the Modern Western World

MIND-WANDERING

Neuroscientists have discovered that most individuals, when not engaged in a task, shift into a default resting state characterized by mind-wandering. Most of modern neuroscience has studied what specific brain areas and circuits become either activated or deactivated during a specific task or condition. However, it became increasingly clear that when an individual was not engaged in anything particular, there was a very specific underlying pattern of activation and deactivations in certain areas and circuits. Thus, while the individual was ostensibly "at rest" the brain itself was nevertheless quite active in very specific ways, and the particular way the brain remained quite active came to be known as the default mode network (DMN) and the specific internal state or experience came to be known as mind-wandering mode. This default mode has been considered "a physiological baseline of the human brain" (Gusnard & Raichle, 2001, p. 688).

Individuals naturally shift into mind-wandering mode when they cease engaging in or get distracted from the task at hand, become passive, intend to rest or close their eyes, and/or turn away from an active external orientation (Gusnard & Raichle, 2001; Mason, et al., 2007; Raichle et al., 2001; Raichle & Snyder, 2007). According to Smilek, Carriere, and Cheyne (2010) episodes of mind-wandering are characterized by blocking external sensory experience from awareness along with "cortical deactivation of areas [of the brain] responsible for processing the external visual world" (p. 788). Mason et al., (2007) state, "We propose that mind-wandering constitutes a psychological baseline that emerges when the brain is otherwise unoccupied" (p. 394). Yet, they emphasize that from the perspective of brain activity, this default mode is not exactly a resting state in that the cortices of the brain are still very active (p. 393). Bucker, Andrews-Hanna, and Schacter (2008) add, "the default network is the most active brain system when individuals are left to think to themselves undisturbed" (p. 30).

Mind-wandering is characterized by a very specific kind of mental content. Mind-wandering entails "spontaneous cognition... stimulus-independent thoughts... momentary lapses in attention" (Bucker et al.,

2008, p. 16). In mind-wandering the mind drifts away from the external task at hand in favor of "inner thoughts, fantasies, feelings, and other musings" (Smallwood & Schooler, 2006, p. 946). Studies on the content of mind-wandering have shown that most of these musings are highly self-referential. In other words, mind-wandering thoughts frequently center around the self, namely spontaneously emerging personal autobiographical memories, reviewing recent past experience, anticipation of immediate future experiences, and fantasies and reveries about the self (Buckner et al., 2008). However, these self-referential thoughts and imaginings are not exactly goal-directed nor are they like ruminations. According to Christoff et al., (2016) ruminative thinking is "fixed on a single theme [in contrast to mind-wandering where thoughts] are free to move hither and thither [p. 719]. [In other words, during mind-wandering mode, the mind really does wander but is] more deliberately constrained than daydreaming but less deliberately constrained than creative thinking" (p. 719).

Mind-wandering is rarely accompanied by meta-cognitive awareness that one is caught up in mind-wandering mode, but sometimes it is. (Smallwood & Schooler, 2006; Smallwood et al., 2007). The most frequent experience is that an individual shifts into mind-wandering mode, and doesn't really know that he or she is caught up in internal self-referential wanderings, and after some period of time shifts out of it or recognizes that the mind has been wandering. Much less frequently the mind shifts into mind-wandering mode and retains some meta-cognitive awareness so that the individual follows the self-referential thoughts, memories and imaginings. Under this very specific condition the brain recruits both the neurocircuitry associated with mind-wandering and that associated with executive control (Christoff et al., 2009). Nevertheless, they found that "mind-wandering is most pronounced when it lacks meta-awareness" (p. 871).

The degree to which mind-wandering occurs under conditions of purposeful executive control is unclear. According to Smallwood and Schooler (2006) during mind-wandering "executive control shifts away from primary tasks to the processing of personal goals…[it] involves executive control yet seems to lack deliberate intent" [p. 946]… Thus,

Chapter 2: The Varieties of Dysfunctional Attention in the Modern Western World

mind-wandering is a paradox: mind-wandering clearly shares many features of traditional executive systems, yet some of these episodes occur in the absence of explicit intention" (p. 953).

Studies on the patterns of activation and deactivation of specific brain areas and circuits have yielded highly consistent findings. Most important, the main finding across all studies is that mind-wandering mode entails the activation of the medial prefrontal cortex (mPFC), the area of the brain responsible for self reference and self experience (Buckner et al., 2008; Gusnard et al., 2001; McGuire et al., 1996). More recent findings have shown that mind-wandering mode entails multiple interacting subsystems of the brain (Fox et al., 2015). One subsystem entails activation of the medial prefrontal cortex (mPFC), posterior cingulate cortex (PCC), infralateral pariental cortex (ILP) and temporo-parietal junction (TPJ), and the precuneus. As mentioned above, mPFC activation is strongly associated with sense of self and self-referential thinking. PCC activation is associated with self-evaluation and judgment. Infralateral pariental cortex and TPJ activation is associated with switching from external to internal engagement. Precuneus activation is associated with imagination, fantasy, and daydreaming. Together this very specific pattern of activations suggests: a switch away from engagement with the external world or task at hand, an internal preoccupation with self referential thoughts and evaluations, and imaginings. Since the temporo-parietal junction (TPJ) is commonly associated with task-switching, its continual activation is consistent with switching from one thought to another. The other subsystem entails activation of the medial temporal lobes and retrosplenal cortex, which are commonly associated with the retrieval of personal, autobiographical memory (Buckner, et al., 2008; Gusnard & Raichel, 2001; Mason et al., 2007; Raichle et al., 2001. Both of these patterns of neurocircuitry are well integrated and show functional connectivity (Fransson & Marrelec, 2008; Grecious et al., 2009). A third subsystem sometimes but not usually activated is the fronto-pariental executive control system. This occurs when mind-wandering is accompanied by some degree of meta-cognitive monitoring and/or intention to engage these internally-based self-referential thoughts (Andrews-Hanna et al., 2010; Fox et al., 2015).

Killingsworth & Gilbert (2010) studied the frequency of mind-wandering in the general population and found it to be disturbingly high. They created a cell phone application so that they could develop a large data base: "nearly a quarter of a million samples from about 5,000 people" contacted at random moments throughout the day (p. 932). They found that "Mind-wandering occurred in 46.9% of the samples" and that the "frequency of mind-wandering in our real-world sample was considerably higher than is typically seen in laboratory experiments" (p. 932). In other words, the typical individual spends nearly half of waking time in mind-wandering mode, in an internal, self-preoccupied state.

Given the enormous amount of time a given individual spends in mind-wandering mode scientists have raised the important question as to what is the adaptive purpose or function of mind-wandering and default mode network brain activation? Does the DMN have an evolutionary adaptive purpose? Unfortunately, scientists don't yet agree on the answer. According to Smallwood and Schooler (2006) mind-wandering functions to "leave the primary task in favor of an alternative personally relevant goal...executive control becomes disengaged from a primary task during mind-wandering and becomes directed toward the processing of internal information, such as memories" (pp. 954-956). While most scientists agree that mind-wandering predominately entails preoccupation with internal, self-referential thought (Bucker et al., 2008; Gusnard et al., 2001; Whitfield-Gabrieli et al., 2011) Spreng and Grady (2009) believe that mind-wandering functions to support review of autobiographical memory and project the self into the past, the future, and into the minds of others (p. 1121). Others have speculated that mind-wandering might play an important role in creative thinking and problem solving (Fox et al., 2015) and in daydreaming (Christoff et al., 2016). Given the central role that mPFC activation plays in mind-wandering, Gusnard (2005) believes that mind-wandering plays an important role in "maintenance of a sense of self" (Gusnard, 2005, cited in Sonuga-Barke & Castellanos, 2007, p. 979).

Yet, despite a search for the adaptive use of mind-wandering, others have emphasized the very clear negative consequences of mind-wandering. Given the enormous amount of time the average individual

Chapter 2: The Varieties of Dysfunctional Attention in the Modern Western World

is preoccupied with mind-wandering during the day, Sonuga-Barke and Castellanos (2007) state it is likely that habitual mind-wandering will persist, intrude into, and therefore distract an individual from active engagement in the tasks of everyday life. In other words, habitual mind-wandering becomes strong competition to goal-directed task-focus and maintenance. All too readily the average individual switches off the task at hand in everyday life back to some internal seemingly aimless self-referential preoccupation. Killingsworth & Gilbert (2010) found that habitual mind-wandering was significantly associated with everyday unhappiness. They say, "mind wandering…may have an emotional cost…happiness is…living in the moment…people were less happy when their minds were wandering than when they were not [and]… a wandering mind is an unhappy mind" (p. 932). They emphatically state that mind-wandering is "the cause not the merely the consequence, of unhappiness" (p. 932). Not only were negative mood states significantly related to mind-wandering in their study, Christoff et al. (2009) additionally found that mind-wandering was associated with personal conflict and unresolved matters (p. 8722). Thus, mind-wandering may be an adaptive attempt to process personal unfinished emotional business (Traue & Pennebaker, 1993). In this sense, mind-wandering may have a direct relationship to the development of psychopathology and certain psychiatric conditions (Anticevic et al., 2012). A similar concern is echoed in the meditation traditions of the East, like Buddhist meditation where the dysfunction of the ordinary mind is seen as the primary source of suffering. More specifically, the untrained mind is an unhappy mind (H.H. The Dalai Lama and Cutler, 1998).

Gao et al. (2009) investigated when the default mode network (DMN) develops over the course of the life cycle. They found that "a primitive and incomplete default network is present in 2-week-olds" (p. 6790). "By two years of age, the default network becomes similar to that observed in adults, including the medial prefrontal cortex (mPFC), posterior cingulate cortex/retrosplenial (PCC/Rsp), inferior pariental lobule, lateral temporal cortex, and hippocampus regions" (p.6790). This study has very important implications for the education of children. The findings strongly demonstrate that the neurocircuitry of the default mode network (DMN) and mind-wandering is nearly fully developed by the second year of life. Thus, toddlers, preschool children, school-aged children, and adolescents likely suffer from the negative effects of mind-wandering the same as adults do. Therefore, it is critical that attention training to offset habitual mind-wandering is initiated in childhood and not just offered to adults.

In 1990 one of the authors (DB) participated in a Mind-Life science dialogue with His Holiness, the Dalai Lama. At the week-long conference one of the Western faculty members mentioned the phenomena of negative self-talk, the automatic incessant negative evaluations of oneself. His Holiness did not understand the concept and spent a long time talking in Tibetan with his two translators trying to conceptually understand what negative self-talk was. At the point of understanding, he turned to us Western faculty with some concern and said, "Why would you let the mind get like that?" Then it became clear to us that negative self-talk was likely a culture-bound Western phenomenon, and that mind-wandering as a default option was not universal, especially not prevalent in a culture where training the mind is given to children.

MULTITASKING

THE MYTH OF MULTITASKING

Multitasking refers to the ability to perform more than one task at a given time. Multimedia exposure in this generation has substantially complicated the normal development of attentional skills and has imposed upon this generation a large range of multitasking demands. According to Wallis (2010) there are three types of media multitasking: 1. Combining a media task with a real life task; 2. Combining tasks from two or ore different media; and 3. Engaging in multiple tasks within the same media.

For example, children who grow up with a television in the background as compared to those without background television have substantially reduced duration of sustained attention during free play periods by age 4 (Schmidt et al., 2008). Parents estimates of how much time their children watch television at a young age significantly predicts

Chapter 2: The Varieties of Dysfunctional Attention in the Modern Western World

which children will have developed significant attentional problems by age 7. In that study, 10% of the children has attentional problems by age 7 (Christakis et al., 2004).

In another study, Brasel and Gips (2011) studied multimedia children who had become accustomed to watching television and a computer screen at the same time. Those children had learned the bad habit of switching rapidly back and forth between one thing and another at a very high rate. Those children who had trained themselves to engage in multiple media presentations, for example, television, computer screen cell phone, instant messaging, and e-mail, typically perform worse than low media children on attentional tasks because of a "reduced ability to filter out interference from irrelevant stimuli" (Lin, 2009, p. 15521).

A number of laboratory studies have been conducted on the effects of heavy media multitasking on task performance. Ophir et al. (2009) used a Media Survey Questionnaire to identify high and low media multitasking children. They found that high compared to low media multitasking children performed worse on tests requiring task-switching, because they readily allowed extraneous information into their working memory and were significantly more likely to respond to stimuli outside of the immediate task. The greater the range of media multitasking the child engaged in, the greater the task interference. They say, "the data suggest that HMMs [heavy media multitaskers] are less likely to filter irrelevant representations arising from either external or internal sources" (p. 15585). Cain et al. (2016) also studied the effects of heavy media multitasking in adolescents. Subjects were given a variety of laboratory measures of academic performance, working memory, intelligence, and growth set. Results showed "poorer performance on measures of academic performance, poorer performance on laboratory measures of working memory capacity… more self-reported impulsive behavior, and lesser growth mindset… and worse statewide standardized test scores" [in heavy vs. light adolescent multitaskers]" (p. 1938). Moisala et al. (2016) studied performance on two different tasks—a sustained speech listening task and a reading task—while either trying to maintain sustained attention to one of the tasks in the presence of distractors from the other sense modality, or concurrently dividing attention between the two tasks. Heavy as compared to light media multitaskers did worse in the presence of distractors from the other modality in the single attentional task, but not on the divided attention task. This poorer performance in heavy multitaskers was associated with activation in the right prefrontal cortex. The authors conclude, "the distracted attention condition required more effort and executive control from the participants the higher their MMT score was [p. 119]…more effort or attentional top-down control was needed…to focus on a focal task in the presence of a distractor" (p. 120). In adults, switching between two tasks, as compared to repeated trials of the same task, resulted in significantly slower performance in the task-switching condition. Task switching entailed activation of the lateral prefrontal system (Dove et al., 2000; Kimberg, Aguirre, ad D'Esposito, 2000; Sohn et al., 2000).

Uncapher, Thieu, and Wagner (2016) investigated the effects of multitasking on working memory and long-term memory in adolescents and young adults. Heavy as compared to light media multitaskers "showed reduced WM [working memory] performance regardless of whether external distractors were present or absent…that WM deficits likely exert effects on LTM [long-term memory]… [had] higher impulsivity… [and] as a consequence goal-irrelevant information may compete with goal-relevant information, reducing task performance" (p. 489).

Not all laboratory results of heavy media multitasking on performance have been negative. Alzahabi and Becker (2013) conducted a laboratory study on the effects of media multitasking on switching between two tasks (numbers and letters) or performing two tasks simultaneously (both numbers and letters). Results showed no difference between heavy and light media multitaskers on the dual task, and that "heavy media multitaskers were better able to switch between tasks in the task-switching paradigm" (p. 1485). These data suggest that at least some heavy media multitaskers learn greater skill in switching between tasks. The authors state, "frequently multitasking with media provides vast experience alternating between tasks, which results in an ability to rapidly shift between tasks that generalizes" (p. 1492). Likewise in her review of the effects of internet use on cognitive development on adolescence. Mills (2016) states that "these new technologies appear to be associated with

Chapter 2: The Varieties of Dysfunctional Attention in the Modern Western World

greater integration into peer groups and even increased cognitive abilities such as faster task-switching" (p. 10). Similarly, Pardo (2015) did not find that heavy media multitaskers produced significantly more errors on a sustained attention task in the presence of distractors than did light media multitaskers.

Baumgartner et al. (2014) investigated the relationship between media multitasking and executive functioning in early adolescents ages 11-15. Measures of executive functioning included tests of: working memory, task-switching, and the ability to inhibit response to distractions. The authors found a clear difference between self-report and laboratory measures of executive functioning. Where deleterious effects of multitasking were self-reported for all areas of executive functioning, there were no significance differences found on laboratory measures of working memory or task shifting, Surprisingly, heavy multitaskers as compared to light media multitaskers performed marginally significantly better on laboratory tests of distraction inhibition (p. 1138). The authors raise the possibility that "media multitasking may be positively related to specific components of cognitive functioning" (p. 1140). Baumgartner et al. (2018) also reported results of two longitudinal studies on the effects of multitasking on attention in early to middle adolescents, ages 11-16. They found that attentional problems were only found in early as compared to middle adolescents. They also found that adolescents with pre-existing attentional problems "are more likely to engage in media multitasking [p. 22]… [and] are more easily distracted by media and may find it difficult to focus their attention in the presence of media distractors" (p. 20).

Sanbonmatsu et al. (2013) have made an important distinction between multitasking activity and perceived multitasking ability. They found that "perceived ability to multi-task…was found to be significantly inflated" (p. 1). In fact, there was no significant relationship between actual multitasking performance and perceived multitasking ability. In other words, an individual's belief that he or she is good at multitasking is an illusion. Moreover, they also found that high levels of multitasking were especially prevalent in children who were high in sensation-seeking behaviors and who were impulsive.

Spink, Ozmutlu, and Ozmutlu (2002) studied children who frequently used the Internet to search for information. It had become a habit for them to depart from the original search task to search for multiple, often completely unrelated things on the web. Loh and Kanal (2015) state that the Internet is "reshaping human cognition" (p. 1) but not in a good way. They argue that children who have grown up in the digital era compared to those who did not "gravitate toward shallow information-processing behaviors characterized by rapid attention shifting and reduced deliberations. They engage in increased multitasking behaviors that are linked to increased distractibility and poor executive control abilities" (p. 1). Shallow processing entails "quick scanning, reduced contemplation, and memory consolidation" (p. 11). Such shallow information-processing they say "can disrupt the development of deep reading skills (e.g. inferential reasoning, critical analysis, reflection etc.) (p. 2).

In a study of dual task performance in children Irwin-Chase and Burns (2000) compared performance on single and dual tasks in 8 and 11-year-olds. There were no age differences when the tasks had equal priority, but there were clear age differences when each task had different priorities. The older children were more able than younger children to appraise the significance of the task and better control and allocate attention to the more relevant task.

Clearly, evaluating the effects of media multitasking on cognitive development in children and adolescents is complex. Most researchers concur that the effects are moderately negative. In a comprehensive review on the effects of media multitasking on youth van der Schur et al. (2015) conclude that media multitasking has a "small to moderate negative effect" on cognitive and attentional control, academic performance, and socioemotional functioning (p. 204). However, there are exceptions. One exception is that some heavy media multitaskers actually improve their skill in task-switching at least on certain tasks, and some heavy multitaskers are exceptional super-taskers. The other exception is that children and adolescents with certain vulnerabilities, like low self social esteem, attention deficit disorder, and impulsivity, may be especially prone to the deleterious effects of media multitasking.

Chapter 2: The Varieties of Dysfunctional Attention in the Modern Western World

Super Multitaskers

However, not all children show deleterious effects from multitasking. Watson & Strayer (2010) had subjects perform a dual task of operating a driving simulator while simultaneously remembering word lists and doing mental mathematical calculations. They found that a small group of subjects (2.5%) responded exceptionally well to all the tasks simultaneously. These exceptional subjects became known as "super taskers." They say, "Super taskers have a strikingly remarkable ability to successfully perform two attention-demanding tasks that over 97% of the population cannot perform without incurring substantial costs in performance" (p. 482). It has also become clear that while most children who frequently engage in media multitasking show deficits in sustained attention, some children who frequently engage in playing action videogames actually improve their attentional skills through playing these games frequently. For example, Green & Bavelier (2003) found differences between children who had played action videogames with high versus low frequency. Such games typically require frequent task switching. They found that high as compared to low frequency videogame players were better at sustained and divided attention tasks because playing the videogames so much had inadvertently trained them to ignore distraction and handle streams of infomation more efficiently.

Why is Multitasking Typically Associated with Poor Performance?

There are two very different styles of information-processing. We either process information over time (serial processing) or we process is simultaneously (parallel processing). However, serial or temporal processing is the default option for most individuals in most situations. Multitasking puts a strain on serial processing. According to Pashler (1994a/b) dual performance tasks reach a "stubborn bottleneck." He explains, "When two tasks need the mechanism at the same time, a bottleneck results, and one or both tasks will be delayed or otherwise impaired" (1994a, p. 221). The bottleneck is attributable to attempting to share the same processing resources at the same time for both tasks (1994b). Tombu et al (2012) presented evidence of a "unified attentional bottleneck" across all multi-tasking (p. 1), and that most subjects performing multiple tasks recognize a "problem state" in trying to do several things at once (Borst, Taatgen & van Rijn, 2010, p. 363). With respect to high frequency media multi-taskers, Salvucci and Taatgen (2008) found that subjects tended to switch from one task to another along "streams of thought as threads of processing" (p. 101). Katidioti and Taatgen (2014) add that switching between topics in media multitaskers is rarely planned but is rather "opportunistic and depends on availability of cognitive resources."

THE NEUROSCIENCE OF MULTITASKING

Studies on the neurocircuitry of multitasking have not yet identified a consistent pattern of neurocircuits associated with multitasking deficits. Dreher et al. (2008) found that the very front of the frontal cortex, the fronto-polar cortex (Brodmann area 10) is activated while trying to hold a primary goal simultaneous to a secondary goal, and that neurological patients with damage to this specific area have difficulty with multitasking. Findings also suggest that normally operative purposeful executive control during multitasking may actually contribute to the task interference. For example, Dux et al. (2009) identified the IFJ inferior frontal junction (Brodmann area 9) as the location of the capacity limiting bottleneck. He found that training in dual task performance was significantly associated with reduced IFJ activation, as subjects re-routed information away from the slower purposeful approach associated with prefrontal cortex activation. When the cortical and subcortical circuits supporting normal executive control are deactivated through multitasking training, multitasking deficits decline (Garner & Dux, 2015). As effective multitasking is learned, the neurocircuitry normally associated with habitual task performance, namely the striatum, is activated (Lin, 2009; Rothbart & Posner, 2015). Training subjects to effectively multi-task may also entail activating meta-cognition in order to change strategies to a better control strategy than simply rapidly shifting between tasks. For example, Verghese et al., (2106) found that training a subject

Chapter 2: The Varieties of Dysfunctional Attention in the Modern Western World

in accurate dual task performance was associated with activation of the meta-cognitive circuitry, namely the left dorsolateral prefrontal cortex.

MULTITASKING IN CHILDREN

There is considerable cause for concern that normally expected attention development in the current generation of developing children may be negatively affected by excessive multimedia exposure. For example, Pea et al. (2012) conducted an extensive on-line survey of girls between the ages of 8 to 12 years old, who had grown up in the digital era. They found that girls of this age spent almost 11 hours per day involved with some sort of multimedia multitasking and significantly less time in actual face-to-face communication with peers. Furthermore, excessive preoccupation with video, television, online communication, and media multitasking "were consistently associated with a range of negative socio-emotional outcomes," whereas the infrequent "face-to-face communication was consistently associated with a range of positive socio-emotional outcomes" (p. 334). Thus, excessive preoccupation with social media multitasking may have an erosive effect on social competence and well-being. Furthermore, children with ADHD as compared with children who do not have ADHD may be especially vulnerable to the negative effects of media multitasking. Siklos and Kerns (2004) found that children ages 7-13 with ADHD as compared to those without ADHD in engaged in multitasking performed significantly worse than normal children. They had clear difficulty planning their time during multitasking performance. They attempted fewer of the required tasks and seldom looked at the clock to pace their performance. For them multitasking presented a clear challenge to executive planning.

REACTIVITY

After Buddha Shakyamuni was enlightened under the Bodhi tree, he walked to the next town, Sarnat, and gave his first teaching on the Four Noble Truths. The first truth is the truth of reactivity. In Pali the word *dukka* means "reactivity," but is often translated as "suffering." Buddha was trying to convey that in each moment of experience the mind moves toward what it likes to make more of it, and moves away from what it dislikes to make less of it. This incessant "reactivity" is built into ordinary information-processing. It is easy to observe. The problems with translating dukka as "suffering" is that such a translation leaves out the method. By translating *dukka* as "reactivity" it preserves the method: Buddha intended that if one were to observe moment-by-moment experience, it is possible to see the reactivity of the ordinary mind and to change it. According to early Buddhism reactivity is built into ordinary information-processing. A practitioner can observe and change it.

In Western psychology, likewise, reactivity is seen as a bias built into ordinary information-processing. According to Thomas and Chess (1977) reactivity is a "primary reaction pattern or initial reactivity" to stimuli (p. 39). Thomas and Chess see reactivity as "constitutional," defined here as "the relatively enduring biological makeup of the organism influenced over time by heredity, maturation, and experience. Reactivity refers to the excitability, responsivity, or arousability of the behavioral and physiological systems of the organism" (Rothbart & Derryberry, 1981, p.40). Rothbart and Derryberry (1981) define reactivity as the "intensity of a child's reaction to stimuli" based on the "overall level of arousal" (pp. 43-44). This reactivity can be seen across a variety of response systems, such as the motor system, vocal response, and facial display. While reactivity to stimuli is built into each individual, it is also clear that there are important individual differences in the level of reactivity of a given individual. According to Rothbart (1989) there are important individual differences in intensity in reaction to a given stimulus. Intensity is defined as "energy level of responsiveness" (p. 61). Newborns are programmed to seek an optimal level of stimulus intensity. According to Lawson and Turkewitz (1980) newborns fixated on a visual pattern of a varying number of cubes in a sound or no sound condition. They found:

> ...the addition of the sound to visual stimuli results in a shift in preferential looking with increased preference for the low-in-

Chapter 2: The Varieties of Dysfunctional Attention in the Modern Western World

tensity stimulus and decreased preference for the high-intensity stimulus. Such results suggest that the newborn's optimal or preferred amount of stimulation is determined by the total amount or intensity of stimulus input, regardless of whether this is contributed to by stimulation from one or more than one modality. (p. 1297)

Rothbart (1991) presented a model on the developement of reactivity and self-regulation (p. 66). She defined temperament as:

> ...individual differences in reactivity and self-regulation that are assumed to have a constitutional basis....By *reactivity*, we mean the arousability of multiple physiological and behavioral systems of the organism (e.g., somatic, endocrine, autonomic, and central nervous systems) as reflected in response parameters of threshold—latency, intensity, rise time, and recovery time. By *self-regulation*, we refer to processes that act to modulate reactivity, including at the behavioral level selective attention and responsiveness to cues signaling reward and punishment, behavioral inhibition to novel or intense stimuli, and effortful control. When we say temperament is *constitutionally based*, we are referring to the relatively enduring aspects of the makeup of the organism, influenced over time by heredity, maturation and experience. (p. 61)

Rothbart adds that early regulation of the child is largely done by the mother:

> ...early on "the young infant...[is] very much influenced by other-regulation... [the mother acts by] stimulating the infant through play and soothing...other-regulation, is in turn influenced by the reactivity of the child. (pp. 61-62)

She adds:

The newborn infant demonstrates a number of regulatory activities, including selective attention and movement toward and away from arousing stimuli...early approach and withdrawal processes... (Lawson & Turkewitz, 1980)... tendency of some infants to fall asleep under conditions of high intensity or prolonged stimulation...[is] further evidence of early self-regulation [p. 62].... Irritability of newborn later predicts insecure attachment [p. 63] infants; irritability or susceptibility to distress has been identified as a dimension of temperament that is present from birth [p. 63] negative reactivity is present early, shows some stability over time, and...predicts forward to both distress and self-regulation strategies such as withdrawal and avoidance that might serve to decrease distress [p. 63]... By 2-3 months, a second major dimension of reactivity can be added to negative reactivity: the child's susceptibility to the positive emotions or *positive reactivity* as shown in smiling and laughter, and probably also in motor and vocal reactions [p. 64]... We have found that positive reactivity in the home to increase from 3 to 9 months... By 2-3 months a "bio-behavioral shift" [occurs]... "the child has come to react to the external world in a new and more positively responsive way. By 2-3 months, individual differences in attention span or *duration of orienting* to external stimuli are clear... *Approach* is a dimension of temperament that can be measured once the infant's motor capacity makes movement toward objects possible... We see that at least two dimensions of variability operating in situations where novel and/or intense stimuli are presented: the first is the child's approach tendency, and the second is inhibition of approach. Thus a child who shows strong positive reactivity and approach under safe and familiar circumstances may nonetheless, by the last quarter of the first year of life, show non-approach and distress toward a novel and intense stimulus. (pp. 64-65)

Chapter 2: The Varieties of Dysfunctional Attention in the Modern Western World

Rothbart identifies six dimensions of temperament: irritability, reaction to novelty (approach, withdrawal, distress), positive affect, activity level, rhythmicity (regularity of sleeping, eating, elimination, food intake), and attention span (p. 66). According to Derryberry and Rothbart (1997) personality differences arise in part from reactivity underlying neural systems (p. 633). As the child develops, initially reactive forms of regulation are supplemented by an increasing capacity for voluntary or effortful forms of control (p. 633). By 2 to 4 years of age, the child shows "increasing ability to control their focus of attention and motor activity" (p. 67). Over time two systems develop—an appetitive and avoidance system. Derryberry and Rothbart (1997) say there is an "'appetitive system' that mobilizes approach behavior to stimuli that predict positive events…and [an] active avoidance system based on behavioral inhibition. (p. 635)

Other Western psychologists have also written further on this reactivity built in to information-processing. For example, Arnold (1960) states that immediately following stimulus perception is an "intuitive appraisal" and an "action tendency" (p. 182) or reactive tendency to like or dislike the stimulus event. If attended to further, [it] results in a "felt action tendency manifesting as the tendency to approach or avoid the object. Next comes an automatic "secondary appraisal" of the pleasantness or unpleasantness of these physiological changes that results in the perception of an "emotional state," and then either an immediate impulsive action or an enduring motivation state.

According to McDevitt and Carey (1981) temperament, including reactivity, shows "significant stability" from 6 months to 3 years of age (p. 343). Level of reactivity to stimuli by the child also interacts with intensity of care-giver stimulation. Gandour (1989), for example, found that activity level as a dimension of temperament interacts with level of maternal stimulation in such a way as to affect exploratory behavior. High active children with high stimulation caregivers show less exploration than high active children with low stimulation caretakers (p. 10960. They conclude, " high level of caretaker stimulation may have a negative influence on some of the mastery behaviors of high active 1-year-olds" (p. 1096).

Gray (1991) demonstrated how these three temperament systems—behavioral inhibition system; fight-flight system; and the behavioral approach system. correspond with three dimensions of personality from Eysenck and Eysenck (1985); high trait anxiety, high aggressive-defensiveness, and high positivity, respectively.

Thus, both Buddhist and Western psychology agree that moment-to-moment reactivity to stimuli generates suffering. The difference is that Buddhism sees reactivity as built into the information-processing system, so as to effect everyone equally, while Western psychology, sees important individual differences in intensity of reactivity to stimuli.

LACK OF COHERENCE OF MIND; PSYCHIC ENTROPY AND THE DISORDERED, NOISY ORDINARY MIND

The concept of psychic entropy is attributed to Carl Jung. The term entropy was originally taken from physics. Entropy is the degree of disorder within a system. It is a natural tendency for energy to dissipate and become disordered when it is not being directed. Jung believed that psychic energy in the mind behaved in the same way as physical systems. Without direction psychic energy fails to flow. With direction psychic energy becomes more orderly and flows.

Csikszentmihalyi (1997) revived Jung's concept of psychic entropy and did extensive modern research on its opposite, namely flow experience. Csikszentmihalyi defines psychic entropy as a natural tendency for the mind to become disorganized and aimless, and for extraneous thought to become random in the absence of intentions, goals, and motivations that serve to organize the mind. He says:

> Emotions refer to the internal states of consciousness. Negative emotions like sadness, fear, anxiety, or boredom produce "psychic entropy" in the mind, that is a state in which we cannot use attention effectively to deal with external tasks, because we need it to restore an inner subjective order. Pos-

Chapter 2: The Varieties of Dysfunctional Attention in the Modern Western World

itive emotions…are states [wherein]… psychic energy can flow freely into whatever thought or task we choose to invest it in…. intentions, goals, and motivations…. focus psychic energy, establish priorities, and thus create order in consciousness. Without them mental processes become random, and feelings tend to deteriorate rapidly. (pp. 21-22)

To pursue mental operations to any depth, a person has to learn to concentrate attention. Without focus, consciousness is in a state of chaos. The normal condition of the mind is one of informational disorder: random thoughts chase one another instead of lining up in a logical sequence. Unless one learns to concentrate, and is able to invest the effort, thoughts will scatter without reaching any conclusion. (p. 26)

    According to Csikszentmihalyi, the key to overcoming psychic entropy, and the key to organization of mind, is systematic training of concentration. The more intense and sustained the concentration, the greater the organization of conscious experience. This increased sense of organization of mind is captured in the term *flow*, which implies orderliness—the opposite of psychic entropy. Csikszentmihalyi rediscovered what has been know for thousands of years in the meditative traditions: systematic training in concentration results in increased organization of mind and orderliness to the unfolding of experience, as captured by the Eastern concept of a stream-enterer (Buddhaghosa, 1976), much like the Western concept of flow.

    To test the prevalence of psychic entropy Faupel (1989) reasoned that psychic entropy would be especially prevalent during adolescence because "loss of motivation, unfocused attention, passivity, and bad moods" (p. 375) are especially apparent during this developmental age range. Faupel developed an Adolescent Psychic Entropy Scale based on Csikszentmihalyi's research. Although the sample size was small the results confirmed the existence of psychic entropy in this adolescent population, both for girls and boys. Further research is needed before it is established that adolescents "have a higher probability for psychic entropy" (p. 378), but the fact that adolescents report high psychic entropy was established by this study.

In Buddhism the ordinary mind is described as lacking a quality of calmness. This means that for most individuals when the mind is idle there is a good deal of background noise of extraneous thought—thought that is relatively aimless and disorganized, not goal-directed. There are of course individual differences in the degree of calmness or background noise. Some people's minds are relatively quiet, and others have many tracks of extraneous thought going on simultaneously so that their minds are rarely ever quiet. Training the mind in concentration is said to result in "calmness" of all the background noise of extraneous thought irrespective of the degree of extraneous background noise. One result of systematic concentration training is that extraneous thought elaboration winds down and eventually more or less ceases. Concentration training results in longer and longer duration episodes of stillness characterized by the absence of any extraneous thought elaboration, and shorter and shorter duration bursts of extraneous thought elaboration. This goal of the relative absence of extraneous thought elaboration is captured in the Tibetan name for concentration training *zhi gnas* "calming-staying meditation," wherein the mind stays continuously and completely on the concentration object and the background noise of extraneous thought becomes completely calm.

While psychic entropy is described by Csikszentmihalyi as a condition of mind that characterizes anyone who lacks goal-directedness and concentrative focus, other research suggests that certain clinical populations show more extreme disorganization of mind, namely individuals with insecure attachment. In their research on the Adult Attachment Inventory (AAI) Mary Main and her colleagues emphasize *coherence of state of mind*. They discovered that secure adults describe early attachment relationships in an organized, coherent manner, but insecure adults do not. Main and Goldwyn (1998) define coherence as "a connection or congruity arising from some common principle or relationship; consistency; [or] connectedness of thought, such that parts of the discourse are clearly related, form a logical whole, or are suitable or suited and

Chapter 2: The Varieties of Dysfunctional Attention in the Modern Western World

adapted to context" (p. 44).

In scoring the AAI, Main and her associates apply Grice's (1975) categories that define cooperative, rational discourse: namely, truthful in *quality*, succinct but complete in *quantity*, *relevant* to the questions asked, and presented in a clear and orderly *manner*. Hesse says, "Discourse is judged coherent when a subject appears able to access and evaluate memories while simultaneously remaining plausible (consistent, or implicitly truthful) and collaborative" (1999, p. 404). Secure adults describe memories of early attachment relationships in a rich, accurate, and organized manner. Their descriptions stay relevant to the questions asked in the interview. Their discourse about attachment depicts a singular internal working model for each attachment figure. In contrast, insecure, dismissing adults do not describe early attachment relationships in a very coherent manner. Their descriptions of early attachment figures are rarely supported by evidence. Even when they do provide illustrative memories, they are often over-idealized, unrealistic or they lack sufficient detail. Such descriptions are typically too succinct to provide a clear picture of early attachment figures. Insecure, preoccupied adults are exceedingly verbose. Their descriptions of early attachment relationships are filled with irrelevancies, passive speech, and jargon, and their descriptions are often excessively long and wandering. Insecure, disorganized adults present a contradictory mixture of discourse showing characteristics of both dismissing and preoccupied speech.

Overall, dismissing, preoccupied, and especially disorganized adults show low coherence of discourse in describing their early attachment experiences on the standardized Adult Attachment Interview. On a 1 to 9 scale measuring *coherence of discourse* in response to the AAI questions, insecure individuals generally score below 3 and secure individuals generally score above 7. Thus, the way a person organizes or cannot organize his or her thoughts and discourse about early attachment relationships is considered to be a primary indicator of secure versus insecure attachment. Base rates of secure attachment in Europe and North America consistently show that about 62% of adults have secure attachment, and that 38% have insecure attachment—either dismissing, anxious preoccupied, or disorganized attachment. These figures suggest that approximately one out of three adults has significantly low coherence of mind, and that extreme psychic entropy in adults is at least in part a function of a insecure infant-caregiver attachment bond, and its disorganizing effect on developing states of mind. On the other hand, it is promising to note that effective treatment of attachment disturbances in adults leads to significant increases in coherence of mind (Brown & Elliott, 2016).

Lack of Meta-cognitive Awareness

Flavell defines meta-cognitive knowledge as follows:

> Meta-cognitive knowledge consists primarily of knowledge or beliefs about what factors or variables act and interact in what ways to affect the course and outcome of cognitive enterprise... [meta-cognition] pertains to knowledge of the type of strategies likely to be effective in achieving goals or solving problems. (p. 907)

Meta-cognition entails awareness of one's own state of mind, the capacity to monitor that state, and the capacity to reflect on strategies used to solve problems. Meta-cognition has played an important role in education since it was discovered that children solve problems more efficiently after being taught to reflect on the meta-cognitive strategies used in solving problems.

Gergely and Watson (1996) have shown how parental affective attunement is central to the development of mentalizing capacity in children. Gergely and Watson observed that somewhere between 9 and 12 months children develop the capacity to detect the other's intention toward a goal and perceive the other as an intentional agent (p. 1182). This intentional stance allows the child to represent beliefs, desires, and emotions of others. They say:

> The mother plays a vital interactive role in modulating the infant's affective states...the quality of maternal interactions

exert a strong regulative influence on the infant's affective state changes...Mothers are generally rather efficient reading their infant's emotion displays and sensitive mothers tend to attune their own affective responses to modulate their infant's emotional states." (p. 1187)

Secure mothers with their spontaneous facial affect displays frequently match their infant's affect display, and show increased coordination and synchronization of matches with facial display, gesture, and vocalizations.

More importantly, Gergely and Watson see this interactive process as a kind of "training" for the infant via affective mirroring. The key to understanding this process pertains to: contingency detection, maximizing, and marking. Contingency detection refers to the infant's discovery that the caregiver's response is in part the outcome of, or contingent upon the infant's behavior. From this the child infers that he or she is an "active causal agent" (p. 1196). Marking refers to the caregiver "producing an exaggerated version" of emotional expression (p. 1198). According to Gergely and Watson marking is critical to the child's learning that the momentary emotional display is about his or her internal state, and not about the caregiver's emotional state. In this manner the child is said to "decouple" the emotion from that of the caregiver, and becomes "sensitized" to his or her immediate introceptive cues so as to infer internal emotional state from those cues. Gergely and Watson state:

> The repetitive presentation of an external reflection of the infant's affect-expressive displays serves a vital 'teaching' function that results in the gradual sensitization to the relevant internal state cues as well as to the identification of the correct set of internal stimuli that correspond to the distinctive emotion category that the baby is in. As a result of this process the infant will eventually come to develop an awareness of the distinctive internal cues that are indicative of categorical-emotion-states. This process is like what occurs in biofeedback

training wherein "The internal state changes are mapped on to an external stimulus equivalent directly observable to the subject...parental affect-mirroring provides kind of natural social biofeedback training for the infant and plays a crucial role in emotional development. (p. 1190)

Parental-affective mirroring depends on contingency detection and amplification.

Markedness produces an additional development, with respect to mentalizing capacity. Gergely and Watson claim that "the infant will construct a separate representation" for the marked as compared to the actual facial affective display of the caregiver, and that this new representation "will come to function as secondary representational structure" (p. 2000). This secondary inter-subjectivity is the foundation of mentalization. Gergely and Watson summarize by saying that parental affective mirroring of affects serves four separate developmental functions: 1. Sensitization to internal states; 2. Building secondary representations as representations; 3. Regulation of child's internal emotional state; and 4. Developing a generalized affective communication code based on the capacity to pretend, play, and know representations as representations (p. 1205). While reflective capacity is mainly the internalization of consistent parental attunement to the internal state of the child, the development of the dorsolateral prefrontal cortex in the child around 8 or 9 years of age plays an important role in perspective-taking and other developing self-monitoring skills.

Main (1991) found that insecure as compared to secure children had far less development of meta-cognitive capacities. She found that insecure as compared to children of similar age are less able to see their thoughts, beliefs, and mental models as representations, are less able to meta-cognitively monitor thoughts, beliefs, and models as not reality and as potentially erroneous or distorted. Insecure children exhibit frequent "failures of corrective meta-cognitive monitoring" (p. 135). Additionally, insecure children are likely to develop multiple, contradictory internal working models for attachment. Interviews showed that secure but not insecure 6-year-olds understood the privacy of thought when asked a series of questions like, "What is thought? Where are thoughts located? Do other people know what you are thinking when they can't see you?"

Fonagy, et al. (1998) developed a Reflective Function scale to assess the capacity to perceive oneself and others in terms of mental states. The scale assesses: awareness of mental states; awareness of mental states underlying a given behavior; awareness of a developmental and intergenerational perspective; and awareness of mental states in relationship to the interviewer. The RF scale is scaled from minus 1 to plus 9, with ratings below 3 indicating low reflective capacity, 5 indicating moderate reflective capacity, and 7 or higher indicating marked reflective capacity. They found that the mean RF score in the general population was 5.8 (moderate). In a prison sample the RF scores were very low (2.5). They also found that psychiatric patients with a personality disorder or dissociative disorder diagnosis rarely scored above 3 on the RF scale. However, it was not uncommon to find that individuals who had been in extensive psychotherapy or psychoanalysis typically scored high (above 7). These data suggest that meta-cognitive reflective capacity is at best moderate for the majority of individuals. Based on the finding of very low reflective capacity in personality and dissociative disorder patients, the Tavistock group developed an entire approach to psychotherapy designed to improve reflective capacity in personality and dissociative disorder patients, namely mentalization-based treatment (MBT). Initial outcomes data using MBT has been very promising. This suggests that even individuals with very low reflective capacity can be taught to improve their reflective capacity.

These findings also suggests that meta-cognitive monitoring is not highly developed in the general population and needs to be improved.

LACK OF WORKING MEMORY

Working memory is "the ability to keep information online during a short period of time" (Westerberg, 2004, p. 6). Baddeley and Hitch (1974) defined three components of working memory:

(1) A temporary storage system for holding speech information called the "phonological loop." This system temporarily stores speech that is heard for short periods in a phonological store before it decays. Verbal rehearsal prevents its quick decay so that such speech information remains in the store. Similar sounding words and longer words are more difficult to retain (Henry, 2012). The phonological store is in the posterior pariental area, and rehearsal is associated with Broca's speech area in the frontal gyrus (Westerberg, 2004).

(2) A temporary storage system for holding visual and spatial information called the "visuospatial sketchpad." This system temporarily stores visual and spatial information to be used during cognitive tasks, and information in this store also decays rapidly unless rehearsed. The visuospatial system is associated with activation of the prefrontal cortex and posterior pariental area (Tammes et al., 2013; Westerberg, 2004). Fougnie (2008) sees the phonological loop and visuospatial sketchpad as a kind of "mental workspace where important information is kept in a highly active state, available for a variety of other cognitive processes" (p. 3), and that these storage areas are distinct from central attention.

(3) A central executive attentional system that controls the use of working memory information. This executive attentional system is used in: planning and problem-solving; shifting attentional set; fluid intelligence; inhibition; working memory; self-monitoring; dual-task performance; and random number generation (Henry, 2012). Consistent with the working memory model, Fougnie (2008) found that attention played "a limited role…in the maintenance of information…only central attention was found to be necessary for manipulating information in working memory" (p. 1). Temporarily maintaining information is associated with the ventrolateral prefrontal cortex (Westerberg, 2004), and also the pariental system (Gazzaley & Nobre, 2011). The monitoring dimension of the central executive monitoring system is likely the dorsolateral prefrontal cortex (Kane & Engle, 2002). The working memory system entails both the "ability to manipulate and store information at the same time" (Henry, 2012, p. 25), for example, trying to keep track of your shopping list (storage) while mentally calculating the price of the items

Chapter 2: The Varieties of Dysfunctional Attention in the Modern Western World

you have bought so far (manipulation). The executive attentional system entails both the ability to sustain goal-directedness and to resolve competing attentional demands, and "the dominance of each depends on WM capacity" (Kane & Engle, 2003, p, 47). The executive attentional system associated with working memory has a limited capacity (Conway & Engle, 1996; Engle, 2002), and span of working memory predicts attention control (Kane & Engle, 2003).

(4) Later it was discovered that the working memory system sometimes draws upon long-term memory (Ericsson & Kintsch, 1995), so that a fourth component, the "episodic buffer," was added to revisions of the original working memory model (Baddeley, 2000, 2007, 2012). This episodic buffer "binds" together information from different sources within the working memory system…to join this information together into a coherent memory episode" (Henry, 2012, p. 31). This buffer also serves as a back-up storage system to the phonological loop and visuospatial sketchpad. Henry (2012) summarizes this model saying, "The working memory model was developed to account for how to temporarily manipulate and store information during thinking and reasoning tasks in everyday life"(p. 34).

The phonological loop is typically assessed with digit span or word span tests or by having subjects remember unfamiliar sounds. Asking subjects to remember unfamiliar sounds minimizes rehearsal effects and is a purer measure of storage span in the phonological loop. Rehearsal effects begin around age 7. The visuospatial sketchpad is assessed with the Corsi Block Tapping test wherein the experimenter points to various blocks arranged randomly in different spatial locations following which the subject must point to the same blocks in the same order. In the Visual Pattern Test subjects are shown grids of varying sizes with some of the boxes filled in and some not filled in. The subject is required to point to the boxes filled in for each grid shown, from smaller to larger grids. The test assesses visual span. Executive attention is assessed using complex span tests that require storage and manipulation of information at the same time. An example of a complex span task is remembering a span of digits in reverse order, which requires storage of the original numbers as well as manipulation of the order of recall.

There is considerable evidence that working memory storage increases with developmental age. With respect to the phonological loop "children can repeat back around three words in the correct order at age 5 years; four words by age 9 years; and five words by 11 years" (Henry, 2012, p. 70). From ages 4 to 10 years of age children can hold longer words and acoustically more similar words in working memory as they get older, and can process acoustical information at a faster speed (Hulme & Tordoff, 1989). Working memory is not present in 5-year-olds, somewhat in 7-year-olds, and definitely in 10-year-olds and adults, familiar words are easier to retain in the phonological store because of the development of recall strategies as part of developing executive control (Turner, Henry, and Smith, 2000). With respect to the visuospatial sketchpad, Corsi span increases to 5 by age 11 and to 5.5 items by age 15 (Isaacs & Vargha-Khadem, 1989; Kemps, de Rammelaere, & Desmet, 2000). The visual component of the sketchpad develops around age 5 and the spatial component develops in later childhood (Hamilton, Coates, & Heffernan 2003). There is a clear shift from ages 4-5 to 7-8 from a preference for visual codes to verbal codes in remembering pictures, and a shift to the use of more complex memory strategies by age 9 (Henry, 2012, p. 113; Kemps, de Rammelaere, & Desmet, 2000). Spatial working memory develops up to around age 13 to 15 and doesn't develop much after that (Luciana, Conklin, & Hooper, 2005). With respect to central executive attention, the capacity to exhibit self control to inhibit unwanted responses develops early. Andrews et al. (1999) studied preschool children from ages 2-5 years old using A-Not-B and a delayed response task, wherein children had to exercise working memory to locate a hidden reward while inhibiting a prepotent response to locate the reward in the wrong location. They found that "performance steadily improved in preschool children between 23 and 66 months of age" (p. 191) and that the foundations for both working memory and response inhibition were well established during the preschool years. They attribute these changes to the initial development of the dorsolateral prefrontal cortex in late infancy (p. 179). Casey et al. (1997) studied response

Chapter 2: The Varieties of Dysfunctional Attention in the Modern Western World

inhibition using a Go-No-Go task in children ages 7-12 and adults 21-24 years old. During the response inhibition task, fMRI neuroimaging revealed activation of the prefrontal cortex in both children and adults, but "significantly greater" activation for children than adults. The primary location of activation was the dorsolateral PFC and orbital PFC, suggesting that working memory is associated with holding information in working memory (dlPFC) and inhibiting extraneous responses (mlOFC). Welsh, Pennington, and Groisser (1991) found that executive functions such as establishing a set, planning, and speed of responding developed around 8 years of age. Bayliss et al. (2005) found that processing speed and working memory storage improved around 8-10 years of age. St. Clair-Thompson and Gathercole (2006) found that behavioral inhibition and the ability to update working memory were well developed by age 11 to 12 years old. Van der Sluis et al. (2007) found that set shifting and updating information in the working memory system was well developed by age 9-12. Gathercole et al. (2004) assessed working memory in over 700 children ranging from 4 to 15 years of age. They found that working memory starts to develop around age 4, and was nearly as developed by age 6 as it was in adults. They say, "the central executive, the phonological loop, and the visuospatial sketchpad are in place by 6 years of age at least" (p. 187). Verbal rehearsal develops around age 7, and executive attention continues to develop in later childhood and throughout adolescence and reaches a plateau around age 14 or 15 years (Holmes, 2012).

The development of working memory is important in that it predicts national curriculum test scores on mathematics and reading (Bull & Scerif, 2001; St. Clair-Thompson & Gathercole, 2006; van der Sluis et al., 2007). Individual differences in the capacity of the phonological loop predict reading span in college students (Daneman & Carpenter, 1980). Working memory skill also enhances inductive reasoning (Kail, 2007). Working memory is also significantly related to fluid intelligence (Voelke & Roebers, (2016).

Some children grow up with consistently poor working memory. Siegel and Ryan (1989) studied working memory in normal, reading disabled and arithmetic disabled 7-13-year-olds. While working memory capacity increased with age in normal children, reading disabled children showed a general deficit in working memory, and arithmetic disabled children showed a specific working memory deficit in processing numerical information. Thus, children with different learning disabilities showed different patterns of working memory deficits. In Gathercole et al. (2008), 4-5-year-old and 8-9-year-old children were screened for poor working memory. 3.4% of the 4-5-year-olds and 2.4% of the 8-9-year olds had very poor working memory, but did not have clinically significant ADHD. Using behavioral teacher ratings Gather-Cole et al. found "The majority of children with low working memory scores obtained atypically high ratings of cognitive problems/inattentive symptoms, and were judged to have short attention spans, high distractibility, problems monitoring the quality of their work, and difficulties in generating new solutions to problems" (p. 214). In a larger study by this same research group Alloway et al. (2009) studied the cognitive and behavioral effects of children with very poor working memory. A total of 3,189 5-11-year-olds were screened with a variety of tests for working memory. A total of 308 of the children, approximately 10% of the sample, had very poor working memory, but did not have clinically significant ADHD. These poor working memory students as compared to normal students were significantly more likely to have problems with attention (short attention span and high distractibility), problem-solving deficits, and problems monitoring their school work (p. 606). Learning was more impaired in older than younger children with poor working memory "raising the possibility that, without early intervention, children may find it difficult to catch up with their peers in key areas of learning" (p. 617). The authors conclude, "this study has established that children with working memory problems identified via routine screening have an extremely high risk of making poor academic progress and have a highly distinctive profile of inattentive behavior and forgetting that disrupts their classroom functioning" (p. 619). Gathercole (2016) summarizes, "Poor working memory skills are relatively commonplace in childhood, and have a substantial advance impact on children's learning" (p. 1). Such children are rarely seen by teachers as having memory problems and instead are seen as having attentional problems. Holmes (2012) lists

Chapter 2: The Varieties of Dysfunctional Attention in the Modern Western World

the major signs of children with poor working memory:

> These include: poor academic progress, difficulties following multi-step instructions, failing to complete common classroom activities that require large amounts of information to be held in mind, problems keeping their place in demanding and complex activities such as writing, and high levels of inattentive and distractible behavior." (p. 8)

In adults Kane et al. (2007) found that undergraduates with poor working memory as compared with those with high working memory could not sustain concentration on challenging tasks, were less able to sustain goal-directed thought and behavior, and had significantly more frequent episodes of mind-wandering. Conway, Cowan, and Bunting (2001) used a complex span task to distinguish between high and low working memory span adult subjects. Just about half of the adult college age subjects had low, and the other half had high working memory span. The 50% base-rate of low working memory is alarmingly high. In a selective listening test, in which the subject's name was inserted into an unattended, irrelevant message, 65% of low-span as compared to 20% of high-span working memory subjects reported hearing their own name in the irrelevant message. These findings suggest, "The critical factor seems to be the ability to block information from the irrelevant message. High-span subjects are more capable of this and were therefore less likely to hear their names, and they also were less susceptible to a consequential disruption of irrelevant task performance" (p. 334). Working memory also is worse in older as compared to younger adults mainly because of slower processing speed, starting around age 20 and worse by the 80s (Salthouse, 1994, 1996). Park et al. (2002) found that processing speed and working memory begin to decline as early as the 20s in young adults.

One of the unfortunate effects of modern technology has been the decline of working memory. Children who grew up in the 1950s and 1960s did not have calculators and therefore had to practice doing mental arithmetic in their heads. It was also common in the 1950s and 1960s for children to memorize longer and longer poems. Practicing mental arithmetic and memorizing longer and longer poems enhances the span of available working memory. Discontinuing mental arithmetic and memorization skills in school causes a decline in working memory span. For example, a Japanese study compared the effect of playing sports videogames, resting, and doing repetitive mental arithmetic on working memory span. "They found that whereas the games only really activated the visual and motor cortices, the arithmetical exercises activated the frontal lobes...The arithmetical exercise, however, demands a great deal from working memory, and therefore activates the frontal lobes.... computer games do not" (Kawashima, cited in Klingberg, 2009, pp. 139-140). In other words, this generation of youth has become lax in methods that might sustain and even improve working memory span.

THE EFFECTS OF MULTIMEDIA
THE RAPID RISE OF MULTIMEDIA EXPOSURE

The rapid rise of multimedia in the past three decades has radically changed the landscape of the development of attentional skills. The American Academy of Pediatrics developed guidelines for infant and toddler television viewing. Nevertheless, researchers found that "A substantial number of children [from 0 to 35 months old] begin watching television at an earlier age and in greater amounts than the AAP recommends" (Certain & Kahn, 2002, p. 634).

At two points in time the Kaiser Family Foundation surveyed families and children about the use of media—both in 1999 and again in 2005 (Roberts, Foehr and Rideout, 2005). The purpose of each survey was to document the rapidly changing media environment to which children of the information and technology world were being exposed (Roberts et al., 2005, p. 3). In just six years, from 1999 to 2005, the price of personal computers fell drastically so that many children and adolescents could now own their own personal computers. The speed of the Internet remarkably increased. Music became digitalized and big screen TVs had become commonplace. This led Roberts et al. to conclude that many American households had become "media saturated" (p. 10). They add, "Clearly, in 2004, TVs, VCRs, radios, and audio CD/

tape players have reached ceilings, with penetration of each medium approaching 100% of young people's households" (p. 10). Furthermore, such media saturation had little to do with socio-economic status. They noted, "those of lower SES were significantly more likely to have their own TV" (p. 15). They also found, "83% of kids in sample owned a videogame console" (p. 17)... and that the "TV was usually on in background in half of homes" (p. 18). They found that in 2006 the average daily children's exposure of TV was about three hours/day and the average total media exposure was 4.5 hours/day. Exposure to music media was especially prevalent in adolescence. Multi-media exposure—computers, videogames, e-mail, chat rooms—were common in about half of the 2006 sample of children (p. 31).

Evidence for multi-media use in the 2006 sample of children was very common. They say, "Today's young people frequently use two, three, or more media at the same time" (p. 35) with 5-6 hours/day total multi-media exposure being common for the 2006 sample of children from ages 8 to 18 (p. 36). Multi-media multitasking was common in this generation of youth. Roberts et al. say, "large numbers of U.S. kids, *do not* limit themselves to one medium at a time...when watching TV, they *also* listen to music, read, or use a computer...58% of kids report media multitasking most of the time, or some of the time when reading, 63% when listening to music, and 65% when using a computer" (p. 36), "8- to 18- year-olds spend substantial amounts of time with media" (p. 39), and screen media continue to account for most of kids' overall media budget (48%)" (p. 40).

By 2006 "15% of sample were heavy media multitaskers...a phenomenon that appears to be increasing...26% of the time that young people use media, they use two or more media simultaneously" (pp. 54-56). It is likely that the percentage of heavy multimedia multitaskers has increased even more in the last decade since the 2006 survey. Already by 2006 some of the negative effects of multimedia exposure were beginning to be noticed. Roberts et al. found that those children that spent more time with print media [reading] as compared to those spent time with videogames were significantly more likely to get grades of As and Bs and heavy multimedia multitaskers were significantly more likely to get Cs and Ds (p. 47).

We forget an earlier generation of research on the performance of vigilance tasks. In the 1960s a hot topic was the discovery that sensory and perceptual deprivation enhanced performance on sustained vigilance tasks. For example, blindfolding subjects during an auditory vigilance task enhanced performance, especially for male subjects (Stroh, 1971, p. 29). In this current generation of multimedia stimulus overload, we forget the wisdom of this earlier generation of research, namely, that deprivation in the face of multimedia exposure is an established solution to sustained attention.

The Effects of Word Processing and Multimedia Learning

Word processing improves quality of writing (Grace-Martin & Gay, 2001). In one study 3rd and 4th graders used either a special word processor or wrote normally on paper after being given a topic to write about. Those who used the word processor as compared to those who didn't showed a significant increase in the quantity of words in these essays and had a higher quality of writing (p. 102).

With respect to multimedia instruction, it has been assumed that presenting both text and pictures is a more efficient way of learning. However, since text and photos represent different aspects of working memory, it can't be assumed that simultaneous presentation of instructional text and photos is beneficial to working memory and may represent a load problem (Schuller, Scheiter, and van Genuchten (2011). Kalyuga, Chandler, and Sweller say, "if learners are required to coordinate and simultaneously process redundant material such as written and spoken text, an excessive working memory load is generated" (p. 567). Furthermore, simultaneous presentation of to-be-learned material in both verbal and pictorial formats may not be useful, it creates some degree of attentional interference between the information of the two formats and learners often forget which source the material came from (Brunye et al., 2006).

Chapter 2: The Varieties of Dysfunctional Attention in the Modern Western World

THE HARM AND BENEFITS OF VIDEOGAMING

Greenfield (2014) says that the difference between passive TV watching and videogame playing is that videogames are interactive. She says, "What happens on the screen is not entirely determined by the computer; it is also very much influenced by the player's actions…the appeal is active control and mastery in the presence of a goal" (pp. 73-74). She concludes that certain videogames train sensori-motor skills and hand-eye coordination" (p. 77). For example, the popular game *Pac-Man* teaches "inductive reasoning skills" (p. 78). She adds, "Pictorial images in general tend to elicit parallel processing… [p. 80]. Because many games have different levels of play such games constantly challenge players to higher levels of mastery" (p. 87). However, while such games foster certain skills, they come with a cost of diminished meta-cognitive reflection. Greenfield says, "The real-time action games may foster parallel processing skills and fast reaction time but may also discourage reflection (If you stop to think while playing *Space Invaders* you're lost)" (p. 87).

The effects of videogame playing on attention have yielded mixed results. One robust positive finding is that playing certain videogames significantly improves visuo-spatial skills. For example, in an early study Gagnon (1985) randomly assigned college students to a videogaming or non-gaming control condition. Subjects had 5 hours of videogame practice. Gagnon found, "The scores on the two videogames were found to be correlated with different spatial test scores" (p 263). Males scored higher than females on the resultant spatial tests after playing the videogames. Another study found positive visuo-spatial effects for both boys and girls. Dorvall and Pepin (1986) had both boys and girls play eight sessions of the videogame Zaxxon. They found significant improvements in posttest spatial relations scores for both boys and girls.

Many videogames emphasize negotiating spatial relationships. For example, McClurg and Chaille (1987) had 5th, 6th, and 9th grade students play computer games that emphasized three-dimensional rotation in space. They found, "certain computer games may enhance the development of spatial ability as measured by the Mental Rotation Test" (p. 95). Feng, Spence, and Pratt (1990) found that boys were generally better than girls at spatial rotation skills, but that after playing certain videogames, "playing an action videogame can virtually eliminate this gender difference in spatial attention and simultaneously decrease the gender disparity in mental rotation ability" (p. 850). The positive effects of certain videogames on spatial skills are strongest for children initially weakest in spatial skills. For example, Subrahmanyam and Greenfield (1996) compared the effects of action videogames emphasizing spatial relationships to computerized word games. They found, "Videogame practice was significantly more effective than the word game, in improving spatial performance on the posttest assessment…[and were]…more effective for children who started out with relatively poor spatial skills" (p. 13). Similarly, De Lisi and Wolford (2002) had 3rd grade boys and girls play videogames and tested them with a two-dimension mental rotation test. They found significant improvements in spatial skills in both girls and boys, especially in those children with initial low mental rotation skills.

There is some evidence that the best improvements in visuo-spatial skills come form long-term, not short-term videogame playing. Greenfield, Brannon, and Lohr (1994) assessed "whether videogames could contribute to the development of spatial representational skills" (p. 87). They found that not short-term but long-term videogame expertise had "beneficial effects on the spatial skill of mental paper folding" (p. 87). In that study the videogame was *The Empire Strikes Back* that requires navigation through three dimensional space on a flat screen (p. 100). Similarly, West et al. (2008) found that only "prolonged engagement in a demanding visual task" during an action videogame "enhances several visual and cognitive processes….[and] increases sensitivity to salient visual events that capture attention" (p. 1167).

Certain videogames may also enhance visuo-spatial working memory capacity. For example, Green and Bavelier (2007) tested subjects ability to accurately identify a target surrounded by distractors in a video flanker task. They studied subjects with high videogame players (VGPs) versus subjects with no videogame experience. They found, "VGPs possess sufficient resources to perform the target task, with resources still re-

Chapter 2: The Varieties of Dysfunctional Attention in the Modern Western World

maining to spill over to the distractors. These results indicate that VGPs possess enhanced attentional capacity" (p. 534). Videogame playing "enhances the number of items that can be unerringly apprehended" (p. 534)... "Thus, 10 days of training on an action game is sufficient to increase the capacity of visual attention, its spatial distribution, and its temporal resolution" (p. 536).

There are several areas of application of improved visuo-spatial skills through videogaming. First, visuo-spatial skills are important during certain military maneuvers, so that frequent action videogamers may be better suited for military training. Second, visuo-spatial skills are critical to any type of surgery. For example, Rosser et al. (2007) found that videogame play contributed to performance excellence in laparoscopic surgery (p. 181). They say, "the impact on training surgeons videogame capabilities were more important than traditionally recognized factors, such as years of training and number of laparoscopic cases" (p. 184).

Certain action videogames also require holding a good deal of information in working memory. In this sense, certain games may actually improve working memory in high videogame users. Klingberg (2009) says, "Maybe we live in a society in which games, media, and information technology are putting an ever-increasing load on our working memory. This, in turn, is improving the average working memory and problem-solving skills of the population at large, which in turn ups the load and the complexity. Is the human norm being raised?" (p. 155).

Regular videogame playing may also train certain attention strategies. For example, Greenfield et al. (1994) found, "videogame experience was a causal factor in improving strategies of divided attention [p. 105]....[It] reduced the cost in attending to a low-probability location in a task that demands divided attention... gamers reported using strategies of visual attention" (p. 119). Pillay (2003) found that certain videogames that taught cause and effect relationships "tended to encourage means-end analysis strategies, whereas adventure games encouraged inferential and proactive thinking" (p. 336). Doolittle (1995) found that certain computer games that required players to solve certain riddles resulted in greater cognitive flexibility.

With respect to the effects of videogame playing on multitasking the results are mixed. Kearney (2005) found that videogame players "showed a statistically significant improvement in their multitasking abilities" with certain types of videogames," for example, *Counter Strike*. However, Greenfield (2009) found, "Under multitasking conditions, cognitive processing was less mindful and more automatic" (p. 70).

Overall, the results of regular videogame playing are mixed. First, whether the results are positive or negative in part depends on the specific videogame a child plays, and what the demands of the videogame entail. Second, it is quite clear that excessive videogame playing is rarely useful and constitutes a kind of addictive behavior. Heavy usage of videogames is significantly associated with poor academic achievement, low self-esteem, and poor social skills (Roe & Muijs, 1998, p.181). On the other hand, moderate use of videogames is more beneficial than high utilization. For example, Durkin and Barber (2002) found that low vs. high or no utilization of videogames in 16-year-olds resulted in "family closeness, activity involvement, positive school engagement, positive mental health, substance use, self-concept, and friendship network" (p. 373). Third, a robust finding is that many interactive videogames encourage visuo-spatial skills, hand-eye coordination, and the use of strategies. Fourth, videogames with predominately visual and motion features that fail to encourage strategy development may encourage a regression to attentional capture and exogenous orienting attention over maintaining executive attentional control, although there are exceptions (e.g. Chisholm, et al., 2010). Greenfield (2009) summarizes the effects of videogame playing by saying that regular but not excessive videogame playing is associated with "a new profile of cognitive skills… [namely the] sophisticated development of visual-spatial skills…[and] new weaknesses in higher-order cognitive processes: abstract vocabulary, mindfulness, reflection, inductive problem-solving, critical thinking and imagination" (p. 69).

THE EFFECTS OF WEB BROWSING ON LEARNING

Grace-Martin and Gay (2001) assessed the effects of web brows-

Chapter 2: The Varieties of Dysfunctional Attention in the Modern Western World

ing and mobile computing in both a communication science class and computer science class. They found, "Across both courses, the *longer* the average browsing sessions students engaged in during class the *lower* the final grades they tended to receive....This suggests that longer browsing sessions during class tend to be a liability for students' academic performance regardless of the nature of the students or the course" (p. 103). Similarly, Hembroke & Gay (2003) studied two groups that heard the same class lecture, while one group used their laptops during the lecture "to engage in browsing, search, and/or social computing behaviors during the lecture" and the group kept their laptops closed for duration of lecture. They found, "Students in the open laptop condition suffered decrements on traditional measures of memory for lecture content.... the more time spent browsing class related pages resulted in lower recall scores" (p. 10). Browsers frequently went off topic and had "sustained distraction" (p. 14). Frequent browsing during class constituted a kind of "high-tech doodling" (p. 16).

The reason for poor performance is that the web is essentially a distraction from the classroom lecture. For example, Loh, Tan, and Lim (2016) investigated the effects of media multitasking on college students learning a video-recorded lecture in the classroom. Subjects were given a Media Multitasking Questionnaire and then divided into heavy and light multitaskters. Students then saw a video lecture—either a geography or a statistics lecture—followed by a examination of the students' understanding of the course content. Results clearly showed that high scores on the media multitasking index were significantly associated both with increased mind-wandering and lower learning comprehension scores. The results also showed that mind-wandering mediated the relationship between media multitasking and poor learning performance. In other words, multimedia sources served as a significant source of distraction during the lecture presentation, which led to increased mind-wandering, and less depth processing of the lecture material.

Outside the classroom while doing homework, Jackson (2008) found that "Nearly a third of fourteen- to twenty-one-year-olds juggle five to eight media while doing homework" (p. 18). In studying multimedia data steaming Jackson adds, "simultaneous data streams flatten content, making prioritizing all the harder...[multiple data streams] effectively puts a grade-B headline on par with a top news story read by the anchor. Thirty shifting color-coded screen windows vying for our attention make trivia bleed into top-priority work" (p. 91)... Depending too heavily on multitasking to navigate a complex environment and on technology as our guide carries a final risk: the derailing of the painstaking work of adding to our storehouses of knowledge" (p. 93). In a study of multiple data streaming in *CNN News* Bergen, Grimes, and Potter (2005) investigated the effects of having a main news presentation simultaneous to streaming news on the bottom of the main screen. They found, "Ten percent of the factual information contained in news stories was lost to participants. It appears that this multi-message format exceeded viewers' attentional capacity" (p. 311).

Carr (2011) blames the negative findings on computers in the classroom on the invention of hyperlinks, wherein the student leaves a central topic to search after one after another of pop up hyperlinks, and in doing so is likely to lose track of the attentional set and original topic of focus. Carr says that students learn to "scroll and skim and search hyperlinks rather than read in linear fashion...Digital immersion...has even affected the way they absorb information. They don't necessarily read a page from left to right and from top to bottom. They might instead skip around, scanning for pertinent information of interest" (p. 9). "They transition between two very different modes of thinking—linear and faster and disjointed [hyperlink] search. To read a book was to practice an unnatural process of thought, one that demanded sustained, unbroken attention to a single, static object...The ability to focus on a single task relatively uninterrupted" (p. 64). In contrast the Internet is "interactive and bidirectional...[and] multi-sensory" (pp. 85, 90). Carr describes the problem of hyperlinks as follows:

> Hyperlinks also alter our experience of media. Links are in one sense a variation on the textual allusions, citations, and footnotes that have long been common elements of documents. But their effect on us as we read is not at all the same. Links don't just point us to related or supplementary works;

they propel us toward them. They encourage us to drop in and out of a series of texts rather than devote sustained attention to any one of them. Hyperlinks are designed to grab our attention [p. 90].... [They are] "interruption technologies" [p. 91]. Our attachment to any one text becomes more tenuous.... Searches also lead to the fragmentation of online works [p. 91]. By combining many different kinds of information on a single screen, the multimedia Net further fragments content and disrupts our concentration. A single Web page may contain a few chunks of text, a video or audio stream, a set of navigational tools, various advertisements, and several small software applications... We all know how distracting this cacophony of stimuli can be [p. 91].... As soon as you inject a book with links and connect it to the Web... you change what it is and you change, as well, the experience of reading it. An e-book is no more a book than an online newspaper is a newspaper [p. 103].... when we go on-line, we enter an environment that promotes cursory reading, hurried and distracted thinking, and superficial learning. It's possible to think deeply while surfing the Net.... but that's not the type of thinking the technology encourages and rewards [p. 116].... the Net seizes our attention only to scatter it. We focus intensively on the medium itself, on the flickering screen, but we're distracted by the medium's rapid-fire delivery of competing messages and stimuli [p. 118].... The constant distractedness that the Net encourages [p. 119].... The need to evaluate links and make related navigational choices, while processing a multiplicity of fleeting sensory stimuli, requires constant mental coordination and decision-making, distracting the brain from the work of interpreting text or other information...[and] interferes with working memory [p. 123].... With the Net we face many information faucets all going full blast.... We're able to transfer only a small portion of the information to long-term memory, and what we do transfer is a jumble of the drops from different faucets, not a continuous, coherent stream from one source [p.

125].... Two main types of cognitive load issues are extraneous problem-solving and divided attention... Those happen to be two of the central features of the Net as an informational medium [p. 125].... Deciphering hypertext substantially increases readers' cognitive load and hence weakens their ability to comprehend and retain what they're reading.... readers of hypertext often ended up clicking distractedly through pages instead of reading them carefully [pp. 126-127].... research continues to show that people who read linear text comprehend more, remember more, and learn more than those who read text peppered with links [p.127].... comprehension decreased as the number of links increased [p. 128].... The Net is, by design, an interruption system, a machine geared for dividing attention. That's not only the result of its ability to display many different kinds of media simultaneously. It's also a result of the ease with which it can be programmed to send and receive messages [pp. 131-132].... Navigating the Web requires a particularly intense form of mental multitasking. In addition to flooding our working memory with information, the juggling imposes what brain scientists call "switching costs" on our cognition. Every time we shift our attention, our brain has to reorient itself, further taxing our mental resources [p. 133].... Switch from reading to power browsing" [p. 137]... hop quickly from one source to another, rarely returning to any source they had already visited. They'd typically read, at most, one or two pages of an article or book before "bouncing" to another site [p. 136].... Screen-based reading behavior...[is characterized by] browsing and scanning, key word spotting, one-time reading, [and] non-linear readin... skimming is becoming our dominant mode of reading... we are evolving from being cultivators of personal knowledge to being hunters and gatherers in the electronic data forest." (p. 138).

Jackson (2008) adds that when we multitask, "we are like swimmers

Chapter 2: The Varieties of Dysfunctional Attention in the Modern Western World

diving into a state of focus, resurfacing to switch gears or reassess the environment, then diving again to resume focus [p. 79].... you can train yourself until you're blue in the face and you'd never be as good as if you just focused on one thing at a time" (pp. 79-80). Small and Vorga (2008) add, "Our high-tech revolution has plunged us into a state of continuous partial attention...describe[d] as continually staying busy—keeping tabs on everything while never truly focusing on anything. Continuous partial attention differs from multitasking, wherein we have a purpose for each task" (p. 18).

For the current generation "'research' is more likely to mean a *Google* search than a trip to the library. (Palfrey & Gasser, 2008, p. 239). Search entails "grazing" through heaps of information (p. 241). The multiple exposures on *Google Book Search* have complicated the distraction capabilities of the Internet even further. Carr (2011) says:

> Surrounding every page or snippet of text on *Google Book Search* is a welter of links, tools, tabs, and ads, each eagerly angling for a share of the reader's fragmented attention [p. 165].... It's not a library of books. It's a library of snippets... [p.166]. The influx of competing messages that we receive wherever we go online not only overloads our working memory; it makes it much harder for our frontal lobes to concentrate our attention on any one thing. The process of memory consolidation can't even get started. And, thanks once again to the plasticity of our neuronal pathways, the more we use the Web, the more we train our brain to be distracted—to process information very quickly and very efficiently but without sustained attention. (p. 194)

Immersion in technology also negatively affects relationships. Small & Vorgan (2008) say, "for every hour we spend on our computers, traditional face-to-face interaction time with other people drops by nearly thirty minutes. With the weakening of the brain's neural circuitry controlling human contact, our social interactions may become awkward [p. 2]. Genuine face-to-face interaction has been replaced by digital social networks" (p. 3).

Palfrey & Gasser (2008) depict the generation born after 1980 that spend most of their time exposed to technology as "digital natives." They say, "Digital Natives live much of their lives online, without distinguishing between the online and the offline...They are joined by a set of common practices, including the amount of time they spend using digital technologies, their tendency to multitask, their tendency to express themselves and relate to one another in ways meditated by digital technologies, and their pattern of using the technologies to access information and create new knowledge and art forms" (p. 4). According to the authors digital natives are a different generation characterized by a multiplicity of digital identities on social networks, a large dossier of personal information on line, a relative ignorance of privacy wherein privacy of personal information has been sacrificed for internet convenience, and access to an overload of information has taken precedence over the accuracy of that information. According to Palfrey and Gasser this information overload leads to "higher levels of distraction" (p. 191).

Smart Phones and Other Mobile Devices

Smart phones, and related mobile technologies such as iPods and tablets "enable-and encourage—constant connection to information, entertainment, and each other" (Ward et al., 2011, p. 140). Ward et al. add that "Smartphone owners interact with their phones an average of 85 times a day [and]... Ninety-one percent report they never leave home without their phone" (p. 140). According to George and Odgers (2015), adolescents send or receive an average of 60 text messages a day (p. 832), and spend on average 7.5 hours per day consuming electronic media (p. 837).

According to a 2014 pediatric survey of predominately low-income households by Kabali et al. (2015), "Most households had a television (97%), tablets (83%), and smartphones (77%). At age 4, half of the children had their own television and three-fourths their own mobile device. Almost all children (96.6%) used mobile devices, and most started using before age 1" (p, 1044). By age 2 one-third of children no longer need help to navigate a mobile device. They add, "Children use mobile

Chapter 2: The Varieties of Dysfunctional Attention in the Modern Western World

devices to play games, watch videos, communicate, take pictures, and access applications (apps) [p. 1045].... Parents often let their children use mobile devices, when they are busy, need to run errands, or wish to keep a child engrossed in something while out in public" (p.1046). According to Kabali et al. these findings suggest a disturbing pattern of "very early and nearly universal adoption of mobile media devices among children 0 to four years of age" (p. 1047), and that "media multitasking is pervasive, both in school and at home" (p. 1048) in the millennial generation.

This exponential increase in the use of mobile devices by the younger generation has sparked a series of fears about the deleterious effects of device use. George & Odgers (2105) list seven fears about the generation growing up with excessive mobile device use. First, parents worry about who their adolescents are spending time with on-line. However, they found that most adolescents spend their time on-line with their off-line friends, rather than getting lost in the dark web. Second, parents worry about their adolescents becoming victims of cyberbullying but George and Odgers say that cyberbulying has a "much lower prevalence than traditional bullying" (p. 838) and that cyberbullying, when it occurs, significantly overlaps with off-line bullying. Third, parents worry that their adolescents who spend too much time on-line become isolated and do so at the expense of forming real relationships. However, George and Odgers say, "there is little evidence to date that it reduces friendship quality or leads to social isolation." (p. 841) Fourth, while parents fear that mobile devices create a "digital divide between parents and adolescents, some evidence suggests that new technologies can provide adolescents with quick, easy, and remote access to their parents." (p. 841) Fifth, parents fear that their adolescents will post things on line that may damage their sense of self or future lives. George and Odgers say that while, for the most part, there is considerable overlap between how most adolescents present themselves, on- and off-line, there are also "important exceptions" where some adolescents post information of an explicitly sexual or aggressive nature that may cause damage to them in the future (p.844). Sixth, parents worry that their adolescents multitasking on mobile devices may interfere with cognitive performance. George and Odgers say research in this area consistently shows negative effects

(p. 844). Seventh, parents fears that their adolescent children are losing sleep because of the excessive time spent on mobile devices. They conclude, "research to date has consistently shown that mobile device and media usage prior to bedtime is associated with reduced sleep time and quality" (p. 845). The authors conclude:

> First, although there are cases in which new technologies have introduced new risks to adolescent well-being (e.g. by creating a new platform for bullying, interfering with sleep, and creating a digital archive that may carry reputational costs), most behaviors and risks that are present in the online world appear to be mirrored offline. (p. 846)

Overall, parents' fears of negative social consequences for adolescents excessive usage of mobile devices for the most part is not supported, but negative effects on cognition and sleep are supported by research.

Wilmer, Sherman, and Chein (2017) review the research on the relationship between smartphones and cognition, especially with respect to effects on attention, memory, and delay of gratification. Wilmer et al. categorize potential smartphone-related effects on attention into endogenous and exogenous interruptions. They say, "Endogenous interruptions occur when the user's own thoughts drifts toward a smartphone-related activity, and thereby evince an otherwise unsolicited drive toward a smartphone-related activity…Exogenous interruptions occur when some environmental cue captures the user's attention" (p.5). For example, Stothart, Mitchum, and Yehnert (2015) found that when subjects received a cell phone notification of a text during performance of a laboratory-based sustained attention task, the notification prompted "task-irrelevant thoughts or mind wandering" (p. 893) that interfered with attention performance even when the subject resisted responding to the cellphone message. The authors conclude, "cellular notifications, even when one does not view or respond to messages or answer calls, can significantly damage performance on an attention-demanding task…we believe that what underlies this effect is the tendency for cellular notifi-

Chapter 2: The Varieties of Dysfunctional Attention in the Modern Western World

cations to prompt task-irrelevant thoughts, or mind-wandering, which persist beyond the duration of the notifications themselves" (p. 896). Similarly, Ward et al. (2017) studied the effects of the mere presence of a cell phone on performance using a test of working memory and a test of fluid intelligence. They found, "even when people are successful at maintaining sustained attention—as when avoiding the temptation to check their phones—the mere presence of these devices reduces available cognitive capacity" (p. 143)... the mere presence of these devices left fewer attentional resources available for engaging with the task at hand" (p. 149).

Instant messages showing up on a computer screen or a mobile device also serve as an exogenous distractor to the task at hand. Several studies have investigated the effects of instant messaging, on reading. Bowman et al. (2010) found that students who were instant messaging, as compared to students who were not messaging took significantly longer to read a passage, but there were no significant differences in reading comprehension between the two groups. Levine, Waite, and Bowman (2007) found that students who spent more time instant messaging as compared to those who spent less time showed significantly higher distractibility when reading. Levine et al., say, "IMing helps create a cognitive style based on quick, superficial multitasking rather than in-depth focus on one task such a reading...[and represents a] tendency toward the use of continuous partial attention" (p. 565).

Some research has attempted to identify psychological factors that predict heavy use or problematic use of mobile devices. Problematic use was more likely in younger people, in girls more than boys, in youth who are extroverted, and in youth who had lower self-esteem (Bianchi & Phillips, 2005).

NOT WORKING MEMORY; THE NEGATIVE EFFECTS OF THE INTERNET ON WORKING MEMORY

According to Ericson (2013) The Internet crams advertisements and content and links into a single display of multi-various information in a way that diminishes working memory. Nie et al. (2016) found that frequent internet use impaired inhibition of distracting information and contributed to poor working memory in adolescents with internet addiction and/or ADHD (p. 28). According to Klingberg (2009) when people perform multimedia tasks that load working memory, and thus place heavy demands on their mental capacity, they become more easily distracted (p. 73). Individuals with poor working memory are especially unable to distinguish relevant from irrelevant information (Vogel, 2005). In a study of a modern open office suite with computer screens Klingberg (2009) found "personnel were interrupted and distracted roughly every three minutes...people working on a computer had an average of eight windows open at the same time" (p. 4). According to Spitzer (2012) we have entered an age of "digital dementia." He says "most kids today have grown up not needing to remember things like phone numbers because we have devices that do it for us. Instead of taking time to remember we look it up on Google." The overall effect of most types of multimedia exposure, with the exception of certain videogames, is an erosion of working memory.

SUMMARY OF THE POTENTIAL EFFECTS OF MULTIMEDIA EXPOSURE

- Displays of simultaneous multimedia information or multiple tracks of streaming news, frequent pop up distracting advertisements and hyperlinks all diminish the likelihood of maintaining an attentional set and contribute to mindlessness.

- Displays of simultaneous multimedia information with a high amount of distracting information diminishes attention span. Frequent pop up advertisements and alternative hyperlinks trains the mind to frequently engage and disengage concentration. When search engines like Google profile users and send information relevant to a user's profile, it makes it even harder to distinguish the information focused upon from similar distractors. The overall effect is a reduction in concentration ability. Children and adults with ADHD are especially at risk.

Chapter 2: The Varieties of Dysfunctional Attention in the Modern Western World

- Multimedia exposure demands a high frequency of multitasking in which performance on any one task is significantly diminished, especially in children with high multimedia use.

- Exposure to information profiled to the multimedia user trains the mind to become more reactive.

- Heavy multimedia exposure contributes to psychic entropy and diminishes the overall organization of mental experience.

- Mindless searching through multiple hyperlinks and pop ups diminishes overall meta-cognitive monitoring.

- Exposure to simultaneous multiple streams of information and hyperlinked searches with high amounts of distracting information diminishes overall working memory span in most children. However, certain videogames may increase working memory span.

- While certain videogames may increase hand-eye coordination and visuo-spatial skills, certain videogames train a regression to operating predominately out of exogenous orientation of attention to novel visual and motion cues, thereby diminishing predominately operating out of developmentally more advanced executive control of attention. Multiple media presentation of frequent distractors, especially profiled distracting similar information that captures attention, further erodes inhibition of response to distractors.

Chapter 3

Training Attention and Related Skills in Children

by Daniel P. Brown, Ph.D.

Two Broad Categories of Training Attention

In the Indo-Tibetan tradition of Buddhist meditation the mind is said to be like an elephant. An elephant is very intelligent and strong. Yet, an elephant is easily startled, and when afraid it stampedes and can cause a lot of damage. The ordinary, untrained mind is said to be like a stampeding elephant running here and there. However, once trained the elephant-mind is able to show its full strength and intelligence. According to the tradition there are two ways to train an elephant. The first way is to tie a rope around the elephant's neck and tie the other end of the rope to a stake. Every time the elephant wanders off it feels the pull of the rope, and after feeling the pull of the rope many times it learns to stay put. The second way to train an elephant is to not tie the elephant to anything and let the elephant wander freely. Yet, wherever the elephant goes you never take your eyes off of the elephant and track the elephant's movements, moment-by-moment. Tying up the elephant is a metaphor for concentration training. The rope of concentration is tied to a concentration object. Every time the elephant-mind wanders off, the rope pulls the elephant-mind back to the concentration object. There are only two possibilities: either the mind stays concentrated on the concentration object, or the mind becomes distracted and wanders off chasing after a thought or a sensory event. If the meditator pulls the mind back to the concentration object many times the mind begins to settle down and stay concentrated on the object. The objective of concentration training is to stay continuously on the object of concentration and reduce distraction. Tracking the elephant everywhere it wanders is a metaphor for pure awareness meditation. The objective of awareness meditation is to reduce discontinuities or lapses in awareness so as to approximate continuous, uninterrupted awareness. There is no concept of distraction in pure awareness meditation. What occurs moment-by-moment is the next event to become aware of.

Modern neuroscience has essentially corroborated that there are two fundamentally different approaches to meditation. Lutz et al. (2008) found that there are two styles of meditation. What they call focused attention (FA) meditation, or concentration, entails the voluntary focusing of attention on a chosen object of concentration. What they call open-monitoring meditation (OM), or awareness meditation, or mindfulness, entails "non-reactive monitoring of the content of experience from moment-to-moment" (p. 163). Each of these distinct forms of meditation is associated with its own neuro-circuitry in the brain. Concentration training entails activation of the anterior cingulate cortex (ACC). The ACC is generally activated when there are competing attentional demands, like in the Stroop test, where it takes effort to focus on the text and tune out interference by the color of the text. In concentration both the ACC and the dorsolateral prefrontal cortex, associated with meta-cognitive monitoring of experience, is also activated (McGeown, 2016, p. 348). For example, meta-cognitive monitoring is necessary to detect the mind-wandering off the concentration object and to bring the mind back to the concentration object. Brefczynski-Lewis et al. (2007) studied the difference between experienced as compared to novice meditators of concentration. Both groups showed activation of the ACC during concentration. However, only the advanced group showed activation of the dorsolateral prefrontal cortex (dlPFC) associated with meta-cognitive monitoring. Experienced concentrators also showed "less brain activation in regions related to discursive thought and emotions… more activation in regions related to response inhibition" (p. 11483).

Pure awareness or mindfulness meditation is associated with deactivation of the posterior cingulate cortex (PCC) (Garrison et al. (2013). The PCC is generally activated when categorizing or making judgments about experience. In pure awareness meditation the meditator remains in the present moment and tracks ongoing experience moment-by-moment without judgment. Tracking the moment-by-moment changes in immediate experience also requires meta-cognitive monitoring (Hesenkamp & Barsalou, 2012, p. 319). Furthermore, Hassenkamp and Barsalou (2012) also found that when subjects intentionally developed a reflective narrative about themselves, they activated the medial prefrontal cortex (mPFC), the neuro-circuitry associated with sense of self. However, when subjects practiced mindfulness and staying in the experience of the present moment, both novice and experienced mindfulness meditators deactivated the mPFC. Deactivating the neuro-circuitry associated with developing a sense of self and top-down control over states of mind may not be indicated for school age children for whom we want to foster greater self development.

The most popular type of meditation in the West is Burmese mindfulness arising from the teachings of Mahasi Sayadaw. This particular type of mindfulness is actually a hybrid form, which combines concentration with awareness training. Many practitioners initially find pure awareness meditation difficult because the ordinary mind doesn't have enough stability to remain present moment-by-moment. Therefore, Mahasi Sayadaw added an initial stage of concentration on the breath to stabilize attention and at least partially calm extraneous thought activity before attempting to stay in the present moment. Mahasi Sayadaw made a second modification to a pure awareness meditation. He introduced using labeling as a means to approximate greater continuity of moment-by-moment awareness. For example, when a thought is occurring the practitioner says, "thinking," as a way to recognize that thinking is occurring in that moment, irrespective of the content of thought. When a sound is occurring the practitioner says, "hearing," as a way to recognize that hearing is occurring at that moment, irrespective of the content of the sound. Other labels include, "seeing," "sensing," "feelings," and so forth. Kabat-Zinn's (1990) version of mindfulness also added a body scan procedure, and a compassion meditation.

The advantage of this emerging hybrid form of Western mindfulness is that it exposes the novice meditator to a range of ways of training the mind. A potential disadvantage is that since mindfulness is a hybrid form, it is unclear whether such practices actually accomplish the specific type of mind-training purported to be accomplished by pure concentration meditation, namely enhanced selective and sustained attention, or the objective to be accomplished by pure awareness meditation, namely maintaining the attentional set and having greater continuity of awareness moment-by-moment.

A number of studies with adults have included a comparison of concentration and mindfulness training with respect to training selective and sustained attention and continuity of awareness in the moment, moment-by-moment. Failure to detect a second target soon after the first has been called "the attentional blink." Three months of intensive mental training [in mindfulness] resulted in improved second target detection (reduced attentional blink) according to Tang and Posner, cited in Slagter et al. 2007, p 224). According to Tang and Posner, "mental training can result in increased control over the distribution of limited brain resources" (p. 1228). Ordinarily, the human brain has limited ability to process two temporally close meaningful items, accounting for the attentional blink (p. 1233). Similarly, Van Leeuwen, Muller and Melloni (2009) studied the effects of both concentration training and mindfulness using long-term, experienced practitioners from the same center. They found that "meditation practice leads to a reduction of the attentional blink" (p. 593).

A number of studies on training mindfulness in adults have shown little improvement specifically with respect to selective and sustained attention. For example, Anderson et al. (2007) studied the effects of mindfulness-based stress reduction (MBSR) on attentional control. They defined mindfulness as a complex, multi-dimensional process. They explain, "mindfulness involves sustained attention, attention switching, inhibition of elaborative processing and non-directed attention" (p. 449). After completing 8-weeks of mindfulness-based stress reduction (MBSR) there were "no improvements in attentional control relative to the control group" (p. 449). The measures used entail: a continuous performance test for sustained attention; a task-switching test; the Stroop interference test; and an object interference test measuring non-directed attention. Overall, the results showed "no evidence that participation in an extensive 8-week MBSR course affected attentional control [using the three Posner ANT measures]" (p. 459). However, mindfulness associated with non-directed attention resulted in improved scores on the object detection test. They add, "mindfulness may be more closely associated with changes in the quality of awareness of present moment experience than with basic attentional abilities" (p. 460).

Van den Hurk et al. (2010) utilized 20 experts in meditation, whose mean years of practice was 15 years, and also matched controls. Those practicing meditation practiced both concentration training and awareness training. The findings were that "mindfulness meditators showed a better orienting of attention than their matched controls [p. 1176]... reflecting a more flexible [less rigid] orienting of attention" (p. 1177). The study also showed a non-significant trend toward better executive attention (p. 1177).

Jha, Krompinger, and Baime (2007) compared the effects of an 8-week mindfulness MBSR training course, a 1-month intensive MBSR retreat, Tibetan concentration training, and a no meditation control group on alerting, orienting, and selective attention and conflict monitoring using the Attention Network Test (ANT). Those Ss practicing MBSR showed improvement in conflict monitoring, but no improvement on other measures of attention. The Ss practicing pure concentration meditation showed improved scores on selective attention and conflict monitoring, and also improved alerting and exogenous orienting (p. 117). Overall, these comparative studies suggest that pure concentration training, as compared to hybrid mindfulness, is more effective in training selective and sustained attention in adults, and mindfulness is more effective in learning to stay in the present moment, and to maintain an attentional set.

Training Mindfulness in Children; Effects of Attentional Systems

The most programmatic, widespread approach to training the mind in both children and adults is mindfulness training. Mindfulness began with the pioneering work of Jon Kabat-Zinn (1990) and the stress reduction clinic at the University of Massachusetts Medical Center. The use of mindfulness as an adjunct to psychotherapy or as the primary treatment of such conditions as acute and chronic pain, anxiety, depression, and insomnia has become enormously popular. As of 2010 there were over 710 peer-reviewed professional articles on mindfulness-based stress reduction MBSR or mindfulness-based cognitive therapy (MBCT). More recently, numerous programs have introduced one version or another of mindfulness training for children. Since these are mainly school-based programs, mindfulness has been used more extensively than most other methods for training the mind in both adults and children. What follows is a review of the studies on training children to be mindful.

A number of studies wherein children were trained in mindfulness found positive results with respect to selective or sustained attention. Napoli, Krech and Holley (2005) offered 12 sessions of mindfulness over a 24-week period to children ages 6-9 years old as compared to wait list controls. Using the Test of Everyday Attention there were significant effects on selective but not sustained attention. The test of selective attention entailed finding two similar space ships amidst many distractors. The test of sustained attention entailed counting the number of tones to give an accurate total score at the end of all tones heard. A significant increase in selective attention occurred only in the mindfulness group as compared to the wait list control group. Similarly, Mendelsom et al. (2010) found that mindfulness training improved the capacity for sustained attention in fourth and fifth graders. Langer and Meldoveanu (2000) also found that mindfulness training improved attention in children.

Saltzman and Goldin (2008) introduced MBSR to children in fourth and sixth grade as compared to wait list control children. The training emphasized "paying attention to the present moment" (p. 141). Attention performance was objectively assessed using the Attention Network Test (ANT). Results were that MBSR students "showed a significantly greater improvement on the cognitive control of attention component of the Attention Network Test, especially in those students who practiced the most" (pp. 155-156).

In a Dutch study Bogels et al. (2008) investigated the effects of mindfulness-based cognitive therapy (MBCT) for adolescents with externalizing disorders. Subjects were given 8 sessions of MBCT, as compared to wait list control Ss. Measures included the self-report version of the Achenbach Behavioral Checklist, which includes a section on attentional problems, and a self-report on mindfulness experiences (MAAS). They found, "After mindfulness training, children self-reported substantial improvement on personal goals, internalizing and externalizing complaints, attention problems, happiness, and mindful attention and performed better on a sustained attention task" (p. 193).

Weijer-Bergsma et al. (2012) introduced an 8-week mindfulness program to 11- to 15-year-old adolescents boys with ADHD in order to assess the effects of mindfulness on attentional skills. The study included two computerized sustained attention tasks, such as sustained attention to the number of dots appearing on a computer screen, or counting the number of different tones presented randomly. They found, "after mindfulness training, adolescents' attention and behavior problems reduced, while their executive functioning improved by self report and teacher report.... [There were] no improvements on the actual attention tasks. These improvements were maintained at an 8-week, but waned at a 16-week follow-up evaluation" (p. 775).

Zylowska et al. (2007) introduced 2.5 hours of mindfulness over 8 weeks to 16-year-old adolescents and adults with ADHD. There was no control group. In order to adapt the mindfulness training to subjects with ADHD, certain modifications in the training were introduced, such as shorter sitting meditations, and guided audio-recorded meditations. They found a significant decrease in self-reported ADHD symptoms in both adolescents and adults. They say, "Mindfulness is a feasible intervention in a subset of ADHD adults and adolescents and may improve behavioral and neurocognitive impairments" (p. 737). Similarly, Bogels et al. (2008) introduced mindfulness training to adolescents diagnosed with attention and behavior control problems. They reported significant increases in self-reported sustained attention and mindful awareness, although no objective measures of attention were used. Singh et al. (2010) introduced 12 sessions of mindfulness training to two boys both with ADHD. The boys' mothers also took the mindfulness training. They found that training the mother in mindfulness increased the boys' compliance with the mindfulness program. Van der Oord, Bogels, and Peijnenburg (2012) introduced an 8-week mindfulness program to children ages 8 to 12 years old with ADHD. Like the previous study parents also took the mindfulness training. They found, "a significant increase in mindful awareness from pre- to post-test [according to self report on the MAAS] (p. 139). Additionally, "ADHD symptoms, as rated by parents, significantly reduced after the training....[but they] did not find a significant reduction on teacher-rated ADHD symptoms, although the reduction of inattentive symptoms reached significance [on MAAS]" (p. 144).

EFFECTS OF MINDFULNESS TRAINING ON DIMENSIONS OTHER THAN ATTENTION

Flook et al. (2010) developed an 8-week Inner Kids Mindfulness Program to see if mindfulness improved executive functioning in third and fifth graders. Measures included parent and teacher behavioral ratings, but not a test battery of executive functioning (EF). They found, "Specifically, those children starting out with poor EF who went through the...training showed gains of behavioral regulation, meta-cognition, and overall global executive control" (p. 71). According to self-report specifically on attentional skills, there were "improvements in children's abilities to shift, initiate, and monitor" (p. 79).

Wall (2005) introduced mindfulness and Tai Chi into a Boston Public Middle School. The program consisted of 5-weeks of training given to 11-to 13-year-olds. Students self-reported "well-being, calmness, relaxation, improved sleep, less reactivity, increased self-care, self-awareness, and a sense of interconnection or interdependence with nature" (p. 230).

Schonert-Reichel and Hymel (2007) developed a Mindfulness Education (ME) Program for fourth and seventh graders. They believe that age 9-12 is a critical period for quieting mind, becoming aware of emotions, managing negative emotions, and acknowledging self in relationship to others. The program focused on "competencies to recog-

Chapter 3: Training Attention and Related Skills in Children

nize and manage emotions, develop caring concern for others, establish positive relationships, make responsible decisions, and handle challenging situations effectively" (p. 21). The program included a component on "self awareness" and "recognizing emotions and values" (p. 22). Schonert-Reichel and Lawlor (2010) reported significant improvements of teacher-rated attention/concentration and social/emotional competence from pre to post-test.

Huppert and Johnson (2010) investigated the effects of MBSR on well-being in adolescent boys. They found, "a significant improvement on measures of stress reduction, mindfulness and, psychological well-being, related to degree of individual practice undertaken outside of the classroom." Heeren and Phiippot (2011) found that 8 weeks of training in MBCT as compared to wait list control subjects reduced maladaptive ruminations and increased adaptive ruminations (p. 8).

Mendelson et al. (2010) developed a school-based 12-week mindfulness intervention program in an urban school for disadvantaged fourth and fifth graders. They found it had a positive impact on problematic responses to stress including ruimation, intrusive thoughts, and emotional arousal" (p. 985). Kuyken et al. (2013) developed the British Mindfulness in Schools Program for children ages 12-16. They found "fewer depressive symptoms, greater well-being, less stress" (p. 126).

Singh et al. (2003) developed the Meditation on the Soles of the Feet for conduct disorder and learning disorder children. They reported increased control over behaviors. Lee et al. (2008) developed a pilot 10-12-week program of MBCT for children 9 to 12 years of age. The pre-/post- differences suggested the program could be "a potential treatment for internalizing and externalizing symptoms in children" (p. 15).

Boderick and Metz (2009) developed a pilot program, Learning to BREATHE, for adolescents to foster emotion regulation. They found, "decreased negative affect and increased feelings of calmness, relaxation, and self-acceptance (p. 35)... greater awareness of their feelings as they were being experienced" (p. 42). Broderick and Frank (2014) add, "Mindfulness teaches ways of relating to thoughts, feelings, and experiences from a decentered meta-level that can ultimately allow for better selection of problem-solving strategies and more effective responses to problems" (p. 33). The specific targeted age was intended because it "capitalizes on youth's growing meta-cognitive skills by explicitly teaching about mindfulness" (p. 37).

EFFECTS OF MINDFULNESS ON ACADEMIC PERFORMANCE

Beauchamp, Hutchins, and Patterson (2008) introduced a 5-week pilot mindfulness program for high school adolescents diagnosed with learning disabilities. They reported, "decreased state and trait anxiety, enhanced social sills, and improved academic performance" (p. 34) based on teacher ratings of academic performance. In another study Linden (1973) reported mindfulness meditation improves reading achievement. Bennett and Dorjee (2015) investigated the effects of an 8-week MBSR program on well-being and academic achievement in 16 to 18-year-olds. Not immediately after the course but at 3-month follow-up there were significant differences in academic scores between MBSR and controls, and MBSR students "were able to meet…their predicted grades" (p.1213).

REVIEWS ON THE EFFECTS OF MINDFULNESS

Burke (2010) reviewed 15 studies and concluded, "Overall, the current research base provides support for the feasibility of mindfulness-based interventions with children and adolescents, however, there is no generalized empirical evidence of the efficacy of these interventions…[There needs to be a] shift away from feasibility studies…[and to] adopt standardized formats for interventions" (p. 133). Harnett and Dawe (2012) reviewed 24 studies, and conclude, "There is increasing evidence that mindfulness-based therapeutic techniques can have a positive impact on a range of outcome variables" (p. 175), but noted the lack of a suitable instrument to measure mindfulness.

Rempel (2012) specifically reviewed the use of mindfulness with children and youth, on a "broad range of outcomes" (p. 215). They note, "mindfulness-based practices can have a positive impact on academic performance, psychological well-being, self-esteem and social skills in children" (p. 216). Weare (2013) reviewed 20 studies on mindfulness with children. They state mindfulness is "capable of improving mental health and well-being, mood, self-esteem, self-regulation, positive behavior, and academic learning" (p. 141). Zenner, Herrnleben-Kurz, and Walach (2014) conducted a systematic review and meta-analysis of mindfulness-based interventions in the schools. They conclude, "mindfulness-based interventions in children and youths hold promise, particularly in relation to improving cognitive performance and resilience to stress" (p. 124). In one of the most recent reviews Burke (2009) says, "Several of the reviewed studies include valuable and detailed examples of adaptations made to meet the age-related needs of younger participants" (p. 42). Felver et al. (2016) conducted a systematic review of mindfulness-based interventions for youth specifically in school settings. They remind us that one important limitation in many of these studies is that most findings rely on self-report rather than performance tests. Despite this limitation, at this point it is fair to say, "The existing literature suggests that MBI is a feasible and acceptable modality of intervention for use in school settings" (p. 40).

What Does Mindfulness Actually Train?

Even while mindfulness-based interventions have become increasingly popular in school programs, it has not been clearly established exactly what attention and performance outcomes are being targeted because of the diversity of definitions and practices subsumed under the term "mindfulness-based." Kuyken et al. (2013) remind us, "Only a small number of studies measured the construct of mindfulness itself... While the interventions being evaluated can be classified as 'mindfulness-based', there was in fact a large variation in both the content and the dose of the interventions evaluated" (p. 10). He adds, "It is important...[to] focus more on understanding the mechanisms responsible for change" (p. 13). To the extent that it is possible, it is important to identify the exact definition of mindfulness used in a given study in order to see what is actually being trained. For example, the original definition of mindfulness in the early Buddhist theory of mind literature, the

Abhidhamma, is not forgetting the task at hand. This definition, in Western terms, is very close to the construct of maintaining or forgetting the attentional set. Some contemporary proponents of mindfulness come close to this definition in their use of the term "mindlessness," although a clear distinction between *mindlessness* (forgetting the attentional set) and *distraction* (not forgetting the attentional set but becoming distracted while still engaging in the task) is rarely made. For example, Brown and Ryan (2003) define "mindlessness" as the absence of mindfulness. Similarly, Sherretz (2011) says, "The opposite of mindlessness is being mindful" (p. 93).

Defining mindfulness more traditionally as not forgetting the task at hand is a very different definition of mindfulness than the definition at the heart of MBSR. The popularity of the MBSR training spread a definition of mindfulness as being "mindful of the moment and non-judgmentally" (Kabat-Zinn 1990, p. 4). Similarly, Flook et al. (2010) define mindfulness as "attention to the present moment-by-moment experience." Some definitions of mindfulness are overly general, so as to subsume under mindfulness many different attention systems. For example, Rempel (2012) defines mindfulness as "a way of directing attention" (p. 202). Other definitions of mindfulness are too specific, so as to define mindfulness in terms of the content of what the individual is being aware of. For example, Weare (2013) defines mindfulness as "being aware of the inner processes involved in doing, feeling, thinking and being aware of impulses…. Essentially…[mindfulness is] meta-cognitive" (p. 142). Sometimes definitions of mindfulness emphasize awareness of body sensations. For example, Huppert and Johnson (2010) subsume the MBSR body scan, mindfulness of breathing, awareness of sounds, understanding the transient nature of thoughts, and walking meditation all as examples of mindfulness. Similarly, Bogels et al. (2008) define mindfulness as "mindful walking, the body scan, sitting with the breath, [being] mindful without judging, but also includes mindfulness training 'trust exercises'" (p. 198). In Broderick and Metz's (2009) Learning to BREATHE program there are six practices subsumed under mindfulness: body awareness; understanding and working with thoughts; understanding and working with feelings; integrating awareness of thoughts; feelings, and body sensations; reducing harmful self-judgments; and integrating mindful awareness into daily life (p. 38). The definition of mindfulness expands even further in Ellen Langer's work where included under the definition of mindfulness is a kind of open-mindedness associated with creativity. Langer (1993) says, "Mindfulness is a state of mind that results from drawing novel distinctions, examining information from new perspectives, and being sensitive to context. It is an open, creative probabilistic state of mind [p.44]... mindfulness is the capacity to see any situation or environment from several perspectives" (p. 44).

Langer and Piper (1987) see mindlessness as a kind of closed-mindedness. They say, "Mindlessness is marked by the rigid use of information during which the individual is not aware of its potential novel aspects... [it] occurs from making premature cognitive commitments to information presented in a single instance" (pp. 280-281). Curiously, this definition of mindfulness is exactly opposite of the traditional *Abhidhamma* definition of maintaining the attentional set. Langer, for example, further says, "To be vigilant, in contrast, one has to have a particular stimulus in mind, an expectation of what the stimulus is rather than what it could be [p. 44]... By letting the stimulus vary, attention need not be paid—it is freely given" (p. 47). Similarly, some definitions of mindfulness go beyond being present in the moment to emphasize novelty. For example, Langer and Moldoveanu (2000) say, "mindfulness [is a]... process of drawing novel distinctions" (p. 1). However, if you are anticipating novelty, or anything, you are not staying in the present moment but rather imposing a preference as to what to experience. Langer and Modoveanu expand the definition of mindfulness even further to include what is typically subsumed under meta-cognitive monitoring. They say mindfulness is being "more aware of the context and perspective of our actions rules and routines that lead to mindless behavior." In their work, they even claim under the definition of mindfulness the alerting attentional system when they add, "[it is] a heightened state of involvement and wakefulness or being in the present" (p. 3). Lastly, mindfulness has been defined as an attentional capacity comparable to concentration training. Meiklejohn et al. (2012), for example, define mindfulness as "directed attention to the breath or another attentional anchor, upon noticing this drift, brings attention back to anchor" (p. 2).

The price paid for the increasing popularity of mindfulness is that the definition has become all-inclusive, and therefore, has drifted further and further away from any direct relationship to basic attentional systems. The critical question, from our perspective is: does mindfulness training, however defined and practiced, lead to improvements in *very specific* attentional skills. Until this question is more adequately addressed, we run the risk of claiming mindfulness includes everything, but does nothing specific. More specifically, in terms of the three primary attentional systems, does mindfulness training improve alertness? Orienting? Selective attention, and conflict resolution? Sustained attention? Does it decrease mind-wandering? Does it reduce the interference normally resulting from multitasking? Does it improve meta-cognitive monitoring? Unfortunately, the current research has given little answers to these questions. In all fairness, using the most popular definition of mindfulness in MBSR as non-judgmental awareness of the present moment, MBSR does seem to accomplish staying more present in the moment. However, we must ask ourselves the fair question, is this the most important skill we want to train in a generation of children who can barely attend to anything? In our view, the endeavor spent training children is better spent training improved selective and sustained attention, working memory, and executive control, as these pertain more directly to academic and life success.

CONCENTRATION TRAINING; SELECTIVE AND SUSTAINED ATTENTION

Lutz et al. (2008) enumerate the basic skills of concentration training: sustaining attention to a selected object; detecting mind-wandering; and disengaging from distractors. Skilled concentration entails both skill in selective and sustained attention, but also in meta-cognitive monitoring of the process. For example, Brefczynski-Lewis et al. (2007) investigated the difference between experienced as compared to novice practitioners of Indo-Tibetan concentration meditation. Both advanced and novice concentrators showed activation of the anterior cingulate cortex (ACC) while concentrating. Increased ACC activation from attentional training was also reported by Tang and Posner (2009, p. 225). While advanced as compared to novice concentrators "had less bran activation in regions related to discursive thought and emotions... more activation in regions related to response inhibition" (p. 11483), the main difference between the advanced and novice concentrators was the skilled application of meta-cognitive monitoring by advanced concentrators. Advanced practitioners use meta-cognitive monitoring both to detect distraction more immediately and to monitor and self-correct strategies so as not to develop bad habits that reduce the effectiveness of concentration. Similarly, Lazar et al. (2000) found activation of the dlPFC typically associated with meta-cognitive activity in various kinds of concentration meditation such as concentrating on the breath or on a mantra.

Effective training in concentration meditation may affect the volume and structure of the neuro-circuits known to be activated in concentration training, namely the ACC and dlPFC. For example, after just 11 hours of a kind of concentration training, Tang et al. (2010) observed changes in white matter associated with the connectivity to and from the ACC. These changes in neuroplasticity suggest that concentration, once trained, becomes a lasting skill that doesn't deteriorate and is generalizable to many aspects of daily life.

In contrast to the many studies of mindfulness-based training in schools, there are surprisingly few studies on training concentration in children, even where concentration training more directly addresses skill development in selective and sustained attention. Valentine & Sweet (1999) conducted a comparison of the effects of concentrative and mindfulness meditation in college students on sustained attention using an auditory counting test of sustained attention as compared to controls. They found both meditation groups had superior performance on sustained attention in comparison to controls (p. 59). However, when a stimulus was presented in an unexpected way, mindfulness of the present moment as compared to concentration was the better method. They say, "when the stimulus was unexpected mindfulness meditators showed superior performance to concentrators" (p. 59). With respect to selective attention they found, "Both groups of meditators were apparently better able to ignore distracting thoughts than the untrained controls [p. 66].... long-term meditators show further increments in attention in comparison with short-term meditators" (p. 67). In the comparison, group mindfulness training also includes concentration on the breath so that the differences between concentration and present moment training may have been confounded. In contrast, however, most of the studies on mindfulness, although they include concentration of the breath, do not show significant improvements on measures of selective or sustained attention (see Goyal et al.'s 2014 meta-analysis of meditation). They conclude there is "insufficient evidence that meditation, mostly mindfulness, had a positive effect on attention" (p. 357).

A number of studies have demonstrated that concentration meditation improves selective attention and the ability to resist distraction. Kubose (1976) taught his subjects 3 weeks of breath-counting meditation. He found a "significant reduction in the frequency of intrusions... over sessions...[meditators were] better able to ignore irrelevant stimuli" (p. 8). MacLean et al. (2010) randomly assigned subjects to an intensive retreat or a wait-list control condition using a counter-balanced design. The intervention consisted of 3 months of traditional Indo-Tibetan concentration training. The effects of concentration meditation were assessed using a vigilance or continuous performance task. The results showed that intensive retreat concentrators as compared to control subjects showed "reliable improvements in visual discrimination... [and] improved vigilance" (p. 836). However, they add, "we did not find compelling evidence to suggest that our meditation training led to direct beneficial changes either in the ability to sustain attention or in the qualitative nature and efficiency of meta-cognitive processes" (p. 836). The improvement in sustained attention was limited to the continuous performance task. They noted "improved vigilance during sustained visual attention" (p. 829).

With respect to Transcendental Meditation (TM), a type of concentration training, Spanos et al. (1979) found that experienced TM medita-

Chapter 3: Training Attention and Related Skills in Children

tors reported many fewer intrusions than novices during TM meditation practice. Rani and Rao (1996) taught TM as part of a school curriculum for 9 to 11 year old children. The TM children showed improved sustained attention on a star counting task. Wisner, Jones, and Gwin (2010) introduced TM as a cognitive behavioral intervention to "manage behavior, thinking, and emotions in adolescents" (p. 156).

There have been some promising results training concentration in children and adults with ADHD. Grosswald et al. (2008) used transcendental meditation (TM) to reduce symptoms of ADHD and to reduce stress and anxiety in students ages 11 to 14 years of age with ADHD. After 3 months of twice daily of TM, "Results showed...significant reductions in stress, anxiety, and improvements in ADHD symptoms and executive function on a self-administered version of the Child Behavioral Checklist, and on teacher behavioral ratings of executive functioning. There were also significant improvements in selective attention/reduced interference on a Stroop-like task, and significant improvements on a continuous performance task measuring sustained attention. Grosswald et al. conclude TM, "May contribute to improved behavior regulation and executive function" (p. 4).

Semrud-Clikeman, et al. (1999) gave attention and problem-solving training to 8 to 12 year olds with ADHD. They measured attentional performance using visual and auditory continuous performance tasks. They found significant improvements on both tasks after 18 weeks of hourly training once a week. Esso and Thomson (2000) introduced a Pay Attention training program to 7 to 11 year olds with ADHD. A variety of attentional measures were used such as coding, digit span, and mazes. There were several test of sustained visual and auditory attention using a continuous performance format. The measures were "designed to train different levels of attention, including sustained, selective, alternating, and divided attention in young children and includes both visual and auditory activities" (p. 282). The overall findings showed "improvement in measures of attention and academic effort but not in hyperactivity" (p. 273) [and that training] "can be effective for improving performance on several psychometric measures of sustained, selective, and higher levels of attention...[there were] also improvements in academic efficiency" (p. 287); "the most improvement was noted on task of selective attention...[and] measures of simple sustained attention" (p. 288).

Abikoff, and Gittelman (1987) found that "contingent positive reinforcement" was important in treating ADHD. Amon and Campbell (2008) used relaxation, breathing techniques, and biofeedback as part of the sessions that also used video game training of attention with ADHD vs. normal control children whose mean age was 9.5. They found "children with AD/HD... demonstrated significant reductions in... AD/HD" according to self-report (p.72).

Farmer et al. (2002) reviewed evidence of treating childhood with externalizing disorders. They say, "For ADHD the strongest empirical evidence support was for pharmacological treatments. Psychosocial treatments alone demonstrated some positive results, but smaller than those demonstrated for medication treatments" (p. 1272).

Overall, concentration training for children holds promise for improving selective attention and sustained attention in children, especially when standard attentional performance tests instead of self-report are used as outcome measures. However, far more work needs to be done in this area, specifically on concentration training in children.

TRAINING TO REDUCE MIND-WANDERING

The purpose of training with respect to mind-wandering is to counter the extent to which habitual mind-wandering spills into engagement of the everyday external world and world of others and also into the tasks at hand. Anticevic et al. (2013) state that the purpose of training is to develop "DMN suppression" (p. 6), i.e., to reduce habitual and frequent preoccupation with mind-wandering to the extent that it interferes with full engagement with everyday life and the tasks at hand.

Both types of meditation—concentration and mindfulness—are associated with a reduction in mind-wandering (Garrison et al. 2013; Holzel et al., 2011). Hassenkamp and Barsalou (2012) describe how variability in initial concentration training is because of the shift to the default mode of mind-wandering. However, as the practitioner becomes more skilled, mind-wandering is greatly reduced. They add that repeated activation of meditation-related neuro-circuitry leads to "functional connectivity changes within attentional networks" (p. 3). Heeren and Phillipot (2011) found that the clinical benefits of mindfulness were mediated by a reduction in ruminative thinking, a component of mind-wandering.

Pagnoni (2012) used Zen meditation as a way to teach attentional skill development. He utilized a group of adult practitioners of Zen meditation and a control group of subjects who had never practiced meditation. Those subjects who simply meditated on their breath as compared to non-meditating controls showed significantly lower activation in the ventral posteromedial cortex. Since the prefrontal cortex is the main region of interest in mind-wandering mode, this important finding seems to suggest that Zen concentration on the breath suppressed DMN activation and likely lowered preoccupation with internal self-referential thinking. Pagnoni concluded that Zen meditation had "a regulatory effect… on DMN spontaneous activity" (p. 7). Similarly, Taylor et al. (2012) studied advanced and novice adult Zen meditators. fMRI revealed that advanced as compared to novice Zen meditators had "reduced medial prefrontal cortex (mPFC) activity, a central default mode network (DMN) component…. [and also]… functional connectivity changes between core DMN regions possibly reflecting strengthened present-moment awareness" (p.1). They emphasized that these changes in the DMN and mind-wandering "extend beyond the state of meditation *per se*" (p. 9).

Brewer et al. (2011) studied the effects of Burmese mindfulness meditation on the DMN and mind-wandering. Results showed that mindfulness meditation as compared to non-meditator control subjects showed significant deactivation of the posterior cingulate cortex (PCC) and medial prefrontal cortex (mPFC)—main components of the neuro-circuitry of DMN activity and mind-wandering. Additionally, analysis of functional connectivity showed a "stronger coupling in experienced meditators between the PCC, dACC, and dlPFC (regions previously implicated in self-monitoring and cognitive control)…consistent with decreased mind-wandering" (p. 20254). These findings suggest increased executive control over mind-wandering. However, the weakness in the study was that it used a meditation practice that confounded three type of meditation, namely concentration meditation, choiceless awareness meditation, and loving kindness meditation, so that it becomes difficult to detect which approach to meditation was associated with the main effect.

Garrison et al. (2015) state that "Meditation involves maintaining attention on immediate experience and away from distractions such as self-referential thinking and mind-wandering...meditation has been associated with reduced activity in a network of brain regions implicated in self-referential processing, known as the default mode network (DMN).... Reduced DMN activity during meditation appears to be consistent across different meditation practices" (p. 712). In this study experienced mindfulness meditators were compared to non-meditator control subjects. Both groups were given an active cognitive task of assigning adjectives to the self, which presumably would be associated with activation of the self-referential system mediated by the mPFC. Mindfulness meditation as compared to controls was associated with significantly lower activation brain regions of the DMN associated with mind-wandering. Deactivations were found in the ACC, fusiform gyrus, middle temporal gyrus, precuneus, and PCC. The results suggest that mindfulness meditators "differ in their resting state DMN processing" (p. 717). Unfortunately, the type of Burmese mindfulness utilized in the study confounded three types of meditation—concentration, choiceless awareness, and loving kindness meditation. While all three types had a similar effect on reducing DMN activation and reducing mind-wandering as compared to control non-meditators, it should be noted that one result was deactivation of the anterior cingulate cortex (ACC)—an area typically activated by concentration meditation. It may be that the confounding of several types of meditation weakened concentration training, so the results are opposite to those expected.

Unfortunately, there have been no studies on training children in DMN suppression or reduction of mind-wandering. However, the studies with adults suggest what to target and what to avoid. Pure concentration meditation like Zen appears to be superior to Burmese mindfulness that confounds concentration, choiceless awareness, and loving kindness. From a neuro-circuitry perspective, pure concentration training entails top-down executive control over mind-wandering, as mediated by activation of the anterior cingulate cortex (ACC), along with increased meta-cognitive monitoring of mind-wandering, as mediated by the activation of the right dorsolateral prefrontal cortex (rdlPFC). Pure concentration, additionally, does not necessarily eradicate self-referential activity, as mediated by the activity of the mPFC, as much as it controls it.

On the other hand, Burmese mindfulness isn't recommended for two reasons. First, mixing concentration, choiceless awareness, and loving kindness was not found to activate the ACC, so apparently, this mixture of meditation does not lead to top-down executive control over the DMN and mind-wandering. Second, with respect to applying mindfulness to training children, mindfulness is associated with significant deactivation of the mPFC, a main brain region associated with sense of self. Since an important objective of child development is fostering a strong sense of self (Brown & Elliott, 2016), methods that significantly reduce mPFC activation may run contrary to this objective. In contrast, pure concentration training develops top-down executive control over mPFC activation, as mediated by ACC activation, and also executive control over preoccupation with self-referential thinking and mind-wandering, while at the same time not necessarily suppressing the mPFC and the experience of self. It seems to us that the desired objective in training children is mastery and executive control over mind wandering as an extreme and frequent habit, while at the same time fostering healthy self development. Awareness-based meditation that fosters what in Buddhism is called "no self" (Pali *anatta*), seems to deactivate the mPFC and the self-representational system, so that in our opinion it is not the best or well thought out approach. While it is now quite popular to introduce mindfulness into the school system, there needs to be better consideration on what attentional systems we are trying to train, based on scientific findings.

Training Multitasking

Multitasking training increases processing speed and improves ability to multitask. Dux et al., (2009) say, " Our ability to multitask is severely limited: task performance deteriorates when we attempt to undertake two or more tasks simultaneously,...extensive training can greatly reduce such multitasking costs" (p.127). Multitasking appears to increase the speed of information-processing in the medial prefrontal cortex (mPFC). Training induces a switch from slow, deliberative processing in "general purpose" brain networks to fast, automatic processing in task-specific neural circuits. Training is often accompanied with decreased activation in prefrontal cortex (p. 127). They add, "training may lead to efficient multitasking by functionally separating neurons devoted to each sensory-motor task, thereby resulting in independent, parallel processing pathways within the prefrontal cortex" (p.131). They summarize, "the effect of training is to speed up information processing" (p. 134). With respect to the change in role for the mPFC they clarify that the mPFC still plays a role "but a more efficient one" (p.134).

Verghese et al. (2016) further adds that the left dorsolateral prefrontal cortex, associated with analytic meta-cognitive monitoring, plays an important role in dual task training. They see the left dlPFC in response to multitask training and signifying "cognitive control" (p. 2638). Erickson et al. (2007) found both left and right activation of the dlPFC occurred in multitask training.

A number of studies on multitask training have reported favorable results. In an early pilot study Spelke et al. (1976) trained two subjects to read stories while writing lists of words. After 17 weeks of training, performance on each of the dual tasks approached the same level as performance on each single task. Minear and Shah (2008) reported that task-switching improves with training, but that there is little improvement in switching costs. In other words, multitasking performance improves but there is still a residual negative effect on performance. Levy et al. (2012) studied the effects of Zen awareness training on multitasking behavior. After 8 weeks of training, subjects "stayed on tasks longer and made fewer task switches, as well as reported less negative emotion" (p. 45).

In a study of multitask training in 8-to10-year-old children, 18- to 26-year-olds, and 62- to 76-year-olds, Karbach and Kray (2009) studied the pre/post effects of task-switching training on the Stroop interference task, and on a dual task entailing reading versus counting numbers at the same time. They found that multitasking training resulted in a significant transfer of learning to a new but similar task, especially in children and adults as compared to the elderly.

Lee & Taatgen (2002) see multitasking as a kind of skill acquisition. Many have interpreted this skill as the consequence of developing strategies to reduce the cognitive load characteristic of trying to do a number of tasks at once. Mayer and Moreno (2003) enumerate various training strategies used in multitask training: off-loading from one sensory system to another; segmenting; pre-training; weeding out extraneous elements; providing cues for processing; and eliminating redundancy. These are all ways to "minimize an unnecessary cognitive load" (p. 50). Ruthruff et al. (2003, 2004) explain that multitasking training works because it reduces the bottleneck when one or more of the simultaneous tasks is carried out automatically (p. 33), the time of processing one task as compared to another is shortened, and/or doing one task as compared to a second is postponed. The explanation that multitask training works to the extent that deliberate processing shifts to automatic processing is given some support by neuroscience findings. For example, Chein and Schneider (2005) found that multitasking practice deactivates regions associated with attentional control, like the ACC and mPFC (p. 610). Kelly and Garavan see practice as a way of "redistributing" brain activations and deactivations (p.1089).

Fischer and Plessow (2015) interpret effective multitasking as a consequence of shifting from serial to parallel processing. They say, "efficient multitaskers are able to adopt a parallel processing strategy" (p. 8), i.e., to process information for each task simultaneously rather than temporally over time. In support of this interpretation Sigman and Dehaene (2008) say that the human information-processing system is designed to use both serial and parallel processing, and in certain situations there is "coexistence of serial and parallel processing within [the same] cognitive task" (p. 7585). The default approach to processing is serial or temporal processing, but multitasking invites the brain to switch to parallel or simultaneous processing, which bypasses the temporal processing bottleneck. This switch requires some re-organization of neurocircuitry activations and deactivations. Sigman and Dehaene describe "A massive cluster in the superior temporal cortex reflected in perfect parallel processing" (p. 7597). According to this interpretation multitasking training entails a radical shift in information-processing strategies in such a way that the bottleneck problem becomes less relevant.

Training to Reduce Reactivity

There have been very few studies specifically designed to reduce moment-by-moment reactivity to ongoing experience. Barnes, Treiber, and Davis (2001) studied the impact of 2 months of Transcendental Meditation (TM) training on adolescents' reactivity to ongoing experience. They measured ongoing cardiovascular reactivity in a resting condition and in response to a relevant stressor to adolescents, namely, a simulated stressful driving test. After 2 months of 15-minute, twice daily TM practice there was a significant reduction in pre/post cardiovascular reactivity in both the resting and stress conditions in TM group as compared to a health education control group (p. 597). Wall (2005) introduced 5 weeks of mindfulness and Tai Chi training into the Boston Public Middle School for 11- to 13-year-olds. The program was said to increase self-reports of "well-being, calmness, relaxation, improved sleep, less reactivity, increased self-care, self-awareness, and a sense of interconnection or interdependence with nature" (p. 230). Surprisingly few mindfulness studies have directly addressed reducing reactivity (for exceptions see Mendelson et al. (2011) and Huppert & Johnson, 2010). Since mindfulness entails deactivation of the posterior cingulate cortex (PCC), typically associated with categorizing and making judgments about ongoing experience, it would seem that mindfulness training holds considerable promise in helping certain children to become less reactive.

Training Meta-cognitive Monitoring

In one of her definitions of mindfulness reviewed above, Langer (1993) includes "examining information from new perspectives, and being sensitive to context...mindfulness is the capacity to see any situation or environment from several perspectives" (p. 44). Since perspective-taking and awareness of context are essentially higher level meta-cognitive skills (Brown et al., 2016), Langer sees mindfulness training in part as a means to train certain higher meta-cognitive skills. In our previous review of the Boderick and Metz (2009) Learning to BREATHE program for adolescents they include in the training "greater awareness of their feelings as they were being experienced" (p. 42). Essentially, they have included meta-cognitive monitoring as a component of the BREATHE program. Elsewhere Broderick and Frank (2014) make more explicit that they intend training in meta-cognitive monitoring. They say, "Mindfulness teaches ways of relating to thoughts, feelings, and experiences from a decentered meta-level that can ultimately allow for better selection of problem-solving strategies and more effective responses to problems [p. 330].... [Mindfulness] capitalizes on youth's growing meta-cognitive skills by explicitly teaching about mindfulness" (p. 37).

Similarly, Ritchhart and Perkins (2000) include a number of higher-level meta-cognitive skills in their "mindful classroom." They describe "three high-leverage instructional practices" cultivated by mindfulness: looking closely [cultivating an openness to new information (p. 31)]; exploring possibilities, and perspectives, and introducing ambiguity (p. 27); and developing a disposition toward mindfulness (p. 29). They say, "The cumulative effect of such open and active instructions is to make students more aware of or sensitive to the ambiguous or conditional natures of the world—that knowledge and understanding are always in flux" (p. 34). They then give an example of mindful teaching of math that emphasizes being mindful, or meta-cognitively aware, of the strategies used to solve problems. They recommend, "Rather than memorizing procedures.... explore a math problem through perspectives" (p. 44).

Knowles, Goodman and Semple (2015) use mindfulness to train meta-cognition in elementary school children ages 8-12 who operate at the level of concrete operational intelligence. They teach "four foundational skills: 1. cultivating present-focused awareness; 2. identifying thoughts, feelings, and body sensations; and 3. differentiating judging from noting;

and 4) decentering" or seeing thoughts as "just thoughts" (p. 20). They define "meta-cognition" as "awareness of one's own thinking processes" (p. 2521). Grant (2015) also sees it best to train meta-cognitive skills at this very same age:

> As children approach the developmental age of 8 or 9 years of age the faculty of discernment becomes stronger....children of this age have a number of wonderful emerging qualities. With increased discerning awareness comes increased meta-cognition, the ability to witness their own thoughts, feelings, motivations, and actions, and to begin to reflect on them. This capacity tends to arrive earlier for girls than for boys and develops more fully in the preteen and teen years...we support children in their developing sense of self and help them to recognize, strengthen, and mature their naturally emerging qualities. (pp. 103-104)

Overall, much more work needs to be done on training meta-cognitive skills in children.

TRAINING IN MENTALIZATION

It has become increasing clear that the capacity to mentalize has important implications for mental health, and that children who score extremely low in reflective capacity are highly likely to grow up manifesting a personality or dissociative disorder in adulthood (Brown et al., 2016). According to Verheugt-Pleiter, Zevalkink, and Schmeets (2008), "non-clinical children just start to develop their ability to mentalize and relatedly an "autobiographical self" at around age 4" (p. 153). Unfortunately, some children poorly develop or never develop this important ability.

Ensink has reviewed a variety of ways to assess mentalization in children adapted for developmental age (Lindquist, 2013). In Canada Ensink reported that the overall level of reflective function in abused as compared to non-abused children is significantly lower. Early detection and treatment of mentalization deficiencies in children is a necessary prevention of mental health problems.

With respect to mentalization-based treatment (MBT) in children, Midgley et al. (2012) in the United Kingdom have described a form of time-limited MBT for children in their book (2012). Mentalization-based treatment for children (MBT-C) consists of 12 individual child therapy sessions and adjunctive parent sessions designed "to enhance skills in mentalizing, both in the parent and the child" (p. 6). Children ages 5 to 12 years old are selected for MBT-C based on either the under-development of mentalizing capacity and/or a significant break-down in mentalizing capacity (p. 41), especially seen in children with trauma and/or attachment disorders. Treatment begins with a detailed 1-3 session assessment to create a "mentalizing profile" (p. 72, 106) The formulation derived from the assessment is shared with both the child and parents. The general goal of MBT-C is "promoting a core developmental process," namely mentalizing capacity (p. 65). It is especially important that the therapist develop a consistent stance of mentalizing, so as to model healthy mentalizing for the child and parents. The therapist provides a secure base and a collaborative context with a consistent focus on the child's state-of-mind in order to foster the development of mentalizing. They say, "the focus will be more on promoting the underdeveloped capacity for mentalizing or paying attention to the situations in which explicit mentalizing breaks down" (p. 73). Through this process the child will "create a coherent narrative" about the problems and about the therapeutic process itself (p. 77). They add, "The overarching aim of time-limited MBT-C is to help develop and enhance mentalizing processes, helping the child to become aware of and regulate emotions and to mentalize about difficulties that they might face." Encouraging pretend play becomes a way to encourage children to reflect on and represent emotional states. The therapist remains carefully attuned to the child during free play, and tries to mirror, contingently mark, wonder out loud about, and clarify and name the child's states-of-mind during play episodes. In MBT-C children are encouraged to "think together" (p. 101) by "marking" the salient emotions and mentalizing about them in the spot. Special care is devoted to develop mentalizing capacity in the child around misunderstandings, ruptures, and other break downs that occur in the therapy. All MBT-C interventions are pitched at the right developmental level of the child.

In Norway, Tanum Johns uses an inter-subjective approach to enhance mentalization and self-agency in developmentally delayed children.

In the USA, Twemlow, Fonagy, and Sacco (2005) developed a Peaceful School program based specifically on fostering mentalizing around school-based bullying. Teachers, victims, by-standers, and bullies are taught to use mentalizing skills and "reflective time" to counter school-based bullying and to foster a positive atmosphere in the classroom. This promising program was introduced in 9 elementary schools for over 3,600 children. Similarly, in Denmark, Bak et al. (2015) developed a web-based Resilience Program that provides psychoeducational material on mentalization, resilience, and self-regulation skills. A 3-day version of resilience training was introduced as a pilot program in 60 Danish schools for over 9,000 children. The program resulted in a significant reduction in episodes of force and violence in the school system.

In the Netherlands, Verheugt-Pleiter, Zevalkink, and Schmeets (2008) assess attention development, emotion regulation, and mentalization in children and then using a developmentally-adapted version of MBT as treatment. They call their approach "mentalization-based child therapy" (p. 1). The target populations for mentalization-based treatment are: children with pervasive developmental problems, children with cumulative trauma, children with insecure attachment, and children unable to mentalize (p. 23). Attachment status is assessed using the Attachment Story Completion Test (ASCT, p. 33) and the draw-a-family test. The main focus of treatment is "promoting mentalization" (p. 47). Both children and parents participate in the program. The focus of fostering mentalization in parents is: "giving reality value to the inner experiences of parents with their child, learning to observe and read the child's inner world, working in the here and now, and repairing misattunement" (p. 69). The treatment approach for children focuses on three broad areas in the overall progression of treatment: attention regulation,

Chapter 3: Training Attention and Related Skills in Children

then affect regulation, and then mentalizaton training. Attention regulation training entails helping the child become aware of and describe: physical states; mental states; threat feelings; and animosity. The child is taught to become more aware of the conditions that provide safety in relationship and inter-subjectivity in interaction. The child is also taught to become aware of the conditions that provide for intentional behavior, such as being aware of the intention associated with nonverbal behaviors, visual orientation, and gestures. Affect regulation training entails setting boundaries in play; introducing fantasy and pretend mode into play; giving value to the reality of emotional states; and helping the child reflect on and develop second-order representations for affective states.

Upon the foundation of attention and affect regulation mentalization training completes the treatment. The interventions include: discussing the thoughts and feelings of attachment figures, and of the child; reflecting on the mental contents of the child, such as while the child is talking or during pretend play or making connections between antecedent states and behaviors or between different states of mind in the child; and bringing into the child's awareness the mental processes associated with interactions with others and the therapist.

Many of these treatment approaches offer parallel mentalization training for parents and children. These MBT programs adaptive for children include: emphasis on the therapeutic stance that fosters mentalization, facilitating a range of mentalization-oriented interventions in children, and fostering reflective capacity in parents (Lindquist, 2013).

TRAINING WORKING MEMORY

Considerable work has been done on developing programs for training working memory in children. There are three main approaches: 1. training multiple dimensions of working memory (WM) with a range of tests; 2: training using a single task of WM to expand WM span; and 3. strategy training. The most widely used approach to training WM isnchildren has been through the development of the CogMed computer-driven training system by Klingberg and his associates. CogMed includes 8 different approaches to train verbal and visuo-spatial WM, such as backward digit span training, training in tracking of visual objects, memory of location of visual-spatial events, listening recall (Alloway, 2007).

Klingberg et al. (2005) used the CogMed training system with 7- to 12-year-old children who showed deficits in executive function and WM associated with their ADHD. As Klingberg et al. say, the WM training resulted in "significant treatment effect both post-intervention and at follow-up. In addition, there were significant effects for secondary outcome tasks measuring verbal WM, response inhibition, and complex reasoning.... This study shows that WM can be improved by training in children with ADHD" (p. 177). In a study on the neuroscience of WM training Olesen, Westerberg and Klingberg (2003) found increased prefrontal and parietal activity after CogMed WM training. In a replication of this finding they also found that the main changes in neuro-circuitry were associated with the span board, visuo-spatial, and Stroop training tests (Westerberg & Klingberg, 2007, p. 186). They add, "practice of WM tasks over several weeks induces a gradual improvement in performance.... generalized to a non-practiced visuo-spatial WM task and a non-practiced reasoning task" (p. 190). In a replication study Klingberg (2010) found that significant changes in brain activity occurred in the frontal and parietal cortices and in the basal ganglia as a result of the CogMed training. Some of the positive effects went beyond the specific tasks of the CogMed training system. Klingberg says, "WM training can induce improvements in performance in non-trained tasks that rely on WM and control of attention" (p. 322).

Thorell et al. (2009) used the CogMed system of WM training for preschool 4 to 5 year old children in Sweden. They conclude, "WM training in children was effective even among preschool children, insofar as it has significant effects on non-trained WM tasks within both the spatial and the visual domains, as well as significant transfer effects on laboratory measures of attention" (p. 111). Holmes et al. (2009) offered WM training to 8- to 11-year-olds with ADHD. The WM training was for 20 days. They conclude "training led to substantial gains in all components of WM across untrained tasks. Training gains associated with central executive WM persisted over a 6-month period gains in verbal and visuo-spatial WM were maintained over 6 months" (p. 833). Beck et al. (2010) used the CogMed WM training system with 7- to 17-year-olds with ADHD. Training consisted of a 5-week intensive WM training. They found, "Parent ratings of changes indicated that participants improved on inattention, overall number of ADHD symptoms, initiation, planning/organization, and working memory…Working memory training appears promising as an intervention in improving executive functioning and ADHD symptoms" (p. 825). After 25 sessions of both verbal and visuo-spatial WM training conducted in home, "About one fourth to one half of the sample showed clinical significant changes on the measures of executive functioning and ADHD symptoms" (p. 834).

Dunning, Holmes and Gathercole (2013) selected children with low working memory for CogMed WM training. The children averaged around 8.5-years old. They were given 45 minutes/day CogMed training over 20-25 training sessions. They conclude, "WM training significantly boosted performance on untrained WM tasks in children with low WM. This enhancement was substantial in magnitude and was partially sustained for 12 months [p. 5]…[with] greatest improvements on complex span measures strongly associated with academic achievement in literacy and mathematics" (p. 9). Holmes and Gathercole (2014) conducted two field trials on 8- to 9-year-olds and 9- to 11-year-olds using 20-25, 45-minute CogMed training sessions. They reported, "improvements on the training activities were equivalent to those observed in the research trials" (p. 447)… training gains transfer improvements in National Curriculum assessments in English and math" (p. 448). [There was] "significantly greater progress at school across the academic year in math and English" (p. 440). Holmes, Gathercole, and Dunning (2009) see the training effect as a result of the intensity of training across all-important areas of WM. They say, "Adaptive training that taxed working memory to its limits was associated with substantial and sustained gains in working memory, with age-appropriate levels achieved by the majority of children. Mathematical ability also improved significantly 6 months following adaptive training" (p. F1). In Sweden Dahlin (2010) used a derivative of the CogMed system over 20-25 days of 30-40 minutes training/day. There were, "Positive effects on reading comprehension. The overall treatment effect size was quite substantial (0. 91).

Some of the evidence has been negative. For example, Elliott, Gathercole et al. (2010) identified primary school children between the ages of 4-5 and 8-9-years-old having WM problems. Using an AWMA computer WM training program, which included mixed verbal and visuo-spatial tasks, after a year "there was no evidence that either of the intervention programs had resulted in greater WM or academic performance" (p. 227).

Waas, Scerif and Johnson (2012) found that cognitive training with the CogMed system was "especially more effective, the earlier the training is applied" (p. 360). They add, however, "substantially altering cognition is hard...studies targeting younger participants are more likely to transfer training effects" (p. 380).

A second approach to training WM is to use a single task. The most widely used task has been the n-back WM task, designed specifically to increase the span of WM. In a neuro-circuitry study of the n-back task Takeuchi et al. (2010) found that training in WM n-back task was associated with increased white matter connectivity to intraparietal sulcus and anterior corpus callosum. Verhaegen et al. (2004) trained WM with 10, 1-hour sessions on n-back task. After 10 weeks WM span increased from 1 to 4. They say, "Our data suggest that the focus of attention can be expanded [from one] to hold four items with practice" (p. 1134). When examining neuro-circuitry changes they discovered that the smaller WM span was associated with activation of the ventrolateral PFC and the larger WM span was associated with activation of the dorsolateral PFC (p. 1335). Redick et al. (2013) offered 20 sessions of dual n-back task, and also used a placebo control group who received no practice. They found that while subjects in the training group but not the control group showed improvements with practice on both the n-back and visual search tasks, (p. 372) there was no transfer of learning to the application of fluid intelligence in daily life. They conclude, "Despite improvements on both the dual n-back and visual search tasks with practice, and de-

Chapter 3: Training Attention and Related Skills in Children

spite a high level of statistical power, there was no positive transfer to any of the cognitive ability tests" (p. 359).

There is one study that claims that mindfulness training increased WM. Jha et al. (2010) trained adults in mindfulness to see how it would affect WM. They state, "the current study suggests that WM may be bolstered by MT [mindfulness training] practice" (p. 62). Little is known about the effects of mindfulness on WM and more work needs to be done along these lines.

An important question is the extent to which WM training actually contributes to how we apply our intelligence in everyday life—what is called *fluid intelligence*. Jaeggi et al. (2008) define fluid intelligence as "the ability to reason and solve new problems independently of previously acquired knowledge." The critical question of WM training is to "transfer from training on a demanding working memory task to measures of Gf [fluid intelligence]" (p. 6829). In their experiment the findings were significant. Four training groups trained with the n-back task to expand WM span. They found an "impressive learning curve in all four experiments" (p. 6831). They note that WM generalized from performance on the various WM tasks to a quite different area, namely fluid intelligence (p. 6832). Jaeggi et al. (2010) replicated the original study using two different training groups. They found "both training groups improved more on Gf [fluid intelligence] than controls, thereby replicating and extending our prior results" (p. 625). Jaeggi et al add, "WM training is important to the field of intelligence because it shows that training can improve fluid intelligence" (p. 6790). Jaeggi et al. (2011) offered cognitive training on the n-back task to 8- and 9-year-old elementary and middle school children. They found that "only children who considerably improved on the training task showed a performance increase on untrained fluid intelligence tasks…[and the gains were] intact 3 months later" (p. 10081). They found, "Our findings show that transfer to Gf [fluid intelligence] is critically dependent on the amount of participants' improvement on the WM task" (p. 10083). Sternberg (2008) also showed that fluid intelligence is trainable. They say, there are "dosage effects, with more training leading to greater gains" (p. 6791).

A number of additional studies have investigated the transfer of WM training effects to academic performance. St.Clair-Thmopson and Gathercole (2006) offered WM training to 11- and 12-year-olds using a variety of executive function tests—shifting, updating, inhibition, and WM. They found that "WM was closely related to mathematics achievement... inhibition [skills were] related to general academic achievement" (p. 755).

However, most of the studies investigating if WM training can be generalized to academic achievement have yielded negative results (Chein & Morrison, 2010; Dahlin, et al. 2008; Holmes, Gathercole & Dunning, 2009; Thorell et al., 2009). Likewise, Chooi and Thompson (2012) after 8 or 20 days of dual n-back training to expand WM span, found "no significant changes in fluid intelligence and WM" (p. 531).

A third approach to training WM is strategy training. Turley-Ames and Whitfield (2003) used strategy training for WM. Half the subjects received specific strategy training and half did not. They found that WM span increased using rehearsal strategies, as compared to control group that used no strategies. They also found that rehearsal was more effective than other strategies, like imagery, or semantic strategies. Subjects who began the training with low WM span benefitted the most from rehearsal strategies, as compared to subjects with high WM spans who did not benefit as much (p. 466). Other approaches have used encoding strategies (Carretti et al., 2007), articulatory rehearsal (Ford et al., 1984), and chunking (St. Clair-Thomson et al., 2010).

In their review of the research on WM training Morrison and Chein (2011) say "the results from individual studies encourage optimism regarding working memory training as a tool for general cognitive enhancement" (p. 46). They describe "two distinct approaches—strategy training and core training.... core WM training studies seem to produce more far-reaching transfer effects... The idea is that training can effectively expand this central workspace of the mind" (p. 46). With respect to strategy training they say, "Studies of strategy training strongly support the claim that the amount of information remembered on measures of WM can be increased by teaching strategies such as rehearsing out loud... or telling a story to make stimuli salient" (p. 48). With respect

Chapter 3: Training Attention and Related Skills in Children

to the core training approach they say, "core training paradigms are commonly designed to: 1. limit the use of domain-specific strategies, 2. minimize automatization, 3. include task/stimuli that span multiple modalities, 4. require maintenance in the face of interferences, 5. enforce rapid WM encoding and retrieval demands, 6. adapt to varying levels of participants' varying level of proficiency, and 7. demand high cognitive workloads" (p. 49). The brain regions typically associate with WM training are the dorso-lateral PFC, posterior parietal cortex, and basal ganglia (p. 56). In conclusion they say, "Specifically, does WM training yield generalized cognitive enhancement? In the case of core training, our answer is a tentative, yes" (p. 57).

Melby-Lervag and Hulme (2013) conducted a meta-analysis of 23 WM training studies. They conclude, "the programs produced reliable short-term improvements in working memory skills. For verbal working memory, these near-transfer effects were not sustained at follow-up, whereas for visuo-spatial working memory, limited evidence suggested that such effects might be maintained.... [There was] no convincing evidence of the generalization of working memory training to other skills.... memory training programs appear to produce short-term, specific training effects" (p. 270). In another meta-analytic review on single approach training (Au et al., 2015) conducted a meta-analysis of 20 n-back studies. They found a "small but significant positive effect of n-back training on improving Gf [fluid intelligence]" (p. 366).

TRAINING EXECUTIVE FUNCTIONS

Moyes (2014) says, "Students with executive function deficits are often targeted for behavioral consequences when they do not follow through with expectations of the classroom teacher" (p. 19). These students show deficits in several EF, such as behavioral inhibition, meta-cognition, WM, organizational skills, attention. The question becomes can normal children and children with specific EF deficits improve executive functioning through EF training? A number of studies have addressed the question of whether or not it is possible to train a variety of executive functions (EF) in children. Diamond et al. (2007) developed the Tools of the Mind program for EF training. The program contains forty EF-promoting activities pertaining to core EF skills (p. 1387). The training was given to preschoolers as compared to other preschoolers who did their usual school curriculum. Outcome was assessed with a Dots task and Flanker task entailing inhibition of distractors. They found, "EFs can be improved in 4- to 5-year olds in regular public school classes with regular teachers" (p. 1388).

Rueda et al. (2005) offered 5 days of EF training to 4- and 6-year-olds because there is a "substantial development of executive attention between 3 and 7 years of age" (p. 14931). Training consisted of tracking objects, anticipating the location of movement in space, selecting a multi-attribute item from a field of distractors, a Stroop-like interference exercise, and an inhibition of a pre-potent response task. Outcomes were assessed using the Attention Network Test for children (Child ANT). Rueda et al. say, "We found evidence of a change in the executive attention network in the direction of reduced difficulty in resolving conflict. … The training effect overall was about half as large as the one due to the 2 years of [child] development" (p. 14935). Rueda, Checa, and Combita (2012) trained preschool children in executive attention. The training consisted of 10 sessions of EF training for a group of 5-year-olds utilizing computerized training of attention, and a delayed gratification task that required decisions about rewards given. They conclude, "the brain circuitry involved in executive attention is activated faster and more efficiently after training" (p. 203).

In Sweden Thorell et al. (2009) offered EF training to 4- and 5-year-old preschoolers trained in either visuo-spatial WM or motor inhibition using a go/no go task. Training lasted 15 minutes per day for 5 weeks as compared to a no-training control condition wherein control Ss played computer games for the same amount of time. Thorell et al. found, "Children trained on working memory improved significantly on trained tasks; they showed training effects on no-trained tests of spatial and verbal working memory, as well as transfer effects to attention. Children trained on inhibition showed a significant improvement over time [p.106]… we found that 15 minutes of visuo-spatial WM training per day for 5 weeks had significant effects on both trained and non-trained WM tasks within both the verbal and spatial domain" (p. 112).

Owen et al. (2010) developed a 6-week computerized training program in brain training that trained five different EF tasks: reasoning, planning, attention, WM, and problem-solving. This brain training program has been tested by over 11,000 adult subjects. The conclusion was largely negative for generalizing learning for this version of popular brain training. They say, "these results provide no evidence to support the widely held belief that the regular use of computerized brain trainers improves general cognitive functioning in healthy participants beyond those that are actually being trained" (p. 777). They add, "Although improvements were observed in every one of the cognitive tasks that were trained, no evidence was found for transfer effects to untrained tasks" (p. 775).

What Do We Want to Target for Training and Why?

As we have seen, although mindfulness training is very popular, it claims to do too much and it's skill-set doesn't readily map onto the priorities for training attention in children. In this generation of children, the priorities are to train the executive attentional system and the executive function system, and reduce mind-wandering. The executive attentional system specifically means training selective attention and enhancing resistance to distraction; extending the capacity to sustain attention while minimizing episodes of engagement/disengagement/re-engagement during a period of sustained attention; and training meta-cognitive monitoring. Furthermore, the main models for understanding peak performance or flow take heightened attentiveness, as mediated by ACC activation, as the foundation for states of excellence (Csikszentmihalyi, 1997; Orlick, 1980). For these reasons training the executive attentional system should be a main target for training. Therefore, we have selected and adapted the main method for concentration training of children and adults in the Indo-Tibetan meditation tradition because this approach offers very detailed instructions on detecting and resisting distraction, cutting off mind-wandering; sustaining the duration of concentration;

reducing dividing attention; and maintaining optimal alertness.

Training executive function includes working memory, organization and planning, and inhibition of response. In the Indo-Tibetan tradition children learn working memory through the discipline of memorizing longer and longer chants and prayers each day. Then, at the age of 9 to 10 years old certain children are selected for special classes in formal concentration meditation training. It is especially important to train WM in modern Western children. In previous generations children trained working memory through memorizing longer and longer poems, and by doing mathematical calculations in their heads. In this generation, children grow up using calculators instead of doing mental calculations, and are exposed to bits of information. Rather than training to memorize more and more, there are very few occasions to learn to expand working memory capacity, unless that gap is filled by formal WM training. Since there are a variety of effective available computerized training programs to train either WM specifically or EF in general, this book will not address these skills in much detail. However, we strongly recommend that schools introduce some form of computerized working memory (WM) or executive functioning (EF) training as a part of a regular curriculum.

Additionally, we strongly recommend some form of training children in mentalizing and reflective capacity. Examples of such programs have recently been developed specifically around classroom bullying and violence containment like the Peaceful Schools experiment (Twemlow et al., 2005) and the Thoughts in Mind program (Bak et al, 2015; Midgley & Vrouva, 2012). However, since meta-cognitive capacity is of vital importance in teaching problem-solving skills, we recommend that some sort of training program in meta-cognition be introduced into the school program. In our case, we have incorporated meta-cognitive training into the concentration training, in general with respect to identifying states-of-mind, and in particular, with respect to detecting mind-wandering.

Furthermore, there are certain groups of children at risk who will require special training. First, it is advisable to consider a program of executive attention training for children with ADHD. In this case, the methods can be adapted both for developmental age and for condition (e.g. offering audio-taped guided concentration training for ADHD children, so that they are constantly reminded from the outside how to keep the focus). Second, children with insecure attachment, especially disorganized attachment, are likely to have impaired meta-cognitive monitoring skills and poor mentalizing capacity (see Brown et al. 2016). The question is whether or not short, effective training programs can be introduced into the school system designed to enhance mentalization and meta-cognitive capacity.

In the next chapters we will discuss these training approach in greater detail. The main section of the book will introduce a program for training the executive attention system in children and adolescents of four age groups: early preoperational 4 to 6-year-olds; late preoperational 6 to 8-year-olds; concrete operational 8 to 12-year-olds; and adolescents beginning the stage of formal operational intelligence. The next chapter will address how we have adapted the training presentation for each of these developmental age-groups.

In summary, we recommend school-based training in:

- Selective and sustained concentration.
- Meta-cognitive awareness of states-of-mind in general, and detecting mind-wandering, and being aware of problem-solving strategies in particular.
- Computer-based training of working memory (WM) and executive function (EF).

This combination of skills will best result in: performance excellence; improved academic performance; greater fluid intelligence; increased detection of and reduction of mind-wandering; reduced multi-tasking and divided attention; and enhanced emotion-regulation, self-control, and resilience in the classroom.

Chapter 4

Training Concentration in Adults
by Daniel P. Brown, Ph.D.

THE BASIC SKILLS OF CONCENTRATION

There are two great Eastern systems for training concentration. Patanjali's *Yoga Sutras* (Mishra, 1973) were written somewhere between 650-850 A.D. Asanga's *Nine Stages of Staying* (Tib. *sems gnas dgu*) was written in 506 A.D. According to the title, there are nine stages pertaining to the degree of staying concentrated on the object of concentration. The *Nine Stages* constitutes one of the oldest and most comprehensive systems for concentration within Buddhism. The complete text was "downloaded" as a series of visions from the future Buddha, Maitreya, to the meditator Asanga while deep in meditation. The *Nine Stages* has served as the main form of practice of concentration meditation for all schools of Indo-Tibetan Mahayana meditators for over 1500 years. Thousands of meditators have used it as standard concentration training. Figure 1 is a graphic depiction of this path of the nine stages. From the graphic, it can be readily seen why these stages of concentration are called "the elephant path." For a classic account of the stages of concentration the reader is refereed to *Calm Abiding and Special Insight Meditation* (Lodro, 1998). What follows is not a traditional Tibetan description of the stages but a Western account derived from one of the authors (DB) teaching concentration for 46 years in the West.

The starting point for training concentration is the ordinary wandering mind. The ordinary mind is likened to be like a wild elephant that is stampeding, i.e., incessantly chasing after thought and sensory experience. The main problem of the ordinary mind, in the meditation tradition, is called "chasing after mode" (*rjes su 'brang ba*). In the graphic, Figure 1 the meditator is patiently following after the wild elephant with two tools. One hand holds a rope to tie the ordinary mind onto a concentration object. This is called the rope of concentration. Whenever the wild elephant wanders off, it feels the pull of the rope, and is reminded that it is tied to the concentration object. Likewise, whenever the mind wanders off it is pulled back to the concentration object by the rope that holds the mind on the concentration object. Every time the mind wanders off it feels the pull of the concentration rope back to the concentration object. After awhile the mind learns to stay on the concentration object for longer and longer duration without wandering off. The other hand holds an elephant prod, which symbolizes meta-cognitive awareness. The meditator repeatedly prods himself with his meta-cognitive intelligence in order to detect mind wandering, to stay on task, and to assess meditation strategies so as to self-correct unproductive habits of concentration.

There are three main tools used in concentration: 1. directing the mind to the concentration object; 2. engaging the concentration object more intensely; and 3. applying meta-cognitive awareness to detect distraction and stay on task. In this sense, beginning concentration is much like learning to drive a car for the first time. Once turning on the ignition and stepping on the accelerator, the first task is to learn to use the steering wheel to keep the car on the road. By repeatedly adjusting the steering wheel the car stays on the road. Likewise, by repeatedly directing the mind to the concentration object, the mind stays on the concentration object for longer and longer duration. It is a good idea to view this task in terms of movement: either there is the intentional movement of steering the mind back to the concentration object, or there is the spontaneous movement of the mind chasing after some distraction, such as thought or sense experience.

Second, once directing the mind toward the concentration object the meditator increases the effort to notice all of details of the concentration object. This skill is called "intensifying" (*sgrims pa*). Intensifying entails more close engagement of the concentration object. Intensifying utilizes more effort, but is mainly defined in terms of staying more closely engaged with the details of the concentration object, or becoming more intimate with the concentration object. Using our car analogy intensifying is like learning to use the accelerator of a car. By giving the car more fuel the car stays closer to the road. Likewise, when intensifying correctly, all of subtle details of the concentration object ordinarily unnoticed come into focus and the mind stays much more closely engaged with the concentration object.

One of the authors (DB) used to take his boys to a dude ranch in Idaho. When his boys were inexperienced as riders, the pack-horses would frequently wander off the trail to eat grass and bushes. At some point the boys learned to hold the reigns tighter, so as not to give the horse too much free play with the reigns. Then, the horse stopped wandering off the trail. Similarly, intensifying is like holding the reigns of the mind tighter so that the mind no longer has the free play to chase after distracting thought or sensory experiences, so as to stay on the path of concentration.

In Kurasawa's classic film *The Seven Samurai* a village of farmers in the middle ages of Japan hear a rumor that there is a band of robbers who swoop into the villages around the time of the rice harvest, plunder the village, and steal harvest. The farmers ask a group of seven samurai to help them defend their village. After building a defensive perimeter and training the farmers in self-defense, each day and night a group of farmers and samurai are on watch. After many days pass the head samurai one day turns to the other farmers on watch with him and says, "Tonight will be the night of the invasion." Do you think the farmers watched the same way that night? Whatever they did differently is an example of intensifying. Intensifying is sometimes described as a kind of mental vigilance so that the thief of thought never steals away concentration. Intensifying is the key to rapid and deep concentration.

Third, returning to the driving metaphor, a third important factor in learning to drive is the level of meta-cognitive awareness brought to the task. Drivers with low meta-cognition repeatedly make the same mistakes and rarely self-correct them because they lack meta-cognitive awareness of the ineffective strategies they are using. In contrast, drivers with high meta-cognitive awareness readily become aware of the strategies they employ during the novel task of driving, and when these strategies are ineffective, they make an adjustment until they find a strategy that works. Likewise, the best meditators readily monitor the quality of their meditation, make adjustments, and are constantly improving the quality of their meditation. However, meditators that lack meta-cognitive intelligence rarely reflect on the quality of meditation, and rarely identify habitual bad habits during meditation. There is a *sufi* tale that says, "A log sits very quietly and still on a wood pile for many years, but never realizes god, so don't sit like a log, sit intelligently." Brefczyski-Lewis et al. (2007) found that the main difference between beginning and advanced concentration meditators was whether the meditator activated the right dorsolateral-prefrontal cortex, the meta-cognitive neuro-circuitry of the brain. The difference between beginning and advanced meditators had little to do with number of years meditating, but mainly to do with whether meta-cognition was utilized as a skill, as a way to self-correct and improve concentration strategies.

In Woody Allen's film *Annie Hall* someone at a party calls the emergency 911 number because he forgot his secret TM mantra. There is no secret mantra, except for marketing hype. In fact, in the Asanga tradition of concentration the type of meditation object selected is far less important than the quality of staying on that concentration object. However, some meditation objects are better suited for certain types of individuals. The best recommendation for Westerners, who are frequently over-identified with thought, is to use a body-based, sensory-based objects like the felt sense of the breath or the felt sense of the body. Maintaining such a focus on a body-based object discourages over-identification with thought. In our approach we use what is referred to as the three-point object of concentration: focus on the felt sense of the arising breath, then the felt sense of the falling breath, and then the felt sense of the body as a whole between the full cycle of the breath. Concentration on the body in the intervals between the cycle of breaths prevents the meditator from resuming chasing after thought and mind-wandering while waiting for the next arising breath.

The name of Asanga's text is called *The Nine Stages of the Mind Staying*. The title clearly shows that the degree and quality of staying on the concentration object is most important, not the type or characteristics of the concentration object. Asanga's teacher, Maitreya wrote five great sutras in Mahayana Buddhism. All five sutras emphasize the same point: don't confuse experiences for the task at hand. For example, some meditation traditions say that you should concentrate on the breath at the tip of the nostrils. Others say follow the breath down the air passages as far as possible. Others say focus on the breath deep in the belly. The problem with these instructions is that once a particular location is fixed upon, the meditator is likely to miss concentrating on the breath when it is located elsewhere. However, if the task at hand is to track the breath, wherever it seems to be located, then it becomes easier to continuously stay on the breath irrespective of location. Likewise, some think that the breath should be soft, rough, warm, cool, etc. However, such use of categories restricts the meditator into looking for certain qualities and dismissing all the changes in the quality of the breath that don't fit into the selected categories. However, if the task at hand is to stay continuously irrespective of the quality of the breath, it becomes easier to track the breath continuously irrespective of all the changes in the quality of the breath. The title clearly defines the task at hand, namely staying concentrated irrespective of the location or characteristics of the breath.

Another basic tool of meditation is the body posture. Benson (1975) conceptualized meditation as a kind of "relaxation response." Since that time it has been customary to view meditation as a kind of relaxation therapy. However, that view is essentially inaccurate. Consider the relaxation posture at the end of a yoga class. What happens to the mind? The mind wanders and you get sleepy. In other words, too much relaxation activates mind-wandering mode and makes the task of concentration training more difficult. Around the same time that Benson coined the relaxation response, Akishige (1970) conducted a study of muscle activation during adopting a meditation posture in beginning and advanced Zen monks. He found that, from the perspective of the striate musculature, meditation is not at all relaxing, but more accurately is seen as the even output and distribution of muscle work. It takes a good deal of muscle work from large muscles in the body, like the lattisimus dorsi, erectus spinae, and psoas, to hold the upper trunk throughout concentration. This muscle work has two beneficial effects: it maintains a certain level of alertness, and is significantly correlated with less rather than more mind-wandering. When we say that the body posture is the foundation for training concentration this means that it is easier to train concentration while maintaining a good body posture because the mind stays more alert and the mind wanders less.

The term for concentration training in Tibet is *zhi gnas*. *Zhi ba* means "calm," and refers to the progressive calming of the extraneous background noise of thought. *Gnas pa* means "staying" and refers to staying for longer and longer duration on the concentration object. The mind stays; the background noise becomes calm. The term literally means, "staying-calming meditation," in that the mind stays concentrated on the concentration object and the background noise becomes calm.

THE STAGES OF CONCENTRATION TRAINING

There are nine stages for concentration training in the Asanga system, as depicted in the graphic, Figure 1. The elephant path is depicted as a winding path. There are four straight paths that depict when the meditation goes well. These four are: the path of reflection, the path of mindfulness, the path of meta-cognitive awareness, and the path of enthusiastic perseverance. Each straight path ends in a curved path, which symbolizes a place where the meditator encounters some new difficulty.

The first stage is defined in terms of the mind staying less than more of the session on the concentration object. A good marker of progress is the percentage of the meditation session the meditator stays on the concentration object, as compared to chasing after distraction. At this first stage the meditator largely learns to use the skill of directing the mind like a steering wheel turning repeatedly back to the concentration object. Over time the meditator learns to stay for longer and longer duration on the concentration object.

Chapter 4: Training Concentration in Adults

Michael Forte did one of the first doctoral dissertations in the country on meditation in 1979 (Forte, 1979). He had novice meditators focus on a candle flame for 20 minutes. Each subject had a mercury switch on their baby finger. They were instructed to twitch the baby finger whenever a distraction occurred. The computer was able to analyze the pattern of distraction over time as the meditators learned concentration. Forte noted three phases over time: 1. Frequent and effortful re-direction of the mind back to the concentration object when distracted; 2. The duration of staying on the concentration object got longer, and also the duration of becoming lost in mind-wandering got longer; and 3. Mind-wandering more or less ceased and the meditator stayed continuously on the object. In teaching concentration training for over 40 years we have observed these same patterns in most of the beginning meditators.

The second stage is defined in terms of the mind staying more than less on the meditation object, i.e., over 50% of the concentration session. The difference between stage 1 and 2 is the skillful application of intensifying. On the graphic, Figure 1, the transition between the first and second stage is depicted by a curve and the path is covered with flames. The flames symbolize intensifying. Through intensifying the mind remains so busily engaged in tracking the fine details of the concentration object so closely that there is little occasion to chase after distractions. Intensifying rapidly deepens the duration of staying on the concentration object. The goal of the second stage is to stay on the concentration object somewhere between 80-100% of the concentration session. In other words, the goal is continuous staying over time. As concentration becomes easier, the meditator is on the first straight path of reflection. The task of the meditator is to have his or her meditation experiences exactly reflect what was pointed out, reflecting these experiences like in a mirror.

After staying on the concentration object relatively continuously and after there seems to be a drop in the background noise of thought, the meditator goes through a period wherein there seems to be a lot more background noise. There is a danger at this point of mistakenly concluding that concentration is deteriorating. The meditator is actually sharpening his or her meta-cognitive awareness to become aware of the kind of continuous subtle engagement in background thought. At this point the meditator comes to realize the problem of "partial staying" (*gnas cha*). Partial staying occurs when the meditator divides attention between the concentration object and background noise of ongoing thought. It is likely, for example, that the meditator has apportioned 20% of his or her attention on the concentration object and 80% on the background noise. However, since the meditator is likely to "stay" on a piece of each rising and each falling breath, the meditator is likely to develop a mistaken view that he or she is staying on each cycle of the breath as a concentration object, which is not incorrect. However, in so far as the meditator is apportioning attention between the concentration and back ground noise of thought, concentration will not develop any further until the meditator stops dividing his or her attention and develops complete, as compared to partial staying. There is a risk that the meditator fails to bring meta-cognitive awareness to recognize the problem of partial staying, and can remain at this level of concentration with this bad habit for years. That is why the graphic depicts another curve between the second and third stage, because partial staying is difficult to overcome without the right instructions.

The new achievement of the third stage is the development of both *continuous* staying over time, and *complete* staying at any given point in time, cross-sectionally. The best method for reducing the habit of partial staying and apportioning attention between the concentration object and the background noise is to break the meditation object into more and more points to concentrate on. In this way the meditator is so busily engaged in keeping track of all the points that there is little occasion to apportion attention to the background noise. For example, if the meditator was concentrating as the focus on the three point object—rising breath, falling breath, and felt sense of the body between the full cycle of breaths—the meditator now focuses on the seven point object, which is the same object but with more points to focus on: the moment of arising, full duration, and end-point of the rising breath, the moment of arising, full duration, and end-point of the falling breath, and the felt sense of the body after the falling breath. In keeping track of all the seven points there is little occasion to sustain engagement with the background noise of thought. The best result is that the meditator accomplishes not only continuous staying over time but complete staying at any given point in time, and there is a substantial drop in the background noise of thought. Once the meditator has mastered the problem of partial staying he or she has mastered the third stage of staying—continuous staying over time and complete staying at any given time. At this stage the meditator seldom loses track of the concentration object, and the meditator now enters the second straight path, the path of mindfulness, wherein he or she rarely loses track of the concentration object.

Nevertheless, at this stage the meditator still struggles with episodes of drowsiness and/or agitation. Drowsiness and agitation are two sides of the same coin. They both represent the extremes of arousal level that cause the rope of concentration to slip from the concentration object. Consider the analogy of sailing. After returning from sailing on a very windy day it becomes difficult to secure the rope onto the cleat on the dock because the boat is bouncing around too much. Likewise, when the arousal level is too high the mind becomes agitated and bounces around, and the rope won't stay tied. When there is no wind it is possible to tie the rope too loosely, so that even the smallest current pulls the rope from the cleat. Likewise, when the arousal level is too low, the mind becomes drowsy, and the rope of concentration keeps slipping off the concentration object.

At stage 4, the skilled meditator learns to master the episodes of drowsiness and agitation so that ongoing concentration is characterized by balanced, sustainable energy. There are two approaches to develop balanced energy in concentration—prevention and remedies using during actual meditation. Prevention includes: maintaining good sleep hygiene, eating in moderation prior to meditation, and adopting a good posture during concentration training, especially keeping the upper trunk upright. The remedies used during actual concentration training vary according to the magnitude of the drowsiness and agitation. If the drowsiness is very subtle, just being meta-cognitively aware of it will sometimes cause it to disappear. If the drowsiness is extreme, like a state of possession, it is best to adjust the posture, and try to continue the meditation standing up. If the intensity of the drowsiness or agitation is in the mid-range, the meditator uses the visualization of the vast expanse or the close, contracted space, respectively. For example, if while concentrating on the three-point object—rising breath, falling breath, and felt sense of the body as a whole between the cycle of breaths—the meditator becomes drowsy, in the foreground the meditator maintains the focus on the three-point object, but imagines that this event—rising, falling, body posture—is occurring against the backdrop of an infinite expanse of space filled with light. The meditator holds the backdrop of the expanse of space filled with light simultaneous to concentration on the three-point object until the energy level becomes elevated and the drowsiness completely subsides. Then, the meditator stops visualizing the vast expanse, focuses fully on the three-point object, and continues the concentration meditation free of drowsiness. The beauty of the vast expanse visualization is that you never have to leave the concentration object to eliminate the drowsiness. Conversely, if the meditator becomes agitated, in the foreground the meditator maintains the focus on the three-point object, but imagines that this event—rising, falling, body posture—is occurring against the backdrop of close, contracted, dark, still space, much like meditating in a cave, and holds the backdrop of the close contracted space simultaneous to concentrating on the three-point object until the energy level becomes clam and still, and the agitation completely subsides. Then, the meditator stops visualizing the close, contracted space, focuses fully on the three-point object, and continues the meditation free of agitation. The meditator continues like this until drowsiness and agitation no longer occur, and he or she has attained a state of balanced energy. This is mastery at the fourth stage.

In the older literature on concentration training the stages of concentration were divided into two main stages—concentration with support and concentration without support. These terms refer to the perception of the concentration object. At first the concentration objects appears solid, and therefore, serves as a support to concentrate upon. However, at a more advanced level of concentration the concentration object will appear much less solid, like moving energy in space, and thereby serves less support as a concentration object. Therefore, it becomes more difficult to maintain concentration upon a concentration object that is forever changing. In the later literature of Mahayana Buddhism this shift was referred to as the shift from the coarse to the subtle level of mind. The coarse level of mind refers to elaborated mental content—specific thoughts, emotions, sights, sounds, etc. The subtle level of mind refers to a level of mind prior to the elaboration of specific content, wherein unfolding events remain in an unelaborated state, called "mind-moments."'Mind-moments are very fleeting movements, or bursts of energy, or light that occur prior to their being constructed or elaborated into specific mental content. As one *sutra* says, you experience a hundred thousand mind-moments in the blink of an eye. At some point the concentration object is no longer solid and the meditator perceives the concentration object as an entire world of dynamic energy and momentary vibrancy. Nevertheless, there is a residual imprint of the original concentration object, so it becomes possible to deepen concentration on the imprint, even though the concentration object is much less solid and has become much less of a support to concentration. In Asanga's system the first four stages pertain to concentration with support, and the last five stages pertain to concentration without support.

There are several conditions, which must be met for the meditator to shift concentration from the coarse to the subtle level of mind. First, the meditator must be free of subtle dullness. Subtle dullness occurs when the meditator maintains continuous and complete staying on the concentration object but the concentration object becomes increasingly vague and the mind apprehending the concentration object loses brightness. Imagine that concentration is like a flashlight. To train concentration the meditator repeatedly directs the flashlight and engages the concentration object very closely. However, the cumulative effect of using the flashlight is that the batteries wear down. Similarly, the cumulative effect of repeated concentration is that the mind stays continuously and completely on the concentration object, but also that the object becomes vague and the mind becomes dull. Because the batteries wear down slowly there is no point of contrast to know that the light has become weak. Similarly, subtle dullness is in part defined by a lack of meta-cognitive awareness: the meditator thinks he or she is in a deeply concentrated state, which is not incorrect in terms of degree of staying, but lacks meta-cognitive awareness that the state has become quite dull. Subtle dullness is also a still, comfortable state, so there is a risk of becoming attached to the state. Subtle dullness is depicted by a rabbit sitting on the back of the elephant in the graphic in Figure 1. This symbolizes how the thick-skinned elephant is not likely to recognize the small rabbit on its back. Moreover, the rabbit is warm and fuzzy. This symbolizes how subtle dullness can be a warm fuzzy still state that becomes an attachment in itself.

Repeated intensifying is a cause of subtle dullness. The main cause, however, is extreme sensory and social isolation, so that subtle dullness becomes a major problem for the cave and hermitage yogis who spend years in retreat. Then it is called the sinking mind, because the meditator sinks into a quiet stuporous state, yet maintains uninterrupted staying on the concentration object. The sinking mind to an advanced meditator is comparable to a major league baseball player in a batting slump. Therefore, although going on long silent retreats may seem the ideal for meditation, in actuality, the extremes of sensory and social isolation make the problem of subtle dullness all the more problematic in long silent retreats.

The main problem regarding subtle dullness is that the meditator has lost meta-cognitive awareness of the dullness. It has to occur to the meditator that he or she is in a dull state. In Zen, subtle dullness is remedied by hitting the meditator sharply on the shoulders with a stick. The sudden crack of the stick is likely to shift the meditator into a state of increased alertness. In the pointing out relational style, the teacher suddenly says to the meditator during meditation, "Wake up! Guard against subtle dullness. Brighten the mind." The sudden reminder will cause some surprise, the meditator will shift to a level of much greater alertness, the dullness will dissipate, and the meditator will activate his or her meta-cognitive awareness, and will have come to see clearly how

Chapter 4: Training Concentration in Adults

much dullness had crept into the concentration.

The second condition that must be met to shift from coarse to subtle level of mind is to add much greater intensifying. Remember that intensifying doesn't mean more effort but rather looking more closely into the concentration object. At this point the meditator needs to look so closely into the concentration object—the breath, the body—that what opens up is an entire world of dynamic energy and momentary vibrancy, and liveliness. In other words, the meditator must see beyond the seeming solidness of the breath and the body to see the dynamic energy of the mind-moments that make up the breath and the body. Imagine looking at a lit light bulb on the ceiling. At first glance the light seems constant. Now look more closely, and you will see all of the dancing energy around the bulb, and what at first seemed constant becomes a world of dancing energy. The meditator learns to see the concentration object—the breath, the body—in the same way as looking at the light bulb: at first as something seeming constant, and then as lively, dynamic energy. If the meditator has brightness of mind and through intensifying looks so closely into the concentration object, he or she will open up the subtle level of mind, and will continue concentration at the subtle level. This shift from concentration with support to concentration without support, or the shift from coarse to subtle level of mind, marks the 5th stage of the path of concentration. This is a huge shift, as depicted by the curve in the graphic between the 4th and 5th stage.

It is important that the meditator be aware that the rules of operation at the coarse and the subtle level of mind are opposite to each other, in certain respects. First, at the coarse level of mind it takes a large output to make a big effect. For example, it takes repeated intensifying for the mind to learn to stay continuously and completely on the concentration object. At the subtle level of mind, the opposite is true: the smaller the output, the bigger the effect. At the subtle level of mind very fine-tuned adjustments in the level of intensifying/easing up cause the biggest changes. This difference is analogous to launching a space capsule. It takes three large booster rockets to blast the space capsule beyond the gravitational field. Then, very small jets are needed to dock the capsule to a space station, and too much thrust will make the space capsule soar miles beyond the space station. Second, at the coarse level of mind, intensifying causes the mind to stay on the meditation object. At the subtle level of mind the opposite is true: easing up causes the mind to stay on the meditation object.

At stage 5 the concentration object—the breath, the felt sense of the body—becomes a field of dynamic energy and momentariness. During the transition between the coarse and subtle level of mind concentration is not yet stable. The experience tends to fluctuate between subtle, unelaborated mind-moments at times, and the elaboration of thought at other times. Over time the experience remains mostly in a stable, unelaborated state, wherein there is lots of energy and movement but very little content, except for very fleeting thoughts, mostly associated with keeping the concentration on track.

Once the subtle level of mind is both stable and continuous, the meditator eases up ever so slightly. By easing up just a little bit, the residual fleeting thought drops away, and the meditator discovers that it is no longer necessary to intensify for the mind to stay concentrated. In fact, the residual fleeting thought associated with keeping the meditation on track is not only unnecessary, it also causes a kind of subtle agitation of mind. At the 6th stage, subtle agitation drops away through the skill of easing up. However, a common mistake is to ease up too quickly or too much, and as a result thought elaboration will burst into the field of experience and the concentration will become scattered. If this happens, all that the meditator needs to do is to re-set the same level of intensifying. By looking much more closely and intensely the meditator will open up the subtle world of dynamic energy and momentary vibrancy once again. The meditator waits until concentration becomes stable at the subtle level, and then attempts easing up once again, this time very finely. If the magnitude of easing up is very slight, the residual fleeting thought elaboration will drop away. Because this level of practice requires making many fine-tuned adjustments of intensifying/easing this straight path on the graphic is called the path of meta-cognitive awareness.

If easing up is very slight another thing occurs. The concentration starts to continue by itself, automatically. Once getting a glimpse of automaticity, the meditator eases up again very slightly. If easing up is not too much, the concentration becomes even more automatic. If easing up is too much there will be a burst of thought elaboration, at which point the meditator must resume intensifying. By easing and waiting, then easing again, the meditator can establish a completely automatic concentration, wherein the concentration continues by itself. Using our car analogy, the meditator has found concentration cruise control, the 7th stage of concentration. This significant change is depicted by another curve in the graphic between stages 6 and 7. The last straight path is called the path of enthusiastic perseverance because the meditator discovers a new-found confidence about mastering concentration.

At this stage the concentration approximates evenness. Prior to this level the quality of concentration varies a good amount. At this stage most of that variability subsides and concentration approximates a steady state. This steady state is called "concentrative evenness" (Tib. *mnyam bzhag*; Skt. *samadhi*). The technical terms in both Tibetan and Sanskrit are best translated as "established or staying evenly."

The 8th stage of concentration is called one-pointedness, but the name doesn't quite capture the main experience. The main experience is an orderly flow. While approximating concentrative evenness the meditator makes finer and finer adjustments of intensifying/easing. If the adjustments made are very fine-tuned—no more than a subtle intention—the meditator will discover a connection between the level of intensifying/easing and the frequency of unfolding experience. By experimenting he or she will discover a range of experience wherein the unfolding energy and momentary vibrancy is distinctly orderly, like a flowing river. The great Tibetan yogi Milarepa once said, "at first it is like a snowball rolling down the Himalayas faster and faster, and then it is like the slow moving mouth of the Ganges River." This is a description of the *frequency* of unfolding. The aim is to discover the range of the most obvious orderly flow and stabilize automatic concentration at that level. However, at this stage of practice smaller output yields bigger results. If the adjustment is too big, it has a masking effect, and the meditator will fail to discover the interconnection between the adjustment of intensifying/easing and the frequency of unfolding experience. At the 8th stage the meditator discovers the orderly flow of one-pointed energy.

At this stage there is a tendency to automatically track the easy flow of orderly energy and to lose track of the original task, namely staying concentrated on the concentration object—the breath and the body. However, to make the correction at this stage, all that is required is the intention to concentrate on the concentration object, and the residual imprint of the breath, the body immediately appears among the energy and flow, so it is still possible to remain continuously and completely concentrated automatically on the concentration object. Finding the residual imprint of the concentration object is much like finding the deeper channel at the mouth of a great river, were the water spills out in all directions, and yet, by looking carefully it is still possible to locate the deeper channel amidst the spillage of water everywhere. Likewise, with nothing more than the intention of awareness, it becomes possible to maintain perfect concentration on the residual imprint of the original concentration object—the breath, the body.

When putting the intention on finding the deeper channel the meditator discovers something else about the nature of awareness. At the coarse level of mind it is common to confound three different conditions—thought elaboration, directed attention, and the lightning speed intention of awareness. In common everyday experience we think of these three conditions simply as thought. However, once thought elaboration stops through concentration training the meditator at some point begins to discover that he or she is operating not out of thought, but out of the intention of awareness. In Western psychology, a tachistoscope is an electronic board that can flash events in a viewing hood in thousandths of a second. At one point we used a T-scope to measure the speed of the mind in advanced meditators. Under standard luminance conditions, thought elaboration is slow—from 3,000 to 500 msec. Directed attention takes about 250 msec. However, the lightning speed of the intention of awareness is as fast as the T-scope will measure, say under 10 msec. Once thought elaboration relatively ceases, as a func-

Chapter 4: Training Concentration in Adults

tion of concentration training, the meditator learns to operate out of the intention of awareness. We call this shifting the "basis of operation" (*spyod yul*) out of thought mode to pure awareness mode. Consider the following example from Major League Baseball. A 90 mile/hour fastball takes 400 msec to reach the plate. That means that if a baseball player is thinking at the moment the ball arrives at the plate, he can't locate the ball. However, if he directs his attention (250 msec.) free of thought, he can locate the position of the ball. Even better, the baseball player can train himself to operate out of the lightning speed of the intention of awareness. Tony Gwynn hit for the second highest career batting average in the history of baseball. He trained himself by standing at the plate while the pitching machine threw in 150 tennis balls at 150 miles per hour, one after the other, even though no recorded bat speed, even for a great hitter, has reached hitting the ball at 150 miles/hour. He wasn't trying to hit the balls, but rather to train his high-speed awareness to locate the position of the ball. After training himself to make the lightning speed of awareness his basis of operation while at the plate, when the pitching machine after that threw 95 mile/hour fastballs, they appeared to be slow and he could match most fastballs with his remarkable bat speed. Likewise, at the 9th stage of concentration the meditator learns to make the lightning speed of the intention of awareness his or her basis of operation. He or she discovers that whatever awareness intends, the mind immediately does just that and only that, without any interference, and without any distraction by extraneous thought activity or reactivity. This newly acquired skill at the 9th stage is called making the mind "serviceable" (*las su rung*).

Thought and awareness share certain common features, the main difference being speed. The main common feature is directionality. You can think along certain lines or reason in a certain direction. Similarly, the lightning speed intention of awareness is like a directed laser beam that reaches its intended direction immediately. One of the authors (DB) teaches concentration training to superior, district, and family court judges. One time a judge nervously said, "I am so busy I have to write up my case findings while shaving and brushing my teeth. How will stopping thought elaboration help me?" I asked him to wait until the end of the training, I would provide him with an experiential answer to his concern. After most of the class reached the 9th stage, wherein there is no thought elaboration and wherein the meditator learns to operate out of the lightning speed of awareness, I said to the class, "Now, bring to mind a case that you have to write up your findings on and compose those findings in your mind. Come to see what it is like to direct thought with the intention of awareness, free of all extraneous thought elaboration." The class was stunned to see that thought elaboration could be directed so clearly by awareness, absent all extraneous thought distraction, and was amazed how easily the writing flowed. This is what it means to make the mind serviceable.

Neuroscientists have come to appreciate the neuroplasticity of the brain: if you repeatedly use certain neuro-circuits they increase in volume and change their structure; if you don't use certain neuro-circuits they lose volume and change structure. Thus, for example, those who train concentration and develop some skill show an increase in the overall volume of the anterior cingulate cortex (ACC), an increase in the white matter or connectivity to and from the ACC (Tang et al., 2010), and also an increase in the gray matter of the ACC (Holzel et al., 2011). Translated experientially, this means that once the brain neuro-circuitry for concentration develops, concentration becomes a stable skill that becomes applicable in all everyday tasks and is no longer limited to meditation sessions.

Chapter 4: Training Concentration in Adults

Figure 1: The Nine Stages of the Mind Staying; The Elephant Path

Part II

Concentration Meditation Training According to Developmental Age

Chapter 5

Adapting Training to the Developmental Age of the Child

by Daniel P. Brown, Ph.D.

As children develop they go through a set of distinct stages of development. In Chapter 1 of this book, we reviewed the research on the development of attentional systems. Piaget (1950) was the first to describe distinct stages of intellectual development in children: 1. Sensorimotor intelligence (ages 0-2); preoperational intelligence (ages 2-7); concrete operational intelligence (ages 7-11); and formal operational thinking (ages 11 +). Brown (1993) described distinct stages of emotional, self, and relational development. The stages of emotional development are: affect expression (at birth); affect experience (6-12 months); affect tolerance and development of a sense of self (12-24 months); affect verbalization (24-36 months); affect defense and the problem of affect recognition (36-48 months); affect orientation, the affective self-in-the-world (4-10 years); adolescent affect language (12-18); and adult affective development (18+). Kegan (1982) described the stages of self-development: the impulsive self; the imperial self, wherein peer relationships predominate; the interpersonal self, characterized by mutuality; the institutional self, exemplified by the adult in relation to work institutions; and the inter-individual self that adopts a wider perspective of inter-connectedness. Brown and Elliott (2016) describe two main stages in relational development: a stage wherein attachment representations develop (18-24 months); and a later stage where complex schemas and emotional ideas develop about relationships—what are called core conflict relational themes.

The implication of all this work on the stages of development is that any training must be adapted to the developmental age of the child. In this book we have introduced concentration to: 4- to 6-year-olds with early preoperational thinking; 7 to 9 year-olds representing late preoperational thinking; 9- to 12-year-olds representing concrete operational thinking; and adolescents representing formal operational thinking. We will discuss some of the main differences at each of these levels of development, and how to best adapt the concentration training to match the developmental age of the child.

THE MAIN CONSIDERATIONS OF EARLY PREOPERATIONAL DEVELOPMENT

It is possible to begin training pre-concentration in younger children ages 3-6, who are at the early stage of preoperational intelligence (Piaget, 1950). At this age-range attention span is quite limited. The young child is mainly operating out of the exogenous, rather than the endogenous attentional system, and is therefore very sensitized to noticing external stimulus-characteristics. Because of their short attention span, things like pop-up stories and the actions of puppets are useful learning tools. *Sesame Street* is based on this assumption of short attention span: by introducing short episodes, one-after-the other, in different modalities (people, puppets, words and numbers, etc.) it is possible to capture a child's attention for 25 minutes. Likewise, it is best to introduce short training sessions, using different modalities such as engagement with the teacher, working alone on some assigned imagination, sharing with the class, etc. It is advisable to involve the child of this age not only in engaged fantasy and imagination, but also get the child involved in his or her body, such as actually taking the posture of the elephant, or the sleeping lion. Late preoperational thinking is very much present-focused, and more perceptually- than mentally-based. Such children are better at developing rich, action-oriented imagined scenarios with open-eyes. Asking children of this age to close their eyes to concentrate usually is ineffective (Wall, 1991) and they can develop a pretend or fantasy scene in rich detail with open-eyes. Pretend play and imaginative pretense are well developed by this age range. Asking the child to imagine or pretend, action-oriented scenes and fantasies is especially easy for these children, provided the scenes are of short duration.

The child's orientation to the world is highly egocentric. Imitative behavior is also well developed by this age range. Therefore, framing interventions in terms of what film and sports heroes and superheroes might do in a similar situation, or what puppets might do, enhances the child's level of involvement. The child can learn from a "concentration superhero," one who has mastered paying careful and sustained attention, and through that has special powers in learning and earns the respect of peers.

THE MAIN CONSIDERATIONS OF LATE PREOPERATIONAL DEVELOPMENT

Attention has made the transition from exogenous to endogenous attention, but the 6- to 7-year-old does not yet have full executive control over attention. Attention span tends to be shorter and periods of seemingly sustained attention are best characterized by engagement/disengagement/and re-engagement. Therefore, it is advisable to keep training sessions short, and to keep switching the mode of engagement.

At this stage of development pretend play is well developed. Most of the discoveries and explorations about life occur through the medium of play. Fantasy development is highly evolved, and most fantasies are action-oriented and strongly emotionally-laden . Focus is more on the present than the future. In this sense it is advisable to frame the concentration training in terms of assignments to imagine along certain lines. Fantasy, pretend play, and imagination become the main medium of learning at this age. Imaginative involvement is especially strong at this age. At this level of development fantasy is best when it is action-oriented. At the late preoperational stage, the child greatly expands his or her awareness of and involvement with peers. Therefore encouraging the child to share experiences of concentration training with classmates is especially important at this age.

The Main Considerations of Concrete Operational Development

The development of concrete operational intelligence constitutes a huge shift from a focus on external perception to a focus on the developing internal world. This is the age when the child develops an interiorized view of emotions, and is able to see the context in which emotions occur (Brown, 1993). This is the age that the child develops a clear sense of "mind," and a large array of subtly nuanced emotional states. The sense of self is stronger and more developed. At this stage, inner experience is enhanced by closing the eyes in order to tune out external distractions.

At this stage the voluntary executive attentional system is much more developed than previously. The child has a greater attention span, and is more able to detect and resist distraction, and actively inhibit irrelevant stimuli than at an earlier age. This is the age where formal concentration training becomes possible. The duration of concentration can be longer than for younger children because of a greater capacity for sustained concentration.

Because the child at this age shows a greater skill in mental operations, the teacher can introduce the main tools of concentration—directing the mind, intensifying, and applying meta-cognitive awareness to detect distraction and mind-wandering—as abstractions, and the child should be capable of understanding these tools at a level of abstraction and mental representation. This is the age where the child understands metaphors (Gentner, 1988; Wall, 1991), so that it is possible to introduce metaphors into training concentration, like using a steering wheel, or unfolding experience like a flowing river. The metaphor of focusing the mind like a spotlight, and zooming in on the subtle details of the concentration object makes sense at this age. This is also the age where the child is capable of articulating and utilizing a range of attentional strategies, so it is advisable to introduce the concept of attentional strategies at this age. A main theme to emphasize is the capacity for voluntary control over attention at this age. Furthermore, the teacher can encourage the child to explore his or her internal experience less in

Chapter 5: Adapting Training to the Developmental Age of the Child

terms of action-oriented fantasies and imaginings, but more as a direct meta-cognitive observation of states-of-mind, and how concentration affects states-of-mind. Distinctions between how things appear or seem, and how they are in reality, get more clearly delineated. Cause and effect relationships at this age tend to be somewhat concrete, so it is advisable that the teacher introduce an exercise and encourage the child to immediately observe and describe its effect.

At this age meta-cognitive development greatly matures, and along with this comes the capacity to take perspective, have empathy, and hold different points of view. At this age the child is capable of understanding that remaining concentrated and engaging in mind-wandering can happen simultaneously (partial staying), and also understand the multi-tasking as a problem of divided attention between different states. Encouraging the child of this age to take various perspectives on the experience of concentration training is helpful. Also at this age a child can have simultaneous, even contradictory emotions about the same experience (Harter, 19).

This is also the age where the child develops a wider range of coping and problem-solving strategies. The teacher can encourage the child of this age to develop new strategies to better handle whatever problems occur during concentration training. Children at this age are better able to reason through their approach to concentration training.

In our interviews of children at Rahob Monastery in Tibet the author (MB) found that this age range (8-11) is approximately when selected children are sent to a special monastery for formal concentration training. In Tibet, as in Western culture alike, it is understood that the changes in intellectual development characteristic of this age, concrete operational thinking, is the prerequisite for formal concentration training.

The Elephant Path: Attention Development and Training in Children and Adolescents

Chapter 6

Introduction to the Program for Children ages 4 Through 12

by Michelle G. Bissanti, M.Ed.

The following is part of a program created, developed and taught by Michelle Bissanti for children ages 4-12. While the program incorporates Michelle's experience as an educator over the past 25 years, it also draws upon her study, practice and research encompassing a rich repertoire of yoga, meditation and compassion practices. This chapter will introduce key components of her program encompassing the principles of Body, Mind, and Heart across the ages. Her subsequent chapters will highlight the aspects that support concentration training through The Elephant Path practices at various developmental ages. The concentration meditation practices were drawn from and inspired by her study with Daniel P. Brown, Ph.D. and his extensive work developing Indo-Tibetan meditation techniques for Western students.

THE THREE-FOLD PRACTICES — BODY, MIND, HEART

As younger children begin to develop a bodily-based yoga practice, the practice of meditation naturally emerges from that. From a yoga and meditation practice the heart naturally opens. The overall program centers around three principles: Body, Mind, and Heart. The practice of yoga and meditation is an anchor, in the most fluid sense, allowing one to be in the world in their most authentic way. Yoga invites children to explore the union of body and mind; while yoga addresses the body and physical postures, meditation invites the children to discover a sense of stillness, develop concentration, and nurture an awareness of their own mind. The development of a yoga and meditation program supports a strong body, a conscious mind, and invites the heart to open allowing its natural sense of compassionate connection to flourish. While subsequent chapters emphasize the Mind Practice and concentration, the Body Practice is introduced here as an important preparational practice for children, and the Heart Practice is included as an outcome and benefit of these practices. The Body and Heart Practices are important to consider as they make up a large and important part of the practice session and support concentration practice.

Often times our Western idea of practice is that it leads us to a point of perfection, a result outside of ourselves, or something different than what or who we already are. However, these practices lead to the discovery of one's inner true nature, the essence that has always been a part of you. One of the most important messages going into this work with children is that it is a practice. It is a learning process that looks different for each practitioner given their place developmentally along the path and what is needed in each moment. Helping children to realize and embrace these developmental and individual differences is key. "I can't" is an expression that seems to flow so easily from their lips as they are trying something new. Whether in reference to how deeply they can move into a stretch, whether they can attempt a challenging pose, or engage in a nice deep breath, it seems to offer protection from failure. While not discouraging children from saying it, they can be encouraged to give it a try and reminded that everyone's practice is unique and looks different. In this way, the student comes to see his or her own practice and know it as only he or she can. Children develop awareness that the practice is right here, in each moment, and that who you are and what you need is already present for you. Over time, the deep knowing and connection to the practice grows louder than the voice that limits, doubts, or hinders. Children begin to see their practice developing in each moment, supporting the moment at hand. Children come to see that they are their own teachers. The class teacher is at best a facilitator, a guide, a support, to hold space for them to see what they actually already know. What develops over time is a constant connection between the mind and the body working together, informing and leading one another, and providing just what the child needs along the way.

Chapter 6: Introduction to the Program for Children ages 4 Through 12

BODY PRACTICE—A SOUND BODY

<u>Tools and Props that are useful when implementing the Body Practice:</u>

Mat

Small rock(s)

Singing Bowl or Chime

Body Ball

Hoberman Sphere

Meditation Cushion

Feathers

Puppets

Small beanbags or beanbag animals

Paper

Pencil

Music

As it became clear during field studies in Tibet and Nepal, it was very important to begin with a body practice for the Western child. The body is precious. We must care for it as it is the vessel that will carry us through this lifetime. Long ago, during the time of hermitage and cave yogis, rigorous yogic exercises were practiced preparing the body for long periods of sitting meditation. Nurturing and caring for the body through the practice of yoga allows for physical pliancy. It makes the body fit to hold a proper meditation posture. There are so many issues facing Western children today around poor body image, low self-esteem, and the struggle to navigate the social images that define a 'healthy body'. Yoga brings the attention back to the body you were born with and the opportunity to see it as a valuable, essential part of the experience of being human. It is not about comparing your body to another peer but about connecting to and feeling comfortable with the body that is yours. It is about tending to the body gently, with awareness, and also about knowing when to push harder, and when to ease up. As children develop the ability to guide their bodies through various yoga postures with awareness, they are able to develop strength, flexibility, balance, and coordination at their own pace. As children develop this relationship with their bodies over the course of their childhood years, they are nurturing healthy bodies that support the development of self-esteem, confidence, and a well-developed sense of self. Ultimately children come to know their bodies with a sense of balance, acceptance, and ultimately a great deal of respect.

For the younger children a sense of play is a valuable and important ingredient. The child's experience is meant to be expressive and fun. The practice allows children to discover the joyful realm of their body. While there are a variety of tools that they are introduced to, the most important tool at this stage of development is the body. The goal is to offer opportunities for children to move freely, creatively, easefully in their body. Yoga poses were originally derived and inspired from animals and aspects of nature. Children respond inherently and enthusiastically to these themes. Our connection to the natural world is the mainstay and foundation supporting, inspiring and weaving through these practices for children through the concrete operational years. Using the senses is an obvious and intuitive place to start with children. It is the way that we experience the world, and it is an easy access point to the body for children. As the practice develops through the ages, the senses continue to

Chapter 6: Introduction to the Program for Children ages 4 Through 12

be important tools. While there are endless exercises and ways in which yoga can be brought to and shared with children, the following are some of the key components and tools that build the foundation for a practice.

The mat. What is initially a unique and exciting experience for the youngest children is the opportunity to settle onto a yoga mat. Undoubtedly during the first weeks of class, the mat is a wonderful distraction. They are eager to choose their mat and spend a great deal of time playing with it, rolling up in it, and using it in any way they can. This is an important experience for the children as they establish their own relationship with the mat as a tool for their practice. As they become more engaged with their yoga practice, the children begin to recognize the mat as an important tool, one that they respect, and often yearn to come to. It is a natural boundary defining "their space." For some children, this can feel intimidating, for others it is a welcome and treasured experience. In most instances this might be one of the only times in a child's school day where they have their own sacred space. And while they are still in connection and interaction with their peers, they have a space where ultimately, they can decide what their body needs. The mat is used at the beginning of class as a place to settle, center, and rest into the moment. Much of the day the body seems to want to pull us into movement. The practice at the beginning of class is an invitation to stillness, where the body and mind have time to settle, transition, rest. They have a moment to realign and prepare for practice. The mat becomes a source of comfort as the child is not too far from their friend but in a space that is their own. Children begin to intuit a healthy sense of boundary. It is from the mat that the practice unfolds. Their mat is now a sacred tool, a step into the vastness of these practices. As children get older it becomes second nature, intuitive; when they reach their mat a sense of centered calm is often automatic, effortless, and children begin to gain the awareness that this feeling of calm and connection, achieved on the mat, is always here, always available.

Rock Pose, also known as Child's Pose, serves as a transition for younger children as they switch gears, letting go of one moment and becoming present in the next. Often for children when a transition is marked by a routine of some sort it helps to frame the next moment. Imagining themselves to be as still and strong as a rock appeals to the pretend play and imaginative skills of the early preoperational child. As children settle onto their mat in Rock Pose, they imagine the specific qualities of a rock—stillness, silence, and strength. As they rest in this pose, similar to the pose they were in while in their mother's womb, they take a moment to reflect on these qualities and consider that they are qualities of mind that they also possess. They may not experience them all the time, but they come to see that settling into rock pose and bringing the three qualities to mind can allow the qualities to come forth into their experience. The children allow their body to feel heavy and allow the mat and the earth beneath them to hold them. The curling inward of the body, the forehead to the mat, the gaze inward, are all aspects of this pose that allow the child to settle, let go, and safely come to the present moment.

The **Singing Bowl** is another tool that can be used to mark the beginning of practice. Once the children have settled into Rock Pose and brought their attention to the physical body by remembering their own qualities of stillness, silence, and strength, the sense of sound can offer further settling. As the singing bowl is gently struck, the children shift their attention to the sound, following the duration of the sound carefully until they can't hear it any longer. Then, they slowly roll up into a sitting posture. The children are intrigued by the singing bowl and by the length of the sound. Following it helps to direct the mind inward. As students become skillful, and diligent with these two practices, they can very quickly prepare themselves for their practice with a sense of independence and confidence.

Once settled into class the most important tool that we bring to yogic posture practice is the breath. The breath is our life force. It is often awe-inspiring for the children when they begin to notice their breath and realize that the breath is the constant that connects them to life. Together, the body and breath breathe themselves in just the rhythm that is needed in each given moment. The breath is one of their greatest teachers and a route to the present moment. The youngest children experience breath work as an expressive, engaging experience. In taking a tall posture, preparing their body, and then engaging in a variety of breath patterns inspired by animals and natural objects they are familiar with, they come to learn that different methods of breathing can provide a different response to the body. Lion Breath, for example, invigorates and wakes us up, while Snake breath can soothe and relax. Lion breath involves sitting with a tall posture in easy pose. The child extends their arms in front with hands just above the knees and takes in a deep breath. As the child exhales they fold forward bringing their palms to the floor in front of them and pushing their breath out forcefully with their mouth open. Snake breath involves sitting in a tall posture and bringing hands to prayer position in front of the heart center. As children inhale they raise their arms up above their head, moving their hands side to side like the slithering movement of a snake. As they exhale they make a "ssssss" sound expelling their breath through their mouth. These quick playful breathing exercises are a child's first experience of the breath as a tool. As they progress with their practice, they are introduced to other breathing techniques and strategies that support the path to the breath as a tool during concentration meditation.

From this point as children have had the opportunity to settle, they can enter into an expressive, joyful experience with their body. Their body is a concentration object, and they come to know this object as an expression of joy. Children begin to learn a variety of poses that reflect and resemble animals and other aspects of nature. Each pose offers the body a specific benefit, whether it is a stretch, an opportunity to develop balance, strength, or allow the body to relax. While the children come to know the correct positioning of the body in each pose, they come to discover the gift that each pose provides. Like the introduction of breath work, they come to learn that some poses energize, some strengthen, while others relax.

When children are comfortable with a number of poses they learn a Sun Salutation, a series of poses performed in sequence. Sun Salutation is a greeting for the sun. Long ago Sun Salutations were performed to greet the day and are seen as an expression of gratitude for the day before us. With the younger children the Sun Salutation is usually done after breath work and stretching as a way to move the body, develop coordination, and a sense of wakefulness in the body. By the age of 7, children begin to direct their attention to the form of their body in each pose and learn to move from one pose to the next with a sense of fluidity and ease. The inhalation and exhalation are used as the body moves into, through, and out of a pose. The children connect their attention to body, breath and movement striving to bring the body to a place of a "just right" point. This is a place where the body feels challenged and stretched but not painful. There are so many things being activated here from the child's ability to listen, move the body through a set of instructions, and attend to their body by keeping their attention on the movement through each pose. Stretching, flexibility, balance, and strength are all explored through practice of yoga postures, introducing children to a rich repertoire of poses designed to address certain skills and areas of the body. These are all opportunities to link the mind to the body and develop an awareness of the body.

From this point, balance poses are explored. The children begin with Mountain Pose. Standing strong with their feet on the mat, a tall spine, and their hands at their side or in prayer position, they are able to ground, to feel their connection to the earth, and the qualities they share with a Mountain: strength, stability, and steadiness. They recognize that, like a mountain, when a force or challenge comes at them, they have within themselves the ability to remain steady. From this point of unshakability, the student can move into balance work with confidence. The children explore balancing on one leg in poses like Tree Pose and Airplane Pose. When beginning, using a focus point or a focus friend enables them to use their sense of sight to settle on an immovable point to focus on. There is a sense of mirroring, in that what the child focuses on he or she can become or connect to with those aspects within themselves. Balance Poses can be practiced individually, in partners, or groups.

After the individual body practice on their mat, children enjoy coming off the mat to interact with one another in partner poses, group chal-

Chapter 6: Introduction to the Program for Children ages 4 Through 12

lenges, creative dance, and games. Because the children have had time to tend to themselves through their individual practice, their ability to cooperate and recognize the needs and ways of supporting one another comes more naturally, intuitively, and easefully. These social interactive practices encourage cooperation, communication, support for one another, and healthy social emotional development. In addition to these structured practices, children enjoy the opportunity for unstructured, playful, free expression through activities such as dance, creating poses, creative movement, and other free flowing opportunities.

As children progress, developing independence and individuality with their practice, and familiarity with their body, there is the opportunity for challenge and goal setting. Children identify areas they would like to work on developing and set goals for themselves and their practice. Children enjoy making these choices for themselves and exploring the ways they can achieve their goals and invite their body more deeply into their practice.

Yoga class ends with the practice of *Savasana*. *Savasana* literally means corpse pose. It is an opportunity for deep relaxation before the child transitions off their mat and back into their day's routine. It is truly a practice of letting go. After movement through a yoga practice it offers an opportunity to rest in the fruit of your practice. During *Savasana* children typically rest on their back or belly. They bring their attention to the felt sense of their body on the mat. The body is long, and legs and arms are slightly apart. The child can close their eyes if they wish. Once the child connects with the feeling of their body on the mat they begin to let go, release any holding in the body, and allow their body to sink into the mat, or feel held by the earth beneath them. The body sometimes feels heavy, and eventually the child can release and rest comfortably into the moment. Sometimes a gentle leg-shake or a roll of a body ball along the spine, if the child is on their belly, can aid in the release and relaxation process. Children are invited to allow their mind and breath to be free. The breath settles into its natural rhythm with the body.

The basic foundational components of class continue over the years as children move through the concrete operational stage and beyond to formal operational thinking. There is a predictable routine, that for many children, offers a sense of safety, confidence, and enthusiasm. There are also many opportunities to explore creative ways to engage children in yoga practices. As you listen, observe, and get to know the children you are working with, they will guide the way. Here are some comments from children about the body-related practices:

"Yoga makes me feel like all my problems go away and all that is left is the pose I am doing" (age 10).

"When we do yoga poses we are showing thanks to nature and the animals that inspired the pose" (age 6).

"Yoga makes me feel empty, like I have nothing in my body. I don't worry about things. I can worry about them another day. It makes my mind clear" (age 7).

Mind Practice—A Conscious Mind

Tools and props that are useful when implementing the Mind Practice:

Meditation cushion

Singing Bowl or Chime

Glass jar, sand, and beads

Paper, pencil

The Elephant Path photo or image

Buddha Board

Chapter 6: Introduction to the Program for Children ages 4 Through 12

A meditation practice is a natural unfolding for a child practicing yoga postures. Yoga incorporates the direction of the mind to the body as it flows through poses, with body and mind working together. The Elephant Path practices introduce children to concentration meditation. Concentration is the ability of the mind to focus on one thing without distraction and to sustain attention. Concentration training is the practice of developing the mind's ability to focus and stay on a specific concentration object. This is different from mindfulness practice, which is a noticing of what is happening or present in each moment that arises. Repeated practice of concentration builds the "mind muscle" which fosters sustained attention, focus, detection of distraction, clarity, confidence, self-esteem, resilience, and the development of meta-cognition enabling children to operate from a place of confidence and knowing. What keeps us from this clarity of mind and knowing in the present moment are distracting sense experiences, thoughts, and emotions. While they are the gifts of being human and necessary for our relative day-to-day existence, the Elephant Path practices offer tools, strategies, and skills to allow for the deeper nature of the mind to shine through alongside sense experiences, thought, and emotion.

Children naturally bring two important ingredients to these practices. They bring their true nature and beginner's mind. According to Buddhism, Buddha nature is an inherent inner intelligence that is believed to be the birthright of every sentient being. It allows us to connect with an innate intelligence and to see the interconnection of everything and everyone. It is the teacher within, deeply knowing. The practice of concentration allows the clearing of distraction and the opening of a pathway to this deeper nature that is beyond conceptual thought. From this perspective, children innately have the potential to grasp these practices with ease, as they haven't spent a lifetime entangled in the habitual distractions of day-to-day life. It is easier for them to remember their deeper nature.

Children bring the beauty of beginner's mind to these practices. "Young children think and act freely, discovering and inventing their world from moment-to-moment. Experiencing many things for the first time, they approach even the most mundane events with interest and curiosity. They take in both vast views and tiny details, and every day brings learning and surprises. A beginner's mind feels open and aware. When we cultivate it, we free ourselves from expectation, but we experience greater anticipation. An open mind can relieve stress and preconception." (Cohen, 2004) "When we start to learn anything for the first time, we are fresh, curious, and open to all possibilities. Our mind is not yet solid with concepts, opinions, and certainties. This beginner's mind is awakened mind itself, which is beyond concepts and opinion." (*Lion's Roar*, 2015) The combination of beginner's mind, the skillfulness of concentration, and the tools of the elephant path practices become the pathway to our inner knowing of our deeper nature. The seeds of these practices are already burning bright in a child's heart mind, and these practices point the way.

THE ELEPHANT PATH

As mentioned in Chapters 3 and 4, in the Tibetan Buddhist tradition, the practice of developing the mind's ability to focus with single-pointed concentration is depicted in a Tibetan painting entitled The Elephant Path. The actual title of Asanga's text for training concentration in Tibetan is *sems gnas dgu* [*The Nine Stages of the Mind Staying*]. The painting illustrates nine stages of mental development, instructions for staying-calming practice or *gzhi gnas* in Tibetan. The painting is a beautiful visual tool for children that both motivates and illustrates the concentration practices. The path depicts three traveling companions, the elephant, the practitioner, and the monkey. The companions begin their travels along a path up the side of a mountain. Each stage of the path depicts a different level of concentration development. The practitioner represents the meditator, setting out on the path of concentration training. He is carrying a rope to tie the mind to the concentration object and an elephant prod to symbolize the meta-cognition with which he will guide and tame the elephant. The elephant represents the mind. A wild elephant can be very dangerous if afraid and stampeding. However, an elephant, once tamed, will obey its master better than any other animal and do so with great strength and intelligence. The footprint of the elephant is larger than any other animal. If tamed, our mind will serve us in positive ways that extend well beyond us as individuals. (Dharma Fellowship Library - Deep Calm Abiding, 2005-2015) The monkey symbolizes the mind's incessant distraction, inability to focus, scattering of thoughts, and mind-wandering. The monkey is full of tricks and surprises, hoping to come between the practitioner and the elephant, leading the way up the mountain. Once the practitioner reaches the elephant, the elephant slows down, until finally the practitioner leads the way. The monkey is still there but travels alongside the elephant, transforming into clarity as the elephant-mind becomes purified as symbolized by the color changing from blue to white. The practitioner and the elephant continue along the path together until finally the practitioner rides the elephant and the mind is naturally settled.

The Elephant Path practices for children are developed with careful attention to the developmental needs and level of each child. Children entering the late preoperational stage are first introduced to these three characters in the painting and begin to come to know these three characters as they exist in their own practice. When the Elephant Path is first introduced children are intrigued by this beautiful piece of artwork, the intricacy and skillfulness that it reflects and most importantly that it depicts and holds within it the stages of concentration practice. It becomes a puzzle that they are very eager to uncover, understand, and discover the key to. There is a playfulness to it and a sense of intrigue that engages the children. They are very eager to learn more, understand the symbolism, and connect this beautiful set of instructions to their own life and practice.

There are many benefits that flourish through these practices: a connection to one's inner stillness and silence, a sense of calm, attention, focus, awareness, physical and mental pliancy, confidence, self-esteem, resilience, clarity, compassion, innate wisdom. The development of meta-cognition is an important benefit of the Elephant Path concentration. Meta-cognition involves higher-order thinking, the ability to be aware of one's awareness and state-of-mind, and problem-solving strategies. These practices go beyond mindfulness practices in that they encourage a "stepping back" to directly become aware of one's own state-of-mind. "Beginners must learn to direct their meta-cognitive awareness to their thinking to discover how they are approaching the new task of concentration with thought and must learn to modify the thinking so as not to develop bad habits of concentration. As they master those alternative patterns of thought that support the development of concentration skill, the need for meta-cognition reflection as a steering mechanism diminishes." (van Gelder, 2009) Furthermore, children learn to use their meta-cognition to detect when a distracting thought occurs and when they get into chasing after mode, i.e., chasing after the thought and losing the concentration focus. Over time, the effort put forth toward meditation practice, the trust developed between student and teacher, and the self-confidence that develops within the child, become a foundation for the development of meta-cognitive skill.

As teachers strive to support the social emotional development of students, these practices offer a vital platform. While social emotional development includes the ability to pay attention, manage emotions, perspective-taking, and empathy, children need the skills and practices to navigate a healthy route to these endpoints. They need to be able to think about their thinking. As challenging emotions arise, they need to be able to recognize them, identify a strategy, and redirect. Development of meta-cognition enables these action steps to come forth from within, from the internal perspective, eventually with automaticity. Rae Jacobson says, "Kids need to be able to make the transition from 'I can't' to the proactive, 'How can I?'...Reflecting on our own thoughts is how we gain insight into our feelings, needs, and behaviors and how we learn, manage, and adapt to new experiences, challenges, and emotional setbacks." (Jacobson, 2017) With meta-cognition comes the development of resilience. Skills, strategies, instructions, become second-nature and the child develops automaticity around how to proceed in each moment. They see the moment clearly, as it is, and self-direct, proceeding from a place of inner knowing. With the development of meta-cognition, self-confidence, self-esteem, self-awareness, resilience, independence, and self-advocacy skills emerge.

Instruction is given following the pointing out style in the Indo-Tibetan lineage traditions. The pointing out style is an ancient way of teaching meditation that is firmly grounded in the teacher-student relationship. The teacher offers richly detailed instruction and explanation just before concentration. Then the students engage in a concentration meditation, carefully guided by the teacher. The student describes their meditation experience, and the teacher monitors, corrects, and guides their progress. Pointing out refers to a style of teaching meditation that is strongly relationally-based. In this way, the children are encouraged to learn in a guided relationship and then to talk about their immediate experience of concentration practice. Nevertheless, it is often challenging, as it can be difficult to talk about and describe something that you can't see as an actual physical object. Typically, the children share their experiences and are then given direction as to how to continue their concentration practice, what to put emphasis on, or are offered specific strategies for concentration. Because everyone's experience is unique, children are encouraged to listen to one another's reflections but recognize that they might be very different than their own experiences. It is very important to encourage all the children to share their experiences so that you can tailor the instructions to just what each child might need to support them around their concentration.

The relationship that is built between student and teacher is unique, supportive, and trusting. The child progresses at their own pace, developing different techniques over time, and with support of the teacher, practice, and their own meta-cognition, the path is revealed. These practices, the path, become a way of being, a direction of moving in the world, a reflection of conduct and thought. One develops trust in the path, the practice, as it continues to unfold providing just what you need along the way, sometimes not as you expected.

THE THREE JEWELS—BUDDHA, DHARMA, SANGHA

In Indo-Tibetan Buddhism the Three Jewels represent the three essential ingredients of concentration training and other meditative practices (elements on the Buddhist path). The Buddha symbolizes someone who has fully trained the mind, as anyone can. Ultimately these practices point the way to our inner knowing, our Buddha nature or innate intelligence. Dharma refers to the corpus of teachings passed down from generation to generation in the same way, because they are uniquely effective in training attention. Sangha refers to the supportive community of practitioners. In the Buddhist tradition the sangha is a community of friends practicing together. The sangha can be your family, fellow practitioners, or your school community. The essential qualities of a sangha are mutual awareness, understanding, acceptance, harmony, non-competitive joy for other's accomplishments, and love. These qualities are necessary if it is a true sangha (Thich Nhat Hanh, 2017). There is a deep connection that develops and a realization that you are not practicing alone, but are part of a family, brothers and sisters supporting one another.

Considering the first jewel, the Buddha, there is a metaphor in Buddhist tradition to depict innate Buddha-nature: A sprout resides within the seed. While you can't see the sprout or experience the sprout in any way with your senses, the sprout is nevertheless always there as a potential. Its essence is known. With moist soil, nutrients, sunlight, and care, the seed sprouts, pushes up through the soil, and blossoms, just like the bee knows the essence of the flower to be honey (Khandro Rinpoche, 2017). Held within you is your deeper nature, your inner knowing, intuition, discernment, wisdom, compassion. When this is nurtured and recognized, it shines forth. Ultimately these practices point the way to your own mode of knowing. As teachers we hold the space for children to stand in wonder, amazement, curiosity, and awe while nurturing and guiding the way toward learning, discovery, realization. Providing opportunities for children to witness and discover this, fosters wonder, motivation, and realization. Nature offers endless opportunities for understanding the blossoming of innate nature: planting a seed that sprouts; nurturing a caterpillar as it transforms to a butterfly; or observing a bee gathering honey.

In regard to the Dharma, the teachings and the teacher, it is essential for the teacher to have familiarity with these practices and a personal meditation practice. It is difficult to truly teach anything if you do not

Chapter 6: Introduction to the Program for Children ages 4 Through 12

have understanding of it as a direct experience. It is most beneficial if the environment that you teach in is supportive to the practice. An uncluttered, open space, with natural light and natural objects is conducive as it supports a sense of calm and ease. Nature is an essential and wonderful classroom for these practices. Taking children out in nature provides a direct connection to the inspiration and roots of these practices. Children welcome the opportunity to step out of their environment, outdoors and into the natural world, which offers new stimuli and often an easier path to their inner presence.

Providing a safe and nurturing classroom community is important. Setting an intention together at the beginning of the year provides a lovely foundation. Offering the question, "How do you want to feel in your community?" provides the opportunity for children to ask for what they want and need. Children are typically quick to share their ideas, which might be qualities like safe, peaceful, kind, fun, thoughtful, allowed to feel what you feel, simple, exciting, warm. Once a reasonable list of qualities is developed, these qualities are held by all as an intention and become part of the values everyone holds for the space, community, and the development of the practice. The knowledge, dedication, and care of the teacher, as well as the intention set together with students create a strong foundation from which the practices can be taught and realized by the students.

In terms of building a supportive "sangha", or practice community that extends beyond the walls of the classroom, it is important to involve the greater school community and families. There are many ways in which a community can practice together. One example is a school-wide Sun Salutation and meditation. This is a wonderful opportunity to come together to offer gratitude for the gift of a new day and to set an intention as you step into the day together. This can be led by children or teachers at the beginning of the week, at school wide and community events, or within classrooms. Closing these practice sessions with an expression of gratitude and intention fosters a feeling of support and connection. For example, you might bring your hands held palms together at your heart. Hands can be drawn to the forehead while sharing the words, kind thoughts. Then drawn to the lips with the words, kind words. Finally, drawn back to the heart with the words, follow your heart. You might share the word '*Namaste*' which means the divine light in me honors the divine light in you or from my heart to your heart. It is with this positive intention that the community steps into the day together, and that the practice is carried into the day, not only for the benefit of each individual, but for the benefit of everyone. Inviting parents and families to events and gatherings like this and offering home practice opportunities are important in creating an extended, supportive community for children.

The following are reflections about the practice of a community Sun Salutation:

"Every Monday morning we do a whole school Sun Salutation where a few children go over the loudspeaker to recite the Sun Salutation. It is so amazing because it is the entire community doing this together and we are starting off our week with intentionality and purpose. It's a beautiful moment together where we are able to start our day by practicing Yoga" (Early Childhood Teacher).

"Every Monday morning everyone in the school gets together and does a Sun Salutation. It gets us ready for the week ahead. I think it is special because I feel one special part in the whole community" (age 9).

"As soon as we did our Sun Salutation I knew I was going to have a good day right at that moment. I knew everyone would have a good day and feel the energy in the air" (age 11).

"When we do *Namaste* it always makes me smile. It is like we are sharing something. I know that everyone is connected. Everyone is safe, and everyone has a friend" (age 6).

Chapter 6: Introduction to the Program for Children ages 4 Through 12

HEART PRACTICE—CONDUCT OF A COMPASSIONATE HEART

The Dalai Lama has said, "If every child in the world would be taught meditation, we would eliminate violence from this world within one generation." This world and our children deserve these practices. In the Buddhist tradition, one of the most reliable indicators of the fruition and level of your practice is conduct in everyday life. Who are you off the mat? How do you carry yourself and interact with the world around you when you are out of the yoga studio and engaged in everyday life? In many ways this might be the most challenging practice because you aren't just working with the activity of your own mind and body, you are also negotiating the energy, behavior, personalities of others and the world around you. That is the true gift of these practices, the fruition of your practice for the benefit of all beings. We live in an interconnected world. Our actions affect others, just as other's actions affect us. What kind of effect do your actions and words have on others? Are you aware of moments when your practice can be of benefit to others? Helping children to recognize that their practice ripples forth touching others is a profound and beautiful realization for children. Heart Practice exercises and activities will be explored in Chapter 9.

Chapter 7

The Practice for Early Preoperational Children (Ages 4-6)

by Michelle B. Bissanti, M.Ed.

Elephant Path Preparation

In the early years, children's experience of the Elephant Path is largely a preparational practice for subsequent concentration practice to come in later childhood years. You might imagine children at this stage of development at the base of the mountain of the Elephant Path experiencing the joy of the body and mind united in practice. Free of the need to exert effort to know or witness the mind, children at this early stage of development are engaging in practices that introduce the body and mind, almost like meeting a new friend. They are encouraged to meet these practices with a sense of wonder, free to move and explore in their own way, supporting and allowing the child's wonder-like view of their world, or beginner's mind.

Yoga postures are important at this stage of development, as the focus is the child's experience of and relationship to the body, the vessel they were born into, in a healthy, accepting, respectful, joyful way. The child's concentration object is the body itself. There are moments of stillness and movement in the practice, and in each experience the child is invited to bring their attention to the body and to those moments of stillness and movement. For the youngest children, stillness is primarily experienced concretely through poses like Rock Pose, Child's Pose, and opportunities to focus on breathing exercises. We experience the world through our senses, and children at this stage of development are invited into these practices through the senses, experience, and inquiry. These practices are of short duration to introduce children to silence, stillness, and to a connection to the heart. When the children are able to rest in stillness, their attention can be drawn to the heart, and the children can notice how they are feeling or reflect on a specific question, drawing from the feeling that arises in their heart.[1] We call these meditations, resting the attention in the heart. These short heart meditations develop a child's awareness and ability to notice feeling as it arises.

The objective of this introductory practice is to experience wonder and joy in the body and natural environment, experiencing of the senses as a tool to the present-moment, awareness of personal space and we space, awareness of the breath as a tool, development of focus, noticing and identifying feelings arising, and discovering relaxation, stillness, and silence.

Personal Space

The mat creates a sacred space and time for these practices. It becomes an important cue to evoke the right state-of-mind for the practice. A calm and peaceful space helps the child to recognize those qualities within themselves. Young children can be very stimulated by visual cues. Therefore, finding an uncluttered, clear space is helpful. A yoga mat is a useful tool because it offers a supportive surface for a yoga practice, but more importantly because it offers a personal space for the child. Over time, as the child arrives at the mat, there is a knowing that arises from within that this place is sacred and precious. It offers a space and a moment to turn attention from the outer focus to connect with inner being. When children feel safe and secure, operating from a place of inner being, qualities of self-esteem, confidence, connection, and groundedness can emerge.

Arriving to the Mat: Rock Pose

Rock Pose serves as a transitional pose for children allowing them to arrive on their mat and to their practice. Beginning practice with this pose creates a routine that can be helpful in guiding children to rest into the present moment. When this pose is first introduced to children it is helpful to have them hold a river rock. A rock that fits easily in the palm

---

1. Geshe Sonam Gurung, 2014 personal communication.

of their hand is the best size. Being able to use the sense of touch can be very helpful to students in this age group. Encourage children to notice the stillness and silence within the rock.

As the child comes into Rock Pose, they will sit in a kneeling position with knees together or apart, whichever is most comfortable. After taking a deep breath in, while exhaling, fold forward over the legs, resting the forehead on the floor, and arms on the mat along the side of the body. If it is uncomfortable to fold fully forward, the child may place their elbows on their knees or floor in front of them and place their head in their hands, gently allowing the palm of the hand to cup the eyes. This pose shifts the attention inward. As the body curls inward, the forehead comes to the mat. The inward gaze creates a sense of calm, allowing the child to settle, let go, and safely come to the present moment. Children can be invited to close their eyes if they wish.

Once settled in Rock Pose, ask the children to allow their body to be held by the mat. They might feel a sense of heaviness as they bring their attention to the body, but the main realization is that they are being held by the floor, by the earth beneath them, and by gravity. This allows the body to release and muscles to relax. At this stage of development, it can be helpful to gently place your hand on their back. This allows a sense of release and can help the child settle into the pose. Once settled ask children to consider the qualities of the rock: stillness, silence, and strength. Encourage them to notice what stillness feels like within their own body and what their silence feels or sounds like. Simply encouraging the noticing of these qualities in this pose can allow them to come forth into the child's experience.

ROCK GARDEN

After children have been introduced to this pose and the routine of taking it as they come to their mat, it is fun to share the idea of a rock garden. As they settle in it is as if they are taking their place in a beautiful rock garden. Tell the children that you will be taking a walk through the garden, noticing and appreciating all the beautiful rocks in the garden. The children love this idea, and it often motivates them to take this pose. The feeling of community, being a part of the garden, and knowing that you are walking through acknowledging their presence creates a wonderful sense of acceptance and care. It is a nice opportunity to place your hand on their back, making connection, and helping those struggling to settle to ground a bit. Allow the children to rest in the nourishment of this pose as they bring their body to the mat and to their practice. Children might want to keep their river rock with them during practice, as a reminder of the qualities they share with the rock. In this way they symbolically learn to bring the rock qualities of stillness, silence, and strength into their practice and the classroom.

The Singing Bowl Meditation

The singing bowl is an important tool that marks the beginning of practice and introduces young children to the experience of directing the mind to an object through the sense of sound. Once the children have settled into Rock Pose, bringing their attention to the feeling of the physical body by remembering their own qualities of stillness, silence, and strength, they are ready to direct their attention to the singing bowl. Children listen carefully for the sound of the singing bowl. Once the singing bowl is struck and they hear the sound, they follow the sound with their attention until it becomes difficult to hear or until they can no longer hear it. At that point, they can slowly roll their body up into a sitting posture at their own pace. Children enjoy the anticipation of the singing bowl and are intrigued by the length of the sound. As students become skillful and diligent with the practice of Rock Pose and the Singing Bowl Meditation, they can quickly prepare themselves for their practice with a sense of independence and confidence.

Breath work

The youngest children experience breath work as an expressive, engaging experience. Taking a tall posture, preparing their body and then engaging in a variety of breath patterns inspired by animals and objects they are familiar with, they come to learn that different methods of breathing can provide a different response to the body. Using puppets

Chapter 7: The Practice for Early Preoperational Children (Ages 4-6)

or props for the various breathing exercises is helpful and engaging for the children. It gives them a playful visual experience to associate with each breathing exercise. This serves to inspire and motivate the children.

Inviting the children to take a tall posture is important as it allows a full, unrestricted breath to the body. Holding a tall posture also requires engagement of core muscles, which helps to foster a sense of wakefulness, which is beneficial to a concentration meditation practice. Children can sit in Pretzel Pose, with legs crossed, or Easy Pose, resting the body on the legs from a kneeling position. Encourage them to take a tall spine, drawing the top of their head up.

Then, lead the children in any of the following:

Feather Breath: an introduction to the movement and strength of the breath.

Holding a small feather at its base between the thumbs, position the hands about 10 inches in front of the face. First explore a gentle breath, instructing the child to inhale and to exhale gently through the mouth so as to flutter only the light, delicate top of the feather with the breath. Repeat this at least 5 times so the child has a sense of a gentle, calming breath. Then explore a stronger breath, instructing the child to inhale and exhale forcefully through the mouth so as to cause the entire feather to flutter with the breath. Repeat at least 5 times, so the child has a sense of a stronger, more energetic breath.

Bear Breath: calming and relaxing.

Take a tall spine. Allow the eyes to close. Imagine a bear hibernating in a warm, cozy den for the winter. His breaths would be long and slow. Take a long, deep breath into your body as if you were filling up your whole body. Exhale slowly allowing your long, deep breath out. Repeat 5 times.

Balloon Breath: calming and centering.

Sit in a tall posture. Extend arms out to the side resting fingertips on the floor. As you take a deep breath in, stretch the arms up above your head in sequence with your inhale. As you exhale allow the arms to float down, like a balloon gently floating to the ground, resting fingertips on the ground. Repeat 5 times.

Lion Breath: invigorates and wakes us up.

Sit in a tall posture in Easy Pose. Arms are extended in front of you with hands just above your knees. Take a deep inhale. As you exhale, fold forward bringing your palms to the floor in front of you and pushing your breath out forcefully, with mouth open. Repeat 3-5 times.

Snake Breath: soothe and relax.

Sit in a tall posture. Bring your hands to prayer position in front of your heart center. As you inhale raise arms up, in front of your face and above your head, moving hands side to side in prayer position like the slithering movement of a snake. As you exhale make a "ssssss" sound expelling your breath through your mouth. Repeat 3-5 times.

Bumble Bee Breath: awake and relaxed.

Sit in a tall posture. Bring your hands to your shoulders, elbows out like wings. Take a deep breath in. As you exhale make a "bzzzzz" sound with your mouth as you flutter your arms. Repeat 3-5 times.

Bunny Breath: energize and center.

Sit in a tall posture. Hands resting on lap. Take three quick breaths in through your nose. One long exhale through your nose. Repeat 3-5 times.

Observing the energy level of the children as they come to their mat can indicate what type of breath might be best in any given practice session. When the children become comfortable with different breathing techniques you might ask them to check in with themselves and choose what breath to lead with. Encouraging children to make up and share their own type of breath and reflect on the feeling that arises, is fun and important as they develop their own practice.

Another fun exercise is to write the names of various animals and objects such as hummingbird, sloth, kangaroo, jet plane, shooting star, volcano on small squares of paper. The children could create or help add to the list. Fold and place the paper pieces in a small bag or basket. Taking turns, the children draw one and demonstrate what they think that type of breath exercise would be. The other children can guess what they think the name of that breath is. Children love creating their own ideas, experimenting with breath and movement, and trying to guess what their friends are doing. As one child said, "When I have a lot of energy I take bear breaths. When I don't have a lot of energy I do cricket pose and it wakes me up" (age 5).

MINDFUL SHARING

This is an activity that is important at all ages. At this age, the children are very eager to share things that are going on in their lives, ideas, and events. It is a wonderful opportunity to develop supportive listening skills, and the confidence to share with the group. After children have settled in and before engaging in yoga or meditation practices is the best time for sharing. The children have had the opportunity to settle and bring their body and mind to their mat. Often, they have lingering thoughts in their mind or something they feel they want you to know. This quick sharing activity can be the remedy for all those pressing thoughts and helps you understand what is happening or present for individual children. Using a puppet or a special object like a talking stick, encourage children to pass the object around the circle. When they are holding the puppet, it is their turn and opportunity to share. It is also their choice; if they don't wish to share, they can choose to pass the puppet to the next friend. The only person speaking is the person holding the puppet. It isn't a time to ask questions, but simply to listen to the person sharing. Once the puppet has made its way around the circle, children could ask questions or make connections to something someone else shared. This encourages children to listen carefully, holding the space for one another to express themselves. It is also helpful for the teacher to connect with the children, listening to what is present for them.

Knowing what is present for them in the session can be helpful in supporting each student through their practice. There are many ways you can vary or tailor this type of sharing to your group. You could begin by prompting with a question. Sometimes this is helpful to the child who might not know what to say but wants to share. Inviting children to whisper their answer or message to the puppet is another option and is wonderful for children who want to share but not aloud. They feel that their idea has been heard, by the puppet. The experience of being heard can generate feelings of acceptance, care, connection, and safety.

Focus Friends

Once the classroom community has been established and children have begun to embrace the routines of class and practice, "focus friends" are an exciting tool to introduce. A focus friend is a small animal bean bag, a size that can easily be held in the children's hands. The focus friend is used to help hold a steady pose during balance work. It becomes a concentration object as the children patiently prepare themselves for a pose and place their gaze on their focus friend sitting at the top of their mat. The stillness of the focus friend enables them to find that same quality within themselves. As they move into a balance pose like Tree Pose or Airplane Pose, children quickly find that keeping their gaze on something still, supports that same quality within themselves. One child said, "Tree pose is hard to do because you almost could fall down. When you look at something that is still then you won't fall down" (age 4).

Heart Meditation; Resting Attention in the Heart— Seeing Through the Eyes of the Heart

These short meditations are an important introduction for young children beginning a meditation practice. Feelings arise frequently and often quickly in children at this age. For some children it can be a struggle to simply name the feeling, let alone know how to respond to it or let go of it. Inviting children to rest their attention in their heart center allows the children to experience thoughts and feelings as they arise. They begin to connect feelings with experiences or situations that are familiar to them. In this way, children develop a vocabulary and way of expressing what arises in their internal world. The heart center is just to the right of the physical heart. It is less important to find an exact location, but to direct children's attention inward to the energy center where awareness knows itself, where truth resides, where compassion blooms.

Heart meditations are introduced when children have developed a connection to a yoga practice, to their classroom community, and to one another. When children feel safe and trusting, these practices arise easily and sometimes spontaneously. Before introducing a Heart Meditation, it

Chapter 7: The Practice for Early Preoperational Children (Ages 4-6)

is useful to engage the children in conversation about feelings and where they arise. What are feelings? Where do feelings come from? What are feelings you enjoy having? What are feelings that are difficult to have? There are no right or wrong answers. The children are beginning to develop a language for their feelings. Often times the heart meditation might be a question, or a scenario. This can reflect something the children might be experiencing or learning about. It could come from a book that you read together. It is wonderful when the idea for the heart meditation comes from the children. There are many ways that children might share about their meditation. Some children will feel eager to talk about their experience, for others the voice for their practice might come through illustration, movement, or other forms of creative expression.

The following Heart Meditations involve asking a question, posing an idea or scenario, and resting in silence. As children get comfortable and prepare for this meditation it can sometimes be helpful for them to have a focus friend with them. Already having worked with them as an object of focus it can provide comfort and a sense of calm. Ask children to sit in a tall posture or rest in a comfortable position on their back. Ask the children to rest their hands on their heart. This helps to direct their attention to their heart center. If they are using a focus friend, they can place it in their hands, or it could rest beside them. Then ask children to notice their body as it settles and becomes still and silent like a rock and to notice a feeling of calm. Then, pose a question or ask children to reflect or think about an idea. Beginning with examples that invoke positive feelings is a good place to start as children are developing a vocabulary for expressing themselves and a foundation to rest back into when challenging feelings and emotions arise. Encourage them to use visualization, asking questions to guide them. For some the answers or information will come spontaneously, for others there will be some effort exerted. Sometimes encouraging the children to simply rest, to do nothing, will allow an idea or feeling to float forth. Use the singing bowl to bring the meditation to a close. Finally, encourage the children to share about their experience.

The Elephant Path: Attention Development and Training in Children and Adolescents

Here are a few examples of Heart Meditations:

What helps me feel safe, happy, and loved? Once children are comfortable and settled in, ask them to listen carefully to their heart as you ask the question. Imagine the answer your heart offers. Maybe you can see a picture of it. Notice the colors and details of the picture. Notice the feeling of happiness that arises when you think of this. Notice how that feels in your body. What else do you notice? If it is hard to hear what your heart says, simply rest, and see if something floats into your mind on its own. Let the children know that you will sound the singing bowl shortly, and they can thank their heart for sharing and roll up to a sitting posture. Invite children to share. In response to *What helps me feel safe, happy, and loved?* one child said, "My whole family, the beach, and the stars" (age 5). Another shared, "My mom, my dad, my brother, and my gumball machine" (age 4).

In response to the question, *"How can I show kindness with my hands?"* the children's heart responses were: "My heart said to be gentle, be a friend, say you're sorry, and love each other" (age 5). "I would use my hands to enjoy playing in the park, by the mountains, and in nature" (age 5). "I can take care of my heart and I can take care of flowers" (age 4). "Hug, hug, hug" (age 4). "I would use a wand to have my hands do lots of kind things" (age 4). "I can use my hands to take care of nature, like wrapping a bandage on a cat" (age 5).

The above exercise can involve asking the children to imagine a scenario based on a specific feeling. Imagine a time you were really happy. Imagine a really funny time when you laughed a lot. Imagine a time you were so excited for something.

Another approach is called resting in silence. Say to the child, "Maybe your heart has something to say to you. Maybe an idea will float into your mind. What do you hear in the silence? What do you see/feel in the silence?" Directing the children to different senses is helpful as some children experience one sense more easily than another. Allow the children a few moments to simply be with silence, listening, feeling, seeing, sensing whatever might arise. In response to a silence meditation, one child said, "I heard a river in the mountains" (age 5). Another said, "I hear a fire crackling" (age 6). Another said, "I heard my toothbrush going around and paper airplanes flying" (age 6). Still another said, "I hear cats purring and raindrops falling on the ground" (age 6). Another said, "I hear the planets when I go to bed" (age 7).

There are so few moments of silence in a child's day. Offering children this time to intentionally rest in silence can invite a deeper pathway to thoughts and feelings, to something beneath the discursive thoughts. A few moments dedicated completely to themselves can feel so nourishing.

Children who experienced these practices of meditation were asked what meditation is or what it means. One child said, "Meditation let's your heart tell you about life" (age 4). Another said, "We meditate because we want to bring ourselves together, to make our class better. Every time we do a meditation, we calm a little bit" (age 6). Still another said "It is like there's a rope connected to all of us. It is like everyone in the world is connected like a big web" (age 6).

SAVASANA

Savasana is often the culminating pose in a yoga practice and is a deeply relaxing pose. This pose invites children to rest and relax into the fruits of their practice and the sense of joy, calm, and connection they experienced. It helps to prepare them for the transition off their mat and back into their day. The children rest on their back or belly on their mat, whichever feels most comfortable to them. They might choose to snuggle with a Focus Friend or hold hands with the child next to them. They might want their own space. Lights can be dim or off, and soothing music is often helpful as they relax. Once the children are settled, there are a few things that can help them rest more deeply into this pose if they would like. Flower spray is a mixture of water and lavender essential oil. Gently spray a mist of flower spray across their face. This can feel refreshing and soothing, and the lavender scent is calming. If the child is resting on their back, you can offer them a leg shake. Grasp their ankles, lift their legs about a foot off the mat, and gently shake the legs to release any holding. Gently return the legs to the mat giving the feet a gentle rub. If the child is resting on the belly, use a large body ball to massage the spine. Beginning at the tailbone, roll the ball the length of the spine stopping at the shoulder blades. Some children enjoy more pressure on the ball than others so gauge this individually. This gentle pressure along the spine can offer grounding into deeper relaxation. *Savasana* should not be so long in duration that they fall asleep, as you want the children to notice and feel the deep relaxation, sense of calm, and inner joy generated by their practice. If the children drift off to sleep that is fine but encourage a sense of wakeful rest.

For the early preoperational child, these practices encourage exploration and celebration of the mind and body through a sense of wonder, playfulness, individual expression, stillness, silence and deep relaxation. Yoga and movement practices might encompass about seventy five percent of the session. Meditation practices encompass the remainder. The skills experienced, nurtured, and developed during a practice session can be supported and encouraged throughout a child's day. Rock Pose or breath work can be used to encourage transitions, or to encourage calm or settling in. Quick movement exercises or yoga poses can be used when the children need a stretch, feel agitated, or simply want to move their body. A session set aside for these practices is invaluable, but the encouragement and support to bring these practices off the mat, throughout the day, is what will instill ownership and the development of the benefits of these practices in children.

Chapter 8

Concentration Development for Late Preoperational Children (Ages 7-9)

by Michelle G. Bissanti, M.Ed.

Playfulness, a sense of wonder, creative expression, and curiosity continue to be precious ingredients for children moving through the late preoperational stage. They continue to engage in many of the early preoperational practices, which serve as helpful transitional tools as they begin their journey along the Elephant Path with the introduction of concentration meditation.

They continue to spend time developing a yoga practice. The body is the vehicle in which the preoperational child engages in meditation. Tending to the needs of the body is helpful to the success of a meditation practice and development of physical pliancy. Through the yoga practice children direct the mind to the body as it moves through each yoga pose, noticing the body's movement and feeling quality in each pose. The child also experiences the breath as a tool to relax and energize the body, and through the progression of yoga practice the child learns to incorporate the inhalation and exhalation alongside the movement of the body through poses.

The child entering the late preoperational stage has experienced meditation through the experience of stillness, silence, and a sense of calm, and also through the development of focus on an object. Concentration meditation becomes the basis for their practice at this stage, as they learn to keep their attention on their breath as a concentration object. They are introduced to the idea of "mind" and begin to recognize the movement of mind, in terms of its occurring content like thought.

The development of meta-cognition is very important at the late preoperational stage. Concentration meditation strengthens a child's mind muscle. Children develop mental pliancy, i.e., the ability to direct the mind easily and flexibly to a concentration object and carry out a specific task effectively. Late preoperational children develop strategies and tools that help keep the mind focused on the concentration object. Over time they are able to self-reflect, to think about and become aware of their thinking and state-of-mind and develop independence in their ability to direct the mind, largely through adopting a range of specific mental strategies. This marks the development of meta-cognition.

Because children progress at different rates and ways, it is important to be aware of each child's needs. The relationship that you build with each child, and also the sense of trust and ability to support each child, are essential ingredients. Children need to be assured that you will meet them right where they are, and that you are all in this together, as a group of practitioners supporting one another.

Goals and Objectives

There are a number of goals and objectives on training concentration that these practices address for the late preoperational child. From the perspective of the body, the goal is to experience wonder and joy in the body, and how the body and mind work together. Immediate awareness of the sense-experience becomes a tool to experiencing and settling into the present moment. Settling in on the mat becomes the occasion to directly experience personal space and we space. Another objective is to use setting up and settling into the same meditation posture as a cue to prepare for practice. Once the posture is established, the child learns to use the three primary tools of concentration practice. First, the child learns to direct the mind, like using a steering wheel, to the concentration object, in this case the breath and the felt sense of the body. Second, the child learns to engage everything about the breath and body, putting in careful effort to follow them very closely. Third, the child utilizes his or her meta-cognitive awareness to notice the occurrence of thought and the following of thought or sense-experience.

The initial skills of concentration are: identifying the concentration object amidst all the distractions; sustaining concentration on the

Chapter 8: Concentration Development for Late Preoperational Children (Ages 7-9)

concentration object for longer and longer duration; noticing thought and other distractors more and more immediately; skillfully re-engaging the concentration object upon being distracted; distinguishing when the mind is quiet and still (absence of thought activity) and when there is movement of thought.

DEFINING PERSONAL SPACE AND SETTING UP THE POSTURE

Concentration practice begins with defining the personal space of the child and group of children. The mat and meditation cushion provide the personal or sacred space, which is important at this stage of development. As the child's body grows it can be useful to incorporate a cushion or block into a sitting practice. As the child takes a sitting posture on a block or cushion, the hips rest slightly above the knees as this can be more comfortable and conducive to a focused meditation practice.

Rock Pose continues to be an important transitional pose as children at this stage of development prepare the mind and body for meditation. It is an innately familiar pose, and because the head is brought to the mat with the folding inward of the body, it is conducive to generating a sense of calm. Children are instructed to connect with the qualities of stillness, silence, and strength. Placing your hand gently on the child's back can help a child settle into this pose. Once the child is settled in the pose, holding a river rock if necessary, and connecting with a sense of stillness and silence, a series of instructions can be given to direct the child to the present moment.

The metaphor of a balloon floating off into the sky is helpful as children settle in. As children progress with their meditation practice and begin to recognize or identify what keeps them from the moment, they can use visualizations like a balloon carrying away their thought or distraction in order to foster an ability to let go and rest in the moment.

As the child at the beginning of the late preoperational stage relaxes into the pose, instruct them to bring their attention to the feeling of their body on the mat, to the sound of your voice, to any smells, sounds, sensations they might be experiencing right now. Even though some children might be very eager to share their discoveries immediately, ask them to rest in their silence, as they will have the opportunity to share their experience when they come out of this pose. Directing the children's attention to sense-experience in the moment is a natural path to staying in the moment.

As children progress, these instructions can be deepened by instructing them to let go of whatever they were doing before this moment, and any thoughts or anticipation about things to come later in the day. Children can allow these thoughts to float off like a balloon lifting into the sky. Finally invite children to guide their attention to the present moment. Instruct them to bring their attention to the feeling of their body on the mat, and finally to the sensations they are experiencing in the moment. They are instructed to simply notice the moment without trying to change anything. As this settling in and letting go becomes more available they might notice a sense of spaciousness as the body and mind settle. Instruct children to rest in this stillness, silence and spaciousness. As one child said, "Rock Pose is like a time to get settled down and take a few deep breaths. You can use it anywhere when you are overwhelmed, excited, anxious or nervous. It's a way to get calm and be ready for what is after" (age 7). Yet another child said, "Finding our stillness and silence is like sinking into our center" (age 9).

SETTING THE INTENTION

Setting an intention with children at the beginning of practice helps to set a direction, a purpose, a goal. This can fuel a positive tone, belief in an outcome, or aiming in the desired direction. At first, the intention shared might be to simply remind children of the qualities you came up with together for the type of environment or community you wanted to create together. As you come to know your students, the intention can be a goal you know the group is working toward. The intention can be a personal goal the child wishes for themselves, or their practice. An intention might be to bring kindness, courage, and support to our practice and one another. It might be to focus more carefully during concentration meditation.

SINGING BOWL

The Singing Bowl meditation serves as a transition from Rock Pose to class. Instruct the children to listen for the sound of the singing bowl, follow it with their attention, and roll up slowly from Rock Pose to a tall pose with a readiness for breath-work. This sound becomes very familiar and soothing to the children and helps to direct their attention inward.

SITTING POSTURE

The children are introduced to a sitting meditation posture. This is a specific way of sitting that is conducive to concentration practice. Children sit in either what is called "easy pose," kneeling, with body resting on legs, or "pretzel pose," with legs crossed. The spine is straight, crown of the head drawn up, and tailbone pointing down. This pose is difficult for some children at first because it requires an engagement of the core muscles and a tall spine. It requires effort. Over time it becomes easier, and the children come to see the connection between a tall spine and the ability to take a comfortable breath. The lungs are open, and breath flows easily and fluidly. The meditation posture supports a tall, healthy spine, engagement of core muscles, and an easy path for the movement of energy and breath. As they bring their awareness to their body, the children learn to make small adjustments to tend to the needs of their individual body. In time, the children achieve physical pliancy, and holding an upright posture supports optimal alertness and wakefulness. A sitting posture encourages the development of core muscle strength, a tall spine, and control of the body, all of which will serve the physical development of a child.

BREATH WORK

At the late preoperational stage of development, the breath becomes a tool capable of bringing the child to the present moment. It becomes a tool to assist the child in shifting the attention from an outward focus to an inward focus. At this stage of development, the breath becomes one of the most important tools in the child's developing concentration practice. Children at this age come to see the breath as a very precious aspect of themselves. It is their life force. Children at this stage of development are in awe of the fact that the body breathes for them, every moment of the day, regardless of their attention to it or not. It is also thrilling for them as they realize that sometimes the breath speeds up, as if you are running in a race. Sometimes, the breath slows down, as when you are sleeping. These observed changes in the breath seem to suggest to the child that the breath seems to always know what you need in each moment. These observations and realizations about the breath foster a deep appreciation for, connection to, and relationship with the breath, which will serve children as they continue to practice concentration.

Sphere Breath

A Hoberman Sphere is a useful tool as children prepare to shift their attention inward to the breath and as they prepare to let go of any props or tools they previously used to follow their breath. The Hoberman Sphere is a three-dimensional sphere that you can expand and contract. The children use their sense of sight to watch the sphere and match their inhalation and exhalation to the expanding and contracting movement. Before beginning you can talk to the children about what a comfortable breath feels like and looks like. This helps children to get a sense of the pace of a resting, calm breath. You might move the sphere so that it expands and contracts quickly and ask the children what animal might breathe at that rate. A hummingbird, a rabbit, a chipmunk might be some of the responses. Then move the sphere so it expands and contracts slowly and ask the children what animal might breathe at that rate. An elephant or a resting bear might be a response. Then demonstrate what the rate of a comfortable human breath might be. This helps bridge the concept of the pace of a comfortable, calm breath.

Ask the children to take a tall sitting posture and direct their eyes to the sphere that you are holding. As you expand the sphere, they breathe in, and as you contract the sphere they breathe out. As you pull on the sphere to expand it, the children inhale, at the rate that you are expanding the sphere. As you contract the sphere, the children exhale. Repeat 5 or 6 times.

Chapter 8: Concentration Development for Late Preoperational Children (Ages 7-9)

The children come to see the immediate sense of calm that can be felt when shifting attention and focus to a steady, full, easeful movement of breath. For some children it can be very helpful to have them operate the movement of the sphere. The physical sense of touch and movement can strengthen the mind body connection and a sense of calm. As one child said, "When I am having a rough day I use the breathing sphere or my breathing strategy when I am outside or not in the house, and then I don't have such a rough day anymore" (age 8).

Mindful Sharing

This activity is essentially the same as Mindful Sharing with the younger children. For children who have experienced this previously, it is often a welcome change to incorporate a river rock, another natural object, or no object at all in place of the puppet. Some children may prefer the puppet while others might feel they've outgrown it. In any case, giving children an opportunity to share what is present for them or something they wish to bring to the group is valuable as it helps the children settle in and helps you get a sense of what is on their mind. Again, it is a wonderful opportunity to develop supportive listening skills and the confidence to share with the group. After the children have settled in and before engaging in yoga practices or short meditations is the best time for this practice. They have had time to rest in class, experience calm through Rock Pose, and what arises is often deeper, more connected to what is true for them, and less reactive. With this age group, using a river rock, or another natural object, is useful. It is helpful to use the same object each time as the children will associate that object with a time to listen and share. Just like the puppet with the younger children, the object is passed around the circle. It is the child's choice to share. The sharing can be open and reflect whatever they might want to share, or it can be a response to a question or topic. This encourages children to listen carefully, holding the space for one another to express themselves. It is also helpful for the teacher to connect with the children, listening to what is present for them. Knowing what is present for them can be helpful in supporting each student through their practice. It also builds the sense of community as we listen and learn more about one another. An extension you might add for children at this age, once everyone has participated, is to give them the opportunity to share what they heard from a classmate. This is a wonderful way to encourage careful listening and acknowledge one another. Some examples might include. "Nina, I heard that you are excited to see your friend after school." "James, I heard that you rode your bike to school today." It is amazing to see the sparkle on a child's face when they feel heard.

Moving Meditation

Like setting an intention during Rock Pose, a Sun Salutation is a greeting and an expression of gratitude for the day before us. Stepping into the day with gratitude through a Sun Salutation is a beautiful way to link body, mind, and heart. As children move their body into and through each yoga pose, they are experiencing directing the mind. Movement through a Sun Salutation is often guided. The teacher instructs the movement through specific poses, and the child follows. Often children are asked to move through a Sun Salutation on their own. They begin in Mountain Pose allowing their body and mind to settle so that they begin from a point of steadiness, strength, and stillness. Listening to the music and the needs of their body, they move at their own pace through poses of their own choosing. The children are encouraged not to plan out their Sun Salutation or worry about what is to come next. They are encouraged to listen carefully to their body and to move through the poses that feel right, comfortable, or that they feel most drawn to in each moment. If they find that they feel stuck or unsure of what their body might need, they can choose to move through a series of cornerstone poses that all the children are introduced to first when learning a Sun Salutation. The children know these by heart. If along the way they notice that their body needs or wants something else, they can make that change and move through something different. Once children are familiar, confident, and comfortable moving through a Sun Salutation, this becomes a moving meditation that children welcome. They enjoy making their own choices, and come to realize the precious lesson that it can be easy knowing what to do next if they simply listen carefully.

WALKING MEDITATION

It is fun for children to realize that concentration practice does not need to be defined by their mat or meditation cushion. A walking meditation can be a focus on each step taken and the feeling of the foot being placed on the earth, where the sensation and placement of the foot on the ground becomes the meditation object. It can also involve the direction of the senses to the things around you. Have them take a walk around the neighborhood and encourage the children to be completely silent and focus on all of the things they hear, smell, or see. Focus on one sense in a meditation. The children will make a mental note or a written list and record/share their discoveries when they return. They are always eager to see how many things they come to notice. One group of children was amazed with the list of more than 30 different things they heard when taking a short walking meditation. For example, they noticed: crushing leaves, the clanking of a dog's chain, wind in the trees, car tires on pavement, whispering, splashing water, and a nut falling off a tree.

SHAKE IT STANDING MEDITATION

Another body-based movement meditation is called Shake It. Ask the children to stand in Mountain Pose, and allow them to ground and center into silence, strength, and steadiness. Holding their hands out in front of them, have the children notice the felt-sense of their hands. Then, have them shake their hands vigorously. Then, allow the hands to become still. As they close their eyes, have them notice the felt-sense of the hands again, noticing the different sensations. This can continue by having the children direct attention to the arms, feet, legs, body. *Shake It!* A song by Christopher Kavi Carbone leads the children through the movement and shaking of the body in a fun, playful way. The children love this song and find that it wakes them up and directs their awareness toward their body and an inward perspective.

Another variation is to simply allow the entire body to bounce. Keeping the feet firmly planted, slowly begin to bounce by bending the knees gently. Allow the rest of the body to feel loose so that eventually as the children increase the bounce, the shoulders, arms and torso join in the movement. Have the children allow a looseness in the neck as they continue to bounce. Have them gently allow the body to become still and return to Mountain Pose, closing the eyes and noticing the sensations of the body. Usually children will find that they feel more relaxed, loose, and awake.

CONCENTRATION 1: FOLLOWING THE BREATH; IDENTIFYING WITH THE MEDITATOR IN THE ELEPHANT PATH

The breath, our life-force, easily serves as a natural concentration object, as it is always with us. Even the youngest children were using their breath through various breathing techniques. Many of these techniques involve the senses. Here, children in the late preoperational stage now learn to use their sense of sight as they follow the expanding and contracting Hoberman Sphere and match their inhale and exhale to its movement. These techniques foster an easeful relationship with the breath, because they involve use of the senses.

Concentration meditation involves focusing the mind on one object and sustaining focus upon that object. As the children progress, developing physical pliancy and familiarity with the breath, rather than watching an object outside of themselves like the Hoberman Sphere, they

Chapter 8: Concentration Development for Late Preoperational Children (Ages 7-9)

become capable of following the internal movement of the breath. For some children it is difficult to make this shift from external to internal and following something that can't be seen. There are many techniques the children can incorporate to help them follow their breath internally. As children are just beginning concentration practice it is best to keep the concentration sessions short, less than 5 minutes, and increase the length of the session based on progress of the group or child.

Ask children to take a sitting posture. Children can rest their hands on their legs or take a *mudra*. A *mudra* is a traditional hand position used during meditation to encourage a specific energy flow in the body. For children, it is often easiest to simply rest the hands on the legs or rest one palm in another on the lap. Sometimes children enjoy experimenting with a specific hand position that feels comfortable for them. Traditionally Elephant Path meditations are taught with the eyes open. It can be helpful for children to begin with a closed eye position as it limits external distraction and creates a sense of calm. If children are not comfortable closing their eyes, or get sleepy when the eyes are closed, an open eye position can be skillful and helpful. Children can be invited to either close their eyes or simply bring their gaze down to a diagonal point in front of them.

Begin by instructing children to notice the felt-sense of their body. Have the child imagine shining a flashlight throughout his or her body, noticing if there is any discomfort anywhere, if their body feels relaxed and calm. If they feel discomfort, they can make little adjustments. Then, ask the children to draw their attention to their breath. At first, they are instructed to simply notice the breath. Are they breathing fast or slow? Sometimes asking children to rest their hands on their chest or belly can be helpful, as they can feel and connect with the movement of the breath and its effect on moving the belly. Sometimes noticing the breath at the nostrils is helpful. These tactile strategies are helpful for children who find it difficult to find the breath. If a child is unable to find their breath at all, instruct them to simply rest their attention in their silence, the felt-sense of their body or the spaciousness that they feel during the meditation, encouraging them to make the effort to check in now and then to see if they can locate or get a sense of their breath.

As children are able to find their breath, instruct them to count their breaths. An inhale and exhale are counted as one breath. Count a few breaths together as children follow your count. When you feel the children are ready, you can ask them to continue on, counting 5-10 cycles of the breath on their own. The inhale and exhale are counted as one full breath cycle. Ask the children to count their breaths with their fingers. Resting their hands on their lap, they can simply make a fist and draw one finger out for each breath taken. In this way, they keep track of their breath, and you can see how far along the children are. Encourage the children to take comfortable, slow breaths. Many children get anxious or want to be the first to finish so will breathe very quickly. Encourage a calm pace. Once you notice children finishing, instruct the children to rest in the felt sense of their body or continue counting their breath until they hear the singing bowl.

Sound the singing bowl to mark the end of the concentration session and encourage the children to gently open their eyes. Ask the children to share their experiences. While this can be difficult for some children, it is important to encourage them to share so that you have a sense of how they are doing. You can better gauge what instruction or support to offer.

What is the Mind? Identifying with the Elephant on The Elephant Path; Clouds in the Sky

It is important to help the children understand what the mind is at this stage of practice. Many children think that the mind is the brain. Help them to make the distinction that the brain is an organ; it is part of the body. It is a physical object that can be seen and touched. The mind is formless and helps you perceive, understand, and be aware of the world. A Tibetan lama, Rahob Tulku Rinpoche, explained how he helped children understand what the mind is. He asked the simple question, "Where is the mind?" The children at this age typically responded, "I am thinking." He then asked the children to locate where the thinking comes from? Some children didn't know. Some pointed to their body. When he pointed out that without the mind you can't think about the body, they agreed that the mind wasn't a material thing that they could see, but that something was still there. He asked them. "So, where does thinking come from?" Then he asked them to look outside at space, to look at the sky, and asked how clouds move. While some were not sure, others said they moved when the wind came. He shared with them the metaphor that thoughts are like the clouds. They move. The mind is like space or the sky within which they move. Clouds are like thought coming and going. Sometimes the sky fills with clouds and cloudy thinking comes. Then Rinpoche told the children that concentration practice helps you clear away the clouds.[1]

CLOUD MEDITATION

The cloud meditation is a beautiful metaphor for helping children to understand the mind. Take the children outside to an open area. Tell the children that they will have the opportunity to rest on their backs, looking up at the sky. It is best to choose a spot that is unobstructed, without tree branches or anything that might limit the view of the sky. Ask the children to simply look at the sky as a whole, noticing its vastness, spaciousness, taking in the whole sky like a large painting. Then, ask them to draw their attention to a cloud and watch it carefully. What does it do? Does it stay the same? Does it change? Does it move? If it changes, how does it change? After watching one cloud for a while, have the children draw their attention to other clouds. Sound a chime to bring the cloud meditation to a close and share. Children will notice the never-ending, limitless nature of the sky. They will notice movements of clouds across the sky, change in shape, and even clouds disappearing. The cloud metaphor provides a beautiful introduction to the mind and its movement.

MONKEY MIND; IDENTIFYING WITH THE MONKEY ON THE ELEPHANT PATH

Through observing the activity of thought to be like the movement of clouds, children come to notice the quality and activity of their mind

---

1. Personal communication, Rahob Tulku Rinpoche, January 2018.

and its contents. They are likely to discover that some days the mind is quiet, and other days it is loud and full of thought. Some days the sky is full of clouds, while some days it is a crystal clear blue cloudless sky. Some days it is easy to follow the breath. On other days the distractions around us can pull attention away from the object of concentration. As children become more comfortable following the breath, a persistent challenge becomes how to manage external distractions, like sights and sounds; and internal distractions, like thought and emotions. Some days the child will find they are able to hold their attention very close to the breath. Other days they become caught up in noticing distractions around them and activity of thought. "Monkey mind" is a term used to describe the mind that is incessantly distracted. When the extent of distraction becomes monkey mind, it is very difficult to follow the concentration object. It is likely that the child will feel like monkey mind has taken over, causing attention to dart from one thing to another, keeping the mind from the breath. Nevertheless, the child is developing sufficient meta-cognitive awareness to actually know when he or she is caught up in distraction. *Mindful Monkey, Happy Panda* by Lauren Alderfer is a great book to read to children to help illustrate monkey mind. Monkey mind is a concept that the children relate to easily. It can be very frustrating for children when they are experiencing monkey mind and the mind is full of thought and distraction. It is easy to zone out, chase after the thought, or get lost in the daydream.

The mind is an idea maker, it is our creative center, it is the birthplace of thought. The purpose is not to get rid of thought, but simply to notice it, not get caught up in it, and let it be without engaging it or blindly chasing after it. Both the breath and the felt-sense of the body as concentration objects are tools that are within the child and available to them at any moment as they learn to bring their mind to the present moment. It is extremely empowering when a child comes to witness their ability to do this, to watch their mind at work and to make the conscious choice to direct the attention to the breath, or whatever the concentration object might be, or most importantly, to the present moment. The ability to notice one's thoughts is one of the marks of the development of meta-cognition.

Chapter 8: Concentration Development for Late Preoperational Children (Ages 7-9)

The Mind Jar; Noticing the Workings of the Mind

The Mind Jar is a tool that symbolizes the mind. It is a mason jar containing sand and water. The sand symbolizes all the stuff of your mind. As we said, the mind is an idea-maker, a place of creativity, interpretation, and ideas. Like a snow globe, when the jar is settled, the sand is simply resting at the bottom, like the restful, meditative mind. When one shakes the jar, the sand scatters around the jar and it becomes cloudy, busy, swirling with sand particles. This represents "monkey mind" or the mind that is engaged in thought or distraction. Once you set the jar down, like the body resting into a meditation, the sand slowly begins to settle. You can sit patiently and simply watch the jar, like we watch the mind, as each particle floats to the bottom of the jar. When all the particles settle, the water is clear and still again. The particles are still there. They've just come to rest at the bottom. This is reflective of a mind that is truly resting in the present moment. It is a mind that is clear, still, ready for the moment at hand. Using a mason jar or similar glass jar with a lid, water, and sand, you can construct this model of the mind with children. The jar itself represents the vessel that holds the mind. The water represents the space aspect of the mind that thoughts move through. The sand represents the "stuff" of the mind. This includes ideas, thoughts, emotions, distractions, sounds, smells etc.—anything that attracts the mind. Scoop a few tablespoons or about a half-inch to an inch of sand into the mason jar. Fill the jar with water. Secure the lid. Ask the children to describe the mind jar that has been activated. They might share descriptors such as, excited, crazy, cloudy, confused. When asked to describe the mind jar at rest, the descriptors might be calm, silent, still, clear, peaceful, restful. The mind jar becomes an important tool to refer to before and after concentration sessions, as children can begin to compare their mind during their concentration meditation with the qualities of the mind jar. Children are developing meta-cognition, a relationship with their mind, and a familiarity with the mind that is clear and the mind that is distracted.

CONCENTRATION 2: NOTICING THE ACTIVITY OF THE MIND; IDENTIFYING WITH THE ELEPHANT AND THE MONKEY ON THE ELEPHANT PATH

The previous concentration practice, namely following the breath, encourages children to hold the breath close, through the task of counting the breath. This current concentration practice will introduce the 2-point object as a strategy for following the breath. The 2-point object refers to the inhalation and the exhalation as two specific aspects or points of the breath. The children watch the inhalation carefully and the exhalation carefully and direct the mind to each distinct moment or point of the breath in time. Once children are comfortable locating the movement of the breath and are able to keep their attention on it, encourage them to let go of counting the breath and to direct attention to the 2-point object, first the inhalation and then the exhalation. Some children will still need to use the counting method to develop concentration on the breath. Whichever method children are using to follow the breath, encourage them to notice: when it becomes difficult to follow the breath; and when something distracts them from the breath. As they keep the attention focused and sustained on the breath, they are simultaneously noticing with their meta-cognition any movement of the mind away from the breath, and also noticing instances of chasing after thought or sense-experience.

Shifting from counting the breath to following the two-point object can naturally cause a loosening of the focus on the breath or an easing up. Children are likely to notice that any easing up from following the breath will invite distraction. It can be exciting for children as they come to witness the noise and thoughts within or around them, alongside the breath. They begin to notice the tendency of their mind to move toward or chase after something. The attention might shift to a sound in the room, or a thought, or even to a daydream. Use the example of the clouds in the sky. Allowing the thought to move on through as the clouds drift across the sky. Use the Mind Jar as a strategy to allow the distractions to settle. Just as the sand settles to the bottom of the jar, there is an allowing of the distraction to settle and a returning of the mind to the breath.

Chapter 8: Concentration Development for Late Preoperational Children (Ages 7-9)

Ask children to take their sitting posture and gently close their eyes. Ask them to notice the felt-sense of their body. Instruct them to move their attention through their body noticing how their body feels. Similar to the way you might shine a flashlight in the dark, have the children do a quick investigation of the body to see if there are any minor adjustments to make so that they feel comfortable. Ask the children to bring their attention to their breath and begin to notice their breath. Ask them to notice first the rising breath and then the falling breath. Guide the children in a few cycles of the breath where you are describing and counting the 2-point object for them. Then encourage them to continue to follow the 2-point object on their own, at their own pace, as if they are watching the rising and falling of a wave, or the wave washing onto the beach and being drawn back out. Then, invite them to use their meta-cognition to notice if they get distracted or if it becomes difficult to follow the breath. If so, remind them of the clouds in the sky metaphor, or the mind jar, and instruct them to see any distraction as something floating in the background, while bringing their attention back to the breath and allowing the distraction to settle. Encourage the children to sustain focus on the 2-point object. Continue with this instruction for around 10 cycles of the breath. Then, tell the children that when they hear the singing bowl they can bring their meditation to a close and gently open their eyes. Then, ask children to share their experiences.

Some children will find following the 2-point object easy and will report that they were able to sustain their attention on the breath the whole time. Some children may only be able to follow the 2-point object when you gave the instruction reminding them to bring their attention to it. Some children will share that they were drawn away by a distraction most of the time, or that they tuned out the directions. For example, they might have been distracted by a sound outside or an idea that popped into their mind and became a daydream. Encourage the children to share, and reinforce that whatever their experience, they are making progress.

Continue to work on the following the breath meditation, concentrating on the 2-point object as children gain comfort following the breath without the need to count it. Use the metaphor of clouds in the sky and the Mind Jar to allow thoughts to settle.

DEEPENING PRACTICE

Handlebars or Steering Wheel Metaphor: As a useful strategy for redirecting attention to the concentration object, the teacher can use the handlebars or steering wheel metaphor. After some experience with short concentration sessions using the 2-point object to follow the breath, you can introduce the strategy of the steering wheel or handle bars for redirecting the mind back to the breath. As children shift from counting the breath to following the 2-point object without counting, they will notice a natural easing up of the activity of mind. The steering wheel is a strategy that is used to help understand your ability to intentionally move or direct the mind back to your concentration object, the 2-point breath. For children who ride a bike, the idea of the handlebars might resonate. The steering wheel or handlebars are the tools to illustrate keeping the vehicle on track. Just as you use the steering wheel to direct a car back on track, you use your intention to direct the mind back to your breath. The steering wheel on a car or the handlebars on a bike are used to keep the bike on course. When riding a bike, if you want to go straight ahead, you don't hold the handlebars in one position. You make slight adjustments to keep the bike moving on a straight path. As the bike shifts to one direction you use the handle bars to steer it back on course and to sustain it on that course. While this takes effort at first, soon the children don't have to think about it, and they develop automaticity. It is very easy for children to become intrigued with whatever the mind moves to or gets distracted by. Remind the children to use their handlebars or steering wheel to direct their minds to the breath, so that they learn to develop the mind muscle and the ability to direct their mind to whatever the object of concentration is.

Repeat the previous concentration sessions using the 2-point object. Check in with the children frequently to remind them to direct their attention back to their breath. Encourage them to use the steering wheel or handle bars to direct their attention back to the breath. Just as children were directing their mind to their body during Rock Pose and the sound of the bowl during the Singing Bowl Meditation, children are now recognizing their own ability to direct their mind intentionally

Chapter 8: Concentration Development for Late Preoperational Children (Ages 7-9)

to a concentration object. With their attention directed inwardly to the breath, when their mind struggles to stay on the breath, they begin to identify what it is that distracts them. These distractions might be noises around them, sense-experiences, thoughts, feelings, body-sensations. They may notice that there was one particular sensation, thought, or distraction that their mind kept moving to. Sometimes they will notice that their mind darted from one thing to another, inside or outside. The children are noticing the movement of the mind, developing strategies to keep the mind focused, and developing their meta-cognitive ability to self-correct. They are coming to see themselves as the practitioner in the Elephant Path painting. Their mind, like the elephant, if left to its own devices, will run wild. The monkey, their thoughts and distractions, always wants to control, distract, and entice the mind to follow it, to create movement within the mind. The goals at this stage of development are: an ability to direct and sustain focus on the breath as a concentration object; improved meta-cognitive awareness of the movement of the mind when distracted; and the skill to redirect the mind back to the concentration object once distracted.

BABY BIRD VISUALIZATION MEDITATION

It is useful to introduce the baby bird meditation at this stage if children are becoming more aware of and distracted by the mind's movement and are struggling to bring their attention back to the breath, even with the strategy of the steering wheel or handlebars. Instruct the children to take their meditation posture. Have them bring their hands together like a nest, as if they are holding something or scooping a handful of sand. Ask them to hold their hands in front of them at the level of their heart. They can have their eyes closed or open, whichever is most comfortable. Instruct the children to bring their attention to the felt-sense of their body, making any adjustments to feel comfortable in their sitting posture. Lead them in a couple of full breaths in through the nose and exhaling gently through the nose. Allow time for settling in to their posture and directing the attention within.

Then, ask the children to imagine that their hands are a beautiful bird's nest. Ask them to imagine they are holding a baby bird, who has not yet learned to fly. Ask them to picture this in their mind—what the baby bird looks like, the colors, and the feel of the bird in their hands. Ask them to notice the care and attention they would bring to holding this small, fragile creature in their hands. Ask them to notice the effort or intensity with which they would watch the baby bird to ensure that it is safe in their hands. Ask them to take a moment to notice any other qualities that come up as they imagine holding this fragile and precious creature in their hands with utmost care. Instruct the children to take a couple of full breaths into their body as they bring the meditation to a close. Then, ask the children to share their experience with the meditation. Ask them to describe how they were holding and watching the baby bird. Guide the children to recognize the increased effort they brought forth within themselves to focus and attend to ensure the safety of the bird.

During a concentration meditation, as they begin to notice that their mind is being carried away by thoughts and distractions, ask them to see if they can bring to their concentration some of the energy and care that they brought to holding the baby bird. The children will find that applying this effort will allow the mind to stay more closely on the breath.

Resting Attention in the Heart and Silence Meditations: Noticing Feelings and Emotions as they Arise

These awareness exercises are important and skillful at all stages. Feelings and emotions are often the most powerful movements of the mind. Feelings and emotions arise frequently as a response to external stimuli and internal thought. Helping children to gain awareness of their feelings, to give them voice and attention, is important as children develop healthy social emotional skills. Concentration is not meant to get rid of thought, emotion, or other distractors. It is meant to develop skills to allow them to settle sufficiently, so that the mind can be directed to the object of concentration, and in so doing they build the mind muscle, and mental pliancy. Feeling and emotion are often the toughest

Chapter 8: Concentration Development for Late Preoperational Children (Ages 7-9)

to let go of or allow to settle. During heart meditations, children are encouraged to notice the feelings and emotion that arise. Identifying, naming, and understanding feelings allows children to feel resolve and move past them. Not only does this support a healthy awareness of self but also our relationship to and connection with others. As feelings and emotion arise in their concentration meditation, they are better able not to attach to them, but to allow them to settle.

Feeling and Emotion as Movement

As you explore feeling and emotion with children it is helpful to investigate how it is held or expressed through the body. Brainstorm a list of some of the feelings that they frequently experience. Ask the children to move in a way that exemplifies that feeling. You might turn on music, call out an emotion or feeling, and allow the children to move in a way that they might express that feeling. This helps them gain an understanding as to how that feeling moves or is expressed as energy in their body. When children are sitting on their mats you can ask them to close their eyes, consider a certain feeling, and ask where they feel that feeling in their body. A child might say that they feel sadness in their heart. Share with them that you can use your breath to move a feeling through your body the way the clouds move through the sky. As they feel a strong feeling or emotion, have them draw a full, positive breath into their body, into the area where they feel the strong feeling. As they exhale, imagine the strong feeling moving out with the exhalation. Repeat this several times. Ask the child how they feel. Do they feel any difference? It is important to help children to see that feelings and emotions are movements within the mind, just like the clouds in the sky. Strong emotions might arrive like hurricanes or tornadoes, blowing strong but then going away.

One little boy shared that he was not able to concentrate during his meditations because that day he also had his piano lesson after school. He shared that he did not like piano lessons and was always nervous about them. He shared that when he got quiet during concentration sessions and his mind became calm, that the worry grew, and fear would take over his whole mind. Then he could not find his breath. All he could find was the fear. After asking him about his piano lesson he said that he liked playing the piano, and he liked his teacher. When asked where he felt the fear in his body, he said in his belly. When asked if the fear was doing anything to help him. He said, "no," and added that he just wanted to play well and not mess up, but that sometimes he got nervous playing piano for someone else. Reminding him that he is the boss of his own mind, he decided he did not want the fear to hang around and decided that the fear was something he wanted to let go of. When he went back to the meditation we all spent a little extra time noticing the felt-sense of our body. He focused particularly on his belly, noticing the sensation. When we turned our attention to the breath, he held his attention close to the breath, and if fear happened to come up his intention was to let it be and direct his attention to the breath. He found some relief and a lightening of the fear. The following week he came to class and expressed that he was still feeling anxious about his piano lesson. We did a similar practice with his anxiousness, reminding him that he could practice this breathing anytime that he felt the fear and anxiousness coming up. The following week he said it was much better. He barely felt the fear. The following week he came in and said that he would like to play one of his songs for all of us. So, he sat down to play his tune on the piano.

This boy's experience was a teaching for all of us. It was a clear example that some thoughts and feelings are strong. They hang around, feel heavy, as if they want to control us. While it is not about getting rid of the feeling, it is about noticing it, viewing it, utilizing your strategies, and allowing it to subside, to move, possibly to dissolve, like the clouds moving across the sky. In any case, there is a loosening of the grip or attachment to the feeling and a more easeful ability to move through and settle in the present moment.

It is really important for the teacher to be aware of and sensitive to each child's experience as they learn to recognize thought, feeling and emotion, and redirect the mind back to the concentration object. When a child identifies a strong feeling or emotion that might feel overwhelming or very difficult to let go of there might be instances where it is im-

Chapter 8: Concentration Development for Late Preoperational Children (Ages 7-9)

portant to address this privately with the child to offer individual support and care. The skillfulness of the teacher and ability to deeply listen to the child is of utmost importance. Children need to feel safe, secure, and supported at all times.

The Elephant Path: Attention Development and Training in Children and Adolescents

Chapter 9

Concentration Development for Concrete Operational Children (Ages 9-12)

by Michelle G. Bissanti, M.Ed.

At this stage of development, the children are well on their way up the Elephant Path. They are developing a comfortable meditation posture, physical pliancy, and have a greater awareness of the body. The children are familiar with the practitioner, the monkey, and the elephant, and they are becoming aware of the twists, turns, and pitfalls of the Elephant Path. They are developing mental pliancy and the strategies and skills needed for sustained concentration.

Along the first two turns of The Elephant Path, children are experiencing basic concentration meditation, following the breath. They are gaining meta-cognitive awareness of the mind's ability to move toward distraction (chasing-after mode) and are beginning to learn methods for bringing the mind back to the concentration object. Remembering that they are not getting rid of anything, erasing anything, or negating anything, these older children are simply allowing the contents of the mind to settle, and allowing distractions to be something that come and go in the background, so that the mind and attention can return to the object of concentration.

As children progress through concrete operational thinking they are capable of understanding the main experiences of the 3rd and 4th turns of the Elephant Path (See Figure 1: page 195). They have come to know the practitioner, elephant, and monkey well. Now, they are introduced to other elements of the Elephant Path painting: the rope, the flames, and the rabbit. Children at this stage are greatly developing their meta-cognitive capacities. They are acquiring skills and strategies so that when they experience distraction they know that an antidote can be applied.

Over time they develop an awareness of strategies that give them the ability to self-correct problems that arise as they develop concentration. The rope represents sustaining concentration, literally by tying the mind securely to the concentration object. The practitioner has "captured" the elephant-mind with his or her rope. Recall that, the rope is held neither too tight or too loose, but in a comfortable way to hold the mind securely. The flame represents the output of effort or intensifying that is needed for concentration. The rabbit represents the subtle dullness that can develop from too much intensifying. In the painting the color of the elephant changes as the elephant progresses up the path. The initial dark color represents thought and other distractions of the mind. The light color represents clarity of mind and calmness. Sense perception is symbolized in the painting by various objects, such as cloth (touch), perfumed conch (smell), fruit (taste), etc.

The development of meta-cognition at this stage goes hand-in-hand with increased confidence, pliancy, and automaticity. These older children are able to sustain attention for a longer duration than younger children, and they are able to detect and resist distraction more immediately.

In addition to developing concentration meditation, children at this stage are also engaging in activities and meta-cognitive reflection to come to understand themselves and their mind more intimately. They learn healthy ways of interacting with one another and gain the confidence to take their practice off the mat.

While most older children are developing a longer attention span—beginning with 2-3 minute meditations is initially appropriate--this can be increased quickly depending on the group. Generally, 5-15 minutes is the optimal duration for the session. The goal is for the children to have enough time to settle in and sustain their concentration for a longer duration. If the duration of the concentration session is too long, most of the children will be unable to maintain their strategies for focus and will likely get discouraged. Building confidence in the skill of concentration is of utmost importance. Involving the children in selecting the length of time for the practice session is an option, provided what they select is realistic.

Chapter 9: Concentration Development for Concrete Operational Children (Ages 9-12)

Goals and Objectives

While children develop and grasp concepts at different rates and in different ways, there is fluidity, flexibility, and individuality to the progression of these practices and the acquiring of these skills. Here is a list of the skills of concentration training that typically develop at this stage:

- *Development of intention and positive motivation*
- *Physical pliancy (ease of the body settling into the posture and sustaining the posture without discomfort)*
- *Ability to use meta-cognitive awareness to notice when the body posture is uncomfortable and the ability to make adjustments*
- *Ability to follow the breath, and stay concentrated on it with some consistency*
- *Ability to sustain concentration for longer duration*
- *Ability to intensify effort to engage the concentration object more closely*
- *More immediate identification of distractions, such as thoughts, emotions, and perceptions arising*
- *Ease to redirect focus back to the object of concentration once distracted*
- *Mental pliancy, (ease of the mind to attend without interference)*
- *Development of meta-cognition in the form of more immediate noticing of distraction, and ability to reflect on and incorporate a strategy to redirect focus*
- *Increased attention span and sustaining concentration*
- *The occurrence of distinct episodes of calmness (absence of thought) during concentration practice*
- *Taking the practice off the mat, such as applying concentration skills to schoolwork, applying meta-cognitive strategies in everyday problem-solving, and development of positive conduct toward self and others.*
- *Increased capacity to take perspective on the task at hand*
- *Development of social emotional strategies*
- *Awareness of conduct—social emotional skill development, pro-social skills*

Rahob Tulku Rinpoche says, "You are the boss of your own mind." This important teaching can serve as a great motivator for children of this age. As they come to develop their meta-cognitive capacity, familiarity and confidence with the practice, the messages of this teaching, become clear. It is the teacher's responsibility to guide the children along offering the teachings that are appropriate and supportive for each child and group of children. The teacher holds the space for all children to experience these practices, and is committed to guide each child along, providing them with what they need to acquire the tools for understanding.

PREPARATIONAL PRACTICES

At the concrete operational stage preparational practices continue to be important and helpful transitional tools. As children go through developmental, social-emotional, and physical changes, it is important to develop a trusting relationship and to provide the best steps to bridge the way to their practice. Some repetition and routine are important, however, knowing what they need and providing the flexibility to implement the preparational practices that best serve the children builds a strong foundation and sets the meditation session up for success.

Rock Pose, The Singing Bowl Meditation, and the Breathing Sphere are all useful practices that the younger children are familiar with and help children transition, settle in, and prepare for a sitting concentration practice. They may be useful for older children at this age as well. As bodies are changing, Rock Pose can sometimes feel uncomfortable for some students. The short movement activities introduced earlier, like Shake It, Bouncing, or a Walking Meditation can be useful. Guided visualization can also foster a sense of relaxation and calm. They can be used at this stage of development for easing anxiety and stress, developing awareness of the body and the body/mind connection, and letting go of the busyness of the day.

Scanning and Relaxing the Body is a guided exercise that helps to relax the body by taking a close look at the felt-sense of the body, which facilitates the release of any tension or holding. Like Rock Pose, children allow the body to settle on the mat, noticing silence and stillness, and settling in to the moment. At this stage children shift to an inward focus and direct their attention throughout the body to allow relaxation. "The body scan alternates between a wide and narrow focus of attention; from focusing on your little toe all the way through the entire body. The body scan trains perspective-taking in that it entails an ability to move the focus from a detailed attention to a wider and more spacious awareness from one moment to the next" (mindful.org—*The Body Scan Practice*, 2012).

At this stage children are introduced to the inward body scan in the following manner. Instruct children to rest comfortably on their backs, with the legs outstretched and slightly apart, and the arms at their side, about 10 inches from the body. Instruct the children to bring their attention to their bodies resting on the mat. Ask them to notice, with their attention, the felt-sense of their body as a whole, considering the body to be one concentration object. Notice how the body-as-a-whole feels right now. Have the child bring attention to the head to notice the entire felt-sense of the head. Focus on the crown of the head and skull, allowing the head to relax. Direct the child's attention to the outer surface of the face, relaxing the space between the eyebrows, allowing the eye balls to rest in their sockets, opening the mouth wide and allowing it to close gently, and relaxing the jaw. Bring attention to the neck and shoulders allowing the release of any tension. Shift attention across the shoulders and down each arm, upper arm, elbow, lower arm, wrists, hands, and fingers. Allow the arms and hands to relax. Bring attention to the torso, relaxing the chest, then the belly, then the front of the body, the spine and finally the back of the body. Bring attention to the hips, relaxing the entire hip area. Allow the weight of the torso and hips to rest on the earth beneath where the child sits as if they are melting into the floor. Move attention down each leg, upper leg, knee, lower leg, ankle, foot, toes. Allow the muscles of the leg to relax so that the entire leg and foot relax and rest on the floor. Direct attention to the entire felt-sense of your body once again. Consider the body as a whole and notice how it feels. Notice how it might feel different than it did when first resting the body on the mat. Enjoy a few moments to rest into this relaxed body, to also notice the spaciousness and sense of calm. Sound the singing bowl inviting children to slowly move into a sitting posture.

BREATH WORK

Have the child take a few clearing breaths to signify grounding, and centering on the mat. A deep breath in through the nose and out through the mouth can be very settling. The Hoberman Sphere can also be used. Asking a child to lead with the sphere is a wonderful opportunity to foster confidence and leadership. While there are a number of other breathing techniques that are useful, and foster relaxation, a sense of calm, and a letting go of tension or distraction, here are a few examples:

Full body Breath: Have the child take a deep breath and imagine filling the entire body with positive, calming energy. Upon exhaling a full breath, have the child imagine letting go of any tension, worry, or holding. With each exhale direct the child to notice the settling of the body arriving on the mat, a sense of calm, stillness and silence. Repeat three times.

Belly Chest Breath: Have the child take a deep breath to fill up the lower belly first and then the chest and lungs. Upon exhalation the child releases the breath from the chest and lungs first, and then from the lower belly. Children can rest a hand on the belly and a hand on the chest as this tactile detail can help draw awareness to the breath and a sense of calm. Repeat three times.

4, 5, 7 Breath: Have the child inhale for a count of 4, gently hold the breath without effort for a count of 5, and then exhale for a count of 7. Directing the children to notice the sense of calm after each breath or at the end of the sequence can be helpful. Repeat three times

Thinking of the breath as an anchor to the moment is a helpful metaphor at this age. A boat anchored in a harbor will not leave the harbor. It will shift with the movement and rhythm of the water, but it will remain tethered to its location. Similarly, the mind, anchored in this moment, will find its rhythm with the comings and goings of distractions and thoughts, guided by its anchor, the breath. As children settle in, ground, and prepare for meditation, it is helpful to remind them to think of the breath as their anchor. This metaphor will serve as a helpful reminder when they are engaged in a concentration meditation.

SETTING INTENTION AND DEVELOPING MOTIVATION

Ultimately, intention becomes a driving force in a concentration practice. As children begin to develop more mature meta-cognition, the acknowledgment of intention can initiate the strategy, or direction of the mind. Setting intentions at the beginning of each practice helps make the goal of the session explicit and sets a nice tone for the class.

Here are two activities that inspire motivation:

Quality Rocks: Children choose a positive quality that represents a strength, something that is important to them, or something that actively helps them and offers support for their practice. They write this word on a river rock and this becomes a symbol and reminder of a quality they can rely on or that they'd like to bring to their practice. These themes might include: confidence, happiness, courage, or patience.

Personal collages: Children enjoy creating collages that represent their personality, identity etc. Using photos, words, images, drawings, the children assemble a visual collection. They choose a word that represents a quality that they would like to cultivate within themselves. Maybe they already exemplify this quality but want to bring more awareness to it or more effort bringing it into their life. They place this word at the center of their collage. This collage becomes a type of portrait of who they believe themselves to be, how they see themselves in this moment, and what they hope to cultivate and bring into their being. Once a child chose the word patience as something she wanted to experience more of. She illustrated her collage with images of a yoga practice, gardening, and helping animals. Another chose calm and included images of sea turtles, majestic mountains, and the moon. While another child chose confidence with images of colorful tropical birds, a hang glider, and a tree.

Exploring positive qualities by means of creating quality rocks and collages supports the setting of intentions, creates motivation within the children, and fosters an eagerness to develop the concentration practice. Encouraging intention and meta-cognitive inquiry allows for self-reflection as children can acknowledge growth, set new goals, and change intentions as they develop their concentration practice.

PREPARATION FOR THE CONCENTRATION SESSION

Meditation Posture: Take the time to help children find the meditation posture that is most comfortable for them. Easy Pose or Pretzel Pose are the most efficient postures as they support a tall spine and engagement of the core muscles. As children develop and as bodies grow, their meditation posture might change. It is helpful for children at this stage to sit on a meditation cushion, a yoga block, or a blanket. This allows the hips to sit slightly above the knees and can provide more comfort to the body. It is especially important that the upper trunk is held upright and not slumped forward. This posture is important because it promotes wakefulness as it requires just enough engagement of the body to keep it attentive. The hands are resting on the legs, or stacked, one hand resting in the other, just below the navel. This becomes a grounding, centering exercise in-and-of-itself.

Felt-sense of the body: After taking their meditation posture, children engage their minds by noticing the felt-sense of the body. This technique helps to support a comfortable posture, and also helps to direct the mind to the body as a concentration object. Children begin by noticing the feeling of their body on the mat. Connecting with the idea that they are being supported by the mat and the ground beneath them, allows them to settle in and develop a connection to the earth. This offers a sense of stability as they begin the concentration session. Scanning the body is an important step as it allows the children to take careful notice of their bodies and to apply their meta-cognition to notice if there are any areas where they feel tension or contraction. It is simply a task of noticing, where the child scans quickly through their body beginning at the crown of their head and moving through their body to the bottoms

Chapter 9: Concentration Development for Concrete Operational Children (Ages 9-12)

of their feet. As they bring their attention to different areas of the body they are simply noticing the felt-sense. It is exciting for children to realize their ability to feel their body simply with the direction of their mind. As they feel tension or holding in the body, sometimes simply noticing it can allow release, and comfort.

CONCENTRATION 1: FOLLOWING THE BREATH, NOTICING THE MIND AND REDIRECTING

This foundational concentration meditation is the same as the Following the Breath meditation introduced earlier for the late preoperational child. However, for the older concrete operational child, a new element is added in that the instructions now incorporate meta-cognitive awareness of movement of the mind off the breath and also instructions to redirect the mind back to the breath.

The 3-point object can be introduced at this stage as most children are comfortable with the 2-point object and they have now had more experience with the felt-sense of the body through guided visualization. Similar to the 2-point object, the inhalation and exhalation remain as the focus of concentration. At the completion of the exhalation, a third point, the felt-sense of the body as a whole, is added as a point for focus of concentration during the interval between the breaths. For many children this entails no more than a quick noticing. However, as the child becomes more concentrated, the interval between the full cycle of breaths becomes longer. Taking the body as a concentration object during this interval, however long or short, prevents the child from re-engaging with distraction. There should not be any holding of the breath at this point, but rather a simple quick pause to notice the body, and then to the next inhalation, and so on.

As the children settle in to following the breath, the instructor offers frequent reminders to keep the attention on the breath, to watch it closely and carefully, the way you might hold a delicate baby bird. In this way, if the child's attention does leave the breath, the instructor's immediate reminder will initiate their redirection back to the breath. The metaphor of the steering wheel or the handlebars on a bike is used to redirect attention to the breath and felt-sense of the body. Ask the children to take their meditation posture and settle the body with any minor adjustments that might be necessary. Instruct them to bring their attention to the felt-sense of their body, simply scanning through the body as if shining a flashlight, noticing where they might be feeling tense and allowing those areas to relax, and gently allowing a sense of calm to develop. Then, instruct the children to notice their bodies breathing and to locate the breath within the body. Encourage them to notice the quality of the breath. Is it calm or strong, fast or slow? Tell the children there is no need to change or modify the breath in any way, simply allow the body to breathe in its natural way. Instruct the children to begin with the 2-point concentration object following the breath with attention, noticing the rising and falling breath.

Next, instruct the children to direct their attention to the 3-point object, watching the movement of the breath, noticing first the inhalation, then the exhalation, and finally in the interval between the full cycle of breaths to notice the felt-sense of the body. The child at this developmental stage is encouraged to notice the breath without depending on a strategy of counting the breath. For children comfortable with finding the breath this often comes with a sense of ease. For some children the strategy of counting the breath might still be useful if they are distracted and need support settling into the meditation. It is still very useful for the instructor to remind the children frequently to keep their attention on their breath, and to engage the breath very closely through intensifying. Children are told to follow the breath as if watching something very precious. Because the ordinary activity of the mind may draw their attention away frequently from the concentration object, the instructor gives a simple reminder to use the steering wheel or handlebars to turn the mind away from the distraction and back to the concentration object, the breath. The meditation can be brought to a close by asking the children to follow 3 more cycles of the breath or by sounding the singing bowl. Then, ask the children to share their experiences.

The goals and main objective at this stage is for the child to follow the breath with awareness of the 3-point object, sustain concentration for longer and longer duration, and notice distraction and redirect the mind when it becomes distracted. It is advisable at this point to devote some time and care to make sure children have developed physical pliancy and are comfortable in their sitting posture. Many are able to watch the 2- point object and then skillfully switch to the 3-point object. These older children are able to listen to the teacher's directions and redirect to the breath with the strategy given. Once a child attains confidence in these basic skills of concentration, he or she is able to notice and articulate more immediately when the mind got distracted. Some children will notice that they were able to follow the breath at first, but the mind shifted to a daydream or another distraction and they never found the breath again. Whether children share verbally or not, encourage the children to reflect upon what went well and also where they struggled. Ask them to think about what they need to incorporate next time. Maybe they were uncomfortable in their posture and need to make an adjustment. Maybe they need to listen more carefully to instructions. They might need to recognize when to use the steering wheel or handlebars. Encouraging this type of reflection facilitates the development of awareness and meta-cognition.

Concentration 2: Noticing the Movement of the Mind and Identifying Distractions

The mind is an incessant idea-maker. The purpose of concentration practice is never to get rid of thought or feeling or any type of distraction, but simply to notice it and not chase after it so as to sustain concentration on the task at hand. Some children have no problem noticing that their attention left the breath, and that distraction arose, but they have a hard time expressing what those distractions are. Begin by spending time brainstorming with the class to construct a list of the things that typically distract the children's focus. Sometimes this list is discussed right when the children come into class, so that their ideas reflect the things that might have distracted them throughout their day so far. Sometimes, the list can be reviewed immediately after a concentration session so the children are looking closely at what is happening in their mind during a meditation. Other times the children reflect on different times in their day-to-day life identifying the things that typically distract the child. The children are amazed to see how lengthy this list becomes. They notice things they have in common with one another and also the distractors that are unique to them. The list might look something like: my baby sister, a belly ache, feeling sad, feeling excited, worrying about something, sounds, smells, a daydream. Keeping an ongoing list of distractors is helpful as it assists children in recognizing distractions as they arise day-to-day and also in a concentration session. With increased familiarity with what distracts, children learn to see the distraction coming or arising more immediately without chasing after them. These older children are gaining increased meta-cognitive awareness about the content of the mind that most distracts them in daily life. As a result, children become far less captured by any distraction.

In this concentration session the child is instructed to keep the attention on the breath while simultaneously noticing the distracting activity of the mind. Like the practitioner in the Elephant Path painting, who must keep a close watch on the elephant, the child also must become familiar with the tricky monkey of distraction— of thought as well as sense-experience. In the Elephant Path painting the senses are repre-

Chapter 9: Concentration Development for Concrete Operational Children (Ages 9-12)

sented in the objects along the path, for example, a cloth representing touch, or gongs representing sound. The instructor can also give the children an instruction to ease up intentionally. Easing up a lot will cause distracting thoughts to arise and serve as an opportunity for the child to learn how disengaging focus can encourage the emergence of distracting thoughts. One way for children to get a sense of this is to have them visualize riding their bikes up and down a hill. Next, have them imagine taking their feet off the breaks as they are coasting down the hill. Reaching the top of a hill on a bike required strong pedaling, and control, once at the top of the hill, they can ease up just a bit, release the breaks and coast. However, if they ease up too much or too quickly the rider loses control of the bike.

Once the children have settled in to following the breath, ask them to ease up, to loosen their grip on the breath just enough to notice the re-emergence of distracting thoughts and to learn what draws their attention away from sustaining concentration. It might be something outside of themselves or something that arises within. Have them take note of the specific patterns of distraction. Next, direct them to use the steering wheel to draw the attention to the breath for a few cycles of breath, and to reestablish sustained concentration. Then, have them ease up again, enough to notice the re-emergence of distraction. Repeat easing up and redirecting a few times, until the child develops clear meta-cognitive awareness of how easing up and disengaging actually creates distraction. To bring the meditation to a close, sound the singing bowl. Ask the children to share the patterns of distractions they became aware of. Begin making a list of the things that the children share. As the children become familiar with the things that distract, they will begin to meta-cognitively notice them in their concentration, more skillfully engage their ability to redirect, and more swiftly re-engage concentration. This technique is especially helpful for children who have a hard time articulating or noticing distractions. Over time, most children discover that the patterns of distractions change, and new distractions appear. With respect to noticing distraction and re-directing the mind one child said, "Meditation makes me feel settled and relaxed on my mat. It sets a good tone. What helps me bring my thoughts down, not having them go away, just having them settle, is breathing and watching my breath. If I do get distracted I just divert my attention back to my breath" (age 9).

Concentration 3: Strategies and Activities for Dealing with Distraction and Sustaining Concentration; Intensifying

A challenge at this stage is that once children begin to notice their mind, and the distractions it creates, they become intrigued by them and can be eager to chase after a magnificent thought or a daydream. At the same time the older children are developing the skills and strategies to redirect the mind. They are able to detect, to notice thoughts and distractions and apply strategies with more and more immediacy. Over time, an automaticity develops, where the children use their meta-cognition in the immediate moment to direct the mind back to the concentration object. They develop staying, the ability to keep the mind on the concentration object with some consistency. Intensifying practices inspired by the symbol of the flame and practitioner's rope enable close staying on the concentration object. At this stage on the Elephant Path, the practitioner has "captured" the elephant with his rope. There is a curiosity, effort, and enthusiasm that arises in the children when they truly realize the notion that they are the boss of their own mind. The related realization is that the mind is an incessant idea-maker and distractions will present themselves. It is important for the instructor to clarify that the goal is not to get rid of distractions, but to intentionally return to the concentration object. The effort of intensifying leads to close engagement with all of the fine details of the concentration object, less occasion to become distracted elsewhere, and the mind settles on the task at hand.

The Flame and Intensifying Activities

The *singing bowl*, *foggy mountain road*, *tree pose*, and *deer spotting* are activities to engage the flame of intensifying.

Chapter 9: Concentration Development for Concrete Operational Children (Ages 9-12)

Singing Bowl Activity

Instruct children to take their meditation posture. Ask them to turn their attention to the singing bowl, or another object. Ask them to look at it and note the qualities of the singing bowl. Have the children share their responses. They might share the color of the bowl, the shape, size, etc. Then have the children look at the singing bowl, or object again, and instruct them to *really* look at the bowl, to look very closely to every quality it has. Then, ask them to share what was different between both opportunities to look at the singing bowl. For example, in the first opportunity they might have identified that the bowl was round and metallic in color. After the second opportunity they might share the way the light hits the bowl, or a variation in the color they had not noticed before, or a fine detail. They are looking ever more closely at the object, just as they will with the breath during a concentration session. Children enjoy revisiting this activity with different objects and incorporating different senses.

Foggy Mountain Road Activity

Imagine traveling along a steep mountain road amidst a heavy fog. As the children imagine this, ask what they must do to ensure that they travel safely along this path. They must exert much more focused energy. They must intensify the effort they are putting forth to pay much more attention. This effort is as if you are stoking a fire to give it a bit more zest.

Tree Pose Activity

Invite one child to stand in Tree Pose. Once they are steady and strong in the pose with their eyes focused on a fixed point, another child tries to distract them, without touching them. They can make movements, sounds, anything to try to pull their attention away and cause them to lose balance. The child in the pose intensifies their balance strategies to maintain steadiness. Ask the child in Tree Pose to describe what they needed to do to hold their balance amidst the distraction the friend was offering. The children will describe intensifying as an increase in effort, a stronger focus and engagement of holding the pose even more carefully. Children will recognize that it is more than the reminder to try harder or stick with it. In some instances, intention plus effort is needed to fuel the ability to steer the mind back to the concentration object.

The Deer Spotting Activity

Have the children imagine going for a walk in the forest with a forest ranger. Instruct them to imagine some of the things that they might come upon right along the path, such as trees, plants, rocks. At some point the forest ranger says, "Look, there is a deer way off in the distance at the edge of that field at the tree line." Have the children look for the deer. Whatever changed in the quality of looking when looking for the deer illustrates intensifying. The instructions required the child not only to exert more effort in looking, but to look much more vigilantly to notice all the subtle detail to find the deer.

INTENSIFYING MEDITATION

During this meditation, when the mind becomes distracted they will apply the same skill of intensifying used when looking closely at the singing bowl, holding Tree Pose, or looking for the deer amidst distraction. The instructor informs the children that he or she will create some outer distractions during the concentration session, and the children are to practice the flame of intensifying to more closely engage the concentration object. The instructor reminds them that intensifying provides the fuel to steer the mind back to the breath and to notice its detail even more carefully than previously.

Instruct the children to take their meditation posture. Ask them to notice the felt-sense of the body. Ask them to bring their attention to their breath and follow it very closely, the inhalation and exhalation, the rise and fall of the breath, using the 2- or 3-point object. Ask them to notice if their mind is drawn away and to gently redirect it back to the breath with the steering wheel. Then, begin making a noise to distract them, such as noisily moving around the room, or having a conversation. Remind them to allow the distraction to be there, but to use the flame of intensifying to keep their mind firmly placed on the breath, while the sound and distraction continue in the background, the same way they intensified looking closely at the singing bowl or in spotting the deer. Then encourage the children to direct the mind back to the breath, if they haven't already, continuing to follow the rising and falling breath carefully and comfortably. This exercise can be repeated a few times. Encourage them to call on the flame of intensifying when needed. Then, sound the singing bowl to bring the meditation to a close. Ask the children how it felt to utilize the flame of intensifying? What happened when the distraction stopped, how did the effort change?

Metaphors to Illustrate the Activity of Mind

As children develop mental pliancy and become more skillful keeping their attention on the concentration object they might be able to use these metaphors to understand the workings of the mind:

The Practitioner's Rope

Once children are beginning to develop pliancy of mind and a consistency with which they are able to redirect the mind to the breath, it is a good time to reintroduce the rope metaphor from the Elephant Path painting. The rope signifies that the practitioner has "captured" the elephant. This does not mean that there will be no distraction or thought, but rather that the child doesn't easily get caught up in thought so as to lose concentration to the task at hand.

Dog on a Leash Metaphor

Ask the children to imagine holding the retractable leash of a dog. Ask them to describe what you might do if the dog tried to run after a squirrel. They might say that you would hold on tight to the leash or attempt to draw the dog back to you. You would certainly have to apply effort, like the flame. Then ask what you would do if you were in a big open space and you wanted the dog to explore, but still wanted him on the leash. You might push the button allowing more leash line out so the dog could roam farther. You might relax your grip or the effort with which you are holding the leash. There is then a sense of easing up.

Fishing Line Metaphor

Some children might relate to fishing. When you have a large fish on your line, there is a balance between reeling the fish in with consistency and strength and easing up so as not to snap the line or lose the fish. The most skillful thing is to develop a balance between intensifying and easing up. Both are useful depending upon the situation. The strategy of mastering the flame is a skillful tool to incorporate to draw the attention back to the object when strongly pulled by distraction of any kind—outer perceptions or inner thoughts and feelings. If, however, they are feeling that they are holding the meditation object too tightly, so as to feel agitated, then they are instructed to ease up, like taking your feet off the pedals when coasting down a hill on your bike. Eventually, children develop a continuous balancing of intensifying and easing up. Sometimes these adjustments can be subtle. The mind must be awake and alert to have sufficient meta-cognitive capacity to balance the easing up and intensifying more closely to the breath.

The Rabbit of Subtle Dullness

On the Elephant Path painting the rabbit symbolizes subtle dullness. Subtle dullness occurs when concentration is steadily sustained on the concentration object and the background noise of distracting thought remains relatively quiet, but the concentration object is vague, and the mind is dull and lacks alertness. Have the child imagine a time at the beach, sitting on the shore, staring out at the ocean watching the waves roll in. Have the child imagine becoming so mesmerized by the movement of the waves that they do not take in any of the subtle detail and have only a vague general sense of there being waves. While subtle dullness might feel deeply calm and peaceful, the waves as a concentration object have become increasingly vague. Helping children to recognize subtle dullness during a meditation is important as the goal is for the mind to be alert and bright.

Ocean and Waves

Have the child imagine the mind as the vast ocean. As a thought comes, have the child notice it, and then allow it to ride off with a wave. Then, have the child allow attention to float back to the depths of the ocean where it is calm and peaceful. Children begin catching the thoughts more quickly. They begin to see thoughts coming like the wave rolling in from the ocean, and then move out to sea again, so that it is possible to return to the concentration object without getting caught up in the distraction.[1] Like the coming and going of waves in an ocean one child said, "It is like looking through a camera lens at an open field. You see a bird fly by. It comes. You see it, and it goes" (age 12).

Bubbles Around Thoughts

As the child sees a thought coming, have him or her place it in a bubble and let it float off. The child simply visualizes a bubble around the thought, as it carries the thought off. If the thought or distraction seems to be stubborn and too heavy for the bubble, then have the child call on the flame of intensifying.

Freight Train

If a freight train were coming, you wouldn't step in front of it to stop it. Simply sit on the grass beside the train tracks and let the freight train come and go, feel the wind against your skin, hear the roar of the engines, and let it continue down the tracks. Similarly, draw your attention back to your meditation object.

DEEPENING PRACTICE: SHARPENING META-COGNITION ON AND OFF THE MAT

FAVORITE CLOUDS

Over time, children begin to zero in on the things that are the biggest distractors. We refer to this discovery as "identifying my favorite clouds." Clouds are metaphors of thoughts and feelings as they arise, move, and disappear. The child can recognize the things that most often come between him or her and the present moment. These themes can be explored on and off the mat. The child learns to narrow meta-cognitive awareness to the biggest distractors. This is a relief to children, in

---
1. personal communication, Rahob Tulku.

that there are often only a few. This feels workable for them, something they can come to manage.

As children explore the things that most cause distraction, their "favorite clouds," they also explore what reliably brings them back to the concentration object. Off the mat children begin to identify the things that have the ability to bring them right back to the moment. For a child scared during a nightmare, it might be the soothing presence of their mother. When a child complains of trouble concentrating because they are hungry, it might be to take a break to have lunch or a snack. Children begin to see that there are things in the day-to-day moments of their life that can bring them to the present moment and the task at hand. They also begin to see the usefulness of a deep breath, a stretch, or a hug. They begin to develop strategies to help throughout their day. Children in the late concrete operational stage come to understand how the practice of concentration on the mat, including sitting in a meditation posture, following the breath, and allowing the distractions of the mind to settle, can create a sense of calm, clarity, peace that they can take off the mat with them.

Favorite Cloud-Jar Activity

As children come to understand their minds and the things that most often distract them, and finally learn to identify their "favorite clouds," they can make a mind jar that reflects their own mind. Each child gets a jar and sand. These represent the mind and the "stuff" of everyone's mind. Beyond that the child adds glitter to represent some of the ideas, feelings, distractions that are frequent and unique to them. Finally, they choose a small bead or object to represent each of their "favorite clouds." These are added, and the jar is filled with water. Their mind, like the mind jar, can grow and change. What once distracted them might settle, rarely to return. What was once a "favorite cloud" might be replaced by a different "favorite cloud." As their practice develops, the mind's meta-cognitive capacity grows.

Chapter 9: Concentration Development for Concrete Operational Children (Ages 9-12)

GAUGING PROGRESS: TALKING ABOUT THE PRACTICE

As the children become comfortable working with the symbols, strategies and instructions offered through the Elephant Path, they begin to develop a language for talking about and reflecting on their concentration practice. They have developed an awareness of and ability to name what distracts them. They've also developed a vocabulary through the metaphors and activities that help them describe their experience. Another way to gauge progress is to have the children reflect on what percentage of the time they are able to stay focused on the concentration object in a given concentration session. This can offer a quick check in and can be helpful for a child who might have a hard time describing or talking about a particular session. For example, they might notice that they are focused 50% of the time or 75% of the time.

THE BENEFITS OF CONCENTRATION

As children begin to round the path to the third level, they begin to notice the elephant's change in color. The head lightens in color. The elephant, the mind, develops clarity. The practitioner is no longer running after the elephant. The elephant, or the mind, is actually looking toward the practitioner. There is a sense of connection, a deeper relationship of the practitioner to the elephant/mind. The change in color signifies a mind that is becoming clearer, spacious, open. The mind is increasingly able to stay in the moment with clarity.

At some point along the path and the practice, students begin to notice more of the benefits of practice. While a sense of calm, stillness, ease, peacefulness, are qualities that children experience early on, children subsequently notice that these qualities become more available to them and arise with more ease and spontaneity. They notice thoughts and feelings arising more immediately, and with their strategies and meta-cognition, they direct their attention back to the object. As the mind settles, the object comes more vividly into view. Off the mat children are able to be in the present moment with less pull of distraction and are better able to experience that moment with a sense of ease. In the Buddhist tradition one of the benefits of a concentration practice is the cultivation of positive qualities, like patience, trust, and balance of mind. The children begin to identify qualities that they feel they exemplify and positive qualities that they would like to cultivate within themselves. One child, for example, noticed that as her meditation practice in class developed, she began to notice that she was able to let troubling things in her life go. She reflected that when she got in arguments with her mom or friends, she noticed that she wasn't getting caught in them. She felt happier in general. She said, "I started to notice that I don't get so worked up over things that aren't that important. I feel happier. My mind allows the not so important but kind of upsetting things to not be important anymore. They settle. I feel happy" (age 12).

IMPERMANENCE

The concept of impermanence, i.e., nothing is permanent or fixed, is something the children can relate to when they come to see the incessant movement of thought and occurrences of mind.

BUDDHA BOARD ACTIVITY

A Buddha Board is a wonderful tool to use to demonstrate this concept for the children. A Buddha Board is a small board that one can paint on using a small paint-brush and water. When you make a stroke on the board, it appears in black upon a white paper background. After a few moments, the image begins to fade and slowly disappears. The board returns to its original, blank surface. The children enjoy exploring with the Buddha Board and begin to experience the appreciation of the preciousness of each moment as they are viewing an image, appreciating it in the moment, alongside the notion of non-attachment, letting go, knowing that it is impermanent.

PAINTING WITH WATER ACTIVITY

A fun exercise with the younger children is to take them outside with a beach pail of water and paint brushes and invite them to paint on

Chapter 9: Concentration Development for Concrete Operational Children (Ages 9-12)

the sidewalk. There is a natural joy with the young ones and complete acceptance that their creation will evaporate. They are simply thrilled to create their next expression.

THE *MANDALA* PROJECT

A *mandala* reflects our essence and can include the six elements: wisdom, space, wind, fire, water, and earth. "As we rest our gaze upon a *mandala*, the mind becomes as still as a surface of a pool of water." In Sanskrit, *mandala* means both circle and center. It represents the visible world outside of us as well as the invisible world within our mind and body. The circle is one of the most ancient and natural forms. We live in a universe made up of planets, stars, the moon, and the sun. The sun rises and sets in a re-occurring circle. *Mandalas* are one of the most ancient art forms, originating in the 4th century (Tenzin-Dolma, 2013). In the Buddhist tradition, *mandalas* are used for meditation. The creation of a sand *mandala* is a meditation in-and-of-itself because of the amount of patience, focus, determination required for its construction. Sands of different colors are painted into the formation of a *mandala*. Once the intricate piece of artwork is constructed, it is destroyed, symbolizing impermanence and non-attachment.

The children enjoy learning about *mandalas* and are intrigued with the construction and destruction of them. Creating a *mandala* is an opportunity for self-reflection. After learning about the elements, children begin to reflect on their connection to each other and to the natural world. This can happen through conversation, journal writing, and short meditations where children visualize the qualities and characteristics of each element. Here is an example of a meditation on water:

Allow your body to relax into your mat and bring to mind the water element. Take an ocean breath imagining that as you inhale a gentle wave is washing over you, and as you exhale, the wave returns to the ocean. Maybe you can feel some of the qualities of water such as smooth, flowing, moveable. Bring to mind the places where water exists such as the vast oceans, lakes, rivers, streams, ponds, rain, water, snow. As you rest your attention on one of these images sense a feeling of fluidity, strength, ease, moisture, flow. Maybe you can sense raindrops on your face or your feet wading in the ocean. *How does water feel in your body? What colors and shapes do you associate with water? Become aware of how water manifests in your life? Maybe you can sense a feeling of gratitude for the water element.*

As children explore the elements they might also identify symbols and colors that they would like to include in their *mandala*.

Here are some prompts the children can reflect on and respond to as they consider what symbols they would like to include in their *mandala*. "This is an element I am drawn to. This is a color I am drawn to. This is something that makes me happy. This is something I consider to be one of my strengths. This is an area I want to get better at. This is how I want to be with others. This is one of my goals." Children create their *mandala* as a thoughtful reflection of themselves. Because they devoted thought and care to its creation, as a reflection of their true qualities, it has value to them. It can serve as a wonderful focus point for meditation. This activity encourages self-reflection, self-awareness and an appreciation for growth and change.

Mandala Meditation Activity

What follows are instructions for a *mandala* meditation:

Rest your gaze upon your *mandala* for a moment. Let your mind remember why you chose the colors you chose. Why you chose the shapes, objects and design. Bring your attention to the center, remembering the element that you chose. Remember for a moment why you chose the element that you did. Maybe it represents something that is important to you. Maybe it represents a quality that you wish was stronger within you. Maybe it represents something that you wonder about. Take a moment to reflect as to why you chose the element. Then let your mind rest. Close your eyes if you wish. Let the thoughts settle away, let the thinking settle away. Take a few moments to just be. Bring your attention to your breath. Take a full breath in, and out. Slowly open your eyes.

Next, encourage the children to share verbally or write about their

Chapter 9: Concentration Development for Concrete Operational Children (Ages 9-12)

mandala meditation. For example, one child said, "I picked water because I am a summer baby and ever since I was born, I've loved water. When I am in the water I feel free. I feel like nothing is holding me back" (age 11). Another child age 11 said, "Space seems like it is never-ending and something we don't know a lot about. I am curious about a lot of things and space is like that. It matches me." Another child age 12 said, "I chose earth. Life is beautiful but harsh that is why I chose to illustrate it with a rose. The center is the rose, and the thorns are the harsh parts coming off from it." Still another child age 12 said, "I want to be able to flow more freely, go with the flow, and understand things more easily. That is why I chose water."

AWARENESS ACTIVITIES

As older children begin to spend more time developing their concentration practice, it is helpful to spend time engaging in awareness activities and exploring tools to manage stress and anxiety. These activities offer children the opportunity to experience bringing awareness to the present moment as they are interacting with others, off the mat.

LISTENING WITH AWARENESS

Listening with Awareness offers children the opportunity to experience what it means to fully listen, without interruption, without turning the moment back to themselves, and without judgment. The goal is to be fully present for another person.

Pairs or Small Group Listening Activity

The children sit in pairs about a foot away, facing one another, usually in their meditation posture. They are given a question that reflects something about their personal life, usually something very easy to relate to. One child is the listener, with the task of simply listening, keeping eye contact, making no interruption, even refraining from making facial expressions in response to what the other is saying. The other child has a minute and a half to share whatever they want in response to the topic.

Sometimes this feels like plenty of time, other times it feels as if more time is needed to share all that someone knows or feels about the topic. After a minute and a half, the child who is sharing takes the role of listener as the other child shares back what they heard their friend say. Again, the child listening is silent, makes eye contact, does not respond even if the information shared was not exactly correct. The two thank one another and repeat the exercise switching roles. It is an interesting opportunity for the children as they observe whether they are more comfortable sharing or listening and realize how easy or difficult mindful listening actually is for them. This activity is helpful as it offers more information about themselves, their mind, their abilities as a listener, and what it means to be completely present for another person. The most beautiful outcome of a mindful listening activity is the glow in a child's eyes when they feel truly, deeply listened to and heard.

Large Group Listening Activity

Another version of this exercise is to include a group of children or an entire class. This is a nice transitional activity as it brings everyone into a listening, focused perspective. Posing a question or topic, one person begins with an answer. These are usually quick, easy, sometimes only involving a one-word answer. Continue around the circle with the expectation that the only person speaking is the person whose turn it is. The room is very quiet, and each child's voice is being heard, without interruption. If a child does not want to share they simply say "pass," their voice still being heard. When the last person shares, time can be given for specific questions around something someone shared. When a question is asked of someone, the communication is now between two people while the others listen. This activity can be very challenging for children at first as they want to interject and respond to and make connections to the things others are sharing. It takes some effort to simply listen and to remember whom your question or wondering was for. One of the benefits is that children feel very listened to and feel that a space for their voice was held and valued within the group.

Chapter 9: Concentration Development for Concrete Operational Children (Ages 9-12)

MIRRORING WITH AWARENESS

Mirroring invites children to bring their full attention to the movement of another as they mirror the same movement. Instruct the children to sit in pairs across from one another and hold their hands palm to palm with their partner, approximately an inch apart, imagining that there is a glass surface, like a window, between them. One child is chosen as the leader, the other as the follower. The leader begins moving their hands along the imaginary pane of glass as the follower mirrors the movement. Both children are silent. After a short period of time the teacher sounds a chime or signal, and the leader moves their hands back to the starting point and both shake out their hands. Then repeat switching roles. At the end, reflect with the children about their experience. Was this exercise easy or difficult? Was it easier to be the follower or the leader? Why? How was your sense of sight involved? Were there other strategies that you used?

DRAWING WITH AWARENESS

This drawing activity allows for a different mode of expression and requires careful listening. Choose one child to be the design maker. This child creates a simple line drawing on a small chalkboard or whiteboard and keeps it hidden from view of the other children. The design maker gives clear step-by-step instructions to the other children who are attempting to draw the same illustration with a pencil on a piece of paper. The design maker can repeat each direction twice. The classmates listen carefully attempting to match their drawing with what the design maker created. When all the directions have been given, the children show their drawings to the design maker. The design maker takes a moment to look at their classmates' drawings noticing the accuracy. It is often surprising to see how the same instructions were interpreted by different children. The design maker can reflect and share how they might have clarified their directions. Ask the children if they preferred being the design maker or the careful listener, and what the challenges were of each.

Assignments and School-Work with Awareness

Encouraging the children to bring their concentration practice and awareness to their schoolwork both in the classroom and at home is an important goal of their practice off the mat. When you feel that the children have developed some consistency with their concentration practice introduce this practice during a specific assignment. Over time, encourage this practice more frequently throughout the day. Eventually ask them to try it on their own while completing assignments outside of school.

Prompt the children

What if you thought of the assignment in front of you as a meditation? Encourage children to prepare their environment in a way that is conducive to studying. Find a quiet space and a clear work surface. Set a time limit as we do for a concentration session. Gather all the materials that you need. Take your posture, and notice the felt-sense of your body, adjusting if you are uncomfortable. Of course, their posture can be more relaxed than a meditation posture, but the effort to notice and tend to it before beginning is what is important. Take a few deep, clearing breaths. Place your attention on the assignment, and use the flame of intensifying when need be, easing up on the rope if you become agitated. See if you can work in a focused way for the time that you set. Start with an amount of time that you feel you can be successful. Take a break, and return to the assignment, setting your time limit again. As you become comfortable with a certain time frame, increase the amount of time. Shorter, focused work sessions with a break in between are more productive overall than a long period of time feeling frustrated or distracted.

Tea Time with Awareness

Tea Time is an opportunity to practice awareness in a social, connected way while enjoying tea and conversation or a game together. While a traditional tea ceremony has its own intricate history and meaning, we draw upon the qualities of tranquility, respect and harmony. The

Chapter 9: Concentration Development for Concrete Operational Children (Ages 9-12)

children love the opportunity to choose their flavor of tea, prepare the tea together, wait patiently as they enjoy the aroma and once the temperature allows are able to sip their tea, enjoying the flavor. Sitting in a circle, we enjoy our tea together, often choosing to play a game or share conversation together, holding tranquility, respect, and harmony as our intention.

Understanding Anxiety and Stress

Anxiety and stress are often experienced by children at this stage of development. The increase in academic expectations, physical changes, hormonal changes, and negotiating social relationships can challenge a child's connection to clarity and confidence. Emotions driven by thought are more intense. Anxiety is a reaction to a situation that is perceived as stressful or threatening. It is important to help children distinguish when anxiety is a useful and protective signal and when it itself has become the problem. Discussing the fight or flight response can help children understand their bodies response to stress. Posing specific scenarios, role playing, and asking the children to distinguish what they think the best response might be helps to encourage dialogue and understanding of different situations. Children are able to see how certain responses might in fact be appropriate given a specific scenario while others might become an overreaction. Children learn meta-cognitive perspective-taking and are able to identify their thinking and appropriate responses or next steps. For example, the stress caused by an increase in school assignments and the feeling that it is overwhelming, might require a stepping back, taking a larger perspective, and developing a plan to move forward and through the situation. Sometimes it is useful and supportive for children to ask for help during these moments. The strategies and tools of the Elephant Path practices can help to guide the child to a place of calm, in which developing clarity becomes possible. This clarity and meta-cognition enable the child to move forward with self-awareness and resilience. Encourage children to ask for help when needed as they learn to navigate challenges and implement the Elephant Path practices.

When the pace of the day or schedule might require a quick strategy to tend to a stressful moment, there are a number of stress and anxiety tools that a child might utilize quickly to shift their perspective. These include taking a deep breath, taking a drink of water as sometimes dehydration can cause stress, humor and laughing, a hug, witnessing or showing kindness, and bringing to mind a positive quality like trust, and patience. It is fun for the children to explore these quick tools. For example, you might plan a session where the children explore humor. Ask the children to reflect on their state of mind at the beginning of the session. Spend time sharing funny stories, telling jokes, watching funny video clips, or reading funny scenes from books. Then ask the children to reflect and notice how they are feeling at the end of the session. There is without a doubt a feeling of joy, light heartedness, and ease.

Heart Practice: The Conduct of a Compassionate Heart

As mentioned earlier, the most reliable indicator of your practice is your conduct in everyday life. We live in an interconnected world, and the essence of these practices are for the benefit of all beings. The following activities and exercises cultivate an awareness of these practices in everyday life and a compassionate heart. These practices develop naturally and automatically for children as an expression of their practice. Through thoughtful intention and willingness to listen with their heart to themselves and the world around them, they experience the beautiful fruition of these practices rippling forth to touch and benefit others.

Before You Speak, Before You Act

This aspect of the practice with children begins with the passage from the poet Rilke who said, "Before you speak, before you act, allow your words and actions to pass through three gates: Is it true? Is it necessary? Is it kind?" Body and speech are servants of the mind. Speech and actions are the way in which we interact with the world. Your speech and your actions matter, not only to your own well-being, to the health and well-being of those around you, and our collective world. If you are able to answer yes to those questions, then you can be sure you are making a good choice, one that is best for the circumstance before you. As children practice this and bring it into their daily lives, this quote becomes a foundation from which to step. The point is to be aware of your speech and actions, showing care and attention. Over time children find this filter becomes second nature. If they engage in a way that was hurtful or unnecessary, they notice it very quickly, sometimes in the moment it arises, and can adjust in a conscious way. At the same time, developing your sense of awareness enables you to see the moment with more clarity and the opportunity to be less reactive.

Intention

Just as children can set their intentions as they settle onto their mat and prepare for practice, setting an intention before leaving the mat invites the movement of the practice off the mat for the benefit of oneself and others. Before closing practice, children can rest their attention in their silence, in their heart center, as they set an intention for the day ahead. Setting an intention is like pointing yourself in a positive direction. Maybe the intention is to be present in each moment. Maybe it is to share kindness, or to find joy in your day. Whatever it is, have the children take a moment to set their intention. Sound the chime or singing bowl to mark the end of this exercise.

Namaste – Closing the Practice

Namaste is a Sanskrit word that expresses a heartfelt gesture. '*Nama*' means bow. '*As*' means I. '*Te*' means you. Literally, it means, "I bow to the divine in you." It symbolizes recognition of the spark and light within each of us. The light in me honors the light in you or from my heart to yours. Sharing the word *Namaste* at the end of the practice is a thoughtful way of honoring the practice and heart of one another. Following *Namaste*, you might share the words, "Kind Thoughts, Kind Words, Follow Your Heart," while instructing children to bring their hands together at the forehead, then hands to the lips, and finally to the heart. This sets a kindhearted, positive tone for taking the practice off the mat.

SPONTANEOUSLY ARISING PRACTICE

It is exciting for children to notice the moments when their practice naturally or intentionally appears in the day-to-day. As we become more aware in each moment, we find that the practice or tool that is necessary for that given moment will present itself. It is important to encourage children to notice these spontaneous moments off the mat, and offer them the opportunity to share or reflect about it at the beginning of each class. Sometimes it is as simple as a child realizing that they took a few full body breaths before beginning their swim meet, or a child taking Cricket Pose in their bed in the morning when they are having a difficult time waking up, or, the little boy who encouraged his father to take a few balloon breaths when his tensions rose at a sporting event after his team lost. Maybe it is the girl who, in the midst of a disagreement with her mom, decided to go to her room, take her meditation posture, and follow her breath until she felt a sense of ease, calm, and clarity arise. The spontaneity can arise as exquisitely as a child who became aware of homeless people while walking down the street, and through her awareness was inspired to act. After returning with her mother to inquire what the people might need and how she could help, she organized a fundraiser to purchase the supplies and items for them.

Every moment that a child recognizes their practice off the mat, there is a strengthening of awareness and meta-cognition, an ownership of practice, an enhanced understanding of their deep and familiar connection to these practices, to their place in this world, and their connection to all beings. Your actions, your words, the way you carry yourself in this world matter. The children come to see that within their essence is an ocean of being, connected to all, capable of spreading gift waves to the world beyond.

Chapter 9: Concentration Development for Concrete Operational Children (Ages 9-12)

Heart Meditations

As a community and within individual classes there are many opportunities to engage in the heart practice together. As mentioned previously, the youngest children begin to learn about meditation practice by resting their attention in their heart and simply noticing feeling, thought, question, story, wonder, or whatever might arise. Heart meditations can also inspire wishes, dreams, hopes for others, and for our greater world. They can be powerful moments to tap into inner knowing, compassion, and connection to others. Whether the children are sitting in a meditation posture, or resting on their backs in *Savasana*, they take an inward perspective, allowing their body and mind to settle and resting their attention in their heart. Children have such a direct, pure connection to their heart, and an unconditional, fluid, eager desire to share their heart's wishes with others.

Mantras, Heart Rocks, Prayer Flags, Daily Wishes and Nuggets of Goodness are examples of projects that were inspired by heart meditations.

Mantras

Traditionally a mantra has been a tool to help rest the mind into meditation, but over time it has come to be thought of as an intention. As mantras were explored with a group of children they became very eager to create their own mantras. After engaging in a series of meditations, including visualizations and resting the attention in the heart, the children began to formulate mantras. For some children it was helpful to consider an intention, wish, or blessing for themselves, and then expand that view to include others.

Here are a few of their mantras:

मय ए वेय ने ह वे सु पोत मेअ न ग ् अ तु : तो लवे अ ह य लफ़े

"May everyone have support, meaning, and truth to live a happy life."

मयथेरेबेमोरेएं विरो मे सतो द बितुं ्द यनी सतोथेपरू

"May there be more environments to distribute daily needs to the poor."

मय एवेये ँ अतरुं हवे जोय, हपिने स, अ अ होमे

"May all creatures have joy, happiness, and a home."

Heart Rocks

This practice for late preoperational and concrete operational children involved an action inspired by the heart. The children engaged in a series of meditations where they quieted the mind and allowed their attention to rest in their heart center. They reflected on the idea that if they could offer one gift to another human being, not a physical gift, but a heart gift that could never be lost, what would it be? Once they identified this gift they thought of a word or phrase that would best represent it. Next, the children chose a river rock, and wrote the word or phrase on the rock and added an illustration if they wished. The children considered who was meant to receive this rock. Some wanted to give it to a parent, others a friend or neighbor. Some children wanted to leave it somewhere for someone to find. Some wanted to keep the rock for themselves. Wherever they felt the rock would be of benefit was where the rock was meant to be. We talked about how it might feel to offer it out, not knowing who or if it would be received. The children took their rocks with them, and we agreed to share the journey of our rocks at some point. Over a number of weeks, the children shared their tales. One child was thrilled to share that she left it on her father's desk. Another left it on a neighbor's porch. One child left it on the handrail to a church. Another took hers on her vacation and left it at a playground. The children's delight and joy at each stage of this practice was beautiful, and it was a deeply inspiring example of kindness and compassion rippling forth to influence another. Some of the children's heart rock messages said, "Shine like a star. Be kind. You are beautiful. Dream big. Peace. Be brave. Today you will inspire and imagine. Joy. Sunshine and sea."

Chapter 9: Concentration Development for Concrete Operational Children (Ages 9-12)

Prayer Flags

According to some lamas, prayer flags date back thousands of years in the Bon and Buddhist traditions. The tradition says that the flags hold prayers and good wishes that will be carried by the wind to reach all sentient beings. After studying about prayer flags the children meditated on a wish that they had for the world. They narrowed their wish down to one word or phrase and designed a prayer flag that represented their wish. We strung these together and hung them as an offering and inspiration. After the earthquake in Nepal, we decided we wanted to reach out through our heart practice to the people of Nepal, specifically the group of children that were living at The Himalayan Children's Home who I had met the previous year when I visited their school to learn about their practices. Each child designed a prayer flag with their own special wish for the children or for the people of Nepal to give them hope and remind them that they are not alone. We gathered over 200 prayer flags and sent them off to the children. The children in Nepal sent back a photo and thankful wishes which were so meaningful to the children here, representing the connection and ripple of kindness generated through the heart practice.

DAILY WISHES; NUGGETS OF GOODNESS

This is a fun and special heart meditation exercise where children reflect on kindnesses, offerings, wishes that might brighten someone's moment or help them connect to their own heart and know they are not alone. Their ideas and wishes were written on strips of paper, folded up, and placed in a basket. This became the *Nuggets of Goodness* basket. Anytime someone felt that they needed a nugget of goodness they could take one from the basket. They could take it with them, offer it to someone else along the way, or return it to the basket for someone else to receive. Examples of such nuggets are: "Be you. You are loved. Shine like a star. Have hope. I hope your day blossoms like a flower. Dream big. Be kind. You are beautiful. Peace to you."

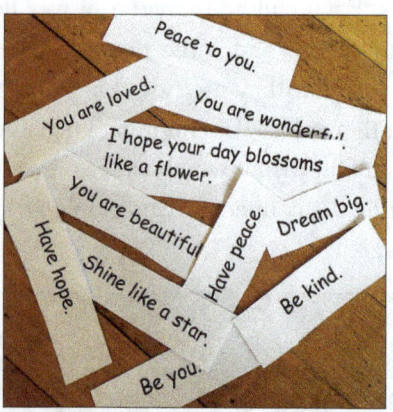

REFLECTION

I've had the privilege of witnessing the profound gift, the possibility, and the benefit of these practices for the Western child. As I mentioned earlier, these are practices that develop over time, with effort, intention, guidance, and commitment. The benefits can appear very subtly from practice session to practice session, but over time they have the ability to affect the very way that one operates and interacts in the world. They shape one's very being. Just like anything else, when you come to it over and over again, it permeates to deeper levels of understanding and knowing. These practices point the way to your true nature. When

Chapter 9: Concentration Development for Concrete Operational Children (Ages 9-12)

you operate from a place of true nature, you are not lead through life by reaction, closed-minded thinking, and disconnection from the beings and world around you. You operate from a place of knowing, clarity, interconnectedness, and compassion. One parent shared that she was amazed by how her daughter independently brought her practice into her life, academics, sports and creative arts endeavors. She said that she had visibly "built muscle" in areas of focus, resiliency, grit, care and empathy for her community and natural environments. She shared that she knows that these are skills that her daughter will have for a lifetime. Teachers reflected about how much their students understand about their inner lives as a result of this program, and that they are able to use the strategies they've learned to navigate challenging moments and feelings. Teachers felt that this program was critical to supporting students' identity and building school community. They found it crucial to the education of the *whole* child, considering children's mental well-being, physical health, and the mind-body connection.

The beauty of these practices begin for children as they discover joy and freedom in the body. As children recognize the nurturing effect of a calm mind, they open to the practices and tools that help to build the "mind muscle" and recognize their own meta-cognitive ability to "be the boss of their mind." Through the realization and development of a healthy inward perspective, one can turn one's awareness outward with clarity, confidence, deep knowing, and acceptance. As mentioned earlier, the true fruition of these practices is one's conduct. Who are you? How do you move through and interact with the world and the interconnected sea of beings that we travel this lifetime with? Taking one's practice off the mat, the Heart Practice, is the true fruition of these practices. One moves with compassion and kindness through this world, for the benefit of oneself, but more importantly, for the benefit of all beings. The seeds of these practices are already burning bright within a child's heart mind. It is our role as teachers, parents, and advocates of children, to nurture the seeds, and stoke the fire allowing it to burn brightly as children move through childhood so that they step into adulthood with the clear light of awareness and compassion guiding their way.

Chapter 10

A Concentration Training Program for Adolescents in a Public School

by Jae Pasari, Ph.D.

ADOLESCENCE; DEVELOPMENTAL CONSIDERATIONS

Starting at around age 12 and peaking at age 15-16 the developing adolescent shows a new level of intellectual development, namely formal operational thinking (Wall, 1991). There are distinct improvements in the ability to use both inductive and deductive reasoning. The teacher can give detailed instructions on how to go about, and what to expect from, concentration training, immediately followed by getting the student to read the instructions out loud.

The mid-adolescent has developed a range of emotions, and the beginnings of a personal identity or sense of self comparable to an adult. The main difference is less about ability and more about approach. Adolescents tend to intensify and exaggerate language when describing their experiences, e.g. "That's Amaaazing!" (Brown, 1993). A teacher of concentration training with adolescents must be especially sensitive to and tolerant of the way adolescents talk about their concentration experiences. The other main difference is the teacher's delivery. The adolescent does best with action-oriented interactions (doing things together), and when the teacher is accessible and real.

At this age the adolescent lives in a world of infinite possibilities. The adolescent no longer focuses so much on the immediacy of experience but on what is possible. Therefore, training adolescents in concentration is followed less by asking what they just immediately experienced in concentration and more about its potential and its possibilities generalized to daily life.

The capacity to think in terms of abstractions and possibilities also sets the foundation for a deep concern about how others, especially peers, might evaluate the adolescent. Wall (1991) says, "The ability to consider abstractly the effect that one has on others or the validity of one's own thought processes appears to generate worry about appearances to others. This is a central theme when working with adolescents." (p. 16) Therefore, teaching concentration to adolescents is best done in small groups, rather than one-on-one, in a way that they can be esteemed by fellow peers in concentration training. Ground rules need to be firmly set forth to prevent scapegoating and bullying in and outside the classroom.

Setting the Context

There are a number of opportunities and constraints to consider in the development of a concentration training program for adolescents in an American public school context. While the substance of the training and the level of rigor are the same as for adults, the success of the program hinges on establishing the appropriate social contexts, peer dynamics, and content framing. In this chapter we will describe a concentration training program developed and taught by one of the authors (JP) for 14- to 18-year-olds at a public charter high school in California. This program seeks to model the principles and best practices described in previous chapters within the constraints of this particular school context. This program should be considered a proof of concept pilot project. All outcomes reflect a small sample size (10-25 students per semester over two years) of anonymous, self-reported responses to the training, collected by the instructor.

The school hosting the concentration training program is an academically rigorous, lottery-based, public charter school in California serving grades 7-12. The students represent a wide range of socio-economic backgrounds, but with a high proportion of white, upper-middle income students from highly educated families. The concentration training course was offered as one choice among twenty mini-electives that met once a week for 45 minutes. Students chose one mini course each semester. The concentration course was restricted to 9th to 12th grade students (14- to 18-year-olds) and enrollment ranged from 10 to 25 students each semester over two school years. The class curriculum was repeated from the beginning at the start of each new semester, and while most students were new each time, several students elected to repeat the course, and one student enrolled four times consecutively.

Design Considerations

In designing this program we focused on three core considerations. First, we attempted to incorporate as many aspects of successful adult-based programs as possible, drawing primarily from one of our author's (DB) decades of experience teaching concentration to adults using Indo-Tibetan meditation techniques, complemented with insights from Western psychology and neuroscience. Second, we hoped to make this proven curriculum more accessible for an adolescent audience by framing the program in a manner that made it relevant, "cool," and useful to their lives. Third, we wanted to offer concentration training in a secular way that was still true to its historical and ethical contexts. Thus, we developed a curriculum that carefully framed concentration training not only as a self-improvement technique for increased focus and attention, but also as a step on a path of service that can lead to radical selflessness and compassion.

The first step in this process was to name the course in a way that would attract the interest of students as they were making decisions about which electives to choose. We settled on the course name, *Jedi Mind Control* with the following course description: "Harness The Force to improve your concentration and awareness skills with ancient contemplative practices. Side effects may include improved academic and athletic performance, increased happiness, flow states, and general awesomeness." As we will discuss shortly, the *Star Wars* theme and the Jedi concept gave the course a popular appeal, while simultaneously providing a well-known but fictitious religion to frame the ethical and humanitarian potential of the practice.

CURRICULUM OVERVIEW

The program begins with a *Star Wars*-framed introduction to Eastern and Western psychology that provides the philosophical and ethical/humanitarian contexts for engaging in concentration training. The bulk of the program consists of about a dozen 45-minute class sessions in which students watch and discuss a short video for 15-20 minutes, meditate for 15-20 minutes, and then reflect upon and discuss their experience for the remainder of each period.

In the first class, the instructor begins by projecting a picture of Yoda and asking the class if they know upon whom George Lucas based the Yoda character. It is not expected that any student will know the correct answer (though some get close by guessing the Dalai Lama), so this device is used to pique their attention and teach them about how George Lucas was inspired by Eastern philosophies in general when he developed the Jedi concept, and by Tsenzhab Serkong Rinpoche in particular when he developed the Yoda character (see Figure 2).

Figure 2: Tsenzhab Serkong Rinpoche (left) and Yoda (right)

This is followed by asking students to analyze themes across several quotes from *Star Wars* to see if they can gain insight into the Eastern

Chapter 10: A Concentration Training Program for Adolescents in a Public School

psychology that underlies the way of the Jedi. The following quotes are useful to help students recognize themes of concentration/focus, awareness, absence of thought, and selflessness/compassion:

> "All Luke's life he looked away, to the future, never to his mind, to *what he was doing*." —Yoda

> "*Concentrate* on the moment. Feel, *don't think*. Use your *instincts*."— Qui-Gon Jinn

> "Your *focus* determines your reality."—Qui-Gon Jinn

> "Try not, *do*. Or do not. There is no try."—Yoda

> "*Let go of* your conscious *self*, and act on *instinct*"—Obi Wan Kenobi

> "The Jedi are *selfless*. They only think of others."—Yoda

Students are then introduced to four distinct mental processes: thought, focus, awareness, and meta-cognition. These concepts are taught first from a Western psychological and neuroscience perspective. To set the stage for future lessons and to help students differentiate (often for the first time) these separate mental processes, we focus on delineating each in terms of its location in the brain and its speed. Thinking is described as a slow (500 - 3000msec) process of the secondary association cortices. Concentration (directed attention) is described as a faster (250msec) process of the anterior cingulate cortex (ACC). Meta-cognitive awareness is described as a very fast process (<10msec) associated with activation of the right dorsolateral prefrontal cortex (rDLPFC), and non-judgmental global awareness is also described as a very fast process (<10 msec) possibly related to deactivation of the posterior cingulate cortex (PCC; typically associated with categorizing and judging immediate experience) and activation of certain areas of the parietal cortex. These processes are made more salient by describing them in terms of successful baseball players who are able to hit better using concentration and awareness as opposed to thought, due to the considerable processing speed differences between these cognitive activities (see chapter 4). In other words good baseball players learn to operate out of high-speed directed attention mode rather than thought mode; and the best baseball players learn to operate out of extremely high-speed awareness mode rather than operating either out of thought or directed attention.

The first class closes by having students watch Matt Killigsworth's TED Talk *Want to be happier? Stay in the moment*, which uses a large correlational dataset to strongly suggest that excessive thinking and mind-wandering are the root of everyday unhappiness. Learning about the problems of the ordinary mind becomes the starting point for justification of Jedi mind training.

In the second class period, students begin by watching Donald Hoffman's TED Talk *Do we see reality as it is?*, in which the speaker makes a strong, mathematically-based argument that we evolved not to *perceive* an accurate representation of reality, but to actively *construct* an ongoing, inaccurate, personal version of reality that is more amenable to survival and reproduction than an accurate representation would be. We then reveal that this recent Western insight into the constructive nature of the mind is actually the foundation of several ancient contemplative traditions, including the Eastern philosophies that influenced George Lucas when he was creating *Star Wars* and the Jedi. The idea is further clarified by comparing the Eastern concepts of *emptiness* (here defined as "constructed as a representation by the mind, and thus lacking inherent independent existence") to modern Western constructivist psychology. In other words, what we see, hear, sense, think, etc. are our own mental representations or constructions. A closely related term is reification, defined as the perceptual habit of taking these mental representations as real. Of course the idea that the world is not as it seems has a certain appeal to the adolescent mind and the emergence of formal operational thinking. The main theme, namely that the world is how we construct it, makes sense to the adolescent mind. This theme of reification is illustrated in class using the movie *The Matrix*, in which humans are enslaved in personal utopias created by the possibilities of their own imagination. The Western approach to understanding emptiness through science and math is thus contrasted with the Eastern approach of experiential understanding through contemplative practice.

Students then discuss how experiential (as opposed to intellectual) realization of emptiness might lead to selflessness and other pro-social behaviors, and are presented with a secular translation of at least one contemplative tradition's path to such realization. For example, the following sequence attempts to succinctly describe the path of the Indo-Tibetan Mahamudra and rDzogchen contemplative traditions (where "empty of x" means "in which x is perceived as an unreified construction of mind"). The entire path is introduced in terms of the possible levels of awareness that can be attained through training the mind, which has great appeal to the adolescent formal operational mind:

1. Preliminary practices (enhancing motivation and positive states of mind)
2. Concentration & meta-cognition training
3. Operating from awareness (mindfulness, higher levels of awareness)
4. Awareness-itself, empty of self-representation
5. Awareness empty of thoughts & emotions
6. Awareness empty of the representation of time
7. Non-dual awareness
8. Awareness empty of conceptualization & doing
9. Awareness of everything at once (including itself)
10. Enlightenment (radical selflessness and compassion)

Having been introduced to a complete path, students can now see how the core activities of the class (concentration training and meta-cognition training) fit into their larger, traditional Eastern contexts, and also how they fit within a growing body of Western psychological and neuroscience research on positive and pro-social psychology.

Training adolescents in some of the more advanced awareness-based meditation techniques, and especially in emptiness practices, may be developmentally premature (see chapter 3) and thus are *not* the intended goals of this curriculum. However, we have found that student interest in concentration training improves markedly when framed in terms of emptiness and in terms of a complete path that contextualizes concentration training as more than merely a stand-alone technique for improving focus. We feel that such a framing is also increasingly necessary given the growing chorus of critiques against "McMindfulness," "ecstasis," and other forms of co-opted contemplative practices that commodify meditation to maximize worker productivity, minimize critique of systemic injustice, and potentiate structural spiritual bypassing (Purser and Loy 2013, North 2014, Gelles 2016, Schwartz 2017, Sherrel and Simmer-Brown 2017).

The second class concludes with the assignment of a single-page homework article about the four cognitive processes we have studied thus far (thinking, concentration, meta-cognition, and awareness), a couple of related processes (attunement and flow), and research connecting these processes to positive personal outcomes (happiness, peak performance, processing difficult emotions, stress reduction, and pain reduction). This assignment serves to ground the curriculum in more personal terms, and reconnect the content to more relatable themes after what is often a conceptually challenging exploration of awareness and emptiness.

Students are taught increasingly advanced concentration and meta-cognition techniques starting in the third class. From the third meeting onward, each class session consists of a video screening and discussion for 15-20 minutes, guided meditation for 15-20 minutes, and reflection upon and discussion of student experiences for the remainder of each period (see Table 1).

Table 1: Jedi Mind Control Overview

Week	Presentation	Video	Meditation
1	*Star Wars* Philosophy Neuro-psychology	Matt Killingsworth: Want to be happier? Stay in the moment	

Chapter 10: A Concentration Training Program for Adolescents in a Public School

2	Emptiness & The Path	Donald Hoffman: Do we see reality as it is?	
3	Concentration	Tan Le: A headset that reads your brainwaves	3 pt. object
4	Concentration	Daniel Goleman: Focus, flow, and frazzle	3 pt. object
5		Dan Harris: What do we have all wrong about meditation? & Hack your brain with meditation	3 pt. object Counting
6		Andy Puddicombe: All it takes is 10 mindful minutes	3 pt. object
7		Instant Egghead: Meditation changes the brain ASAP Science: The scientific power of meditation	3 pt. object Meta-cognition
8		Rick Hanson: How to change your brain	3 pt. object
9		Cliff Nass: Are you multitasking your life away?	3 pt. object
10		Dandapani: Unwavering focus	3 pt. object
11		Isaac Lidsky: What reality are you creating for yourself?	3 pt. object
12		Srikumar Rao: Plug into your hard wired happiness	3 pt. object
13		Richard Davidson: The four constituents of well-being	3 pt. object

14		Alia Crum: [Change your mindset, change the game](#)	3 pt. object
15		Abigail Marsh: [Why some people are more altruistic](#)	7 pt. object

A Video Guide to Jedi Mind Training

Week 1: Matt Killingsworth: [Want to be happier? Stay in the moment](#)

Using an iPhone app that surveyed a diverse array of 15,000 people about their happiness at random points of the day, Killingsworth found that happiness correlated negatively with mind-wandering. Even people whose minds wander to pleasant thoughts while engaged in unpleasant activities were *less* happy than those whose minds were focused on the present moment, even unpleasant present moments. Killingsworth also found that mind-wandering was happening about 47% of the time. This talk is useful to illustrate that concentration (on the task at hand) is key to happiness. This provides students with a statement of the problem of mind-wandering and a justification for mind training. It provides stronger motivation to begin practicing concentration skills.

Week 2: Donald Hoffman: [Do we see reality as it is?](#)

Using advanced mathematical modeling and common sense examples, Hoffman demonstrates that evolution leads to the selection of individuals who actively construct a distorted image of reality in a way that maximizes reproductive fitness. Evolution does not lead to the selection of individuals who passively perceive an unfiltered, accurate representation reality. This talk is useful to introduce students to the concept of emptiness from a Western perspective, and to the possibilities of mind. In the context of the course, this is used to further motivate students to engage in concentration practice, since it is a prerequisite to emptiness practice (which is not taught in the course).

Chapter 10: A Concentration Training Program for Adolescents in a Public School

Week 3: Tan Le: [A headset that reads your brainwaves](#)

Le demonstrates how emerging wearable EEG technology is allowing mental control of computer software and physical objects (even cars) connected to the software. A live demonstration vividly shows how good concentration abilities are critical to effectively use these emerging technologies. Thus, this talk also serves as motivation to the students to improve their concentration abilities so that they will be effective users of new technology.

Week 4: Daniel Goleman: [Focus, flow, and frazzle](#)

In this talk, Goleman discusses the importance of finding a point in between being overly distracted (frazzle) and overly exerting attention (focus) in order to achieve a more effective state of flow. This talk is introduced as students have just begun learning concentration techniques, and serves as a reminder of the importance of balancing relaxation with effort to achieve effective concentration. In-depth concentration training is seen as a key ingredient in the occurrence of peak performance and flow states.

Week 5: Dan Harris: [What do we have all wrong about meditation?](#) and [Hack your brain with meditation](#)

In these well produced, semi-animated short interviews, network anchorman Dan Harris describes how and why he became an "evangelist" for meditation. Importantly, he reviews how "normal" meditation has become (among celebrities, corporations, schools, professional sports, etc.), which can help reluctant students get past any resistance they may have based on cultural stereotypes about meditation. In addition, he cleverly defines the core of concentration meditation as "starting over" (re-engaging attention when we notice that it has been lost), which is a useful framing when leading students through practices. The aim of this video is to normalize concentration training, and for students to see concentration training as a necessary component to everyday living and learning.

Week 6: Andy Puddicombe: All it takes is 10 mindful minutes

In this highly engaging talk, former Buddhist monk Andy Puddicombe uses juggling to illustrate the most common obstacles to effective concentration meditation. This presentation is useful because it articulates many (if not all) of the obstacles students face early in their concentration practice, and hopefully makes students more comfortable knowing that their difficulties are common.

Week 7: Instant Egghead: Meditation changes the brain and ASAP Science: The scientific power of meditation

These fast-paced, well-produced videos bombard the viewer with a summary of the ways in which meditation can be good for physical and emotional health. Like the Dan Harris videos from week 5, these are useful arguments to help normalize what may seem like culturally strange practices to Western adolescents.

Week 8: Rick Hanson: How to change your brain

Hanson briefly details how concentration-based meditation leads to growth of specific areas of the pre-frontal cortex, the area of the brain associated with executive control and a strong sense of self. This is a useful review for students and helps to remind them that in many ways, concentration meditation is like a mental workout that builds the brain similarly to how physical workouts build muscle.

Week 9: Cliff Nass: Are you multitasking your life away?

Through engaging, song-filled allegory, Nass details the myth of multitasking, and the importance of complementing social media-based interaction with in-person interactions, especially among adolescents. In particular, Nass uses brain imagery to show how multitasking trains the brain to devote excessive attention to irrelevant stimuli, which is yet another useful argument to motivate students to train their brains to concentrate single-pointedly.

Chapter 10: A Concentration Training Program for Adolescents in a Public School

Week 10: Dandapani: [Unwavering focus](#)

Hindu monk Dandapani points out that while we ask children to focus, we never teach them how to do it, and we don't have a cultural norm around practicing concentration skills. Instead, we inadvertently practice being distracted nearly all of our waking hours. This framing reminds students that "it is not their fault" thus they can't yet concentrate well, and that the simple solution is to learn the techniques and to practice them.

Week 11: Isaac Lidsky: [What reality are you creating for yourself?](#)

In this powerful personal narrative, Lidsky demonstrates how our thoughts about our identity powerfully shape the reality that we end up living. This talk is a useful complement to teaching meta-cognition practices because it gives students added motivation to better notice how their most common (but often unnoticed) thoughts and beliefs about themselves gradually potentiate and constrain their actions in the world.

Week 12: Srikumar Rao: [Plug into your hard-wired happiness](#)

Rao argues that happiness is our innate nature, but that most of us have a flawed "if-then" mental model in which we believe that we have to obtain certain things or be certain ways in order to achieve happiness. Instead of feeding this flawed model or pursuing other models, Rao suggests that our innate happiness naturally emerges when we accept our circumstances and focus on actions instead of outcomes. As students progress in practice and begin to become more aware of their common thoughts and mental models, this talk is a useful reminder of the power of meta-cognition in shaping one's reality and happiness.

Week 13: Richard Davidson: [The four constituents of well-being](#)

Summarizing the latest neuropsychology research, Davidson argues that "well-being is a skill" underpinned by resilience, positive outlook, attention, and generosity. These four traits involve measurable, highly plastic neurocircuits, and are thus trainable. This talk summarizes Killingsworth's findings (week 1) and reminds students about the importance of training attention in the context of other qualities that also potentiate pro-social behavior.

Week 14: Alia Crum: Change your mindset, change the game

By reviewing several surprising studies about the placebo effect and similar psychological interventions, Crum demonstrates the incredibly powerful physical effects of mindset. This talk complements the Lidsky talk (week 11) to remind students about meta-cognition's importance in strengthening concentration, and in establishing agency over the self as distinct from the habitual patterns of the mind.

Week 15: Abigail Marsh: Why some people are more altruistic

Using brain imaging, Marsh demonstrates that extraordinary altruists possess enlarged amygdalas relative to normal brains, and have a less self-centered mental model about their actions in the world as a result. Using a framework similar to the neuroscience-based concentration and meta-cognition videos shown earlier, this talk reminds students about the most important goal of contemplative practice – compassionate action. Combined with summaries of how compassion practices can lead to changes in brain activity (which are circulated in text form at the beginning of the course), this video is a helpful reminder of how training the mind is at the core of who we are, and how we act in the world.

Concentration and Meta-cognitive Training

Students are taught concentration techniques from the first three stages of the Elephant Path (see chapter 4), along with several activities and exercises to train meta-cognition and compassion. The most important modification is not to the techniques themselves, but to the narratives used to explain concentration training. In particular, we replaced the driving analogy used for adults in training concentration

Chapter 10: A Concentration Training Program for Adolescents in a Public School

with a smart phone analogy more appropriate for adolescents. In this analogy, "intensifying" (see chapter 4) is replaced with "magnifying" to describe the activity of looking more closely at the details of the concentration object.

Students are taught that learning to concentrate is like learning to use a smart phone effectively. First, you must learn to keep your attention on important content on your current screen, and *direct* your attention back to important content when notifications distract you. In that sense, the skill of *directing* attention is said to be like using your thumb to swipe your way back to an important screen when you have become distracted by other media content. Second, in order to get the most out of your smart phone, you must be able to *magnify* text and images at certain times to look at them more closely. Thus, *magnifying* is like spreading two fingers apart on the screen to enlarge content and see all its details. Finally, imagine you have installed an app that tracks and displays your phone usage behavior in terms of how often you succumb to notifications and how often you magnify content. Such an app would function much like *meta-cognition* during concentration, which monitors state of mind and the strategies used during concentration, and detects episodes of distraction.

Students are taught to use the three-point object as the principle concentration object. Students are also taught a counting technique from the Zen tradition to layer on top of the three-point object should they find that their concentration is particularly scattered. Students are highly encouraged to practice for 10-15 minutes daily outside of class. Since most students readily admit failing to do so regularly, the more advanced seven-point object is not introduced until the end of the course, and concentration without support is not taught at all. Instruction related to intensification (magnification) increases as the course progresses, culminating in the introduction of the seven-point object.

Core training in the three-point object is prefaced by brief trainings in relaxation and exemplar practice, and is occasionally complemented with concentration-based games. Relaxation training is framed in terms of the benefits of finding the right balance between exertion and relaxation to achieve optimal concentration. Exemplar practice involves having students visualize someone whom they admire for their ability to focus (common examples among students include Lebron James and Kendrick Lamar), and then having them adopt the perspective of that exemplar person for the duration of the concentration, as if it were not the student but the exemplar actually doing the concentration training. Concentration games vary, but the most fun one involves having students compete to see who can count the most beans from one cup into another while other students try to distract them.

To train meta-cognition, students learn to report the amount of time (as a percent) that they are able to remain with the concentration object in each session. Early on in concentration training the best marker of progress is the percentage of the session spent staying on the concentration object as compared to the percentage being distracted. At the first stage the practitioner stays less than 50% of the session on the concentration object. At the second stage the practitioner spends more than 50%, say 70% or 80% of the session on the concentration object. Such reporting can take several forms, and all of them appear to be effective as long as the students feel like they are in a safe, non-competitive environment. For example, students can write down their meta-cognitive assessments anonymously along with any questions they have about the techniques. The instructor can then collect these, report the data from each anonymous self-assessment to the whole class, and answer the anonymously posed questions. This process allows students to see that their level of concentration (whether high or low that day) and their confusion about the techniques are not anomalous. If the students know and trust each other well, students can simply be asked to honestly share their meta-cognitive assessments and practice experiences with the class after each session. Either way, knowing that they will be expected to self-report appears to help students monitor their practice more actively during meditation.

The meta-cognitive "spinning sword meditation" is also introduced in the first half of the course to help train their faculties of awareness and mental pliancy. In this exercise, students are directed to expand their awareness from the single-pointedness of a concentration object to a

Chapter 10: A Concentration Training Program for Adolescents in a Public School

vast field and then to establish that field of awareness as the basis of operation or vantage point. Operating out of that field of awareness, the student learns to detect each and every instance of thinking occurring in the field. Since the mere observation of a thought upon its arising usually causes it to dissipate, students are figuratively striking at thoughts with the "spinning sword" of meta-cognitive awareness. In this manner, students learn to train meta-cognitive awareness to detect instances of distracting thought more and more quickly, and also to detect when they get caught up in chasing-after mode and mind-wandering.

SAMPLE GUIDED MEDITATIONS

The following is a sample of typical language used in guiding students through a meditation. Since each meditation session is short, no single session would contain all of these sections.

Preparations:

Let's begin. Find your phone. Make it silent and put it in your backpack. Place your feet flat on the floor. Sit with your back straight and your hand in your lap or on your desk. Close your eyes or keep them slightly open with an unfocused gaze. Take a couple of deep breaths to relax. Remember that the best concentration is often found in the sweet spot in between relaxation and exertion.

Exemplar practice:

Imagine someone you know, or someone you know of, who is especially focused —someone who is able to maintain excellent concentration. Imagine what this person is like when they are in this extremely focused state. Now, remind yourself that you too can learn to become that focused. You have a malleable brain that responds to mental training just like a muscle responds to physical exercise – it gets stronger. Maintain the image of this person and use them as inspiration for this session. Set the intention to concentrate as best as you can for the next 15 minutes. For just the next 15 minutes, take the perspective of this master concentrator and use it as the motivation to become as focused as they are.

Directing Concentration to the Three-Point Object:

Let your breath be however it is. If it is quick, let it be quick. If it is deep, let it be deep. Don't try to control it in any way. Our task here is not to control our breath, but to control our minds observing the breath. Whatever your breath is like right now, start to notice the three-points in each cycle. For point one, start by noticing your inhalation and all the physical sensations that accompany it. At first, the most obvious sensations are usually around your nostrils and also in your trunk as your lungs fill with air. As soon as an inhalation ends, immediately focus on the second point - the exhalation and all its associated sensations. Then, in the interval before the next inhalation, however long or short, become aware of the third point - all sensations associated with your entire body. As soon as you notice that your attention has been distracted elsewhere, direct your attention back to the three-point object. Each time you direct it back, you are improving your brain's ability to concentrate, and it will strengthen over time just like your muscles do if you lift weights. Be careful not to slow your breath down, hold your breath, or emphasize any part of the cycle deliberately. Instead, track the breath as it is naturally, whatever its qualities and wherever it is located.

Supplemental Counting:

If you find that your attention is particularly scattered, then add the counting technique to the three-point object. Label the next cycle of the three-point object with the number "one" in your mind. Then label the next cycle "two", and so on up to ten. If you can make it up to ten, then repeat by starting at one. If your attention becomes distracted, start again with the last number you can remember, or start again at one if you can't remember the last number. Counting involves thinking, but this can be useful because it reduces the number of thoughts you are having from many down to just one – the number associated with the current three-point object. When your concentration becomes more stable and you are able to count up to ten a few times in a row without distraction, then return to the pure three-point object.

Intensification (Magnification):

If your concentration is strong and you can maintain the three-point object most of the time, then start to magnify the concentration object more. See if you can notice more details about each point of the three-point object. Look at the concentration object more closely until you notice sensations that you overlooked in the past. For just a few

Chapter 10: A Concentration Training Program for Adolescents in a Public School

minutes, convince yourself that the concentration object is the most interesting thing in the world, such that it becomes easy to examine it very closely. By magnifying in this way, and by becoming so busily engaged with all of the subtle details, your mind has fewer occasions to become distracted, and your concentration will become both deeper and more continuous across time.

Seven-Point Object:

Some of you who practice outside of class may have been able to achieve deep and continuous concentration for long periods. If so, you may have also gained the ability to maintain attention on the concentration object while simultaneously having other thoughts. This "split mind" or "divided mind" is actually an impediment to progress, because you are inadvertently apportioning attention between the concentration object and the background noise of thought. Such partial staying can be overcome by deliberate magnification using the seven-point object. Start by noting the exact moment that an inhalation begins. Then immediately switch to the second point – all the sensations occurring during the duration of the entire inhalation. For the third point, notice the exact moment that the inhalation ends. The fourth point requires noticing the exact moment that the subsequent exhalation begins. Then, the fifth point is focusing on all the sensations associated with the full duration of the exhalation, ending with the sixth point – the exact moment the exhalation ends. The seventh point is to focus on the felt sense of the body as a whole in the interval between the full cycle of the breath, before the next inhale begins. By breaking up the concentration object into many small pieces, the mind is kept so busy on the seven-point concentration object that it can no longer maintain other activities while concentrating so deeply.

Training Meta-cognitive Detection of Distracting Thought; The Spinning Sword Exercise:

Drop the concentration object and open your attention from its focused, pin-point state to a broader field of awareness. Take this broad field of awareness as your vantage point, directing this awareness like a spinning sword or light saber. Use your sword of awareness to detect the activity of each and every thought moving through this field of awareness. Through exercising this faculty of meta-cognition, you become the watcher of your own mind. When you notice a thought from this perspective, you will usually find that it dissolves simply by being noticed with awareness. See if you can notice thoughts quicker and quicker as they occur. At first you may only notice thoughts that have become elaborated into daydreams. As you notice thoughts more quickly, you will catch them in less elaborated forms like simple associations or isolated words and images. Eventually, see if you can catch them so fast that they have no discernable content, but only the energy of an emerging thought. Make sure to keep your awareness broad, so that you notice all thoughts, including thoughts about the meditation exercise and how well you are doing. Also, make sure that you are detecting thoughts with awareness, and not just thinking about detecting thoughts.

Closing:

At the sound of the first closing bell, relax your attention but don't come completely out of the meditation. Use your best meta-cognitive abilities to reflect on your experience. How did the instructions match your experience? What percent of the time were you able to stay on the concentration object? Which types of thoughts were the most distracting? How quickly did you detect thought? At the sound of the second bell, bring your practice to a close.

Reporting back:

Version 1: With complete humility, honesty, and curiosity, take a moment to describe your experience to your neighbor and listen to their experience. Once you have finished, raise your hand to share an experience with the class or ask a question about the practice. Version 2: Take a minute to write down at least one question you have about the practice.

OUTCOMES AND IMPLICATIONS

Course surveys were collected at the end of each semester. According to their survey responses students generally reported that the course was valuable to them and that they would recommend it to others. Further, most reported modest improvements in their concentration abilities during class time as the course progressed. However, students generally did not report increased concentration abilities outside of class time unless they established a regular meditation practice outside of class, which was rare. These findings strongly suggest the importance of emphasizing appealing to motivation in working with adolescents, as was done through the series of video-teachings.

A number of students reported that the course was particularly important to them because it helped them dis-identify with negative self talk in their minds, and become more familiar with their habitual thought patterns and the problem of mind wandering. A few students also reported gaining a new perspective on the self and mind, particularly that they no longer thought of their sense of self as wholly defined by the content of their thoughts and emotions. No students reported negative outcomes.

The most common questions posed to the instructor after practice sessions were: How do I avoid falling asleep? Is it ever dangerous or unhealthy to be too concentrated? Doesn't maintaining meta-cognition mean that you can't use all your brain for concentrating? Is it normal to feel such and such type of sensation while doing this? Why is this so hard? Is it safe to do this practice while doing other activities like driving? Are you enlightened?

The main implication drawn by the instructing author (JP) is that bigger outcomes are not likely to be realized unless class time is expanded, or unless the class culture and incentive structure shift so that meditation practice outside of class becomes more common. That said, many students who have graduated continue to send messages of appreciation and express continued interest in learning more techniques.

Final Comment:
Implementing these Practices in Educational Settings

Considering the educational community's mission, values, population, and goals is of utmost importance when implementing any program. These practices come from ancient traditions through lineages that have passed their teachings down from generation to generation. They are adaptable to a variety of settings. Just like it is important to meet children where they are, it is important to understand the educational setting in which you are hoping to share these practices. The teachers, who contributed to this book, have explored sharing these practices in both public and independent settings. They've experienced teaching these practices to children over a short, limited time span as well as over the course of many years. They've experienced teaching these practices as part of a stand alone course, as well as part of a course that is woven into the makeup and program of an educational community. As with any practice, it is important to develop a commitment and a regular schedule from which the practice can deepen. Therefore, when these practices are seen and valued as part of the core curriculum, that is when they can affect the well-being of our children and communities.

The true benefit of these practices can be seen when they are taken off the mat, or the meditation cushion. Involving the teachers, administrators, parents, families, and community members in the development of these practices and programs is also vitally important. As the students develop skill around these practices, meta-cognition, and the awareness of and ability to utilize these practices in everyday life, they truly become a part of their rhythm, and very being. This also must be organically offered to the educational community. Creating teacher meditation workshops or classes, family practice sessions, and school-wide events are great ways to introduce the community to the program and practices in an accessible and inviting way. Once teachers and parents begin to familiarize themselves with the practices, they can better support the children.

Lastly, the competence of the teachers who will be implementing the program and practices is of most importance. It is important to have a direct experience of these practices and an individual daily practice developed over time to truly understand the practices. It is difficult to teach anything if you do not know it deeply.

The Elephant Path: Attention Development and Training in Children and Adolescents

Bibliography

Abikoff, H. & Klein, R.G. (1987). Cognitive training in treatment of hyperactivity in children, *Archives of General Psychiatry*, 44 (3), 296-297.

Ablon, S., Brown, D., Khantzian, E.J., & Mack, J.E. (1993) *Human feelings: Explorations in affective development and meaning.* Hillsdale, NJ: Analytic Press.

Adamson, L.B., & Bakeman, R. (1991). The development of shared attention during infancy, In R. Vasta (Ed.), *Annals of Child Development*, 8, 1-41.

Adler, S.A., & Rovee-Collier, C. (1994). The effect of enhanced attention on infant memory, *Infant Behavior and Development*, 17, 484.

Akhtar, N. (1988). The relations between covert search, filtering, and priming: A developmental study. Unpublished Masters thesis. Dalhousie University.

Alloway, T.P., Gathercole, S.E., Kirkwood, H., & Elliott, J. (2009). The cognitive and behavioral characteristics of children with low working memory, *Child Development*, 80 (2), 606-621.

Alzahabi, R., & Becker, M.W. (2013). The association between media multitasking, task-switching, and dual-task performance, *Journal of Experimental Psychology: Human Perception and Performance*, 39 (5), 1485-1495.

Amon, K.L., 7 Campbell, A. (2008). Can children with AD/HD learn relaxation and breathing techniques through biofeedback video games? *Australian Journal of Educational & Developmental Psychology*, 8, 72-84.

Andersen, D.R., Choi, H.P., & Lorch, E.P. (1987). Attentional inertia reduces distractibility during young children's TV viewing, *Child Development*, 58, 798-806.

Anderson, D.R. & Levin, S.R. (1976). Young children's attention to "Sesame Street," *Child Development*, 47, 806-811.

Anderson, D.R., Lorch, E.P., Field, D.E., Collins, P.A., & Nathan, J.G. (1986). Television viewing at home: Age trends in visual attention and time with TV, *Child Development*, 57, 1024-1033.

Anderson, D.R., Lorch, E.P., Field, D.E., & Sanders, J. (1981). The effects of TV program comprehensibility on preschool children's visual attention to television, *Child Development*, 52, 151-157.

Anderson, D.R., Lorch, E.P., Smith, R., Bradford, R., & Levin, S.R. (1981). Effects of peer presence on preschool children's television-viewing behavior, *Developmental Psychology*, 17, 446-453.

Anderson, N.D., Lau, M.A., Segal, Z.V., & Bishop, S.R. (2007). Mindfulness-based stress reduction and attentional control, *Clinical Psychology & Psychotherapy*, 14, 449-463.

Anderson, P. (2002). Assessment and development of executive function (EF) during childhood, *Child Neuropsychology*, 8 (2), 71-82.

Anderson, V.A., Anderson, P., Northam, E., Jacobs, R., & Catroppa, C. (2001). Development of executive functions through late childhood and adolescence in an Australian sample, *Developmental Neuropsychology*, 20 (1), 385-406.

Andrews, K., Kaufman, P.M., McDiamrid, M.D., & Glisky, M.L. (1999). Executive functioning in preschool children: Performance on A-not-B and other delayed response format tasks, *Brain & Cognition*, 41, 178-199.

Andrews-Hanna, J.R., Reidler, J.S., Sepulere, J., Poulin, R., & Bucker, R.L. (2010). Functional-anatomic fractionation of the brain's default network. *Neuron*, 65 (4), 550-562.

Au, J., Sheehan, E., Tsai, N., Duncan, G.J., Buschkuehl, M., & Jaeggi, S.M. (2015). Improving fluid intelligence with training on working memory: A meta-analysis, *Psychonomic Bulletin Review* 22, 366-377.

Anticevic, A., Cole, M.W., Murray, J.D., Corlett, P.R., Wang, K.I., & Krystal, J.H. (2012). The role of default network deactivation in cognition and disease, *Trends in Cognitive Sciences*, 16, 584-592.

Arnold, M. B. (1960). Emotion and personality. *New York: Columbia University Press.*

Baddeley, A.D. (2000). The episodic buffer: A new component of working memory? *Trends in Cognitive Sciences*, 4 (11), 417-423.

Baddeley, A.D. (2007). *Working memory, thought, and action.* New York: Oxford.

Baddeley, A.D. (2012). Working memory: Theories, models, and contro-versies, *Annual Review of Psychology*, 63 (1), 1-29.

Baddeley, A.D. & Hitch, G.J. (1974). Working memory, In G.A. Bower (ed.), *The psychology of learning and motivation*, Vol. 8 (pp. 47-89), New York: Academic Press.

Bahrick, L.E., Walker, A.S., & Neisser, U. (1981). Selective looking by infants, *Cognitive Psychology*, 13, 377-390.

Bak, P.L., Midgley, N., Zhu.,J.L., Wistoft, K., & Obel, C. (2015). The Resilience Program: Preliminary evaluation of a mentalization-based education program. *New Frontiers in Psychology*, 6, 753.

Bakemanm R., & Adamson, L.B. (1984). Coordinating attention to people and objects in mother-infant and peer-infant interaction, *Child Development*, 55, 1278-1289.

Baker, R.L. & Brown, D.P. (2016). On engagement: Learning to pay attention, *University of Arkansas Law Review*, 36, 337-385.

Barkley, R.A., Grodzinsky, G., & DuPaul, G.J. (1992). Frontal lobe functions in attention deficit disorder with and without hyperactivity: A review and research report, *Journal of Abnormal Child Psychology*, 20 (2), 163-188.

Barrera, M.E., & Maurer, D. (1981). The perception of facial expressions by the three-month-old, *Child Development*, 52, 203-206.

Barnes, V.A., Treiber, F.A., & Davis, H. (2001). Impact of Transcendental Meditation on cardiovascular function at rest and during acute stress in adolescents with high normal blood pressure, *Journal of Psychosomatic Research*, 51, 597-605.

Barrett, S.E., & Shepp, B.E. (1988). Developmental changes in attentional skills: The effect of irrelevant variations on encoding and response selection, *Journal of Experimental Child Psychology*, 45, 382-399.

Baumgartner, S.E., Lemmens, J.S., Weeda, W.D., & Huizinga, M. (2017). Measuring media multitasking: Development of a short measure of media multitasking for adolescents, *Journal of Media Psychology*, 29, 188-197.

Baumgartner, S.E., van der Schuur, W.A., Lemmens, J.S. & De Poel, F. (2018). The relationship between media multitasking and attentional problems in adolescents: Results of two longitudinal studies, *Human Communications Research*, 44, 3-30.

Baumgartner, S.E., Weeda, W.D., van der Heijden, L.L., & Huizinga, M. (2014). The relationship between media multitasking and executive function in early adolescents, *Journal of Early Adolescence*, 34 (8), 1120-1144.

Bayliss, D.M., Jarrold, C., Baddeley, A.D., Gunn, D.M., & Leigh, E. (2005). Mapping the developmental constraints on working memory span performance, *Developmental Psychology*, 41 (4), 579-597.

BBC News 22 Feb, 2002 Turning into a digital goldfish.

Beauchemin, J., Hutchins, T.L., & Patterson, F. (2008). Mindfulness meditation may lessen anxiety, promote social skills, and improve academic performance among adolescents with learning disabilities, *Complementary Health Practice Review*, 13 (1), 34-45.

Beck, S.J., Hanson, C.A., Puffenberger, S.S., Beniner, K.L., & Benninger, W.B. (2010). A controlled trial of working memory training for children and adolescents with ADHD, *Journal of Clinical Child & Adolescent Psychology*, 39 (6), 825-836.

Becker, P.T., & Thomas, E.B. (1983). Organization of sleeping and waking states in infants: Consistency across contexts, *Physiology and Behavior*, 31, 276-292.

Belsky, J., Garduque, L., & Hrncir, E. (1984). Assessing performance, competence and executive capacity in infant play: Relations to home environment and security of attachment, *Developmental Psychology*, 20, 406-417.

Belsky, J., Goode, M.K., & Most, R.K. (1980). Maternal stimulation and infant exploratory competence: Cross-sectional, correlational, and experimental analysis, *Child Development*, 51, 1168-1178.

Belsky, J., & Most, R.K. (1981). From exploration to play: A cross sectional study of infant free play behavior, *Developmental Psychology*, 17, 630-639.

Bergen, L., Grimes, T., & Potter, D. (2005). How attention partitions itself during simultaneous message presentations, *Human Communication Research*, 31 (3), 311-336.

Berger, I., Remington, A. Leitner, Y., & Leviton, A. (2015). Brain development and the attention spectrum, *Frontiers in Human Neuroscience*, 9 (23), 1-2.

Berger, I., Slobodin, O., Aboud, M., Melamed, J., & Cassuto, H. (2013). Maturational delay in ADHD: Evidence from CPT, *Frontiers in Human Neuroscience*, 7, 691, 10-14.

Berlyne, D.E. (1970). Attention as a problem of behavior therapy, In D. I.Mostofsky (Ed.) *Attention: Contemporary theory and analysis*, (pp. 25-60), New York: Appleton-Century-Crofts.

Betts, J., McKay, J., Maruff, P., & Anderson, V. (2006). The development of sustained attention in children: The effect of age and task load, *Child Neuropsychology*, 12, 205-221.

Bhatt, R.S., Bertin, E., & Gilbert, J. (1999). Discrepancy detection and developmental changes in attentional engagement in infancy, *Infant Behavior and Development*, 22, 197-219.

Bianchi, A., & Phillips, J.G. (2005). Psychological predictors of problem mobile phone use, CyberPsychology & Behavior, 8 (1), 39-51.

Blakemore, S-J., & Choudhury, S. (2006). Development of the adolescent brain: Implications for executive function and social cognition, *Journal of Child Psychology and Psychiatry*, 47 (3/4), 296-312.

The Body Scan Practice, *mindful.org*, 2012.

Bogels, S., Hogstad, B., van Dun, L., de Schutter, S., & Restifo, K. (2008). Mindfulness training for adolescents with externalizing disorders and their parents, *Behavioral and Cognitive Psychotherapy*, 36, 193-209.

Bornstein, M.H. (1985). How infant and mother jointly contribute to developing cognitive competence in the child, *Proceedings of the National Academy of Sciences, USA*, 82, 7470-7473.

Borst, J.P., Taatgen, N.A., & van Rijn, H. (2010). The problem state: A cognitive bottleneck in multitasking, *Journal of Experimental Psychology: Learning, Memory, and Cognition*, 36 (2), 363-382.

Bowman, L.L., Levine, L.E., Waite, B.M., & Gendron, M. (2010). Can students really multitask? An experimental study of instant messaging while reading, *Computers & Education*, 54 (4), 927-931.

Brasel, S.A. & Gips, J. (2011). Media multitasking behavior: Concurrent television and computer usage, *Cyberpsychology, Behavior, and Social Networking*, 14 (9), 527-534.

Brefczyski-Lewis, J.A., Lutz, A., Schaefer, H.S., Levinson, D.B. & Davidson, R.J. (2007) Neural correlates of attentional expertise in long-term meditation practitioners. *Proceedings of the National Academy of Sciences USA*, 104, 11483-11488.

Brewer, J.A., Worhunksy, P.D., Gray, J.R., Tang, Y-Y., Weber, J. & Kober, H. (2011). Meditation experience is associated with differences in default mode network activity and connectivity, *Proceedings of the National Academy of Sciences USA*, 108 (50), 20254-20259.

Breznitz, Z., & Friedman, S.L. (1988). Toddlers' concentration: Does maternal depression make a difference? *Journal of Child Psychology and Psychiatry*, 29, 267-279.

Broadbent, D.E., Cooper, P.F., Fitzgerald, P., & Parkes, K.R. (1982). The Cognitive Failures Questionnaire (CFQ) and its correlates, *British Journal of Clinical Psychology*, 21, 1-16.

Brock, S.E., Rothbart, M.K., & Derryberry, D. (1986). Heart-rate deceleration and smiling in 3-month-old infants, *Infant Behavior and Devel-*

opment, 9, 403-414.

Brocki, K.C., & Bohlin, G. (2004). Executive functions in children aged 6 to 13: A dimensional and developmental study, *Developmental Neuro-psychology*, 26 (2), 571-593.

Broderick P.C., & Frank, J. L. (2014). Learning to BREATHE: An intervention to foster mindfulness in adolescence, *New Directions for Youth Development*, 142, 31-44.

Broderick, P.C., & Metz, S. (2009). Learning to BREATHE: A pilot trial of a mindfulness curriculum for adolescents, *Advances in School Mental Health Promotion*, 2 (1), 35-46.

Brodeur, D.A. (1990). Covert orienting in young children, In J.T. Enns (Ed.), *The development of attention: Research and theory.* (pp. 211-226) Amsterdam, Netherlands: Elsevier.

Brodeur, D.A., & Boden, C. (2000). The effects of spatial uncertainty and cue predictability on visual orienting in children, *Cognitive Development*, 15, 367-382.

Brodeur, D.A., & Enns, J.T. (1997). Covert visual orienting across the lifespan, *Canadian Journal of Experimental Psychology*, 51 (1), 20-35.

Brown, D. (2006). *Pointing Out the Great Way: The Stages of Meditation in the Mahamudra Tradition.* Somerville, MA: Wisdom Publications.

Brown, D. (2009). Mastery of mind East and West: Excellence in being and doing and everyday happiness. *New York Academy of Sciences*, 1172, 231-251.

Brown, D.P., & Elliott, D. S. (2016). *Attachment Disturbances in Adults: Treatment for Comprehensive Repair.* New York NY: Norton.

Brown, K.W., & Ryan, R.M. (2003). The benefits of being present: Mindfulness and its role in psychological well-being, *Journal of Personality and Social Psychology*, 84 (2), 822-848.

Brunye, T.T., Taylor, H.A., Rapp, D.N., & Spiro, A.B. (2006). Learning procedures: The role of working memory in multimedia learning experiences, *Applied Cognitive Psychology*, 20, 917-940.

Buckner, R.I., Andrews-Hanna, J.R., & Schacter, D.L. (2008). The brain's default network: Anatomy, function, and relevance to disease. *Annals of the New York Academy of Sciences*, 1124, 1-38.

Buddhaghosa, B. (1976). *The Path of Purification*, Vols 1-2. Trans. B. Nanamoli. Boston MA: Shambhala Publications.

Bull, R., & Scerif, G. (2001). Executive functioning as a predictor of children's mathematics ability: Inhibition, shifting, and working memory. *Developmental Neuropsychology*, 19 (3), 273-293.

Bullock, M., & Lutkenhaus, P. (1988). The development of volitional behavior in the toddler years, *Child Development*, 59, 664-674.

Burke, C.A. (2009). Mindfulness-based approaches with children and adolescents: A preliminary review of current research in an emergent field, *Journal of Child & Family Studies*, 19 (2), 133-144.

Burns, J.J., & Anderson, D.R. (1993). Attentional inertia and recognition memory in adult television viewing, *Communication Research*, 20, 777-799.

Buschman, T.J. & Miller, E.K. (2007). Top-down versus bottom-up control of attention in the prefrontal and posterior parietal cortices, *Science*, 315, 160-162.

Bushnell, E.W. (1985). The decline of visually guided reaching during infancy, *Infant Behavior and Development*, 8, 139-155.

Butterworth, G., & Cochran, E. (1980). Towards an mechanism of joint visual attention in human infancy, *International Journal of Behavioral Development*, 3, 253-272.

Caballero, A., Granberg, R., & Tseng, K. Y. (2016). Mechanisms contributing to prefrontal cortex maturation during adolescence, *Neuroscience and Biobehavioral Reviews*, 70, 4-12.

Cain, M.S., Leonard, J.A., Gabrieli, J.D., & Finn, A.S. (2016). Media multitasking in adolescence, *Psychonomic Bulletin & Review*, 23, 1932-1941.

Canfield, R.L. & Haith, M.M. (1991). Young infants' visual expectations for symmetric and asymmetric stimulus sequences, *Developmental Psychology*, 27 (2), 198-208.

Campbell, S.B., Breaux, A.M., Ewing, L.J., Szumowski, E.K., & Pierce, E.W. (1986). Parent-identified problem preschoolers: Mother-child interaction during play at intake and 1-year follow-up, *Journal of Abnormal Child Psychology*, 14, 425-440.

Canfield, R.L., & Haith, M.M. (1991). Young infant's visual expectations for symmetric and asymmetric stimulus sequences, *Developmental Psychology*, 27, 198-208.

Carlson, E.A., Jacobvitz, D., & Sroufe, L.A. (1995). A developmental investigation of inattentiveness and hyperactivity, *Child Development*, 66, 37-54.

Carlson, S.M., & Moses, L.J. (2001). Individual differences in inhibitory control and children's theory of mind, *Child Development*, 72, 1032-1053.

Carlson, S.M., Moses, L.J., & Claxton, L.J. (2004). Individual differences in executive functioning and theory of mind: An investigation of inhibitory control and planning ability, *Journal of Experimental Child Psychology*, 87, 299-319.

Carr N. (2011). *The shallows: What the Internet is dong to our brains*. New York NY: Norton.

Carretti, B., Borella, E., & De Beni, R. (2007). Does strategic memory training improve working memory performance of younger and older adults? *Experimental Pyschology*, 54, 311-320.

Carriere, J.S.A., Cheyne, J.A., & Smilek, D. (2008). Everyday attention lapses and memory failure: The affective consequences of mindlessness, *Consciousness and Cognition*, 17, 835-847.

Casey, B.J., Giedd, J.N., & Thomas, K.M. (2000). Structural and functional brain development and its relation to cognitive development, *Biological Psychology*, 54, 241-257.

Casey, B.J., & Richards, J.E. (1988). Sustained visual attention in young infants measured with an adapted version of the visual preference paradigm, *Child Development*, 59, 1514-1521.

Casey, B.J., Tottenham, N., Liston, C., & Durston, S. (2005). Imaging the developing brain: What have we learned about cognitive development? *Trends in Cognitive Sciences*, 9 (3), 104-110.

Casey, B.J., Trainor, R.J., Orendi, J.L., Nystrom. L.E., Giedd, J.N., Castellanos, F.X., Haxby, J.V., Noll, D.C., Cohen, J.D., Forman, S.D., Dahl, R.E., & Rapoport, J.L. (1997). A developmental functional MRI study of prefrontal activation during performance of a Go-No-Go task, *Journal of Cognitive Neuroscience*, 9 (6), 835-847.

Certain. L.K., & Kahn, R.S. (2002). Prevalence, correlates, and trajectory of television viewing among infants and toddlers, *Pediatrics*, 109 (4), 634-642.

Chein, J.M., & Schneider, W. (2005). Neuroimaging studies of practice-related change: fMRI and meta-analytic evidence of a domain general control network for learning, *Cognitive Brain Research*, 25, 607-623.

Cheyne, J.A., Carriere, J.S.A., & Smilek, D. (2006). Absent-mindedness: Lapses of conscious awareness and everyday cognitive failures, *Consciousness and Cognition*, 15, 578-592.

Chislolm, J.D., Hickey, C., Theeuwes, J., & Kingstone, A. (2010). Reduced attentional capture in action video game players, *Attention, Perception, & Psychophysics*, 72 (3), 667-671.

Choi, H.P., & Anderson, D.R. (1991). A temporal analysis of free toy play and distractibility in young children, *Journal of Experimental Child Psychology*, 52, 41-69.

Chooi, W-T., & Thompson, L.A. (2012). Working memory training does not improve intelligence in healthy young adults, *Intelligence*, 40, 531-542.

Choudhury, N., & Gorman, K.S. (2000). The relationship between sustained attention and cognitive performance in 17-24-month-old toddlers, *Infant and Child Development*, 9, 127-146.

Christakis, D.A., Zimmerman, F.J., DiGiuseppe, D.L., & McCarty, C.A. (2004). Early television and subsequent attentional problems in children, *Pediatrics*, 113 (4), 708-713.

Christakou, A., Brammer, M., & Rubia, K. (2011). Maturation of limbic fronto-striatal activation and connectivity associated with developmental changes in stemporal discounting, *Neuro Image*, 54 (2), 1344-1354.

Christoff, K., Gordon, A.M., Smallwood, J., Smith, R., & Schooler, J.W. (2009). Experience sampling during fMRI reveals default network and executive system contributions to mind wandering, *Proceedings of the National Academy of Sciences USA*, 106 (21), 8719-8724.

Christoff, K., Irving, Z.C., Fox, K.C.R., Spreng, R.N., & Andrews-Hanna, J.R. (2016). Mind-wandering as spontaneous thought: A dynamic framework, *Nature Reviews. Neuroscience*, 17 (11), 718-731.

Chugani, H.T. (1998). A critical period of brain development: Studies of cerebral glucose utilization with PET, *Preventive Medicine*, 27, 184-188.

Cohen, K. (2004). Beginner's Mind, *Experience Life*.

Cohen, L.B. (1972). Attention-getting and attention-holding processes of infant-visual preferences, *Child Development*, 43, 869-879.

Colombo, J. (1993). *Infant cognition: Predicting later intellectual functioning.* Newbury Park CA; Sage.

Comalli, P.E., Wapner, S., & Werner, H. (1962). Interference effects of the Stroop color-word test in children, adulthood, and aging, *Journal of Genetic Psychology*, 100, 47-53.

Conway, A.R.A., Cowan, N., & Bunting, M.F. (2001). The cocktail party phenomenon revisited: The importance of working memory capacity, *Psychonomic Bulletin & Review*, 8 (2), 331-335.

Conway, A.R.A., & Engle, R.W. (1996). Individual differences in working memory capacity: More evidence for a general capacity theory, *Memory*, 4 (6), 577-590.

Corbetta, M. & Shulman, G.L (2002) Control of goal-directed and stimulus-driven attention in the brain. *Nature Reviews: Neuroscience*, 3, 201-215.

Couperus, J.W. (2011). Perceptual load influences selective attention across development, *Developmental Psychology*, 47 (5), 1431-1439.

Czikszentmihalyi, M. (1997) *Finding flow: The psychology of engagement with everyday life*. New York: Basic.

Cunningham, C.E., & Barkley, R.A. (1979). The interactions of normal and hyperactive children with their mothers in free play and structured tasks, *Child Development*, 50, 217-224.

Dahlin, K.I.E. (2011). Effects of working memory training on reading in children with special needs, *Reading and Writing*, 24 (4), 479-491.

Daneman, M., & Carpenter, P.A. (1980). Individual differences in working memory and reading, *Journal of Verbal Learning and Verbal Behavior*, 19 (4), 450-466.

Davidson, M.C., Amso, D., Cruess, D., Anderson, L., & Diamond, A. (2006). Development of cognitive control and executive functions from 4 to 13 years: Evidence from manipulations of memory inhibition, and task switching, *Neuropsychologia*, 44 (11), 2037-2078.

De Lisi, R., & Wolford, J.L. (2002). Improving children's mental rotation accuracy with computer game playing, *Journal of Genetic Psychology*, 163, 272-282.

DeLoache, J.S., Rissman, M.W., & Cohen, L.B., (1978). An investigation of the attention-getting process in infants, *Infant Behavior and Development*, 59, 1504-1513.

De Oliveira, C.R., Pedron, C. & Gurgrl, L. G., Reppold, C.T., & Fonseca, R.P. (2012). Executive functions and sustained attention, *Dementia Neuropsychology*, 6 (1), 29-34.

Deep Calm-Abiding – The Nine Stages of Abiding. Dharma Fellowship of His Holiness the Gyalwa Karmapa, 2005-2015

Derryberry, D. & Rothbart, M.K. (1988). Arousal, affect, and attention as components of temperament, *Journal of Personality and Social Psychology*, 55 (6), 958-966.

Derryberry, D. & Rothbart, M.K. (1997). Reactive and effortful processes in the organization of temperament, *Development and Psychopathology*, 9, 633-652.

DeStafano, D., & LeFevre, J. (2007). Cognitive load in hypertext reading: A Review, *Computers in Human Behavior*, 23 (3), 1616-1641.

Diamond, A., Barnett, W.S., Thomas, J., & Munro, S. (2007). Preschool program improves cognitive control, Science, 318 (5855), 1387-1388.

Diamond, A., & Goldman-Rakic, P.S. (1989). Comparison of human infants and rhesus monkeys on Piaget's AB task: Evidence for dependence on dorsolateral prefrontal cortex, *Experimental Brain Research*, 74, 24-40.

Dreher, J-C., Koechin, E. Tierney, M., & Grafman, J. (2008). Damage to the fronto-planar cortex is associated with impaired multitasking, *Plos One*, di.org/10.1371/journal.pone.0003227,

Doolittle, J.H. (1995). Using riddles and interactive computer games to teach problem-solving skills, *Teaching of Psychology*, 22, 33-36.

Donnelly, N., Cave, K., Greenway, R., Hadwin, J.A., Stevenson, J., & Sonuga-Barke, E. (2007). Visual search in children and adults: Top-down and bottom-up mechanisms, *Quarterly Journal of Experimental Psychology*, 60 (1), 120-136.

Dorval, M., & Pepin, M. (1986). Effect of playing a video game on a measure of spatial visualization, *Perceptual and Motor Skills*, 62, 159-162.

Dove, A., Pollman, S., Schubert, T., Wiggins, C.J., & Von Cramon, D. (2000). Prefrontal cortex activation in task switching: An event-related fMRI study. *Cognitive Brain Research*, 9, 103-283.

Dunning, D.L., Holmes, J., & Gathercole, S.E. (2013). Does working memory training lead to generalized improvements in children with low working memory? A randomized controlled trial, *Developmental*

Science, 16 (6), 915-925.

Durkin, K., & Barber, B. (2002). Not so doomed: Computer game play and positive adolescent development, *Journal of Applied Developmental Psychology*, 23, 373-392.

Dux, P.E., Tombu, M.N., Harrison, S., Rogers, B.P., Tong, F., & Marois, R. (2009). Training improves multitasking performance by increasing the speed of information processing in human prefrontal cortex, *Neuron*, 63, 127-138.

Elliott J.G., Gathercole, S.E., Alloway, T.P., Holmes, J., & Kirkwood, H. (2010). An evaluation of a classroom-based intervention to help overcome working memory difficulties and improve long-term academic achievement, *Journal of Cognitive Education and Psychology*, 9 (3), 227-249.

Engle, R.W. (2002). Working memory capacity as executive attention, *Current Directions in Psychological Science*, 11 (1), 19-23.

Enns, J.T. (1990). *The development of attention: Research and theory.* Amsterdam, Netherlands: Elsevier.

Enns, J.T. (1990). Relations between components of visual attention In J.T. Enns (Ed.), *The development of attention: Research and theory.* (pp. 1390158) Amsterdam, Netherlands: Elsevier.

Enns, J.T., & Akhtar, N. (1989). A developmental study of filtering in visual attention, *Child Development*, 60, 1188-1199.

Enns, J.T., Burack, J.A., Iarocci, G. & Randolph, B. (2000). The orthogenetic principle in the perception of "forests" and "trees," *Journal of Adult Development*, 7 (1), 41-48.

Enns, J.T. & Girgus, J.S. (1985). Developmental changes in selective and integrative visual attention, *Journal of Experimental Child Psychology*, 40, 319-337.

Ericson, J. (2013) Information overload: How the Internet inhibits short-term memory, www.medicaldaily.com.

Ericsson, K.A., & Kintsch, W. (1995). Long-term working memory, *Psy-*

chological Review, 102 (2), 211-245.

Eriksen, B.A., & Eriksen, C.W. (1974). Effects if noise letters upon the identification of a target letter in a non-search task, *Perception & Psychophysics*, 16 (1), 143-149.

Erickson, K.I., Colcombem S.J., Wadhwa, R., Bherer, L., Peterson, M.S., Scalf, P.E., Kim, J.S., Alvarado, M., & Kramer, A.F. (2007). Training-induced functional activation changes in dual-task processing: An fMRI study, *Cerebral Cortex*, 17, 192-204.

Eysenck, H.J. & Eysenck, M.W. (1985). *Personality and individual differences: A natural science approach.* New York: Plenum.

Evans-Schmidt, M., Pempek, T.A., Kirkorian, H.L., Lund, A.F., & Andeson, D.R. (2008). The effects of background television on the toy play behavior of very young children, *Child Development*, 79 (4), 1137-1151.

Fan, J., McCandliss, B.D., Fossella, J., Flombaum, J.I., & Posner, M.I. (2005). The activation of attentional networks, *Neuro Image*, 26, 471-479.

Fantz, R.L. (1963). Pattern vision in newborn infants, *Science*, 140, 296-297.

Fantz, R.L. (1964). Visual experience in infants: Decreased attention to familiar patterns relative to novel ones, *Science*, 146, 668-670.

Farmer, E.M., Compton, S.N., Robertson, E., & Burns, B.J. (2002). Review of evidence base for treatment of childhood psychopathology: Externalizing disorders, *Journal of Consulting and Clinical Psychology*, 70 (6), 1267-1302.

Farb, N.A. S., Segal, Z.V., Mayberg, H., Bean, J., McKeon, D., Fatima, Z. & Anderson, A.K. (2007) Attending to the present: Mindfulness meditation reveals distinct modes of self-reference. *Social, Cognitive, and Affective Neuroscience*, 7, 109-119.

Faupel, K.C. (1989). Adolescent psychic entropy: A response to unacknowledged fears, *Adolescence*, 24 (94), 375-378.

Felver, J.C., Celis-de Hoyos, C.E., Tezanos, K., & Singh, N.N. (2016). A systematic review of mindfulness-based interventions for youth in school settings, *Mindfulness,* 17 (1), 34-45.

Feng, J., Spence, I., & Pratt, J. (1990). Playing an action video game reduces gender differences in spatial cognition, *Psychological Science,* 18 (10), 850-855.

Fernandez-Duque, D., Baird, J.A., & Posner, M.I. (2000). Executive attention and meta-cognitive regulation, *Consciousness and Cognition,* 9, 288-307.

Fisch, S.M. (2000). A capacity model of children's comprehension of educational content on television, *Media Psychology,* 2, 63-91.

Fisher, R. (2006). Still thinking: The case for meditation with children, *Thinking Skills and Creativity,* 1 (2), 146-151.

Fischer, R., & Plessow, F. (2105). Efficient multitasking: Parallel versus serial processing of multiple tasks, *Frontiers in Psychology,* 201, 1-46.

Fisher, A., Thiessen, E., Godwin, K., Klooss, H., & Dickerson, J. (2013). Assessing selective sustained attention in 3- to 5-year-old children: Evidence from a new paradigm, *Journal of Experimental Child Psychology,* 114, 275-294.

Fisher, R. (2006). Still thinking: The case for meditation with children. *Thinking Skills and Creativity,* 1 (2), 146-151.

Fjell, A.M., Walhovd, K.B., Brown, T.T., Kuerman, J.M., Chung, Y., Hagler Jr., D.J., Venkatraman, V., Roddy, J.C., Erhart, M., McCabe, C., Akshoomoff, N., Amaral, D.G., Bloss, C.S., Libiger, O., Darst, B.F., Schork, N.J., Casey, B.J., Chang, L., Ernst, T.M., Gruen, J.R., Kaufmann, W.E., Kentet, T., Frazier, J., Murray, S.S., Sowell, E.R., van Zijl, P., Mostofsky, S., Jernigan, T.L., & Dale, A.M. (2012). Multimodal imaging of the self-regulating developing brain, *Proceedings of the National Academy of Sciences, USA,* 109 (48), 19620-19625.

Flook, L., Smalley, S.L., Kitel, M.J., Galla, B.M., Kaiser-Greenland, S., Locke, J., Ishijima, E., Kasari, C. (2010). Effects of mindful awareness practices on executive functions in elementary school children,

Journal of Applied School Psychology, 26, 70-95.

Foerde, K., Knowlton, B.J., & Poldrack, R.A. (2006). Modulation of competing memory systems by distraction, *Proceedings of the National Academy of Sciences USA,* 103 (31), 11778-11783.

Ford, C.E., Pelham, W.E., & Ross, A.O. (1984). Selective attention and rehearsal in the auditory short-term-memory task-performance of poor and normal readers, *Journal of Abnormal Child Psychology,* 12 (1), 127-141.

Forte, M.A. (1979). The process of meditation and the retraining of attention. Unpublished doctoral dissertation, Harvard University.

Fortenbaugh, F.C., DeGuitus, J., Germine, L., Wilmer, J.B., Grosso, M., Russo, K., & Easterman, M. (2015). Sustained attention across the life span in a sample of 10,000: Dissociating ability and strategy, *Psychological Science,* 26 (9), 1497-1510.

Fougnie, D. (2008). The relationship between attention and working memory, In. N.B. Johnson (Ed.), *New research on short-term memory,* (pp. 1-45), Hauppauge NY: Nova Science.

Fox, K.C.R., Spreng, R.N., Ellamil, M., Andrews-Hanna, J. R., and Christoff, K. (2015). The wandering brain: Meta-analysis of functional neuroimaging studies of mind-wandering and related spontaneous thought processes. *Neuro Image,* 111, 611-621.

Fransson, P., Aden, U., Blennow, M. & Lagercrantz, H. (2011). The functional architecture of the infant brain as revealed by resting-state fMRI, *Cerebral Cortex,* 21, 145-154.

Fransson, P., & Marrelec, G. (2008). The precuneous/posterior cingulate cortex plays a pivotal role in the default mode network: Evidence from a partial correlation network analysis, *Neuro Image,* 42 (3), 1178-1184.

Frederickson, W.T., & Brown, J.V. (1975). Posture as a determinant of visual behavior in newborns, *Child Development,* 46, 579-582.

Gadberry, S. (1980). Effects of restricting first-graders' TV-viewing on leisure time use, IQ change, and cognitive style, *Journal of Applied Developmental Psychology*, 1, 45-57.

Gaertner, B.M., Spinrad, T.L., & Eisenberg, N. (2008). Focused attention in toddlers: Measurement, stability, and relations to negative emotion and parenting. *Infant and Child Development*, 17 (4), 339-363.

Gagnon, D. (1985). Videogames and spatial skills: An exploratory study, *Educational Communication and Technology Journal*, 33, 263-275.

Gale, A., & Lynn, R. (1972). A developmental study of attention, B*ritish Journal of Educational Psychology*, 42, 260-266.

Gandour, M. J. (1989). Activity level as a dimension of temperament in toddlers: Its relevance for the organismic specificity hypothesis, *Child Development*, 60, 1092-1098.

Gao, W., Zhu, H., Giovanello, K.S., Smith, J.K., Shen, D., Gilmore, D., & Lin, W. (2009). Evidence on the emergence of the brain's default nework from 2-week-old to 2-year-old healthy pediatric subjects, *Proceedings of the National Academy of Sciences USA*, 106 (16), 6790-6795.

Garner, K.G., & Dux, P.E. (2015). Training conquers multitasking costs by dividing task representations in the fronto-parietal-subcortical system, *Proceedings of the National Academy of Sciences USA*, 112 (46), 14372-14377.

Garrison, K.A., Scheinost, D., Worhunsky, P.D., Elwafi, H.M., Thornhill, T.A., Thompson, E., Saron, C., Desordes, G., Kober, H., Hampson, M., Gray, J.R., Constable, R.T., Papademetris, X., & Brewer, J. A., (2013), Real-time fMRI links subjective experience with brain activity during focused attention, *Neuro Image*, 81, 110-118.

Garrison, K.A., Santoyo, J.F., Davis, J.H., Thornhill, T.A., Kerr, C.E., & Brewer, J.A. (2013). Effortless awareness: Using real time neurofeedback to investigate correlates of posterior cingulate cortex activity in meditators' self-report, *Frontiers in Human Neuroscience*, 7, 440.

Garrison, K.A., Zeffiro, T.A., Scheinost D., Constable, R.T. & Brewer, J.A. (2015). Meditation leads to reduced default mode network activity beyond an active task, *Cognitive, Affective, & Behavioral Neurosci-*

ence, 15, 712-720.

Gathercole, S.E. (2016). Working memory in the classroom, *The Psychologist*, 21 (5), 1-6.

Gathercole, S.E., Alloway, T.P., Kirkwood, H.J., Elliott, J.G., Holmes, J., & Hilton, K.A. (2008). Attentional and executive function behaviors in children with poor working memory, *Learning and Individual Differences*, 18, 214-223.

Gathecole, S.E., Pickering, S.J., Ambridge, B., & Wearing, H. (2004). The structure of working memory from 4 to 15 years of age, *Developmental Psychology*, 40 (2), 177-190.

Gay, G., Stefanone, M., Grace-Martin, M., & Hembroke, H. (2001). The effects of wireless computing in collaborative learning environments, *International Journal of Human-Computer Interaction*, 13 (2), 257-276.

Gazzaley, A., & Nobre, A.C. (2011). Top-down modulation: Bridging selective attention and working memory, *Trends in Cognitive Sciences*, 16 (2), 129-135.

Gelles, D. (2016). The Hidden Price of Mindfulness Inc. *The New York Times*. https://nyti.ms/1RtotF6

Gentner, D. (1988). Metaphor as structure mapping. The relational shift. Child Development, 59 (1), 47-59.

George, M.J., & Odgers, C.L. (2105). Seven fears and the science of how mobile technologies may be influencing adolescents in the digital age, *Perspectives on Psychological Science*, 10, 832-851.

Gerhardstein, P., & Rovee-Collier, C. (202). The development of visual search in infants and very young children, *Journal of Experimental Child Psychology*, 81, 194-215.

Giambra, L.M. (1995). A laboratory method for investigating influences on switching attention to task-unrelated imagery and thought, *Consciousness and Cognition*, 4, 1-21.

Gogtay, N., Giedd, J.N. Lusk, L., Hayashi, K.M., Greenstein, D., Vaituzis, A.C., Nugent III, T.F., Herman, D.H., Clasen, L.S., Toga, A.W., Rapoport, J.L, &Thompsom, P.M. (2004). Dynamic mapping of human cortical development during childhood through early adulthood, *Proceedings of the National Academy of Sciences USA*, 101 (21), 8174-8179.

Goldberg, M.C., Maurer, D., & Lewis, T.L. (2001). Developmental changes in attention: The effect of endogenous cueing and of distractors, *Developmental Science*, 4, 209-219.

Gordon, E.M., Lee, P.S., Maisog, J.M., Foss-Feig, J., Billington, M.E., VanMeter, J. et al. (2011). Strength of default mode resting-state connectivity relates to white matter integrity in children, *Developmental Science*, 14 (4), 738-751.

Goyal, M., Singh, S., Sibinga, E.M., Gould, N.F., Rowland-Seymour, A., Sharma, R. Haythorne, J.A. (2014). Meditation programs for psychological stress and well-being: A systematic review and meta-analysis. *Journal of the American Medical Association—Internal Medicine*, 174, 357-368.

Grace-Martin, M., & Gay, G. (2001). Web browsing, mobile computing and academic performance, *Educational Technology and Society*, 4 (3), 95-107.

Graham, F.K., Clifton, R.K. (1966). Heart-rate change as a component of the orienting response, *Psychological Bulletin*, 65, 305-320.

Grant, L. (2015). Child development: Attunement, attachment, and emerging qualities, In C. Wilard and A. Saltzman (Eds.) *Teaching mindfulness skills to kids and teens* (pp.89-105). New York: Guildford.

Gray, J.A. (1991). The neuropsychology of temperament, In J. Strelau and A. Angleitner (Eds.), *Explorations in temperament: International perspectives on theory and measurement*, (pp. 105-128), New York: Plenum.

Graziano, P.A., Calkins, S.D., & Keane, S.P. (2011). Sustained attention development during the toddlerhood to preschool period: Associations with toddler's emotion regulation strategies and maternal behavior, *Infant Child Development*, 20 (6), 389-408.

Green C.S. & Bavelier, D. (2003) Action video games modify visual selective attention, *Nature*, 423, 534-537.

Green, C.S., & Bavelier, D. (2007), Action-video game experience alters the spatial resolution of vision *Psychological Science*, 18, 88-94.

Greenberg, L.M. & Waldman, I.D. (1993). Development of normative data on the test of variables of attention (TOVA), *Journal of Child Psychology and Psychiatry*, 34 (6), 1019-1030.

Green, C.S., & Bavelier, D. (2003). Action video game modifies visual selective attention, *Nature*, 423, 534-537.

Greenfield, P.M. (2014). *Mind and media: The effects of television, video games, and computers.* New York: Psychology Press.

Greenfield, P.M. (2009). Technology and informal education: What is taught, what is learned. *Science*, 323. 69-71.

Greenfield, P.M., Brannon, C., & Lohr, D. (1994). Two-dimensional representation of movement through three-dimensional space: The role of video game expertise, *Journal of Applied Developmental Psychology*, 15, 87-103.

Greenfield, P.M., de Winstanley, P., Kilpatrick, H., & Kaye, D. (1994). Action video games and informal education: Effects on strategies for dividing visual attention, *Journal of Applied Developmental Psychology*, 15, 105-123.

Greicius, M.D.., Krasnow, B., Reiss, A.L., & Menon, V. (2003). Functional connectivity in the resting brain: A network analysis of the default mode hypothesis. *Proceedings of the National Academy of Sciences USA*, 100, 253-258.

Greicius, M.D., Supekar, K., Menon, V., & Dougherty, R.F. (2009). Resting-state functional connectivity in the default mode network, *Cerebral Cortex*, 19 (1), 72-78.

Grice, H.P. (1975). Logic and conversation, In P. Cole and J.L. Moran (Eds.), *Syntax and semantics:* Vol 3. Speech acts (pp. 41-58), New York NY: Academic Press.

Grosswald, S.J., Stixrud, A.W.R., Stixrud, W., Travis, A.F., & Bateh, M.A. (2008). Use of transcendental meditation technique to reduce symptoms of attention hyperactivity disorder (ADHD) by reducing stress and anxiety: An exploratory study, *Current Issues in Education*, 10, 1-16.

Gurung, Geshe Sonam, personal communication, 2014.

Gusnard, D.A. (2005). Being a self: Considerations from functional imaging, *Consciousness and Cognition*, 14, 679-697.

Gusnard, D.A., Akbudak, E., Shulman, G.L., & Raichle, M.E. (2001). Medial prefrontal cortex and self-referential mental activity: Relation to a default mode of brain function, *Proceedings of the National Academy of Sciences USA*, 98, 4259-4264.

Gusnard, D.A., & Raichel, M.E. (2001). Searching for a baseline: Functional imaging and the resting human brain, *Nature Reviews Neuroscience*, 2, 685-684.

Guttentag, R.E., & Ornstein, P.A. (1990). Attentional capacity and children's memory strategy use, In J.T. Enns (Ed.), *The development of attention: Research and theory.* (pp. 305-320) Amsterdam, Netherlands: Elsevier.

Hagen, J.W., & Hale, G.A. (1973). The development of attention in children. In A.D. Pick (Ed.), *Minnesota Symposia on Child Psychology*, vol. 7, Minneapolis: University of Minnesota Press.

Haider, M. (1970). Neuropsychology of attention, expectation, and vigilance, In D I. Mostofsky (Ed.) *Attention: Contemporary theory and analysis*, (pp. 419-432), New York: Appleton-Century-Crofts.

Hale, G.A., & Morgan, J.S. (1973). Developmental trends in children's component selection, *Journal of Experimental Child Psychology*, 15, 302-314.

Hamre, B.K., & Pianta, R.C. (2005). Can instructional and emotional support in the first grade classroom make a difference for children at risk of school failure?, *Child Development*, 76, 949-967.

Hanauer, J.B., & Brooks, P.J. (2003). Developmental change in the cross-modal Stroop effect, *Perception & Psychophysics*, 65 (3), 359-366.

Harnett, P.H., & Dawe, S. (2012). Review: The contribution of mindfulness-based therapies for children and families and proposed conceptual integration, *Child and Adolescent Mental Health*, 17 (4), 195-208.

Harter, S. (1992). Trait versus non-trait conceptualizations of intrinsic/extrinsic motivational orientation, *Motivation and Emotion*, 16, 209-230.

Hassenkamp, W. & Barsalou, L.W. (2012). Effects of meditation experience on functional connectivity of distributed brain networks, *Frontiers in Human Neuroscience*, 6, 1-14.

Heerin, A., & Phillipot, P. (2011). Changes in ruminative thinking mediate the clinical benefit of mindfulness: Preliminary findings, *Mindfulness*, 2, 8-13.

Hembroke, H. & Gay, G. (2003). The laptop and the lecture: The effects of multitasking in learning environments, *Journal of Computing in Higher Education*, 15 (1), 46-64.

Henry, L. (2012). *The development of working memory in children*. Los Angeles: Sage.

Hesse, E. (1999). The Adult Attachment Interview: Historical and current perspectives, In J. Cassidy & P.R. Shaver (Eds.), *Handbook of attachment: Theory, research, and clinical applications*, (pp. 395-433), New York: Guilford.

H.H. The Dalai Lama & Cutler, H.C. (1998). *The art of happiness: A handbook for living*. Great Britain: Hodden & Stoughton.

Higgins, A.T., & Turnure, J.E. (1984). Distractibility and concentration of attention in children's development, *Child Development*, 55, 1799-1810.

Holmes, J. (2012). Working memory and learning difficulties. *Dyslexia Review*, Summer, 7-10.

Holmes, J., & Gathercole, E. (2014). Taking working memory training from the laboratory into schools, *Educational Psychology*, 43 (4), 440-450.

Holmes, J., Gathercole, S.E., & Dunning, D.L. (2009). Adaptive training leads to sustained enhancement of poor working memory in children, *Developmental Science*, 102 (4), F1-7.

Holmes, J., Gathercole, S.E., Place, M., Dunning, D.L., Hilton, K.A., & Elliott, J.G. (2009). Working memory deficits can be overcome: Impacts of training and medication on working memory in children with ADHD, *Applied Cognitive Psychology*, 24 (6), 827-836.

Holzel, B.K., Carmody, J., Vangel, M. Congleton, C., Yerramsetti, S.M., Gard, T., & Lazar, S.W. (2011) Mindfulness practice leads to increases in regional brain gray matter density, *Psychiatry Research: Neuroimaging*, 191, 36-43.

Holzel, B.K., Lazar, S.W., Gard, T., Schuman-Olivier, Z. Vago, D.R. & Ott, U. (2011) How does mindfulness meditation work? Proposing mechanisms of action from a conceptual and neural perspective. *Psychological Science*, 6, 537-559.

Hood, B.M. (1993). Inhibition of return produced by covert shifts of visual attention in 6-month-old infants, *Infant Behavior and Development*, 16, 245-254.

Hood, B.M., & Atkinson, J. (1993). Disengaging visual attention in the infant and adult, *Infant Behavior and Development*, 16, 405-422.

Hornik, R., Risenhoover, N., & Gunnar, M. (1987). The effects of maternal positive, neutral, and negative affective communication on infant response to new toys, *Child Development*, 58, 937-944.

Huang-Pollock, C.L., Carr, T.H., & Nigg, J.T. (2002). Development of selective attention: Perceptual load influences early versus late attentional selection in children and adults, *Developmental Psychology*, 38 (3), 363-375.

Hudspeth, W.J. & Pribram, K.H. (1992). Psychophysiological indices of cerebral maturation, *International Journal of Psychophysiology*, 12, 19-29.

Hulme, C., & Roodenrys, S. (1995). Practitioner review: Verbal working memory development and its disorders, *Journal of Child Psychology and Psychiatry*, 36 (3), 373-398.

Hulme, C., & Tordoff, V. (1989). Working memory development: The effects of speech rate word length, and acoustic similarity on serial recall, *Journal of Experimental Child Psychology*, 47 (1), 72-87.

Humphrey, M.M. (1982). Children's avoidance of environmental, simple task internal, and complex task internal distractors, *Child Development*, 53, 736-745.

Hunterlocher, P.R. (1979). Synaptic density in human frontal cortex—Developmental changes and effects of aging, *Brain Research*, 163, 195-205.

Huppert, F.A. & Johnson, D.M. (2010). A controlled trial of mindfulness training in schools: The importance of practice for an impact on well-being, *Journal of Positive Psychology*, 5 (4), 264-274.

Irwin-Chase, H. & Burns, B. (2000). Developmental changes in children's abilities to share and allocate attention in a dual task, *Journal of Experimental Child Psychology*, 77, 61-85.

Isaacs, E.B., & Vargha-Khadem, F. (1989). Differential course of development of spatial and verbal memory span: A normative study, *British Journal of Developmental Psychology*, 7, 377-380.

Isquith, P.K., Crawford, J.S., Espy, K.A., & Gioia, G.A. (2005). Assessment of executive function in preschool-aged children, *Mental Retardation and Developmental Disabilities Research Reviews*, 11 (3), 209-215.

Jackson, M. (2008). *Distracted: The erosion of attention and the coming dark age.* Amherst NY: Prometheus.

Jacobson, R. Meta-cognition: How Thinking About Thinking Can Help Kids, *Child Mind Institute*.

Jaeggi, S.M., Buschkuejl, M., Jonides, J., & Perrig, W.J. (2008), Improving fluid intelligence with training on working memory, *Proceedings of the National Academy of Sciences USA*, 105 (19), 6829-6833.

Jaeggi, S.M., Buschkuejl, M., Jonides, J., & Shah, P. (2011). Short- and long-term benefits of cognitive training, *Proceedings of the National Academy of Sciences, USA*, 108 (25), 10081-10086.

Jaeggi, S.M., Studer-Luethi, B.,Buschkuehl, M., Su, Y-F., Jonides, J., & Perrig, W.J. (2010). The relationship between-back performance and matrix reasoning—Implications for training and transfer, *Intelligence*, 38, 625-635.

Jerison, H.J. (1970) Vigilance, discrimination, and attention, In D. I. Mostofsky (Ed.) *Attention: Contemporary theory and analysis*, (pp. 127-148), New York: Appleton-Century-Crofts.

Jha, A.,P., Krompinger, J. & Baime, M.J. (2007) Mindfulness training modifies subsystems of attention. *Cognitive, Affective & Behavioral Neuroscience*, 7, 109-119.

Jha, A.P., Stanley, E.A., Kiyonaga, A., Wong, L. & Gelfand, L. (2011). Examining the protective effects of mindfulness training on working memory capacity and affective experience, *Emotion*, 10 (1), 54-64.

Johnson, M.H. (2010). *Developmental Cognitive Neuroscience*, 3rd ed. Oxford, UK: Wiley-Blackwell.

Johnson, M.H., Posner, M.I., & Rothbart, M.K. (1991). Components of visual orienting in early infancy: Contingency learning, anticipatory looking, and disengaging, *Journal of Cognitive Neuroscience*, 3, 335-344.

Jones, L.B., Rothbart, M.K., & Posner, M.I. (2003). Development of executive attention in preschool children, Developmental Science, 6 (5), 498-504.

Kabat-Zinn, J. (1990). *Full Catastrophe Living: Using the Wisdom of Your Body and Mind to Face Stress, Pain, and Illness*. New York: Delacorte Press.

Kabali, H.K., Irigoyen, M.M., Nunez-Davis, R., Budacki, J.G., Mohanty, S.H., Leister, K.P., & Bonner, R.L., Exposure and use of mobile media devices by young children, *Pediatrics*, 136 (6), 1044-1050.

Kail, R.V. (2007). Longitudinal evidence that increases in processing speed and working memory enhance children's reasoning, *Psycholog-*

ical Science, 18 (4), 312—313.

Kalyuga, S., Chandler, P.,& Sweller, J. (2004). When redundant on-screen text in multimedia technical instruction can interfere with learning, *Human Factors*, 46 (3), 567-581.

Kane, M.J., Brown, L.H., McVay, J.C., Silvia, P.J., Myin-Germeys, I., & Kwapil, T.R. (2007). For whom the mind wanders, and when: An experience-sampling study of working memory and executive control in daily life, *Psychological Science*, 18 (7), 614-621.

Kane, M.J., & Engle, R.W. (2002). The role of the prefrontal cortex in working-memory capacity, executive attention, and general fluid intelligence: An individual-differences perspective, *Psychonomic Bulletin & Review*, 9 (4), 637-671.

Kane, M.J., & Engle, R.W. (2003) Working-memory capacity and the control of attention: The contributions of goal neglect, response competition, and task set to Stroop interference, *Journal of Experimental Psychology, General*, 132 (1), 47-70.

Kannass, K.N., Oakes, L.M., & Shaddy, D.J. (2006). A longitudinal investigation of the development of attention and distractibility, *Journal of Cognition and Development*, 7 (3), 381-409.

Karbach, J., & Kray, J. (2009). How useful is executive control training? Age differences in near and far transfer of task-switching training, *Developmental Science*, 12 (6), 978-990.

Katidioti, I., & Taatgen, N.A. (2014). Choice in multitasking: How delays in the primary task turn a rational into an irrational multi-tasker. *Journal of the Human Factors and Ergonomics Society*, 56 (4), 728-736.

Kaye, D.B., & Ruskin, E.M. (1990). The development of attentional control mechanisms, In J.T. Enns (Ed.), *The development of attention: Research and theory.* (pp. 227-244) Amsterdam, Netherlands: Elsevier.

Kaye, K., & Fogel, A. (1980). The temporal structure of face-to-face communication between mothers and infants, *Developmental Psychology*, 16, 454-464.

Kearney, P.R. (2005). Cognitive calisthenics: Can computer games enhance the player's cognitive abilities? *Proceedings of DiGRA Conference: Changing Views—Worlds in Play*. Digital Games Research Association.

Kegan, R. (1982). *The evolving self: Problems and process in human development*. Cambridge, MA: Harvard University Press.

Kelly, A.M., & Garavan, H. (2005). Human functional neuroimaging of brain changes associated with practice, *Cerebral Cortex*, 15, 1089-1102.

Kelly, W.M., Macrae, C.N., Wyland, C.L., Cagler, S., Inati, S., & Heatherton, T.F. (2002). Finding the self: An event-related fMRI study, *Journal of Cognitive Neuroscience*, 14, 785-794.

Kemps, E., de Rammelaerre, S., & Desmet, T. (2000). The development of working memory: Exploring the complementarity of two models, *Journal of Experimental Child Psychology*, 77, 89-109.

Kerns, K.A., Eso, K., & Thomson, J. (1999). Investigation of a direct intervention for improving attention in young children, *Developmental Neuropsychology*, 16 (2), 273-295.

Kerr, A., & Zelazo, P. D. (2004). Development of "hot" executive function: The children's gambling task, *Brain and Cognition*, 55, 158-170.

Khandro Rinpoche, Jetsun, personal communication, 2017.

Kimberg, D.Y., Aguirre, G.K., & D'Esposito, M. (2000). Modulation of task-related neural activity in task-switching: An fMRI study. *Cognitive Brain Research*, 10, 189-196.

Killingsworth, M.A., & Gilbert, D.T. (2010). A wandering mind is an unhappy mind, *Science*, 330, 932.

Klenberg, L., Korkman, M., & Lahti-Nuuttila, P. (2001) Differential development of attention and executive functions in 3- to 12-year-old Finnish children, *Developmental Psychology*, 20 (1), 407-428.

Klingberg, T. (2008). *The overflowing brain: Information overload and the limits of working memory*. New York, NY: Oxford.

Klingberg, T. (2010). Training and plasticity of working memory, *Trends in Cognitive Sciences*, 14, 317-324.

Klingberg, T., Fernell, E., Olesen, P.J., Johnson, M., Gustafsson, P., Dahlstrom, K., Gillberg, C.G., Forsssberg, H., & Westerberg, H. (2005). Computerized training of working memory in children with ADHD: A randomized, controlled trial, *Journal of the American Academy of Child and Adolescent Psychiatry*, 44 (2), 177-186.

Kochanska, G., Coy, K.C., & Murray, K.T. (2001). The development of self-regulation in the first four years of life, *Child Development*, 72 (4), 1093-1116.

Kochanska, G., Murray, K.T., & Harlan, E.T. (2000). Effortful control in early childhood: Continuity and change, antecedents, and implications for social development, *Developmental Psychology*, 36 (2), 220-232.

Kopp, C.B. (1982). Antecedents of self-regulation: A developmental perspective, *Developmental Psychology*, 18 (2), 199-214.

Korkman, M., Kemp, S.L., & Kirk, U. (2001). Effects of age on neurocognitive measures of children ages 5 to 12: A cross-sectional study on 88 children from the United States, *Developmental Neuropsychology*, 20 (1), 331-354.

Korner, A.F., & Grobstein, R. (1966). Visual alertness as related to soothing in neonates, *Child Development*, 37, 867-876.

Knowles, L.M., Goodman, M.S., & Semple, R.J. (2015), Mindfulness with elementary-school-age children: Translating foundational practices from clinic to the classroom, In C. Willard and A. Saltzman (Eds.) *Teaching mindfulness skills to kids and teens* (pp. 19-41). New York: Guildford

Knudsen, E.I. (2007). Fundamental components of attention, *Annual Review of Neuroscience*, 30, 57-78.

Krakow, J.B., Kopp, C.B., & Vaughn, B.E. (1982). Sustained attention during the second year: Age trends, individual differences and implications for development. Unpublished manuscript.

Kubose, S.K., (1976). An experimental investigation of psychological aspects of meditation, *Psychologia*, 19, 1-10.

Kuyken, W., Weare, K., Ukoumunne, O.C., Vicary, R. Motton, N., Burnett, R., Cullen, C., Hennelly, S., & Hupert, F. (2013). Effectiveness of the mindfulness in schools programme: Non-randomised controlled feasibility study, *British Journal of Psychiatry*, 203, 126-131.

Landry, S.H., Chapieskim M.L., & Schmidt, M. (1986). Effects of maternal attention directing strategies on pre-terms' response to toys, *Infant Behavior and Development*, 9, 257-270.

Lane, D.M., & Pearson, D.A. (1982). The development of selective attention, *Merrill-Palmer Quarterly*, 28, 317-337.

Langer, E. J. (1992). Matters of mind: Mindfulness/mindlessness in perspective, *Consciousness and Cognition*, 1, 289-305.

Langer, E.J. (1993). A mindful education, *Educational Psychologist*, 28 (1), 43-50.

Langer, E.J. (2000). Mindful learning, *Current Directions in Psychological Science*, 9 (6), 220-223.

Langer, E., Blank, A., & Chanowitz B. (1978). The mindlessness of ostensibly thoughtful action: The role of "placebic" information in interpersonal function, *Journal of Personality and Social psychology*, 36 (6), 635-642.

Langer, E.J., & Moldoveanu, M. (2000). The construct of mindfulness, *Journal of Social Issues*, 56 (1) 1-9.

Langer, E.J., & Piper, A. I. (1987). The prevention of mindfulness, *Journal of Personality and Social Psychology*, 53 (2), 280-287.

Langsdorf, P., Izard, C.E., Rayais, M., & Hembree, E.A. (1983). Interest expression, visual fixation, and heart rate changes in 2- to 8-month-old infants, *Developmental Psychology*, 19, 375-386.

Lawson, K.R., Parrinello, R., & Ruff, H.A. (1992). Maternal behavior and infant attention, *Infant Behavior and Development*, 15, 209-229.

Lawson, K.R., & Turkewitz, G. (1980). Intersensory function in newborns: Effect of sound in visual preferences, *Child Development*, 51, 1295-1298.

Lazar, S.W., Bush, G., Gollub, R.L., Friccione, G.L., Khaisa, G., & Benson, H. (2000). Functional brain mapping of the relaxation response and meditation, *NeuroReport*, 11, 1581-1585.

Lazar, S.W., Kerr, C.E., Wasserman, R.H., Gray, J.R., Grave, D.N., Treadway, M.T., McGarvey, M., Quinn, B.T., Dusek, J.A., Benson, H., Rausch, S.L., Moore, C.I., Fischl, B. (2005). Meditation experience is associated with increased cortical thickness, NeuroReport, 16 (17), 1893-1897.

Lee, F.J. Taatgen, N.A. (2002). Multitasking as skill acquisition. *Proceedings of the Annual Meeting of the Cognitive Science Society*, 24, 1-6.

Lee, J., Semple, R.J., Rosa, D., & Miller, L. (2008). Mindfulness-based cognitive therapy for children: results of a pilot study, *Journal of Cognitive Psychotherapy*, 22, 15-28.

Lee, K.M., & Peng, W. (n.d.). What do we know about social and psychological effects of computer games? A comprehensive review of the current literature. Unpublished manuscript. University of Southern California.

Levin, H.S., Culhane, K.A., Hartmann, J., Evankovich, K., Mattson, A.J., Harward, H., Ringholz, G., Wing-Cobbs, L., & Fletcher, J.M. (1991). Developmental changes in performance on tests of purported frontal lobe functioning, *Developmental Neuropsychology*, 7 (3), 311-393

Levine, L.E., Waite, B.M., & Bowman, L.L. (2007) Electronic media use, reading, and academic distractibility in college youth, *CyberPsychology & Behavior*, 10 (4), 560-566.

Levy, D.M., Wobbrock, J.O., Kasniak, A.W., & Ostergren, M. (2012). The effects of mindfulness meditation training on multitasking in a high-stress information environment, Unpuplished presentation at the Graphics Interface Conference, May 28-30.

Levy, F. (1980). The development of sustained attention (vigilance) and inhibition in children: Some normative data, *Journal of Child Psychology and Psychiatry*, 21, 77-84.

Lewis, M., Kagam J., Campbell, H., & Kalafat, J. (1966). The cardiac response as a correlate of attention in infants, *Child Development*, 37, 63-71.

Lin, L. (2009). Breadth-biased versus focused cognitive control in media multitasking behaviors, *Proceedings of the National Academy of Sciences USA*, 106 (37), 15521-15522.

Lion's Roar. (2015). Beginner's Mind. What is it?

Linden W. (1973). Practicing meditation by school children and their levels of field-dependence-independence, test anxiety, and reading achievement, *Journal of Consulting & Clinical Psychology*, 41, 139-143.

Lindquist, K. (2013) Mentalization based time-limited psychotherapy with children and parents, Workshop at the Erica Foundation, April 26-27, 2013.

Lodro, Gedun. (1998) *Calm abiding and special insight meditation*. Ithaca NY: Snow Lion.

Loh, K.K., & Ryota, K. (2015). How has the Internet reshaped human cognition? *The Neuroscientist*, 1-15.

Loh, K.K., Tan, B.Z.H., & Lim, S.W.H. (2016). Media multitasking predicts video-recorded lecture learning performance through mind wandering tendencies, *Computers in Human Behavior*, 63, 943-947.

Lopez, F., Menez, M., & Hernandez-Guzman, L. (2005) Sustained attention during learning activities: An observational study with preschool children, *Early Child Development and Care*, 175 (2), 131-138.

Luciana, M., Conklin, H.M., Hooper, C. J., & Yarger, R.S. (2005). The development of nonverbal working memory and executive control processes in adolescents, *Child Development*, 76 (3), 697-712.

Luciana, M., & Nelson, C.A. (1998). The functional emergence of prefrontally-guided working memory systems in four- to eight-year-old children, *Neuropsychologia*, 36 (3), 273-293.

Lui, G.Z., & Chong, S.S. (2011). Meta-cognition & conceptual drifting in interactive information retrieval: An exploratory field study, *Pro-

ceedings of the Association for Information Science and Technology, 48 (1), 1-9.

Luna, B., Garver, K.E., Urban, T.A., Lazar, N.A., & Sweeney, J.A. (2004). Maturation of cognitive processes from late childhood to adulthood, *Child Development*, 75 (5), 1357-1372.

Luna, B., Thulborn K.R., Munoz, D.P., Merriam, E.P., Garver, K.E., Minshew, N.J., Keshavan, M.S., Genovesem C.R., Eddy, W.F., & Sweeney, J.A. (2001). Maturation of widely distributed brain function subserves cognitive development, *Neuro Image*, 13, 786-793.

Luria, A.R, & Homskaya, E.D. (1970). Frontal lobes and the regulation of arousal processes, In D I. Mostofsky (Ed.) *Attention: Contemporary theory and analysis*, (pp. 303-330), New York: Appleton-Century-Crofts.

Lutz, A., Slagter, H.A., Dunne, J.D. & Davidson, R.J. (2008). Attention regulation and monitoring in meditation. (2008). *Trends in Cognitive Sciences*, 12, 163-169.

Mack, A., & Rock, I. (1998). *Inattentional blindness.* Cambridge MA: MIT Press.

Mackie, R.R. (1977). *Vigilance: Theory, operational performance and physiological correlates*. New York: Plenum.

MacLean, K.A., Ferrer, E., Aichele, S.R., Bridwell, D.A., Zanesco, A.P., Jacobs, T.L., King, B.G., Roenberg, E.L., Sahdra, B.K., Shaver, P.R., Wallace, B.A., Mangun, G.R. & Saron, C.D. (2010). Intensive meditation training improves perceptual discrimination and sustained attention. *Psychological Science*, 21, 829-839.

MacLeod, C.M. (1991). Half a century of research on the Stroop effect: An integrative review, *Psychological Bulletin*, 109 (2), 163-203.

Mahone, E. M. (2005). Measurement of attention and related functions in the preschool child, *Mental Retardation and Developmental Disabilities Research Reviews*, 11, 216-225.

Main, M., & Goldwyn, R. (1998). *Adult attachment scoring and classification system*, Version 6.0. Unpublished manuscript, University of California, Berkeley.

Manly, T., Robertson, I.A., Galloway, M., & Hawkins, K. (1999). "The absent mind" Further investigations of sustained attention to response, *Neuropsychologia*, 37, 661-670.

Martin, A., Razza, R., & Brooks-Gunn, J. (2012). Sustained attention at age 6 predicts attention-related problems at age 9, *International Journal of Behavioral Development*, 36 96), 413-419.

Mash, E.J., & Johnston, C. (1982). A comparison of mother-child interactions of younger and older hyperactive and normal children, *Child Development*, 53, 1371-1381.

Mason, M.F., Norton, M.I., Van Horn, J.D., Weger, D.M., Grafton, S. T., & Macrae, C.N. (2007). Wandering minds: The default network and stimulus-independent thought, *Science*, 315, 393-395.

Masters, J.C., & Binger, C.G. (1978). Interrupting the flow of behavior: The stability and development of children's initiation and maintenance of compliant response inhibition, *Merrill-Palmer Quarterly*, 24, 229-242.

Mayer, R.E., & Moreno, R. (2003). Nine ways to reduce cognitive load in multimedia learning, *Educational Psychologist*, 38 (1), 43-52.

McClurg, P.A., & Chaille, C. (1987). Computer games: Environments for developing spatial cognition? *Journal of Educational and Computing Research*, 3, 95-111.

McDevitt, S.C. & Casey, W.B. (1981). Stability of ratings vs. perceptions of temperament from early infancy to 1-3 years, *American Journal of Orthopsychiatry*, 51 (2), 342-345.

McGeown, W.J. (2016). Neuroimaging of meditation, hypnotic suggestibility and hypnosis, In A. Raz and M. Lifshitz (Eds.), *Hypnosis & meditation: Towards and integrative science of conscious planes*, (pp. 343-367). New York: Oxford.

McGuire, P.K., Paulesu, E., Rackowiak, R.S., & Firth, C.D. (1996). Brain activity during stimulus independent thought, *NeuroReport*, 7 (13), 2095-2099.

McKay, K.E., Halperin, J.M., Schwartz, S.T., Sharma, V. (2009). Developmental analysis of the three aspects of information processing: Sustained attention, selective attention, and response organization, *Developmental Neuropsychology*, 10 (2), 121-132.

Meiklejohn, J., Phillips, C., Freedman, M.L., Griffiths, M.L., Biegel, G., Roach, A., & Saltzman, A. (2012). Integrating mindfulness training into K-12 education: fostering the resilience of teachers and students, *Mindfulness*, 3 (4), 291-307.

Melby-Lervag, M. & Hulme, C. (2013). Is working memory training effective? A meta-analytic review, *Developmental Psychology*, 49 (2), 270-291.

Memmert, D. (2006). The effects of eye movements, age, and expertise on inattentional blindness, *Consciousness and Cognition*, 15, 620-627.

Mendelson, T., Greenberg, M., Dariotis, J., Gould, L., Rhoades, B., & Leaf, P. (2010). Feasibility and preliminary outcomes of a school-based mindfulness intervention for urban youth, *Journal of Abnormal Child Psychology*, 38 (7), 985-994.

Menon, V. (2013). Developmental pathways to functional bran networks: Emerging principles, *Trends in Cognitive Sciences*, 17 (12), 629-640.

Midgley, N., Ensink, K., Lindqvist, K., Malberg, N., & Muller, N. (2017). *Mentalization-based treatment for children: A time-limited approach.* Washington, DC: American Psychological Association Press.

Midgley, N., & Vrouva, I. (2012). *Minding the child: Mentalization-based interventions with children, young people, and their families.* London, UK: Routledge.

Miller, J., Ulrich, R., & Rolke, B. (2009). On the optimality of serial and parallel processing in the psychological refractory period paradigm: Effects of the distribution of stimulus onset asynchronies, *Cognitive Psychology*, 58 (3), 273-310.

Miller, P.H., Seier, W.L., Probert, J.S., & Aloise, P.A. (1991). Age differences in the capacity of a strategy among spontaneously strategic children, *Journal of Experimental Child Psychology*, 52, 149-165.

Miller, P.H., Woody-Ramsey, J., & Aloise, P.A. (1991). The role of strategy effortfulness in strategy effectiveness, *Developmental Psychology*, 27 (5), 738-745.

Miller, P.H., & Zalenski, R. (1982). Preschoolers' knowledge about attention, *Developmental Psychology*, 18 (6), 871-875.

Mills, K.L. (2016). Possible effects of internet use on cognitive development in adolescents, *Media and Communication*, 4 (3), 4-12.

Minear, M., & Shah, P. (2008). Training and transfer effects in task switching, *Memory & Cognition*, 36 (8), 1470-1483.

Moisala, M., Salmela, V., Hietajarvi, L., Salo, E., Carlso, S., Salonen, O., Lonka, K., Hakkarainen, K., Salmela-Aro, K., & Alho, K. (2016). Media multitasking is associated with distractibility and increased prefrontal activity in adolescents and young adults, *NeuroImage*, 134, 113-121.

Mondloch, C.J., Geldart, S., Maurer, D., & de Schonen, S. (2003). Developmental changes in the processing of hierarchical shapes continues into adolescence, *Journal of Experimental Child Psychology*, 84, 20-40.

Moody, D.E. (2009). Can intelligence be increased by training on a task of working memory? *Intelligence*, 37, 327-328.

Morrison, A.B. & Chein, J.M. (2011). Does working memory training work? The promise and challenges of enhancing cognition by training working memory, *Psychonomic Bulletin Review*, 18, 46-60.

Moses, P., Roe, K., Buxton, R.B., Wong, E.C., Frank, L/ R., & Stiles, J. (2002). Functional MRI of global and local processing in children, *NeuroImage*, 16, 415-424.

Moyer, K.E., & Gilmer, B.V.H. (1955). Attention spans of children for experimentally designed toys, *Journal of Genetic Psychology*, 87, 187-201.

Moyes, R.A. (2014). *Executive function "dysfunction": Strategies for educators and parents.* Philadelphia PA: Jessica Kingsley.

Napoli, M., Krech, P.R., & Holley, L.C. (2005). Mindfulness training for elementary school students, *Journal of Applied School Psychology,* 21 (1), 99-125.

National Center for Education Statistics [NCES} (1997). The condition of education 1997; No. 12: Public and private schools: How do they differ? U.S. Dept. of Education, Office of Educational Research and Improvement. Washington DC: US Gvernment Printing Office document NCES 97-983.

Nie, J., Zhang, W., Chen, J., & Li, W. (2016). Impaired inhibition and working memory in response to internet-related words among adolescents with internet addiction: A comparison with attention-deficit/hyperactivity disorder, *Psychiatry Research,* 236, 28-34.

Nelson, C.A., Haan, Michelle de, & Thomas, K.M. (2006). *Neuroscience of cognitive development: The role of experience and the developing brain.* New York: Wiley.

Nhat Hanh, T. (2017). The Practice of Sangha, *Lion's Roar.*

Nigg, J.T., Quamma, J.P., Greenberg, M.T., & Kusche, C.A. (1999). A two-year longitudinal study of neuropsychological and cognitive performance in relation to behavioral problems and competencies in elementary school children, *Journal of Abnormal Child Psychology*, 27 (1), 51-63.

Nobre, A,C. (2004) Probing the flexibility of attentional orienting in the human brain. In M.I. Posner (Ed.) *Cognitive neuroscience of attention.* (pp. 157-179). New York: Guilford.

North, N. (2014). The Mindfulness Backlash, *The New York Times.* https://op-talk.blogs.nytimes.com/2014/06/30/the-mindfulness-backlash.

Oakes, L.M., Tellinghuisen, D.J. (1994). Examining in infancy: Does it reflect active processing? *Developmental Psychology*, 30, 748-756.

Oakes, L.M., Tellinghuisen, D.J., & Tjekes, T.L. (2000). Competition for infants' attention: The interactive influence of attentional state and stimulus characteristics, *Infancy*, 1(3), 347-361.

Olesen, P., Westerberg, K., & Klingberg, T. (2004). Increased prefrontal and parietal brain activity after training of working memory, *Nature Neuroscience*, 7, 75-79.

Ophir, E., Nass, C., & Wagner, A.D. (2009). Cognitive control in media multitaskers, *Proceedings of the National Academy of Sciences USA*, 106 (37), 15583-15587.

Orme-Johnson, D.W., Schneider, R.H., Son, Y.D., Nidich, S., & Cho, Z-H. (2006), Neuroimaging of meditation's effect on brain reactivity to pain, NeuroReport, 17 (2), 1359-1363.

O'Sullivan, J.T. (1993). Preschoolers' beliefs about effort, incentives, and recall, *Journal of Experimental Child Psychology*, 55, 396-414.

Owen, A.M., Hampshire, A., Grahn, J.A., Stenton, R., Dajani, S., Burns, A.S., Howard, R.J., & Ballard, C. G. (2010). Putting the brain to test, *Nature*, 465 (7299), 775-778.

Pagnoni, G. (2012). Dynamical properties of BOLD activity from the ventral posteromedial cortex associated with meditation and attentional skills, *Journal of Neuroscience*, 32, 5242-5249.

Palfrey, J., Gasser, U. (2008). *Born digital: Understanding the first generation of digital natives*. New York: BasicPardo, A.C. R. (2017). Social media and cognition, Unpublished masters dissertation, The University of Western Ontario.

Pardo, J.V., Fox, P.T., & Raichle, M.E. (1991). Localization of a human system for sustained attention by positron emission tomography, *Nature*, 349, 61-64.

Park, D.C., Lautenschlager, G., Hedden, T., Davidson, N.S., Smith, A.D., & Smith, P.K. (2002). Models of visuo-spatial and verbal memory across the adult life span, *Psychology and Aging*, 17 (2), 299-320.

Parrinello, R.M., & Ruff, H.A. (1988). The influence of adult intervention on infants' level of attention, *Child Development*, 59, 1125-1135.

Pashler, H. (1994). Dual-task interference in simple tasks: Data and theory, *Psychological Bulletin*, 116 (2), 220-244.

Pashler, H. (1994). Graded capacity-sharing in dual-task interference?

Journal of Experimental Psychology: Human Perception and Performance, 20 (2), 330-342.

Passler, M.A., Isaac, W., & Hynd, G.W. (1985). Neuropsychological development of behavior attributed to frontal lobe functioning in children, *Developmental Neuropsychology*, 1 (4), 349-370.

Patterson, C.J., & Mischel, W. (1975). Plans to resist distraction, *Developmental Psychology*, 11, 369-378.

Paus, T. (1989). The development of sustained attention in children might be related to the maturation of frontal cortical functions, *Acta Neurobiologie Experimentalis*, 49, 51-55.

Paus, T. (2005). Mapping brain maturation and cognitive development during adolescence, *Trends in Cognitive Sciences*, 9 (2), 60-68.

Paus, T., Zijden, A., Worsley, K., Collins, D.L., Blumenthal, J., Giedd, J.N., Rapoport, J.L., & Evans, A.C. (1999). Structural maturation of neural pathways in children and adolescents: In vivo study, *Science*, 283, 1908-1911.

Pea, R., Nass, C., Meheula, L., Rance, M., Kumar, A., Bamford, H., Nass, M., Simha, A., Stillerman, B., Yang, S., & Zhou, M. (2012). Media use, face-to-face communication, media multitasking, and social well-being among 8- to 12-year-old girls, *Developmental Psychology*, 48 (2), 327-336.

Pearson, D.A. & Lane, D.M. (1990). Visual attention movements: A developmental study, *Child Development*, 61, 1779-1795.

Pennington, B.F. & Ozonoff, S. (1996). Executive functions and developmental psychopathology, *Journal of Child Psychology and Psychiatry*, 37 (1), 51-87.

Petersen, S.E., & Posner, M.I. (2012). The attention system of the human brain: 20 years after, *Annual Review of Neuroscience*, 35, 73-89.

Piaget, J. (1950). *The psychology of intelligence*. New York: Routledge & Kegan Paul.

Pick, A.D., Christy, M.D., & Frankel, G.W. (1972). A developmental study of visual selective attention, *Journal of Experimental Child Psychology*, 14, 165-175.

Pick, A.D., & Frankel, G.W. (1973). A study of strategies of visual attention in children, *Developmental Psychology*, 9, 348-357.

Pillay, H. (2003). An investigation of cognitive processes engaged in by recreational computer game players: Implications for skills of the future, *Journal of Research on Technology and Education*, 43 (3), 336-350.

Pillow, B.H. (1988). Young children's understanding of attentional limits, *Child Development*, 59, 38-46.

Plude, D.J., Enns, J.T., & Brodeur, D. (1944). The development of selective attention: A life-span overview, *Acta Psychologica*, 86, 227-272.

Poirel, N., Mellet, E., Houde, O. & Pineau, A. (2008). First came the trees, then the forest: Developmental changes during childhood in the processing of visual local-global patterns according to the meaningfulness of the stimuli, *Developmental Psychology*, 44 (1), 245-253.

Porges, S.W. (1974). Heart-rate indices of newborn attentional responsivity, *Merrill-Palmer Quarterly*, 20, 231-254.

Porporino, M., Shore, D.I., Iarocci, G., & Burack, J.A. (2004). A developmental change in selective attention and global form perception, *International Journal of Behavioral Development*, 28 (4), 358-364.

Posnansky, C.J., & Rayner, K. (1977). Visual-feature and response components in a picture-word interference task with beginning and skilled readers, *Journal of Experimental Child Psychology*, 24, 440-460.

Posner, M.I., & Petersen, S.E. (1990) The attention system of the human brain. *Annual Review of Neuroscience*, 13, 25-42

Posner, M.I., Synder, C.R., & Davidson, B.J. (1980). Attention and the detection of signals. *Journal of Experimental Psychology*, 109, 160-174.

Posner, M.I., Rothbart, M.K., Sheese, B.E., & Voelker, P. (2012). Control networks and neuromodulators of early development, *Developmental Psychology*, 48 (3), 827-835.

Posner, M.I., Rothbart, M.K., Sheese, B.E., & Voelker, P. (2014). Developing attention: Behavioral and brain mechanisms, *Advances in Neuroscience*, May 1, 1-9.

Posner, M.I., Walker, J.A., Friedrich, F.J., & Rafal, R.D. (1984). Effects of parietal injury on covert orienting of attention. *Journal of Neuroscience*, 4, 1863-1874.

Posner, M.I., Walker, J.A., Friedrich, F.J., & Rafal, R.D. (1987). How do the parietal lobes direct covert attention? *Neuropsychologia*, 25 (1A), 135-145.

Power, T.G., Chaieski, L. & McGrath, M.P. (1985). Assessment of individual differences in infant exploration and play, *Developmental Psychology*, 21 (6), 974-981.

Printz, R.J., Tarnowski, K.J., & Nay, S.M. (1984). Assessment of sustained attention and distraction in children using a classroom analogue test, *Journal of Child Clinical Psychology*, 13 (3), 250256.

Ptak, R. (2012). The fronto-parietal attention network of the human brain: Action, saliency, and priority map of the environment, *The Neuroscientist*, 18 (5), 502-515.

Purser, R., & Loy, D. (2013). Beyond McMindfulness. *Huffington Post*. https://www.huffingtonpost.com/ron-purser/beyond-mcmindfulness_b_3519289.html

Raichle, M.E., MacLeod, A.M., Snyder, A.Z., Powers, W.J., Gusnard, D.A., & Shulman, G.I., (2001). A default mode of brain function. *Proceedings of the National Academy of Sciences USA*, 98, 676-682.

Raichle, M.E., & Snyder, A.Z. (2007). A default mode of brain function: A brief history of an evolving idea, *Neuro Image*, 37, 1083-1090.

Rani, N.J., & Rao, P.V.K. (1996). Meditation and attention regulation, *Journal of Indian Psychology*, 14, 26-31.

Raz, A. (2004) Atypical attention: Hypnosis and conflict reduction. In M.I. Posner (Ed.) *Cognitive neuroscience of attention*. (pp. 420-429). New York: Guilford.

Reason, J. (1984). Lapses of attention in everyday life, In R. Parasuraman & D.R. Davies (Eds.), *Varieties of attention*, (pp. 515-549). Orlando FL: Academic Press.

Rebok, G.W., Smith, C.B., Pascualvaca, D.M. Mirsky, A.F., Anthony, B.J., & Kellam, S.G. (1997). Developmental changes in attentional performance in urban children from eight to thirteen years, *Child Neuropsychology*, 3 (1), 28-46.

Redick, T.S., Shipstead, Z., Fired, D.E., Hambrick, D.Z., Kane, M.J., & Engle, R.W. (2013). No evidence of intelligence improvement after working memory training: A randomized placebo-controlled study, *Journal of Experimental Psychology: General*, 142 (2), 359-379.

Reed, M.A., Pien, D.L., Rothbart, M.K. (1984). Inhibitory self-control in preschool children, *Merrill-Palmer Quarterly*, 30, 131-147.

Remington, A., Cartwright-Finch U., & Lavie, N. (2014). I can see clearly now: The effects of age and perceptual load on inattentional blindness, *Frontiers in Human Neuroscience*, 8, 229-241.

Reynolds, J.H. (2004). Attention and contrast gain control. In M.I. Posner (Ed.) *Cognitive neuroscience of attention*, (pp.127-143). New York: Guilford.

Richards, J.E. (1989). Development and stability in visual sustained attention in 14, 20, and 26-week-old infants, *Psychophysiology*, 26, 422-430.

Richards, J.E. & Casey, B.J. (1991). Heart rate variability during attention phases in young infants, *Psychophysiology*, 28, 43-53.

Richards, J.E., & Casey, B.J. (1992). Development of sustained visual attention in the human infant, In B.A. Campbell, H. Hayne, & R. Richardson (Eds.), *Attention and information-processing in infants and adults: Perspectives from human and animal research*, (pp. 30-60), Hillsdale NJ: Erlbaum.

Richards, J.E., & Turner, E.D. (2001). Extended visual fixation and distractibility in children from six to twenty-four months of age, *Child Development*, 72 (4), 963-972.

Rideout, V.J., Foehr, U.G., & Roberts, D.F. (2010). Generation on Media in the Lives of 8 to 18 Year-Olds, *A Kaiser Family Foundation Study*.

Ridderhof, K.R., van der Molen, M.W., Band, G.P.H.., & Bashore, T.R. (1997). Sources of interferences from irrelevant information: A developmental study, *Journal of Experimental Child Psychology*, 65, 315-341.

Ritchhart, R. & Perkins, D.N. (2000). Life in the mindful classroom: Nurturing the disposition of mindfulness, *Journal of Social Issues*, 56 (1) 27-47.

Roberts, D.F., Foehr, U.G., & Rideout, V. (2005). *Generation M: Media in the lives of 8-18-year-olds*. Menlo Park CA:The Henry J. Kaiser Family Foundation.

Robertson, I.A., Manly, T., Andrade, J., Baddeley, B.T., & Yiend, J. (1997). 'Oops!:' Performance correlates of everyday attentional failures in traumatic brain injured and normal subjects, *Neuropsychologia*, 35 (6), 747-758.

Roe, K., & Muijs, D. (1998). Children and computer games: A profile of the heavy user, *European Journal of Communication*, 13, 181-200.

Romine, C.B. & Reynolds, C.R. (2005). A model of the development of frontal lobe functioning: Findings from a meta-analysis, *Applied Neuropsychology*, 12 (4), 190-201.

Rose, S.A., & Feldman, J.F. (1987). Infant visual attention: Stability and individual differences from 6 to 8 months, *Developmental Psychology*, 23, 490-498.

Rosser, J.C., Lynch, P.J., Cuddhihy, L., Gentile, D.A., Klonsky, J., & Merrell, R. (2007). The impact of video games on training surgeons in the 21st century, *Archives of Surgery*, 142, 181-186.

Rothbart, M.K. (1989). Temperament in childhood: A framework. In G.A. Kohnstamm, J. E. Bates, and M. K. Rothbart (Eds.), *Temperament in childhood*, (pp. 59-73), New York: Wiley

Rothbart, M.K. (1991) Temperament: A developmental framework, In

J. Strelau and A. Angleitner (Eds.), *Explorations in temperament: International perspectives on theory and measurement*, (pp. 61-74), New York: Plenum.

Rothbart, M.K., & Derryberry, D. (1981). Development of individual differences in temperament, In M.E. Lamb & L. Brown (Eds), *Advances in developmental psychology* (pp. 37-86), Hillsdale NJ: Erlbaum.

Rothbart, M.K., & Posner, M.I. (2015). The developing brain in a multitasking world, *Developmental Reviews*, 35, 42-63.

Rothbart, M.K., Posner, M.I., & Bolan, A. (1990). Regulatory mechanisms in infant development, In J.T. Enns (Ed.), *The development of attention: Research and theory* (pp. 47-66) Amsterdam, Netherlands: Elsevier.

Routh, D.K., Schroeder, C.S., & O'Tuama, L.A. (1974). Development of activity level in children, *Developmental Psychology*, 10, 163-168.

Rowan, C. (2017). The Impact of Technology on the Developing Child, Rueda, M.R., Checa, P., & Combita, L.M. (2012). Enhanced efficiency of the executive attention network after training in preschool children: Immediate changes and effects after two months, *Developmental Cognitive Neuroscience*, 2s, S192-S204.

Rueda, M.R, Rothbart, M.K., & Posner, M. (2005). Training, maturation, and genetic influences on the development of executive attention, *Proceedings of the National Academy of Sciences USA*, 102 (41), 14931-14936.

Ruff, H.A. (1986). Components of attention during infants' manipulative exploration, *Child Development*, 57, 105-114.

Ruff, H.A., & Capozzi, M.C. (2003) Development of attention and distractibility in the first 4 years of life, *Developmental Psychology*, 39 (5), 877-890.

Ruff, H.A., & Dubiner, K. (1987). Stability of individual differences in infants' manipulation and exploration of objects, *Perceptual and Motor Skills*, 64, 1095-1101.

Ruff, H.A. & Lawson, K.R. (1990). Development of sustained, focused attention in young children during free play, *Developmental Psychology*, 26 (1), 85-93.

Ruff, H.A., Lawson, K.R., Parrinello, R., & Weissberg, R. (1990). Long-term stability of individual differences in sustained attention in the early years, *Child Development*, 61 (1), 60-75.

Ruff, H.A., & Rotbart, M.K. (1996). *Attention in early development: Themes and variations.* New York: Oxford.

Ruff, H.A., Saltarelli, L.M., Capozzoli, M., & Dubiner, K. (1992). The differentiation of activity in infants' exploration of objects, *Developmental Psychology*, 28, 851-861.

Ruff, H.A., & Turkeiwtz, G. (1975). Developmental changes in the effectiveness of stimulus intensity on infant visual attention, *Developmental Psychology*, 11, 705-710.

Ruthruff, E., Johnston, J.C., & Van Selst, M. (2003). Why practice reduces dual-task interference, *Journal of Experimental Psychology, Human Perception and Performance*, 27 (1), 3-21.

Ruthruff, E., Van Selst, M., Johnston, J.C., & Remington, R. (2004). How does practice reduce dual-task interference: Integration, automatization, or just stage-shortening? *Psychological Research*, 70, 125-142.

Salthouse, T.A. (1994). The aging of working memory, *Neuropsychology*, 8 (4), 535-543.

Salthouse, T.A. (1996). The processing-speed theory of adult age differences in cognition, *Psychological Review*, 103 (3), 403-428.

Salvucci, D.D., & Taatgen, N..A. (2008). Threaded cognition: An integrated theory of concurrent multitasking, Psychological Review, 115 (1), 101-130.

Saltzman, A., & Goldin, P. (2008). Mindfulness-based stress reduction for school-aged children, In S.C. Hayes & L.A. Greco (Eds.), *Acceptance and mindfulness interventions for children, adolescents, and families*, (pp.

139-161), Oakland CA: New Harbinger.

Sarbonmatsu, D.M., Strayer, D.L., Mederos-Ward, N. & Watson, J.M. (2013). Who multi-tasks and why? Multi-tasking ability, perceived multi-tasking ability, impulsivity, and sensation seeking, *Plos One* 8 (1), e54402, 1-12.

Sarid, M., & Breznitz, Z. (1997), Developmental aspects of sustained attention among 2- to 6-year-old children, *International Journal of Behavioral Development*, 21 (2), 303-312.

Sarter, M., Givens, B., & Bruno, J.P. (2001). The cognitive neuroscience of sustained attention: Where top-down meets bottom-up, *Brain Research Reviews*, 35, 146-160.

Scherf. K.S., Behrmann, M., Kimchi, R., & Luna, B. (2009). Emergence of global shape processing continues through adolescence, *Child Development*, 80 (1), 162-177.

Schmidt, M.E., Pempek, T.A., Kirkorian, H.L., Lund, A.F., & Anderson, D.R. (2008). The effects of background television on the toy play behavior of very young children, *Child Development*, 79 (4), 1137-1151.

Schooler, J.W., Smallwood, J., Christoff, K., Handy, T.C., Reichle, E.D., & Sayette, M.A. (2011). Meta-awareness, perceptual decoupling and the wandering mind, *Trends in Cognitive Sciences*, 15 (7), 319-316.

Schonert-Reichl, K.A., & Hymel, S. (2007). Educating the heart as well as the mind: Social and emotional learning for school and life success, *Education Canada*, 47 (3), 20-23.

Schonert-Reichl, K.A., & Lawlor, M.S. (2010). The effects of a mindfulness-based education program on pre- and early adolescents' well-being and social and emotional competence, *Mindfulness*, 1(3), 137-151.

Schuler, A., Scheiter, K., & van Genuchten, E. (2011). The role of working memory in multimedia instruction: Is working memory working during learning from text and pictures? *Educational & Psychological Review*, 23, 389-411.

Schwartz, C. (2017). How to hack your brain (for $5000). *The New York Times.* https://nyti.ms/2jLkijX

Schweitzer, K., Zimmerman, P. & Koch, W. (2000). Sustained attention, stimulus discrimination, and the crucial role of perceptual processes, *Learning & Individual Differences*, 12 (3), 271-286.

Selst, V., Ruthruff, E., & Johnston, J.C. (1999). Can practice eliminate the psychological refractory period effect? *Journal of Experimental Psychology: Human Perception and Performance*, 25 (5), 1268-1283.

Semple, R.J., Lee, J., Rosa, D., & Miller, L. F. (2010). A randomized trial of mindfulness-based cognitive therapy for children: Promoting mindful attention to enhance social-emotional resiliency in children, *Journal of Child & Family Studies*, 19, 218-229.

Shallice, T., & Burgess, P.W. (1991). Deficits in strategy application following frontal lobe damage in man, *Brain*, 114, 727-741.

Shepp, B.E. & Barrett, S.E. (1991). The development of perceived structure and attention: Evidence from divided and selective attention tasks, *Journal of Experimental Child Psychology*, 51, 434-458.

Shepp, B.E. & Swartz, K.B. (1976). Selective attention and the processing of integral and non integral dimensions: A developmental study, *Journal of Experimental Child Psychology*, 22, 73-85.

Sherrell, C. & Simmer-Brown, J. (2017). Spiritual bypassing in the contemporarymindfulness movement. *Initiative for Social Equity and Action Journal* 1,(1),7.

Sherretz, C.E. (2011). Mindfulness in education: Case studies of mindful teachers and their teaching practices, *Journal of Thought*, Fall-Winter 79-96.

Siegel, L.S., & Ryan, E.B. (1989). The development of working memory in normally achieving and subtypes of learning disabled children, *Child Development*, 60, 973-980.

Sigman, M., & Dehaene, S. (2008). Brain mechanisms of serial and parallel processing during dual-task performance, *Journal of Neuroscience*, 28 (30), 7585-7598.

Siklos, S., & Kerns, K.A. (2004). Assessing multitasking in children with

ADHD using a modified Six Elements Test, *Archives of Clinical Neuropsychology*, 19, 347-361.

Simons, D.J., & Chabris, C.F. (1999). Gorillas in our midst: Sustained inattentional blindness for dynamic events, *Perception*, 28, 1059-1074.

Singh, M.N., Singh, A.N., Lancioni, G.E., Singh, J., Winton, A.S.W., & Adkins, A.D. (2010). Mindfulness training for patients and their children with ADHD increases the children's compliance, *Journal of Child & Family Studies*, 19, 157-166.

Slagter, H.A., Lutz, A., Greischer, L.L., Francis, A.D., Niewenhuis, S., Davis, J.M. & Davidson, R.J. (2007) Mental training affects distribution of limited brain resources. *PLos Biology*. 5(6): 1228-1235 .

Sonuga-Barke, E.J.S., Castellanos, F.X. (2007). Spontaneous attentional fluctuations in impaired states and pathological conditions: A neurobiological hypothesis. Neuroscience. *Biobehavioral Reviews*, 31, 977-986.

Sowell, E.R., Petrrsom, B.S., Thompson, P.M., Welcome, S.E., Henkenius, A.I., & Toga, A.W. (2003). Mapping cortical change across the human life span, *Nature: Neuroscience*, 6 (93), 309-315.

Sowell, E.R., Thompson, P.M., Holmes, C.J., Batth, R., Jerngan, T.L., & Toga, A.W. (1999). Localizing age-related changes in brain structure between childhood and adolescence using statistical parametric mapping, *Neuro Image*, 9, 587-597.

Small, G.W., Moodey, T.D., Siddarth, P., & Bookheimer, S.Y. (2009). Your brain on Google: Patterns of cerebral activation during internet searching, *American Journal of Geriatric Psychiatry*, 17 (2), 116-126.

Small, G.W., & Vorgan, G. (2008). *iBrain: Surviving the technological alteration of the modern mind.* New York: HarperCollins.

Smallwood, J., Davies, J.B., Heim, D., Finnigan, F., Sudberry, M., O'Connor, R.O., & Obonsawin, M. (2004). Subjective experience and the attentional lapse: Task engagement and disengagement during sustained attention, *Consciousness and Cognition*, 13, 637-690.

Smallwood, J., Fishman, D.J., & Schooler, J.W. (2007). Counting the cost of an absent mind: Mind wandering as an under recognized influence on educational performance, *Psychonomic Bulletin & Review*, 14 (2), 230-236.

Smallwood, J., & Schooler, J.W. (2006). The restless mind. *Psychological Bulletin*, 132, 946-958.

Smallwood, J., McSpadden, M., & Schooler, J.W. (2007). The lights are on but no one's home: Meta-awareness and the decoupling of attention when the mind wanders, *Psychonomic Bulletin Review*, 14, 527-533.

Smith, S.E., & Chattterjee, A. (2008). Visuospatial attention in children. *Archives of Neurology*, 65 (10), 1284-1288.

Smilek, D., Carriere, J.S.A., & Cheyne, J.A. (2010). Out of mind, out of sight: Eye blinking as indicator and embodiment of mind wandering, *Psychological Science*, 21 (6), 796-789.

Sohn, M-H., Ursu, S., Anderson, J.R., Stenger, V.A., & Carter, C.S. (2000). The role of prefrontal cortex and posterior parietal cortex in task switching, *Proceedings of the National Academy of Sciences, USA*, 97, 13448-13453.

Sonuga-Barke, E.J.S., & Castellanos, F.X. (2007). Spontaneous attentional fluctuations in impaired states and pathological conditions: A neurobiological hypothesis, *Neuroscience and Biobehavioral Reviews*, 31, 977-986.

Spanos, N.P., Steggles, S., Radtke-Bodorikm H.L., & Rivers, S.M. (1979). Non-analytic attending, hypnotic susceptibility, and psychological well-being in trained meditators and non-meditators, *Journal of Abnormal Psychology*, 88, 85-87.

Spear, L.P. (2000). The adolescent brain and age-related behavioral manifestations, *Neuroscience and Biobehavioral Reviews* 24, 417463.

Spink, A., Ozmutlu, H.C., & Ozmutlu, S. (2002). Multitasking information seeking and searching processes, *Journal of the American Society for Information Science and Technology*, 53 (8), 639-652.

Spitzer, M. (2012). *Digitale demenz* [*Digital dementia*]. Munich, Germany: Droemer-Verlag.

Spreng, R.N. & Grady, C.I. (2009). Patterns of brain activity supporting autobiographical memory, prospection, and theory of mind, and their relationship to the default mode network, *Journal of Cognitive Neuroscience*, 22 (6), 1112-1123.

St. Clair-Thompson, H., & Gathercole, S.E. (2006). Executive functions and achievements in school: Shifting, updating, inhibition, and working memory, *Quarterly Journal of Experimental Psychology*, 59 (4), 745-759.

St. Chair-Thompsom, H., Stevens, R., Hunt, A., & Bolder, E. (2010). *Improving* children's working memory and classroom performance, *Educational Psychology*, 30 (2), 203-219.

Steele, A., Karmiloff-Smith, A., Cornish, K., & Scerif, G. (2102). The multiple subfunctions of attention: Differential gateways to literacy and numeracy, *Child Development*, 83 (6), 2028-2041.

Steffert, B. & Steffert, T. (2014). Maturational lag in ADHD or maturation deficit? *ADHD in Practice*, 6 (1) 10-14.

Stroh, C.M. (1971). *Vigilance: The problem of sustained attention*. New York: Pergamon Press.

Sternberg, R.J. (2008). Increasing fluid intelligence is possible after all, *Proceedings of the National Academy of Sciences USA*, 105 (19), 6791-6792

Stothart, C., Mitchum, A., & Yehnert, C. (2015). The attentional cost of receiving a cell phone notification, *Journal of Experimental Psychology: Human Perception and Performance*, 41 (4), 893-897.

Subrahmanyam, K., & Greenfield, P.M. (1994). Effect of video game practice on spatial skills in girls and boys, *Journal of Applied Developmental Psychology*, 15, 13-32.

Sykes, D.H., Douglas, V.I., Weiss, G., & Minde, K.K. (1971). Attention in hyperactive children and the effect of methylphenidate (Ritalin). *Journal of Child Psychology and Psychiatry*, 12, 129-139.

Takeuchi, H., Sekiguchi, A., Taki, Y., Yokoyama, S., Yomogida, Y., Komuro, N., Yamanouchi, T., Suzuki, S., & Kawashima, R. (2010). Training of working memory impacts structural connectivity, *Journal of Neuroscience*, 30 (9) 3297-3303.

Tammes, C.K., Walhovd, K.B., Grydeland, H., Holland, D., Ostby, Y., Dale, A.M., & Fjell, A.M. (2013). Longitudinal working memory development is related to structural maturation of frontal and parietal cortices, *Journal of Cognitive Neuroscience*, 25 (10), 1611-1623.

Tang, Y-Y, Lu, Q., Geng, X., Stein, E.A., Yang, Y. & Posner, M.I. (2010) Short-term meditation induces white matter changes in the anterior cingulate. *Proceedings of the National Academy of Sciences USA*, 107, 15649-15652.

Tang, Y-Y, & Posner, M.I. (2009). Attention training and attention state training, *Trends in Cognitive Sciences*, 13 (5), 222-227.

Taylor, V.A., Daneault, V. Grant, J., Scavone, G., Breton, E., Roffe-Vidal, S., Courtemanche, J., Lavarenne, A.S., Marrelec, G., Benali, H. & Beuregaard, M. (2012). Impact of meditation training on the default mode network during a restful state. *Social Cognitive and Affective Neuroscience*, 8, 4-14.

Tenzin-Dolma, L. (2013). Buddhist Mandalas/How to Meditate on Mandalas, London, Watkins Publishing.

Thomas, A. & Chess, S. (1977). *Temperament and development.* New York: Brunner/Mazel.

Thompson, L.A., & Massaro, D.W. (1989). Before you see it, you see its parts: Evidence for feature coding and integration in preschool children and adults, *Cognitive Psychology*, 21, 334-362.

Thorell, L.B., Lindqvist, S., Ntley, S.B., Bohlin, G., & Klingberg, T. (2009). Training and transfer effects of executive functions in preschool children, *Developmental Science*, 12 (1), 106-113.

Thupten Kalsang Rinpoche, Rahob Tulku, personal communication, 2018.

Tipper, S.P., Bourque, T.A., Anderson, S.H., & Brehaut, J.C. (1989) Mechanisms of attention: A developmental study. *Journal of Experimental Child Psychology*, 48 (3), 363-378.

Tipper, S.P., Lortie, C., & Baylis, G.C. (1992). Selective reaching: Evidence for action-centered attention, *Journal of Experimental Psychology: Human Perception and Performance*, 18, 891-905.

Tomasino, B., Fregona, S., Skrap, M., & Fabbro, F. (2012). Meditation-related activations are modulated by the practices needed to obtain it and by the expertise: An ALE meta-analysis study. *Frontiers in Human Neuroscience*, 6, 346.

Tombu, M.N., Asplund, C.L., Dux, P.E., Godwin, D. & Martin, J.W. (2012), A unified attentional bottleneck in the human brain, *Proceedings of the National Academy of Sciences USA*, 108 (33), 13426-13431.

Traue, H.C., & Pennebaker, J.W. (Eds). (1993). *Emotions, inhibition, and health* (pp. 100-115). Boston: Hogrefe & Huber.

Turley, K.J., & Whitfield, M.M. (2003). Strategy training and working memory in task performance, *Journal of Memory and Language*, 49, 446-468.

Turner, J.E., Henry, L.A., & Smith, P.T. (2000). The development of the use of long-term knowledge to assist short-term recall, *Quarterly Journal of Experimental Psychology*, Section A, 53 (2), 457-478.

Turnure, J.E. (1970). Children's reactions to distractors in a learning situation, *Developmental Psychology*, 2, 115-122.

Turnure, J.E. (1971). Control of orienting behavior in children under five years of age, *Developmental Psychology*, 4, 16-24.

Twemlow, S.W., Fonagy, P., & Sacco, F.C. (2005). A developmental approach to mentalizing communities: II. The Peaceful Schools experiment. *Bulletin of the Menninger Clinic*, 69, 282-304.

Uncapher, M.R., Thieu, M.K., & Wagner, A.D. (2016). Media multitasking and memory: Differences in working memory and long-term memory, *Psychonomic Bulletin & Review*, 23, 483-490.

Valentine, E.R., & Sweet, P.L.G. (1999). Meditation and attention: A comparison of the effects of concentration and mindfulness meditation on sustained attention. *Mental Health, Religion & Culture*, 2, 59-70.

Van de Weijer-Bergsma, E., Formsma, A.R., de Bruin, E.I., & Bogels, S.M. (2012). The effectiveness of mindfulness training on behavioral problems and attentional functioning in adolescents with ADHD, *Journal of Child & Family Studies*, 21 (5), 775-767.

Van de Weijer-Bergsma, Formsma, A.R, de Bruin, E.I, Bogels, S.M.(2012). The effects of mindfulness training on behavioral problems, *Journal of Child & Family Studies*, 21, 775-787.

Van den Hurk, P.A., Giommi, F., Gielen, S.C., Speckens, A.E.M. & Barendregt, H.P. (2010) Greater efficiency in attentional processing related to mindfulness meditation. *Quarterly Journal of Experimental Psychology*, 63, 1168-1180.

Van der Ord, S., Bogels, S.M., & Peijnenburg, D. (2012). The effectiveness of mindfulness training for children with ADHD and mindful parenting for their parents, *Journal of Child & Family Studies*, 21 (1), 139-147.

Van der Schuur, W.A., Baumgartner, S.E., Sumter, S.R., & Vaikenburg, P.M. (2015). The consequences of media multitasking for youth: A review, *Computers in Human Behavior*, 53, 204-215.

Van der Sluis, S., de Jong, P.F., & van der Leij, A. (2007). Executive functioning in children, and its relations with reasoning, reading, and arithmetic, *Intelligence*, 35, 427-449.

Van Gelder, T. (2009). Mindfulness vs Meta-cognition, and Critical Thinking. Van Hover, K.I. (1974). A developmental study of three components of attention, *Developmental Psychology*, 10, 330-339.

Van Leeuwen, S., Muller, N.G. & Melloni, L. (2009) Age effects on attentional blink performance in meditation. *Consciousness and Cognition*. 18, 593-599.

Van Selst, M., Ruthruff, E., & Johnston, J.C. (1999) Can practice eliminate the psychological refractory effect? *Journal of Experimental Psy-*

chology: *Human Perception and Performance*, 25 (5), 1268-1283.

Verghese, A., Garner, K.G., Mattingly, J.B., & Dux, P.E. (2016). Prefrontal cortex structure predicts training-induced improvements in multitasking performance, *Journal of Neuroscience*, 36 (9), 2638-2645.

Verhaeghen, P., Cerella, J., & Basak, C. (2004). A working memory workout: How to expand the focus of serial attention from ne to four items in 10 hours or less, *Journal of Experimental Psychology: Learning, Memory, and Cognition*, 30 (6), 1322-1337.

Verheugt-Pleiter, A.J.,E., Zevalkink, J., & Schmeets, M.G.J. (2008). *Mentalizing in child therapy: Guidelines for clinical practitioners.* London UK: Karnac.

Vinter, A., Puspitawait, I., & Witt, A. (2010). Children's spatial analysis of hierarchical patterns: Construction and perception, *Developmental Psychology*, 46 (6), 1621-1631.

Voelke, A.E., & Roebers, C.M. (2016). Sustained attention and its relationship to fluid Intelligence and working memory in children, *Journal of Educational and Developmental Psychology*, 6 (1), 131-139.

Vogel, E.K., McCullough, A.W., & Machizawa, M.G. (2005). Neural measures reveal individual differences in controlling access to working memory, *Nature*, 438, 500-503.

Von Bargen, D.M. (1983). Infant heart rate: A review of research and methodology, *Merrill-Palmer Quarterly*, 29, 115-149.

Wachs, T.D. (1989). The nature of the physical microenvironment: An expanded classification system, *Merrill-Palmer Quarterly*, 35, 399-419.

Wachs, T.D. (1993). Nature of relations between the physical and social microenvironment of the two-year-old child, *Early Development and Parenting*, 2, 81-87.

Walden, T.A., & Ogan, T.A. (1988). The development of social referencing, *Child Development*, 59, 1230-1240.

Wall, V. (1991). Developmental considerations in the use of hypnosis with children, In W. C. Wester, II and D. J. O- Grady (Eds). *Clinical hypnosis with children*, (pp. 3-18), New York: Brunner/Mazel.

Wallace, J.C., Vodanovich, S.J, & Restino, B.M.(2003). Predicting cognitive failures from boredom proneness and daytime sleepiness scores: An investigation within military and undergraduate samples, *Personality and Individual Differences*, 34, 635-644.

Wallis, C. (2010). The impact of media multitasking on children's learning and development: Report from a research seminar. NY: The Joan Ganz Cooney Center at Sesame Workshop.

Wang, T-S, & Huang, H-C. (2013). The design and development of a computerized attention-training game system for school-aged children, Presentation at the IADIS International Conference e-Learning, pp. 486-488.

Ward, A.F., Duke, K., Gneezy, A., & Bos, M.W. (2017). Brain drain: The mere presence of one's own smartphone reduces available cognitive capacity, *Journal of the Association for Consumer Research*, 2 (2), 140-154.

Wass, S.V., Scerif, G., & Johnson M.H. (2012). Training attentional control and working memory: Is younger better? *Developmental Review*, 32, 360-387.

Waszak, F, Li, S-C., & Hommel, B. (2010). The development of attentional networks: Cross-sectional findings from a life span sample, *Developmental Psychology*, 46 (2), 337-349.

Watson, J.M., & Strayer, D.L. (2010). Supertaskers: Profiles in extraordinary multitasking ability, *Psychonomic Bulletin & Review*, 17 (4), 479-485.

Weare, K. (2013). Developing mindfulness with children and young people: A review of the evidence and policy context, *Journal of Children's Services*, 8 (2), 141-153.

Weil, L.G., Fleming, S.M., Dumontheil, I., Kilford, E.J., Weil, R.S., Rees, G., Dolan, R.J., & Blakemore, S-J. (2013). The development of meta-cognitive ability in adolescence, *Consciousness and Cognition*, 22 (1), 264-271.

Weissberg, R., Ruff, H.A., & Lawson, K.R. (1990). The usefulness of reaction time tasks in studying attention and organization of behavior in young children, *Journal of Developmental and Behavioral Pediatrics*, 11, 59-64.

Welsh, M.C., Pennington, B.F., & Grossier, D.B. (1991). A normative-developmental study of executive function: A window on prefrontal functions in children, *Developmental Neuropsychology*, 7, 131-149.

Wertsch, J.V., McNamee, G.D., McLane, J.B., & Budwig, N.A. (1980). The adult-child dyad as a problem-solving system, Child Development, 51, 1215-1221.

West, G.L., Stevens, S.A., Pun, C., & Pratt, J. (2008). Visuo-spatial experience modulates attentional capture: Evidence from action video game players, *Journal of Vision*, 8 (16), 1-9.

Westerberg, H. (2004). *Working memory: Development, disorders and training.* Stockholm, Sweden: Karolinska Institutet.Westerberg, H., & Klingberg, T. (2007). Changes in cortical activity after training of working memory: A single-subject analysis, *Physiology and Behavior*, 92 (1-2), 186-192.

Whitfield-Gabrieli, S., Moran, J.M., Nieto-Castanon, A., Triantafyllou, C., Saxe, R., & Gabrieli, J.D. E. (2011). Associations and dissociations between default and self-reference networks in the human brain, *NeuroImage*, 55, 225-232.

Willard, C., & Saltzman, A. (2015). *Teaching mindfulness skills to kids and teens.* New York: Guilford.

Williams, B.R., Ponesse, J.S., Logan, G.D., Schachar, R.J., & Tannock, R. (1999). Development of inhibitory control across the life span, *Developmental Psychology*, 35 (1), 205-213.

Wilmer, H.H., Sherman, L.E., & Chein, J.M. (2017). Smartphones and cognition: A review of research exploring the links between mobile technology habits and cognitive functioning, *Frontiers in Psychology*, 8, 605, 1-16.

Wisner, B.L., Jones, B., & Gwin, D. (2010). School-based meditation practices for adolescents: A resource for strengthening self-regulation, emotional coping, and self-esteem, *Children & Schools*, 32 (3), 150-159.

Wolff, P.H. (1965). The development of attention in young infants, *Annals of the New York Academy of Sciences*, 118, 815-830.

Woods, A.J., Goksun, T., Chatterjee, A., Zelonis, S., Mehta, A., & Smith, S.E. (2013). The development of organized visual search, *Acta Psychologica*, 143, 191-199.

Wright, J.C., & Vlietstra, A.G. (1975). The development of selective attention: From perceptual exploration to logical search, *Advances in Child Development and Behavior*, 10, 195-239.

Yarrow, I.J., Morgan, G.A., Jennins, K.D., Harmon, R.J., & Gaiter, J.L. (1982). Infant's persistence at tasks: Relationships to cognitive functioning and early experience, *Infant Behavior and Development*, 5, 131-141.

Zeidan, F., Gordon, N.S., Mechant, J., & Goolkasian, P. (2010). The effects of brief mindfulness meditation training on experimentally induced pain, 11 (3), 199-209.

Zenner, C., Herrnleben-Kurz, S., Walach, H. (2014). Mindfulness-based interventions in schools: A systematic review and meta-analysis, *Frontiers in Psychology*, 5, 603—623.

Zylowska, L., Ackerman, D.L., Yang, M.H., Futrell, J.L., Horton, N.L., Hale, T.S. et al. (2007). Mindfulness meditation training in adults and adolescents with ADHD: A feasibility study, *Journal of Attention Disorders*, 11, 737-746.

www.ingramcontent.com/pod-product-compliance
Lightning Source LLC
Chambersburg PA
CBHW050501240426
43673CB00023B/457/J